# PUBLIC ADMINISTRATION

---

## THIRD EDITION

---

*Marshall Edward Dimock*

*Gladys Ogden Dimock*

---

**HOLT, RINEHART AND WINSTON, INC.**

*NEW YORK CHICAGO SAN FRANCISCO TORONTO LONDON*

JF
1351
.D5

*September, 1964*

# Preface

This third edition of our text is a complete rewriting and reformulation of the subject. Like the first edition, it stresses the role of the operating administrator in the belief that most of what is called overhead administration is better covered in courses in American, state, or local government. This edition differs from the preceding ones, however, in paying more attention to the history of the subject, to its relation to society, to the political economy, and to public policy. It also stresses the role of political dynamics and discusses the relevance for public administration of some of the newer insights into motivation and leadership that psychologists are studying. As in the former editions, the unifying theme is what the operating administrator should know in order to continue his education throughout a career in the public service, developing breadth and depth as he progresses.

A course in public administration explains the key terms and concepts of the subject and teaches the areas of knowledge to be integrated if one is to get the feel and develop the art of administration. But perhaps the most important function of such a course is to help the student to develop for himself a philosophy of administration, leaving the acquisition of a detailed knowledge of techniques to experience on the job where its relevance is more quickly appreciated than in the classroom. We also assume that in the modern world a careerist in the public service should ground himself in the structure and dynamics of society and the political economy if he is to grow as an administrator and to have a hand in the solution of society's problems.

No particular school of disciplinary thought is represented here. There is value in all of the various approaches to the subject that follow a particular line: positivism, behavioralism, decision making, human relations, scientific management, and more; but so far, at least, no one of them has come up with even partial answers to the most serious problems of a modern society. Consequently we have adopted the eclectic method, taking from other approaches to the subject the best they can offer, and from these and other sources, trying to fashion a balanced treatment that will make sense to the student.

It is surely important that a science of administration should eventually be developed, for it would greatly contribute to the art and

iii

philosophy of administration. But this book is not such an attempt. To us it seems inappropriate here to adopt a rigorously positivistic approach under the assumption that a science already exists or is about to be invented. Instead, we have been mindful throughout of the needs of the student and employed a vocabulary that will be readily understood.

The book is designed for the beginning course in public administration, covering one semester or possibly two quarters. We believe, however, that training in administration is a venture large enough to require a lifetime of effort on the part of the careerist, and hence we have noted the work and ideas of many authors in the hope that it will stimulate further reading later in the student's development, even if he should not be able to do much collateral reading during the period of the course. For those who may wish to dig further, we have included illustrative case materials and references and a brief annotated bibliography at the end of each chapter.

This is not a technical book, therefore, nor is it a long one. It is intended for the student who thinks he may wish to enter the public service, or who would become a better citizen, or who, as a more knowledgeable businessman or professional specialist, would understand his relation to and concern in the many governmental programs that directly or indirectly affect nearly every aspect of his daily life. Many personal and social aspirations alike depend for their attainment on the skill and statesmanship with which our governing institutions are administered. If the quality of government is to improve, administration also must improve; if taxes are to be kept within reasonable bounds and supply a dollar's worth of service for a dollar's worth of contribution, public administration is a central area of interest and concern to the citizen.

Administration is the practical, productive side of institutional management. Currently, the two largest academic specializations in the field of government are international relations and public administration. But even students in international relations need a course in public administration because international institutions must become more practical before they become more effective. Thus, administration is not really a specialty, but a skill that in the modern world is required almost literally of every individual in every field or profession where human relations and institutional management are involved. Today the number of occupations where these factors are lacking is diminishing to the vanishing point.

M.E.D.

G.O.D.

*Scrivelsby*
*Bethel, Vermont*
*March 1964*

# Contents

**PART FIVE—Administration and the Public**    327

# PART
# ONE

---

# What Is
# Public Administration?

# 1

# The Context
# of Administration

PUBLIC ADMINISTRATION LIES at the center of a web composed of many different relationships that extend to the citizen, to the state, to society and its values, to the economy and its development, and more. The citizen and the future administrator alike should learn to think clearly about these relationships and the values and balances they affect, for they constitute the synthesis that is public administration.

## Public Administration and the Citizen

The two main functions of government are rule and service; in each case, public administration is centrally concerned and so is the citizen. The maintenance of law and order is an example of the function of rule, or control, and the provision of a municipal water supply is an example of service.

The broadest definition of public administration was suggested in 1887 by Woodrow Wilson in a celebrated essay.[1] Public administration, said Wilson, is the practical or business end of government because its objective is to get the public business done as efficiently and as much in accord with the people's tastes and desires as possible. It is through ad-

---

[1] "The Study of Administration," *Political Science Quarterly*, June 1887, vol. 2.

ministration that government responds to those needs of society that private initiative cannot or will not supply.

Consequently, a main relationship of administration occurs at the point of contact between government and the citizen where public controls and services come to fruition. One of the tests of administration is how well it meets these human needs in consonance with the larger interests and values that society prizes.

## The Structure of Government

Another way to get at the relationships that characterize public administration is to think in terms of the separation of powers. An oversimplified version of this basic doctrine of American government holds that the legislature makes the law, the executive carries it out, and the judiciary settles any disputes that may arise. On the basis of the budgets required and the personnel employed by each of these three branches, some 95 percent of government is administration in the executive branch.

In practice, however, government is not so sharply divided among the three branches, nor is the executive branch so exclusively concerned with administration. A broader and more realistic view holds that public administration is concerned with the ends of the state, which means that in addition to executing the law, administration is also concerned with politics, with the ends of the economy, with the values of national life, and with the hearing and deciding of cases and controversies not allocated to the judiciary (a much greater number than those that are so allocated). Consequently, in addition to being practical in a business sense, public administration must also be statesmanlike and philosophical.

Yet another way that administration relates to the ends of the state is in the determination of public policy itself. The reason is that the administrator not only carries out public policy but also recommends it, and he often takes an active part in securing its enactment into law or administrative directive. The only respect in which the career administrator differs from the elected leader who is his boss is that the latter, under the American form of government, always has the last word. Hence the administrator must not only be practical and production-minded, he must also be skilled in human relations, policywise, understanding of the needs of the economy, and appreciative of its value systems.

From the standpoint of the structure of government, therefore, public administration is the area of study and practice where law and policy are recommended and carried out. Once the legislature has approved a policy by enacting it into law, and the judiciary has defined and delimited the law, everything else in formal governmental functioning is the responsibility of the administrative branch.

## Society and the Economy

Yet another relationship of public administration is to the whole of society and its economy—what may be called, in broad terms, the cultural setting. Government is only one of many institutions in the nation that rule and serve: there are also the family, the religious association, the business economy, all of which share with government the wide field of public policy determination, and all at least as concerned as government with administration.

Because of this broad relationship, public administration must constantly and correctly define and redefine its role in society. Not even in the Communist state does government try to do everything; in the democratic state, government does what it should or must, and no more. The three main reasons for this restraint are, first, that democracy encourages voluntarism, and hence government should enter only those areas where voluntarism is inadequate or inappropriate. Second, that public administration acquires its tone and character from the belief systems and values of the society in which it operates, and hence if administration is to be congruent and respected, it must be part of the whole social fabric and not separate from or imposed upon it. And third, that since administration is a practical pursuit and there is a practical limit to what any government can do well, there must be choice among alternatives and priorities, because the laws of optimum size and of diminishing returns apply as much to government as to other human institutions.

Since the societal nexus is so intrinsic a part of its fabric, one might almost call public administration a branch of sociology, although the distinction is important only to show a relationship that should not be overlooked. Public administration is equally a branch of political economy, which is business and government working together to increase the national wealth and to create the conditions that people call the good life. As long as the memory of man knoweth, a sound and prosperous economy has been the *sine qua non* of public policy, and government's role in achieving it has been prominent and indispensable. Because a trained and conscientious corps of public administrators is the necessary instrument of such a system, public administrators must be not only sociologists and political scientists, but also historians and economists.

## Administration a Universal

As a discipline, public administration has a family relationship to a larger body of knowledge, administration. This functional view of administration disregards the question of what kind of administration is in question: business, church, educational, or some other. Carried to its logical limits this view is so broad as to include all human effort—one might even speak of administering oneself—but especially does it connote joint human endeavor in even so simple a task as rolling a stone or planting a garden.

Although there is some danger of pushing this idea too far, it nevertheless can validly be melded into the synthesis toward which this train of thought is leading. It illustrates that administration is basically a matter of cooperation; that it progresses from simple to more elaborate forms of cooperation; that human beings are always involved; and that when cooperation is simple, the human element is more prominent than it becomes later when organization, prearranged rules and signals, and similar matters dominate.

This functional view of administration also reveals overlapping with other institutional specializations. Public administration and business administration are much alike, for example, because both are practical, provide services, and rely on common techniques relating to planning, organization, budgeting, delegation, control, and the like. But there are also prominent differences. Government is sovereign and makes laws; in this area business has only a supporting or opposing role, as the case may be. Government serves the broad public interest; business is more concerned with a private profit. These differences diminish, however, as the similarities and overlappings increase, for technology encourages professionalization and bureaucratization in business and government alike.

Finally, the functional view of administration makes it possible to compare the administrative characteristics of different institutions such as business and government or government and education, and also to compare the administrative characteristics of different national governments, the British and the French, for example, or the Soviet and the German.

The advantage of comparative studies is to focus on common elements in different kinds of administration and to suggest the universality of the discipline. Such studies also suggest the variety that exists among institutions and even among whole cultures, showing how administration takes on the personality and coloration of a given society. There may be a right way of doing something for a given time, place, and situation, for example, but it is at least open to question that this is the only right way for all times, places, and situations.

### The Human Factor

Is administration an art or a science? The question has often been debated with some heat. At this stage in its development it seems possible to say only that administration—in the sense that it is a skill or a technique to be applied—is indeed an art, and that in time some aspects of it may come to be dealt with so systematically as properly to constitute a science.

That administration is an art of a high order seems clear enough. Some individuals, certain groups, and even whole nations seem more able than most to set workable goals, marshal their resources to achieve them effectively and on time, and to operate with a considerable degree of efficiency while strengthening and not detracting from the value system of which administration is a part. In other cases there may be equally high aspirations but a low order of administrative and organizing skills by which to give effect to practical programs.

It has already been suggested that administration is a synthesis, perhaps one of the most intricate and delicate of the syntheses that characterize modern society. The converse of this proposition is that administration is no one thing, like intelligence or power or cunning. Part of the purpose of this book is to explore just what it is that makes for administrative success. Some call this factor the administrative mind, some the integrated or balanced personality, others the balance between mind and value systems, and still others what our forebears use to call character.

While administration is a highly practical, production-oriented, societal concern, it depends ultimately upon the human personality, an area that is far from illuminated by science. A science of administration, therefore, is not a substitute for practical experience and moral behavior, although it could, of course, become a useful source of important factors entering into the ultimate synthesis that must be made.

To keep it useful, however, those who would create a science of administration should avoid specialized vocabularies sometimes designed by professionals to be understood only by the initiated. They should also utilize large drafts of the scientist's modesty and tolerance of other viewpoints. There is great value in the concepts of behavioral science, decision making, group dynamics, operational research, and other systematic approaches, but none of these is broad enough, as yet, to offer a complete guide to administration. The practical man must still make higher syntheses of his own in order to act effectively in the real world.

This view characterized the first attempt to apply the scientific method of administration, the so-called scientific management movement started by Frederick W. Taylor and his disciples at the turn of the present century. Taylor believed that reliable methods could be developed to measure the efficiency of every unit entering into production, and that progressively larger syntheses made from these factors would indicate the most efficient method of completing a given operation. But as any scientist would, Taylor also realized what his system lacked: it overlooked what in the long run may be the most important factor in efficiency, namely, human beings, their motivations and satisfactions, and the methods of getting them to cooperate in a common effort.

## Techniques and Values

Yet another relationship of administration is between technique and value. The objective of public administration is sometimes said to be efficiency; but what is efficiency? Is it merely a high rate of production? If so, what degree of social cost or undesirable side effects may be permitted? If efficiency were merely the relation between input and output, the calculus would be a rather simple one for the engineer with the necessary skills. But production is not the whole of a man's concern in life, and if other elements are overlooked production can be bought at too high a social price. What, for example, happens to freedom? To self-expression and individual growth? To incentive and enterprise and initiative? How important is it that people should willingly assume responsibility instead of having it forced upon them? What is the good life and is it the same for all people at all times? It must be remembered that public administration shares in the determination of public policy, and hence merely to ask these questions shows how impossible it is for the administrator to escape the role of philosopher even if he would.

If, as most writers on public administration seem to agree, the practical yardstick by which to judge the quality of administration is efficiency, then the term had better be defined to include human beings, broad social concerns, and ultimate values—not merely the limited engineering view of input-output. Otherwise the term might better be discarded in favor of a more neutral one such as behavior. Unfortunately, behavior is not a fixed element, in administration or elsewhere, being determined partly by inheritance and partly by the influence of environment. Behavior also involves choice and habit, and these are largely dictated by the social attitudes and values of a given society. So the term "efficiency" will doubtless have to be retained as a key word in the vocabulary of administration, but it should be accorded a broad rather than a narrow definition.

## Stage of Development

The next relationship in administration has to do with the stages of economic development of a nation. Society is an organism; at each stage of its growth certain factors are constant and others are the result of temporary conditions calling for temporary responses. Thus, there is a constant need for certain fixed elements in administration, including people, organization, planning, goals, finances, delegation, supervision, coordination, control, and the like. But as society proceeds from simple to more complex technologies, some of these elements must be more emphasized than others, and the resulting integrations are increasingly complicated. As institutions become more specialized and intricate, goal setting and policy formation must take more factors into account, decision making becomes especially taxing on administrators, and the results of decision making are increasingly fateful for the organization and society alike.

The various degrees of administrative sophistication that are needed may be illustrated in Rostow's five stages of economic growth, beginning with the traditional society and proceeding through the preconditions stage, the take-off stage, and the mature society, finally reaching the mass-production or affluent or consumer-oriented stage, where the United States finds itself today.[2] Traditional societies may be so lacking in even rudimentary administrative know-how that their progress is discouragingly slow. On the other hand, a society such as the American or the Soviet may have solved most of the problems of production but encounters difficulties of synthesis in goal setting, planning, decision making, and human motivation. In these cases the long-range challenge may be even more severe than that faced by the primitive society unlocking the door to the preconditions stage of development.

In other words, administration is an instrument for solving a nation's problems, and the more there are the more must administration progress and adapt to new demands if it is to keep on top of the situation. Indeed, one reason that administration in the United States is of so much interest today is that technology and social tensions are outstripping the number of administrators equipped to cope with the structural changes and adjustments the nation needs at this stage of its development.

This lack of qualified administrators would be much less serious if administration were merely a matter of techniques, procedures, and mechanics. A master with a long whip and enough slaves was able to build everlasting monuments; wars have been won by brilliant strategists and mercenary troops; a fifteenth-century business venture in Europe presented few administrative problems because the scope was limited and competitors few.

But in the space age administration is more than a matter of knowing how to organize and delegate and coordinate, much of which is only common sense anyhow. Increasingly, administration is a double-barreled affair. It means, first, knowing a particular substantive field, often a highly specialized one such as medicine, space exploration, or the disposal of atomic wastes; and second, knowing how to organize and supervise the efforts of others. For most public administrators, a test of effectiveness is the degree to which they blend these two requirements usefully.

---

2 W. W. Rostow, *The Stages of Economic Growth, A Non-Communist Manifesto* (New York: Cambridge University Press, 1960).

## Pyramids and Hierarchies

Then there is the relationship that has to do with levels of operation. Government is a hierarchy arranged like a pyramid. How the relationships within it are worked out goes far to determine the quality of service government can offer at a reasonable price, as well as what happens to freedom and voluntarism. In the United States there are six levels of government, including those at the local, county, state, regional, national, and the international levels—the regional and the international being fairly new. But the very multiplicity of governments, amounting now to more than 100,000 units, adds to the complexities of public administration and to the cost of government at every level.

Within a particular government there may be three different levels of administration as distinguished from levels of government. First, there is the central headquarters office, commonly remote from the citizen-consumer, or client. Then there is the field organization whose main function is operations, and it is here that the consumer and the public official come face to face. Between these two levels there is sometimes an intermediate or regional level constituting the connecting administrative link between headquarters and the field. (This kind of regional unit differs, of course, from the more autonomous regional level mentioned above; some of those—the Tennessee Valley Authority, for example—are separate governmental agencies in themselves, whereas in the connecting-link type of arrangement the regional officials are never independent of central office authority.)

There are some marked differences in administration at the two main levels of administration, headquarters and field. Headquarters is chiefly concerned with over-all policy and the so-called staff activity involving planning, research, and the setting of standards. At the field or operational level, on the other hand, emphasis is on action and day-to-day problem solving. Both kinds of work have their distinctive challenge, and it will be part of our responsibility in a later chapter to explain what these relationships and interdependencies are.

## Blending the Ingredients

The final relationship in administration concerns the ingredients of the discipline itself. Thus, administration deals with

objectives—what to do;
policy—how to do it;
planning—determining the steps by which objectives are attained;
decision making—choosing among priorities and alternative courses of action;

organization—by levels and units, accompanied by job assignments so that everyone shall have a clear mandate;

personnel—recruitment, motivation, human relations at all levels;

budgeting and finance—translating plans into money terms as a basis for control and decision making;

purchase and supply—often a centralized function;

direction—program formulation and the dynamics of leadership;

coordination—synchronizing the program and avoiding duplication;

supervision—directing the work of others;

control—determining whether the enterprise is on target and on schedule, and whether it is operating efficiently;

public relations—explaining the program to all parties of interest so as to sell the service and improve its tone.

The dominant characteristic of this outline is that all these factors of administration are interrelated; none is independent. Consequently, if any one of these factors in the integrated operation lags or breaks down, all the others are likely to suffer.

## Summary

In simple terms, administration is securing cooperation in order to get the work of the world accomplished. As a process, administration is so much a matter of analysis and synthesis that these functions should become second nature to the administrator. As a career, administration is an exciting challenge, for it calls on many aspects of a man's nature and abilities and applies them to sticky social problems. Administration is of concern to every citizen because the service he receives, the taxes he pays, and even the personal freedoms he enjoys depend so largely on what the public administrator does or fails to do. Many of the sharpest social issues of the modern age, including how to combine freedom and organization, revolve around this bureaucratic area of administration, making public administration a central interest of political theory and philosophy.

As noted here, public administration is an aspect of the larger field of administration, but the public variety is distinctive because it deals with the ends of the state, the sovereign will, the public interests, and law, the coercive element in society.

Administration is concerned with relationships and with integrations. To show that integration is the key problem of administration and to try to give the feel of administration, nine of these relationships have been dealt with in rapid sequence. These are to the citizen, to the structure of government, to society and the economy, to administration as an over-all field of knowledge, to the human factor in administration, to techniques and values, to stages of national development, to levels of operation, and to the ingredients that constitute the synthesis of public administration itself.

Administration both serves and controls; it is more than a tool of government, it is also a process; it grows out of and is controlled by the whole cultural pattern of the society in which it operates, a chief aim of which is a viable political economy. Administration is an art and potentially it is also a science, but most of all it is an intricate and challenging synthesis of many elements. It is concerned with values and moral philosophy as well as with techniques. Because society progresses through successive stages of growth, there are variables as well as constants in administration. Government operates at several levels with hierarchy in each. And finally, public administration is an endless chain starting with the definition of problems and the establishment of objectives and winding up with control and public relations, with each step in the process essential to over-all success.

## *BIBLIOGRAPHY AND CASES*

### Annotated Reading Suggestions

The suggestions in this and the following chapters are brief and meant to introduce the student to the "feel" of operating administration as quickly as possible. More extensive bibliographies are found in the indexes of *Public Administration Review, American Political Science Review, Public Management, Advanced Management,* and *National Municipal Review,* and in compilations edited by Sarah Greer, C. Seckler-Hudson, and Laverne Burchfield.

One of the best realistic treatments of public administration is Paul H. Appleby, *Policy and Administration* (University of Alabama Press, 1949). A comparable study, relating to general management and business administration, is Peter F. Drucker, *The Practice of Management* (Harper & Row, 1954). Chester Barnard, *The Functions of the Executive* (Harvard University Press, 1938) is already something of a classic. The role of the operating official is presented in the form of a modified case study by Marshall E. Dimock, *The Executive in Action* (Harper & Row, 1945).

The perennial issues in public administration are presented by Dwight Waldo in *The Administrative State* (Ronald Press, 1948), in his book of readings, *Ideas and Issues in Public Administration* (McGraw-Hill, 1953), and in *The Study of Public Administration* (Doubleday, 1955).

Trends in public administration are dealt with in a series of four articles in *Public Administration Review:* John M. Gaus on theory (Summer 1950), George A. Graham on teaching (Spring 1950), Wallace S. Sayre on administrative values (Winter 1951), and Robert A. Dahl on science (Winter 1947). These articles may profitably be supplemented by Emmette S. Redford's lectures,

*Ideal and Practice in Public Administration* (University of Alabama Press, 1958); The President's Advisory Committee on Management, "Improvement of Management in the Federal Government," *Public Administration Review*, 13 (Winter 1953); and Rensis Likert, *New Patterns of Management* (McGraw-Hill, 1961); all of which deal with the future of public administration.

The challenges of public administration as they affect the whole of society and the national economy are discussed by Marshall E. Dimock, *The New American Political Economy* (Harper & Row, 1962); this book also includes an extensive bibliography relating to economic and other factors.

One of the best short articles on administration and the need to take a wide range of factors into account is Paul H. Appleby, "Making Sense Out of Things in General," *Public Administration Review*, 22 (December 1962). For a more extended treatment, see Marshall E. Dimock, *A Philosophy of Administration* (Harper & Row, 1958).

## Case Studies

One of the best ways to get the "feel" of administration is to study actual cases, a method that has been widely adopted in schools of business and public administration, with a good deal of success.

For the most part, the cases noted here are those of the Inter-University Case Program, which is supported by a number of leading universities and foundations. The first studies in this series were produced by the Committee on Public Administration Cases, 1948-1951. Since 1951 the Inter-University Case Program has published "Cases in Public Administration and Public Policy: ICP Case Series." Between 1951-1963 some fourscore cases were prepared, some of them bearing the imprimatur of the University of Alabama Press.

These studies are relatively short (often fifteen to twenty pages) and separately and inexpensively reproduced. Any or all of them can be obtained at little cost from the Inter-University Case Program, 45 East 65th Street, New York 21, New York.

In the first edition of this textbook we experimentally included condensations of some of these leading cases, and although instructors apparently liked this method, we have concluded that in order not to break the train of the discussion, it is better to separate case references from the text and include them, along with annotated bibliographies, at the end of each chapter. Another advantage of this method is to enable us to deal with most of the case material available. In each instance we try to show something of the content of the case in question and to call attention to any other cases that seem pertinent.

To allocate fourscore or more cases among twenty-three chapters is not an easy job because few cases deal exclusively with a single aspect of public administration, such as organization or personnel or supervision. Nevertheless, a certain classification is possible, and when in doubt we have listed the same case in more than one chapter.

What use is to be made of these cases? They may be read by the student on his own initiative, or they may be utilized in instruction for class report and discussion, or for the preparation of a critique. Our own experience indicates the value of dealing with relatively few cases and going into each one rather more fully than is possible when several are considered in a short period.

The most convenient compendium of cases from the Inter-University Case Program (hereafter referred to as ICP) is edited by Harold Stein, *Public Administration and Policy Development: A Case Book* (Harcourt, Brace & World, 1952). This contains some of the best of the early cases, twenty-six in number and constituting approximately a third of those now available in the ICP series. Since these studies are more readily available than those separately bound, we shall refer to them first in each chapter annotation. Except where the case appears in Stein, *we shall give the ICP number for the case,* in order to facilitate ordering or finding it.

Before studying any one of these cases, however, it is desirable to read the brilliant essay on the case method by Stein himself, that appears in the first fourteen pages of his book. An advantage of the ICP series is that public policy is emphasized along with public administration, which makes for a more dynamic treatment of the subject than might otherwise be so. Additionally, one may wish to consult International Institute of Administrative Sciences, *Essays on the Case Method* (University of Alabama Press, 1962).

Because of the wide-ranging nature of this first chapter, no cases have been included at this point. But hereafter several will accompany each chapter.

# 2

# Perspective
# on the Past

As SOON AS primitive man began to act jointly with his fellows, they had to plan, organize, assign roles, and coordinate, which literally makes administration the oldest of professions (or almost). On the other hand, as a body of knowledge in the university curricula, public administration, like administration generally, is a fairly new field and, as might be expected, it has been the subject of much change and experimentation during the last two generations or so. The purpose of this chapter is to highlight the past, to show where public administration as a field of knowledge came from and where it seems to be heading, so as better to understand it and shape its development. For as in every major field of knowledge there is a growing awareness that time and tradition are the bases on which progress depends.

## Historical Awareness

As an aspect of political philosophy and statecraft, public administration has a long history. Socrates, Plato, and Aristotle all had much to say about administration, although they did not sharply differentiate it from political philosophy and substantive fields such as science, education, or ethics. They were concerned with the city-state and the good life, as well as with the practical means by which the good, the true, and the beautiful might be attained; administration was one of the means. In his Academy,

Plato in effect trained administrators, although he would doubtless have called them philosopher-kings. So also, in another part of the world at about the same time (fifth century B.C.), did Confucius train administrators. Confucius was known as a teacher of ethics, and at that time ethics related primarily to rule and to rulers. The six main rules of public administration suggested by Confucius in order to bring benevolent rule still have a modern ring: First, a ruler should know his country well and try to remove the causes of its troubles. Second, in decision making an official should hold the mean, that is, be objective, fair, moderate, practical, and ethical. Third, an official should try to serve the public interest, avoiding favoritism and partisanship. Fourth, it is government's duty to promote the economic welfare of the people. Fifth, public officials should constantly busy themselves in the conduct of the affairs of the state. And finally, the accomplishment of all these objectives depends upon a high quality of public personnel, officials who are honest, unselfish, and able.[1]

As strong rulers gradually gained centralized authority, the practice of public administration was bound to expand, and so did its problems.[2] There may not have been much teaching of administration or even writing about it, but administration as a practical art had to be developed or nothing of consequence would have been accomplished in the far-flung empires of ancient history. Finally, under the Romans administration was taught as part of Aristotle's politics, or as law, or as ethics. Not even in the thinking of scholars was administration separable from these subjects. Later, formal schools of administration were created. One of the first in the Western world, created in the latter part of the fifteenth century, was part of the slave household in Constantinople of the Sultan of the Ottoman Empire,[3] which at the time extended around most of the Mediterranean and into Europe. Early in the eighteenth century Peter the Great set up administrative colleges in Russia.[4] A hundred years

---

[1] Leonard Shihlien Hsü, "The Rules of Public Administration," *The Political Philosophy of Confucianism* (New York: Dutton, 1932), pp. 121-124, quoted in Albert Lepawsky, *The Art and Science of Organization and Management* (New York: Alfred A. Knopf, Inc. 1949), p. 840.

[2] For example, Papyrus 752 in the British Museum, dated September 13, 288 A.D., is a letter from a high official of the Roman administration in Egypt to the district governor of Middle Egypt complaining of the useless multiplicity of public officials in the administration of the crown accounts. Consequently, "It has therefore become necessary for me to send you instructions to arrange a single superintendent of good standing to be chosen for each estate on the responsibility of the local municipal council, and to abolish all remaining offices, though the superintendent elected shall have power to choose two, or at most three assistants. . . . You will, of course, ensure that only such persons are appointed . . . as can stand public scrutiny."

[3] Arnold J. Toynbee, *A Study of History* (London: Oxford University Press, 1954), vol. III, pp. 35-45, and vol. VII, pp. 361-363.

[4] *Ibid.*, vol. VII, p. 359.

later the British East India Company established a college to train appointees to its administrative service in India.[5]

Nevertheless, formal schools such as these were rare. Rather, emphasis was on statecraft (modern political science); on law and legal systems (out of which administrative law emerged); on political economy, which dealt with the promotion of national wealth and royal power; and on ethics and philosophy. Knowledge and university curriculums were more unified than they are today. The need was for a competent administrative corps capable of ruling, and it did not especially matter how these royal servants acquired their knowledge and indoctrination.

During the Middle Ages, for example, the objectives of a king and his government were wealth, extension of empire, and a certain efficiency in tax collection and similar civic matters. The king's greatest asset, therefore, was a corps of faithful administrators able to get things done. The system called mercantilism appeared in Europe just before and after the Thirty Years' War when the modern state system began to take form. Kings began to establish infant industries such as iron and coal mining, and to encourage colonization as the means of acquiring the wealth with which to dominate their neighbors. None of these policies were possible save as kings also succeeded in developing administrators able to push economic and political development at home and in the New World as well. In Germany and Austria the system was known as cameralism. In France the Physiocrats stressed agriculture as the source of all wealth and well-being.

In 1776 when Adam Smith wrote *The Wealth of Nations,* it was still held that government policies and their administration by statesmanlike measures were the first requirement of a viable economy. Nevertheless, changes were beginning to appear. Two revolutions had occurred in England during the preceding (seventeenth) century, as a result of which royal power had been relaxed and specialization of functions had been taking place. Administration and adjudication, which previously had been one, were now thought of as separate functions in separate government departments. Parliamentary supremacy had been established; political parties increasingly made policies and decisions in areas where formerly the king had been supreme. By the ninteenth century differentiation of function reached the point where an independent civil service, standing apart from king and parliament alike, came to be regarded as public administration per se. In sophistication it was probably in no way superior to the fifteenth-century slave corps of public administrators serving the Ottoman Empire. Both were forerunners of the permanent civil service that exists in many nations today.

During the eighteenth century also, dispersion began to affect the economy. A new merchant and trading community grew up alongside

5 *Ibid.*, vol. VII, p. 365. A detailed study of early civil services in many parts of the world appears in this volume, pp. 344-372.

agriculture; corporations, although created as hitherto by the state, began to be used for individual or private enterprise. A new managerial class, composed of businessmen, arose beside the civil service. The industrial revolution of the early nineteenth century gave economics new power, simultaneously creating new problems of public administration that taxed the ability of government to keep pace with social and economic change.

In America the development of public administration and business alike began, of course, from scratch on seventeenth-century European models, but the new nation quickly caught up with Europe in both areas. By the second half of the ninteenth century, business had followed the railroads to become nationwide in scope and so powerful as to constitute a rival of the state itself. Regulatory laws such as the Interstate Commerce Commission Act of 1887 and the Sherman Antitrust Act of 1890 marked the weakening of laissez faire and a return to government's direct concern for the economy, a policy under which business continued to grow, however, despite the dire predictions of the opponents of these measures. As the size of business units increased, bureaucracy became as typical of them as it was of government. With growing power, businessmen came to share in the governing process of the nation, reluctant as they were to admit this fact. All of which culminated in a social structure where managers in both business and government increasingly hold the real power in the nation, for they control the policies and the decisions on which the nation's fate in large part depends.

It is not surprising, therefore, that the American system is sometimes called the Administrative State, the Managerial Society, or even the Civil Service State. Indeed, it might even be claimed that administration—not merely public administration but all administration—is the ultimate human science, so greatly do the services and the welfare of the people depend upon the environment, the policies, the personalities, and the skills with which managers of all institutions, large and small, public and private alike, discharge their responsibilities.

This is the real challenge in public administration. There has been created an elite, a leadership group, and the spirit and values of society, not to mention its material basis, come to depend on the caliber of the men and women who constitute this elite group.

## The Traditions of Public Administration

Seen in this historical perspective, public administration derives from several interrelated traditions. The first of these is the *political economy* tradition. Administration serves large social and national ends, involving a knowledge of economics and of the principles and measures that produce and sustain wealth.

There is also a *law and legal institutions* tradition. In Europe and other parts of the world, public administration is still taught as part of the law curriculum, and especially administrative law. In France and Turkey, for example, it is only recently that anything like public administration, as taught in the United States, has begun to appear as a separate discipline independent of law schools.

Then there is the *general administration* tradition. Over a period of centuries the problems of organizing, planning, leading, and controlling institutions of all kinds—business, governmental, educational, ecclesiastical, and voluntary—were found to resemble each other in important respects, just as they differed in others depending on the character of the work done.

There is also the *civil service* tradition. As noted above, even before the civil service systems in England, the United States, and other western countries were formalized toward the end of the nineteenth century, a civil service existed in fact if not in name. All the agencies of policy and decision brought to bear upon their practical carrying out are a necessary and indispensable part of the administrative process, however primitive the mechanisms may be in certain instances. Public administration is the powers, the organization, the personnel, and the methods that are involved in giving effect to the will of the state.

Next is the *ethical and philosophical* tradition. If any single element has been constant and dominant from the time of Confucius to the present, it is a concern for political philosophy and for the values and ethics of society. Should power be concentrated or dispersed? Are private interests and the public interest reconcilable? Which is more important, process or human beings? Order or freedom? And must it always be an elite that rules, even one so seemingly objective as the civil service, or is any kind of elite undesirable and unnecessary? Just to raise these questions indicates that today the principal issues of political philosophy originate largely in the administrative process.

Then comes the *engineering and science* tradition, which is increasingly evident as technology develops to the point where a nation enters what Rostow refers to as the mass-production or affluent stage. In our society it is almost literally true that the greatest problems of public administration stem directly from scientific and technological innovation. Indeed, every skill and field of knowledge today is within the ken of the governmental administrator. Modern administration encompasses the whole range of skills, competencies, and bodies of knowledge taught in the largest and best universities of the land.

Then there is the *political* tradition, political in the sense that government differs from other institutions by reason of its ultimate civil authority over a given territory, its monopoly of the law and the law's sanctions, and the fact that all who live within its territory are required to comply with its mandates. None of these factors applies to the management of a business or a university, for example, no matter how large they may be. With public administration, on the other hand, the atmosphere and principles of politics are part of its very stuff and substance.

There is, finally, the *human relations* tradition. Always and everywhere it is outstanding men and women who supply administration with its efficiency and verve. Moreover, as institutions grow larger and inevitably more bureaucratic, and as bureaucracy brings in its train specialization, hierarchy, formal rules and regulations, and impersonality, there is a correspondingly greater need to understand and to deal effectively with the human elements involved. Otherwise they will suffer from the impersonality of the situation, and the indispensable efficiency and verve of administration will be weakened.

What a mélange! No less than eight traditions combine to give public administration its character. Consider their seeming diversity: political economy, law and legal institutions, general administration, civil service, ethical and philosophical beliefs, engineering and science, political dynamics, and human relations. It is little wonder that public administration has been so long in becoming a viable field of study, sufficiently distinct from older bodies of knowledge to be accorded its own place in university structure.

Mélange or not, an effective synthesis of these traditions must be made if society is to prosper or even to survive. Like the general practice of medicine, the parts and the interrelations of the subject must be understood if the whole body is to remain healthy. To neglect one area is to jeopardize the whole system. As Brooks Adams once remarked, administration is "the capacity of coordinating many, and often conflicting social energies in a single organism, so adroitly that they shall operate as a unity." [6]

The fact that the needed synthesis can be made is shown by administrators who seem to have a genius for their craft. No aspect of it is beyond their range. They are people with just the right blend of many elements of personality, mind, and temperament. But especially do they understand the many relationships between seemingly disparate elements that are part of administration.

## Public Administration in the United States

Public administration as a university study in the United States began to develop during the nineteenth century. After Adam Smith's *The Wealth of Nations,* political economy began to divide into two streams; on the one hand the economic, which came down through David Ricardo, and on the other the political and moral, which was largely the work of John Stuart Mill and the Utilitarians, who sought to promote

---

[6] Brooks Adams, *The Theory of Social Revolutions* (New York: Macmillan, 1913), quoted in Lepawsky.

social reform and the good life and hence took an interest in institutions, including public institutions. At about the same time, Darwinian theories of biological evolution brought a concern for organic growth and functioning, social evolution. Auguste Comte, sometimes called the father of modern sociology, developed the idea that social engineering is the key to future social development and that governing skills are by all odds the most important to this end. In the United States economists, political scientists, and sociologists alike gave their main attention during the latter part of the nineteenth century to public policy and social engineering. From all of these areas came the ingredients out of which the future university discipline of public administration was to be fashioned.

Woodrow Wilson, as already noted, stressed the business and operational side of government and gave administration in the United States a new stature and importance. Shortly thereafter, political scientists and economists, most of them trained in the public law tradition of France and Germany, began to develop the field of American administrative law and comparative administrative law. Frank J. Goodnow, first president of the American Political Science Association, was one of these pioneers.

A little later, going beyond the strictly juristic aspects of the subject, interest began to focus on social reform and municipal government. There was discontent with boss rule and municipal corruption, and support for a remedy through "good government" and improved administration. In 1915 Charles A. Beard became Director of the Training School for Public Service and in 1918, Director of the New York Bureau of Municipal Research, which was later to become the Institute of Public Administration under the leadership of Luther Gulick. A host of fine young Ph.D.'s began to go into the field of municipal government, especially municipal administration.

Toward the end of his life Beard said, "There is no subject more important—from its minute ramifications of unit costs and accounts to the top structure of the overhead—than this subject of administration. The future of civilized government, and even, I think, of civilization itself rests upon our ability to develop a science and a philosophy and a practice of administration competent to discharge the public functions of civilized society." [7]

Meanwhile, the modern science of management got underway in 1903 when Frederick W. Taylor read a paper to the American Society of Mechanical Engineers on the principles of modern shop management. Taylor's ideas had a revolutionary effect not only in the United States but throughout the world, including Soviet Russia. His main thesis was

7 Charles A. Beard, "The Role of Administration in Government," *The Work Unit in Federal Administration* (Chicago: Public Administration Service, 1937), p. 3.

that all work processes are separable into units; the efficiency of each unit can be tested and improved; the technique can be extended upwards in organization so that at last whole businesses and governments, even whole societies, may be made more rational and efficient. This was not the whole of administration, as Taylor knew. He believed the most important element to be cooperation, which involves human nature and motivation, and never claimed that the stop watch could deal with this area.

Several developments followed. In 1911 President Taft appointed a presidential Commission on Efficiency and Economy to look into budgets and finance, organization, and greater economy and efficiency of operation in the federal government. Louis Brandeis, later to become a justice of the Supreme Court of the United States, threw himself into the scientific management movement and was joined by a number of Taylor's disciples, such as Harrington Emerson, H. L. Gantt, Morris Llewellyn Cooke, Henry Dennison, Henry Towne, and Harlow Person. These men among others caused the ideas of scientific management and general administration to exert a worldwide influence.

As a result of the Taft Commission report, the federal Budget and Accounting Act was passed in 1921, creating the Bureau of the Budget and institutionalizing public administration in a spectacular way. State governments began to appoint commissions of their own to study organization, structure, duplication, functionalization, staff services, legislative-executive relationships, budgetary systems, and better personnel administration. At the local level the commission and city manager forms of municipal government added impetus to the movement.

Then in 1920 W. F. Willoughby of The Brookings Institution and Johns Hopkins University, published *The Government of Modern States* and in 1927, *Principles of Public Administration*. Willoughby took the view that administration is much the same in business and government; in the federal government, Congress is the board of directors and the President the chief executive; and there are principles that apply to all large-scale organizations including, incidentally, the courts. In 1926 Leonard D. White of the University of Chicago brought out his *Introduction to the Study of Public Administration,* stressing the human side of administration and dealing comprehensively with administration in government. Public administration as a subject of academic study was now fully launched.

## The New Deal and World War II

There is no better illustration of the thesis that administration is a reaction to social need than the upsurge of interest in administration that followed the onset of the Great Depression. Under the inspiring leadership of Louis Brownlow, Charles E. Merriam, and others, a group of specialized agencies in public administration was brought together under the egis of the Public Administration Clearing House on the edge of the campus of the University of Chicago. Influenced by the nationwide human catastrophe of those years, the functions of government had so quickly multiplied that there were not enough skilled administrators to fill many remedial and relief agencies created under the New Deal. Schools of public administration, such as those at Syracuse and the University of Southern California, stepped to the fore to try quickly to train as many men and women as possible in the techniques of administration in the hope that their natural aptitudes and flexibility would make it possible for them to fill a diversity of positions even if they lacked substantive training in all of them.

Illustrating the laws of supply and demand, challenge and response, public administration rapidly became the favored specialization of political scientists. There were almost limitless opportunities in this field for professors to gain practical experience as public administrators or consultants; the Bureau of the Budget and offices of general administration within the executive departments and agencies began to act as central personnel generating stations for the government as a whole. Large sums were made available for research in public administration and from this effort came such notable books as Gaus and Wolcott, *Public Administration and the United States Department of Agriculture,* and Macmahon, Millett, and Ogden, *The Administration of Federal Work Relief.*

At about the same time the Southern Regional Center in Public Administration at the University of Alabama commenced a notable series of lectures and publications from which were to come such fine studies as Gaus's *Reflections On Public Administration,* in which he stressed the importance of ecology, or the relation between natural and human environment as the starting point for the study of administration; and James Fesler's *Area and Administration.* At the University of Chicago, Professors Gaus, White, and Dimock published *The Frontiers of Public Administration,* and a little later Gulick and Urwick brought out their *Papers on the Science of Administration* which was a major landmark because it dealt with general and large-scale administration and the principles that apply to institutional management generally. Among other contributions it included one by Henri Fayol and a discussion of his work. A French mining engineer, in 1916 Fayol had published *Industrial and General Administration* a classic in the field and still widely influential.

Meanwhile, the career aspect of the public service was emphasized in such books as Macmahon and Millett, *Federal Administrators* and White, *Government Career Service.* The National Resources Planning Board was created in the federal government to study and make recommendations for the planned development and use of national resources, as well as to plan and coordinate public works expenditures; from this agency came a wealth of basic publications centering on not only physical resources of all kinds but also human resources and dealing in addition with regionalization, urbanization, the structure of the economy, and the like. New textbooks began to appear, including John M. Pfiffner's *Public Administration*. In 1935 came *Better Government Personnel,* the report of a broad national survey with accompanying volumes, the product of a distinguished research staff headed by Luther H. Gulick.

What in many ways is the capstone of these efforts is the 1937 *Report of the President's Committee on Administrative Management* in the federal government, with supporting volumes. This study was directed by Messrs. Brownlow, Merriam, and Gulick and dealt broadly with every important aspect of federal administration: the institutionalization of the Office of the President, departmental management, regulatory commissions, personnel, budgeting, auditing, government corporations, and more, making this one of the landmarks in public administration in this or any other country.

It was largely due to this broadened and deepened research, teaching, and publishing activity occurring during the New Deal that the country was in a stronger position than it might have been when World War II began in 1939, involving the United States in 1942. During the heyday of "a businessman's civilization," government had been somewhat neglected. Now it was becoming a more effective instrument of national policy and administration.

## Taking Stock after World War II

Because of the panic conditions under which administrators were hastily trained for service during the Great Depression, it was perhaps inevitable that public administration should have come to be considered thereafter largely a matter of technique, emphasizing such things as POSDCORB, a term coined by Luther Gulick in 1937 to signify planning, organizing, staffing, directing, coordinating, reporting, and budgeting. A useful and necessary development at the time, it proved to be too limited for a discipline that was rapidly gaining ground and influence.

The first major reaction against a narrow emphasis on the techniques of administration occurred in 1948 when Dwight Waldo's *The Administrative State* reaffirmed the much older view that if it is to be democratically and value-oriented, administration must find its origins in and be tested by the enduring moral and philosophical insights of its greatest political theorists. This book started what is seen in retrospect as a revolt against the crash training program of the depression. The result has been a greatly broadened orientation for public administration, mainly in the direction of policy, decision making, and the behavioral sciences.

A year after Waldo's book appeared, Paul Appleby's *Policy and Administration* questioned and largely demolished the dichotomy that Frank J. Goodnow began in his *Politics and Administration* as early as 1914 and which others, including one of the present authors, had continued in *Modern Politics and Administration*. Appleby argued that all of government deals with politics, and consequently policy is made at all levels and offices. Although in popular discussion a rough separation between policy and administration is valid, said Appleby, sophisticates should realize that all of administration is concerned with policy and decision making. He noted eight main processes in government: the presidential nomination, general nominations, voting, legislation, adjudication, party maintenance and operation, pressure group activity (or what he called the agitational process), and lastly, the administrative or executive process. Administration is the application and execution of policy as formulated in law.

Meantime, as might be expected, scientific management in business was also undergoing a broadening and humanizing process in response to insistent social needs and forces. Chester Barnard, a businessman, published *The Functions of the Executive* in 1938 and *Organization and Management* a decade later, in which he stressed psychological and behavioral factors. Ordway Tead, already known for his books on leadership and human relations, published *The Art of Administration* in 1951, in which, among other things, he stressed the reconciliation of selfhood and a sense of belonging. In 1954 Peter Drucker wrote *The Practice of Management* in which he emphasized long-range planning and human relations in industry and government.

In the field of administration generally, the behavioral approach, getting its start after World War II, argues that human behavior is more important than the ideal structure of organizations. But it notes also that nonhuman factors, such as organization, profoundly affect behavior and personality alike. At first the behavioral science movement was largely a protest against the easy acceptance of generalizations or "proverbs" that had not been adequately tested and verified, but soon the behaviorists were making generalizations of their own that in many cases sounded surprisingly like some of those heard during the prescientific era.

One of the first books in the behavioral field was Herbert Simon's *Administrative Behavior*, wherein it is argued that all of administration revolves around rationality and decision making. In 1950 a textbook on *Public Administration* by Simon, Smithburg, and Thompson reemphasized the decision-making theme, and thereafter the influence of the behavioral approach spread. The fourth edition of Pfiffner's *Pub-

*lic Administration* (1960), with Robert V. Presthus as coauthor, was also largely converted to the behavioral decision-making approach.

The emphasis on decision making had been anticipated and perhaps encouraged by the Inter-University Case Program, in which actual administrative situations are captured and recorded so as to give the reader the facts with which to appreciate the influences brought to bear upon decision makers at work. (See Case Studies, Chapter 1.)

While this critical appraisal and broadening of approach was going on, two additional comprehensive surveys occurred, the first and second so-called Hoover Commission reports on the organization and administration of the federal government. The first, in 1949, was similar in many respects to the Brownlow committee's survey of administrative management in 1937. The second, in 1955, was additionally interesting because it dealt not only with the *how* but also with the *what* of government, namely, what government should and should not do, what activities might be discontinued, and what policies should underlie these decisions.

## *Trends and Challenges*

Has public administration come of age as an academic subject? Authorities differ, though most would doubtless agree that the discipline has made rapid strides and is now viable.

Throughout the course of its development in the United States there has been a sequence of emphases relating to the character and content of public administration. Thus between 1883 when the Pendleton Act established the federal Civil Service Commission and the early 1900s when the scientific management movement was born, emphasis was largely on civil service reform and cleaning up American politics and administration. From 1900 to 1920 there was a mixture of influences, including scientific management, municipal reform, and commissions of efficiency and economy at the federal and state levels. Between World War I and the outbreak of World War II, emphasis was first on budgeting, then on organization, and then on superstructure or overhead administration. And since 1945 interest has largely centered on human relations, psychological motivation, and behavioristic explanations.

In this sequence, however, no new concentration of attention has superseded any prior one, so that while such factors as civil service, proper budgeting, and rational organization are today taken for granted, there is in addition a ferment of new emphases. One stresses decision making, operations research, and rationality. Another believes that policy and program formulation is the primary area and that administrators should again become political economists and statesmen. Still another, the sociological, focuses on social forces and institutional interrelations, as illustrated by Philip Selznick's discussion of cooptation, or responding to external groups and their needs and purposes.[8] There is also a focus on the nature of bureaucracy or what might be called the innate environment of administration.

The result of this research and speculation is that public administration, like general administration of which it is a subdivision, is today a mix of academic specializations. Among the more important contributions are those of psychology to motivation, human needs and expectations, leadership, the wellsprings of achievement, and the like. Notable work is being done in places such as the Survey Research Center of the University of Michigan, where teams of social scientists headed by men such as Rensis Likert are developing new syntheses and new insights as a result of clinical experiments.

The accomplishment of the administrative practitioner and the academic specialist alike at any particular stage of social and economic development depends largely upon challenge and response, or what Mary Parker Follett called "the law of the situation." Administration is a sociological subject and it will remain organismic. But at the same time public administration is also public policy and decision making and as such inevitably involves economics, technology, and all the areas that create society's opportunities and corresponding problems of adjustment. And finally, public administration is and probably always will be political philosophy and morality because in the last analysis, decision making depends upon value systems that are operational.

For both the practitioner and the student, therefore, it seems safe to conclude that no single system or school of thought is wholly "right" in the sense that it is complete and universal. The challenge, therefore, is to continue to create syntheses of different elements as the subject, the art, and the science, mature through additional insights into institutions and human behavior.

This challenge will be our guideline in this book. Public administration cannot ignore what general administration has to teach, but at the same time administration in a political setting has its own special features and problems, for it must deal with politics and policy if it is to be realistic. Our brief excursus into history seems to bear out the relevance of this conclusion. The present authors are not militantly behaviorist nor are they unsympathetic to behaviorism. But they would keep constantly in mind the question, What does the operational administrator need to know about administrative policy and technique in order to be effective at work and satisfied in his selfhood, and make his best contribution to problem solving and the values that a democratic society would promote?

8 Philip Selznick, *Leadership in Administration, A Sociological Interpretation* (New York: Harper & Row, Publishers, 1957).

## BIBLIOGRAPHY AND CASES

### Annotated Reading Suggestions

No one book gives the complete history of public administration, although Albert Lepawsky's *Administration: The Art and Science of Organization and Management* (Knopf, 1949) goes far back into historical times; see especially Chapter IV, "A History of Administration." See also Woodrow Wilson, "The Study of Administration," *Political Science Quarterly*, II (June 1887), reprinted in the 1941 volume of the same journal; Luther H. Gulick and L. Urwick, eds., *Papers on the Science of Administration* (New York: Institute of Public Administration, 1937); Henri Fayol, *Industrial and General Management* (International Management Institute, 1930); Frederick W. Taylor, *The Principles of Scientific Management* (Harper & Row, 1947); John M. Gaus, Leonard D. White, and Marshall E. Dimock, *The Frontiers of Public Administration* (University of Chicago Press, 1936); Symposium, *New Horizons in Public Administration* (University of Alabama Press, 1945); Dwight Waldo, *Perspectives on Administration* (University of Alabama Press, 1956); and Donald C. Rowat, ed., *Basic Issues in Public Administration* (Macmillan, 1961), especially Chapter I, "The Nature of Public Administration."

### Case Studies

In the Inter-University Case Program (ICP), several studies deal with the historical evolution of administrative problems. One of the best is No. 41, *Little Rock Story* (revised 1959), written by C. Silverman. In thirty-two pages, this study deals with race relations, federalism, and cooperative relationships amongst the agencies of government. Obviously it deals with one of the outstanding issues of the present decade of American politics.

A second study in this series, No. 15, *Gainesville School Problem* (eleven pages) is written by F. T. Adams and deals with a period of transition in educational affairs.

A third case, No. 46, *Echo Park Controversy* (ninety-seven pages) is written by D. Stratton and deals with another kind of issue, the development of conservation in the west. A fourth, No. 38, *New Bedford Manpower Incident,* by K. S. Arnow, illustrates another type of governmental activity.

Finally, the early history of the Rural Electrification Administration, one of the most controversial of the New Deal programs, is narrated by its first director, Morris L. Cooke, a pioneer in scientific management, in his article, "The Early Days of the Rural Electrification Idea: 1914-1936," *American Political Science Review*, 42 (June 1948).

# 3

## A Career
## in Government

THE THREE PRINCIPAL questions that students usually ask about the possibilities of a career in government service are these: What kind of jobs are there? How does one prepare for them? And what are the pros and cons of a career in government? This chapter tries to give some preliminary answers, but the matter is discussed again in many other parts of the book. In the end, the student himself must make his own judgment on the basis of his own synthesis of the factors he considers important.

At the outset, a characteristic aspect of public employment in the United States should be understood. In most other parts of the world a career in government service has prestige. By contrast, in this country until fairly recently public employment was handicapped by a long history of belittlement. The reasons are obvious: Americans fought and won the War of Independence against Britain in order to escape governmental controls that were intolerable, and thereafter government at any level was regarded with suspicion. As a nation of businessmen we have looked on government as the natural foe of laissez faire, even though that doctrine was operative during only a brief period in our history. Individualistic and resourceful, we have been alert to use government when it was to our advantage, while determined to keep it in its place. Until recently it has seemed that the best way to do this was to hold government in low regard. Consequently, working for government also was held in low regard.

Fortunately, these attitudes have greatly changed in the course of the last few decades. Two world wars and a disastrous depression within the memory of a single lifetime created nationwide problems of public policy that only a strong government could solve. These emergencies brought to the administration of government many businessmen who came with skepticism and left, after yeoman service, with respect and admiration for the many able and dedicated public servants and the work they accomplish with little thanks from the public. So great has been the effect of this change in attitude that many businessmen now ask, What can we do to improve the efficiency of government and the respect in which it is held? Many now realize that if government fails effectively to administer programs vital to the public interest—foreign affairs, foreign aid, economic stabilization, taxation, and the like—then private business will not survive no matter how well, for its part, it is administered.

Thus the contemporary climate for a career in government is favorable. The service itself has been improved but much remains to be done, for it must attract to it the best minds and talents from among our young people that the nation has to offer.

### The Importance and Magnitude of Public Employment

Advanced technology and a corresponding complexity in American business and government have created a new elite, the professional manager. In government, this means the three top grades on the General Schedule, GS-16, GS-17, and GS-18.

That there is a serious need for skilled top executives in government is shown by these figures: In 1961 top federal officials assigned over 11,000 positions to executive selection and development programs for the purpose of receiving training for higher responsibilities. It was expected that 3000 (27 percent) of these jobs would become vacant in the following five years, 22 percent by voluntary departures and 5 percent through mandatory retirement.[1] Moreover, the turnover rate among federal career executives is higher than the expected turnover of top-level executives in business. For example, it was anticipated that from 1960 to 1965, 20 percent of the presidents and vice presidents in the 100 largest business concerns would reach retirement age. For government the corresponding figure is 27 percent.[2]

[1] Ross Pollock, "Federal Career Development Needs—An Overview," *The University-Federal Agency Conference on Career Development,* working papers for meetings held at Princeton University, Nov. 2-4, 1961 (Washington, D.C.: Government Printing Office, 1961), p. 1.
[2] *Ibid.*

In the face of this shortage of administrative leadership, an official of a large company once suggested that a partial solution might lie in sharing executives, and it is significant that so makeshift an arrangement could seriously be considered.[3]

Top-level vacancies are especially serious because the type of work involved so largely determines the fate of the country. In 1957 a Brookings Institution study found 3000 to 3600 career officials in positions such as administrative assistant, secretary, chief of a staff office, director and assistant director of a bureau, or chief of an important division. "On this small number," noted the Brookings study, "rests, in substantial measure, the efficiency and effectiveness of the executive branch."[4] It is at this level that the administrative elite deals with the substance of policy, creates the dynamics for carrying it out, and provides the administrative continuity that all institutions must have. In government, unless the career service can be improved, said the Dean of Harvard's Littauer School of Public Administration, government cannot do what the people expect of it, for "A great empire and little minds go ill together." The professional administrator, he continued, must make himself the link between the scientist and the politician in order to reconcile technology with democratic values. And so long as this new elite remains under the direction of the responsible heads of departments and is accountable through them to Congress, the danger of creating an irresponsible bureaucracy is not great.[5]

The magnitude of public employment in the United States may be shown by the fact that eight or nine out of every 100 gainfully employed person now work for government at one level or another. If the military are included, the figure is about one out of every five. The combined figure for employment at state and local levels is greater than for the federal government, and at all levels the total is growing. In the half century between 1902 and 1955, state and local expenditures increased thirtyfold, while the nation's gross national product (GNP) expanded only twentyfold. Local governments alone employ more than 5 million persons, which is 10 percent of the nation's nonfarm workers.

Nevertheless, the federal government is the single largest employer in the nation, its work is the most complex of any, and calls for nearly every modern skill and profession. In January 1958, for example, the federal government employed some 2.4 million civilians and about 2.8 million additional personnel on active military duty. By contrast, the American Telephone and Telegraph Company, the nation's largest pri-

3 Remark to one of the present authors, at the conference noted in note 1 above.
4 Douglas Cater, *Developing Leadership in Government* (Washington, D.C.: The Brookings Institution, 1960), p. 10.
5 Don K. Price, "Administrative Leadership," *Daedalus* (Fall 1961), pp. 750-763.

vate employer, in 1957 had only 800,000 men and women on its payrolls, and only four other American corporations had as many as 200,000: General Motors, General Electric, U. S. Steel, and A & P.[6]

Yet another way to show the magnitude of federal employment is to compare the civilian portion of it to large areas of industry. Thus, in 1961:[7]

|  | Number of Employees |
| --- | --- |
| Federal government (civilian) | 2,384,000 |
| 10 largest industrial corporations | 1,905,000 |
| 50 largest merchandising corporations | 1,148,000 |

Moreover, federal career executives manage the career service itself, which includes most government employees. Thus, also in 1961:[8]

|  | Number of Employees | Percent |
| --- | --- | --- |
| In the career service | 2,051,000 | 86 |
| In the excepted service | 333,000 | 14 |

When the second Hoover Commission reported in 1955 it counted sixty-five separate federal departments, agencies, boards, commissions, and corporations, plus 350 major operating bureaus below the departmental and agency level.[9] Moreover, many federal agencies and departments are as large as many of our giant business corporations. In 1962 civilian employment exceeded 50,000 in nine federal departments and agencies, including the Post Office with 588,477, Army with 393,849, Navy with 348,056, Air Force with 306,181, Veterans Administration with 176,562, Agriculture with 110,511, Treasury with 83,036, Health, Education, and Welfare with 77,242, and Interior with 63,353.

Fortunately not all of these federal employees are located in Washington; in fact, only 10 percent of them are employed there, the majority being distributed among the fifty states and abroad. In 1962 250,000 federal employees were located in California alone, and there were 186,000 in New York, 134,000 in Pennsylvania, 119,000 in Texas, and 104,000 in Illinois. Vermont accounted for only a little over 3000 and New

---

6 Marver H. Bernstein, *The Job of the Federal Executive* (Washington, D.C.: The Brookings Institution, 1958), pp. 205-206.
7 Pollock, *loc. cit.,* p. 9.
8 *Ibid.*
9 Commission on Organization of the Executive Branch of the Government, *Task Force Report on Personnel and Civil Service* (Washington, D.C.: Government Printing Office, 1955), p. 201.

Hampshire for less than 4000. In addition, 160,000 were stationed outside of the country.

Comparisons of employment among the three branches of the federal government—legislative, judicial, and executive—also are interesting. Thus in 1962 Congress had a total of 7887 persons on its payroll, the judicial branch had 5568, while the executive branch has over 2.5 million.

## Kinds of Jobs

In some countries a career in politics can be pursued similarly to a career in the administrative civil service. In Britain, for example, a young man or woman joins a political party and runs for office irrespective of legal residence, in any district where the party thinks the chances of success are good. And whether the party is in power or out, the candidate is continually employed in party work. In the United States, political parties mean less, nor are they organized to guarantee a continuing career to young people of ability. Accordingly most Americans who enter politics do so only after having established themselves in another career—a law practice is probably the most common—which they keep active so as to have something to fall back on when they lose out politically, as sooner or later they usually do.

Consequently the United States lacks the kind of continuity in political activity that would assure a greater degree of policy leadership in the legislative and executive branches alike. This leadership must come, therefore, from the career executives of the permanent civil service, but so far the need has been only partially met.

There are other areas of careerism in government, however, where America has done remarkably well. The city manager movement is one of them. The system was inaugurated early in this century and has now been installed in more than 1800 cities throughout the nation. It is most popular among the larger cities and has been adopted in nearly half of those with a population of 25,000 or more. Professional city managers move from city to city on a career ladder depending on administrative competence instead of the favoritism often shown a home town boy. In 1961 salaries ranged from an average of $7636 in places of less than 5000 population up to a top salary of $30,000 in one of the largest cities. The plan has now spread to other countries including Finland, Germany, Norway, Sweden, Ireland, and Canada.

Another interesting government career possibility is the Foreign Service of the State Department, which once suffered from handicaps similar to those mentioned above but is now greatly improved in prestige and career opportunities, thanks partly to enhanced support from Congress. For obvious reasons there are few more challenging opportunities in the world today than work in the Foreign Service.

The prestige of government employment is high also in professional areas where Americans have acquired an international reputation. Public health, education, medicine, law, and engineering are some of them. Since literally millions of jobs in government at various levels are in some specialized area, this is a favorable development.

An area of special appeal to those who dislike office routine and enjoy the outdoors are many jobs in the Departments of Agriculture and the Interior having to do with the national forests, national parks, supervision of the public lands, reclamation (largely heavy construction), wildlife conservation, resource conservation, soil conservation, and the like. Many different kinds of specialties are needed, both in the field and at the administrative end.

For all white-collar employment in the federal government by occupational groups in 1961, the breakdown was as follows:[10]

| | |
|---|---|
| Total white collar, all groups | 1,533,061 |
| General administrative, clerical, and office | 799,102 |
| Engineering | 105,426 |
| Accounting and budget | 103,425 |
| Mental, dental, hospital, public health | 88,817 |
| Supply | 73,940 |
| Business and industry | 40,808 |
| Legal and kindred | 37,024 |
| Biological sciences | 34,839 |
| Physical sciences | 34,596 |
| Investigation | 31,346 |
| Transportation | 29,273 |
| Personnel administration and industrial relations | 28,038 |
| Education | 19,161 |
| Social science, psychology, and welfare | 18,244 |
| Mechanic | 15,332 |
| Mathematics and statistics | 14,387 |
| Commodity quality control, etc. | 12,874 |
| Fine and applied arts | 8,879 |

[10] U. S. Civil Service Commission, *1962 Annual Report,* p. 27.

| | |
|---|---:|
| Library and archives | 5,936 |
| Veterinary medical science | 2,260 |
| Copyright, patents, and trademark | 1,614 |
| Trades, crafts, and labor | 10 |
| Miscellaneous occupations | 47,130 |

Note that engineering, accounting, and medical care are second, third, and fourth in size, next only to general administrative personnel.

The most interesting and challenging federal positions are in the so-called supergrades occupied by those whom we have referred to as the new elite. These jobs are scattered over forty-nine agencies and many more bureaus. Almost a third of them are in the Defense Department which incidentally accounts for nearly half of all federal employees. Three fourths of the supergrades are in nine agencies in addition to the Defense Department, and these include the Departments of State, Treasury, Justice, Interior, Commerce, and Agriculture, and the Atomic Energy Commission, the Federal Aviation Agency, and the Aeronautics and Space Administration.[11]

In view of the occupational range of federal white-collar employment, it is not surprising that in the top grades (GS-16 and above, or equivalent pay), something like three out of ten careerists are scientists or engineers, generally in supervisory or line positions. For the rest, four out of ten are in other line positions and three out of ten are in various staff and other jobs not in the line. Within each of these categories, the range of duties and responsibilities is enormous.[12]

## Preparation for the Public Service

The foregoing groups of figures show pretty clearly that the new administrative elite in government consists largely of specialists. And since causation is broadly social, this is equally true of industry where as early as 1949 a survey showed that one third of the largest business corporations were headed by engineers.[13]

In public administration, the importance of engineers in the top ranks is comparable. As of 1956, for example, of every 100 engineers employed in the United States, seven worked for the federal government and sixteen for state or local units. Moreover, government at all

---

11 Pollock, *loc. cit.*, p. 2.
12 *Ibid.*, p. 3
13 A study by Dr. Earl B. Norris, reported in James C. Stephens and Gilbert Chester Jacobus, "The Engineer Manager: Training the Technician for Executive Responsibilities," *Personnel* (March 1954), p. 375.

levels employed 43 percent of the nation's biologists, 27 percent of its mathematicians, and 25 percent of its physicists.[14] In government as in industry, these technically trained specialists increasingly rise to the top executive jobs.

As might be expected, therefore, the federal career executive is usually a well-educated person. Whereas in 1952 some 57 percent of business executive had college degrees,[15] the comparable figure for 1650 government executives in GS-16 or higher classification was 75 percent. Ignoring the 500 federal scientists and engineers in this group (one third of whom have Ph.D.'s), 70 percent of the remaining 1150 career executives in these grades were college graduates and 9 percent had Ph.D.'s.

The education of the scientist and the engineer is in their profession of course, but what of the others, the 1150 who are general administrators? They attended over 275 different colleges and took the following courses (up to two majors coded for any individual):[16]

| | |
|---|---:|
| Business and commerce | 305 |
| Economics | 220 |
| Law | 217 |
| Engineering | 142 |
| Physical sciences, geology, and mathematics | 124 |
| Public administration | 81 |
| Political science | 75 |
| History | 53 |
| Agricultural and biological sciences | 44 |
| Education | 38 |
| English | 37 |
| Psychology | 25 |

Note how low on the list are the humanities and the social sciences. In both private and public employment, as William H. Whyte, Jr.,[17] has so

---

14 National Science Foundation, *Trends in the Employment and Training of Scientists and Engineers* (Washington, D.C.: Government Printing Office, 1956).

15 W. Lloyd Warner and J. C. Abegglen, *Occupational Mobility in American Business and Industry* (Minneapolis, Minn.: University of Minnesota Press, 1955).

16 Pollock, *loc. cit.*, p. 6.

17 William H. Whyte, Jr., *The Organization Man* (New York: Simon & Schuster, 1956), chaps. 7 and 8, and pp. 103-104.

clearly shown, the liberal arts graduate gets short shrift in the nation's governing institutions.

At all levels of government, most employment is now under civil service. Consequently, unless one is interested in a political appointment, the legislative service, the judiciary, a diplomatic appointment as minister or ambassador in the Foreign Service (increasingly rare), or one of the excepted positions under the permanent civil service (14 percent of all jobs in the federal service), an understanding of civil service methods is indispensable.

Information as to vacancies and projected entrance examinations announced by the Civil Service Commission is as accessible as the nearest post office; many university professors keep themselves posted in this area. In addition, the Commission maintains its own offices in many cities grouped into a number of regions covering the nation. The federal Civil Service Commission as well as commissions at the state and local levels also publish informative circulars directed at the college student's interest.

Generally speaking, civil service commissions proceed according to specializations. The postal service has its own examinations, for example, the FBI likewise, there is a legal register, and so on. But in other areas where skills are transferable—and this applies to most General Schedule positions—there may be registers (lists of qualified candidates who have passed particular examinations) that may be used throughout government, or nearly so. But here too specialization is a factor, and most promotion systems for secretarial, custodial, postal clerk, professional, and many other types of jobs have been vertical rather than horizontal. The reason for this rather inflexible approach is that classification laws determine the combination and degree of skills needed for each position, in the light of the nation's educational system. This tends to splinter and divide skill groups and to make promotion systems a rather narrow staircase.

Beginning in 1934, however, the Civil Service Commission began to cater to the generalist skills of college graduates. State and local jurisdictions had already bestirred themselves in this direction, or were about to. As a consequence, most civil service commissions today are in active pursuit of the college graduate, even if not as aggressively, perhaps, as some of the largest private corporations. Nevertheless there has been a notable increase in college recruitment for the public service at all governmental levels.

The 1934 innovation was the Junior Civil Service Examination and it was repeated in 1936. Although originally designed to recruit government experts in personnel administration, it was effectively used to place college graduates in other positions as well. In 1937 another significant step was the Social Science Analyst Examination, the scope and purpose of which was obviously wider than the earlier examination. This was aimed at students of public administration, economics, and other disciplines useful in supervisory and staff positions, and for line positions in agriculture, social security, census, labor statistics, and the like.

The principle of recruiting college graduates having been firmly established, it has not only been continued but considerably accelerated. In 1939 came the Junior Administrative Technician Examination, followed by the Administrative Analyst Examination, both junior and senior. From qualified candidates listed on the appropriate registers it was possible to secure college men and women for both administrative and specialist positions.

The examination mainly relied upon today is the Federal-Service Entrance Examination, announced annually and given six or seven times during the course of the school year, to fill beginning professional positions in some sixty occupational fields. Most of these positions are in grade GS-5, but where the candidate is especially qualified by experience or graduate work the appointment may be in grades GS-7 to GS-9. This examination is also used to recruit outstanding candidates for special training in management work. In addition to the FSEE, there are, of course, a number of entrance level examinations announced for specific job titles, such as engineer, chemist, librarian, and the like.

In the past, except in the professional fields and for substantive specializations, the general college graduate examinations have been weighted in favor of the social sciences. They have gradually been broadened, however, to include general aptitudes and the whole range of the liberal arts curriculum. Consequently, many undergraduate majors in mathematics, English, a foreign language, or art have fared as well as majors in the social sciences in these later examinations, which, of course, is as it should be.

Another factor in recruitment is that veterans receive special consideration, which as a matter of fact extends to other matters affecting their employment as well. This preference becomes significant when it is realized that as of 1961, more than half of all federal employees, most of them exservice men and women, received this kind of preference; approximately 17 percent of them had been disabled.

Finally, the Civil Service Commission also encourages college students to try for public employment by offering them summer jobs as well as opportunities to work in the federal service even before graduation. The means is a work-study program under which students alternate between periods of on-the-job training and study on the campus. For the most part, these opportunities are offered to majors in engineering and the physical and biological sciences, but others may also be accepted.

## Conditions of Employment

The federal government has developed a career plan for its employees, the basis of which is the career-conditional appointment system covering employee rights and privileges in such matters as promotions, transfers, reemployment, and the like. After he has passed the entrance examination and has been hired, the employee must complete three years of conditional service before he gains full career standing, the purpose being to discourage candidates who do not wish to make the public service a lifetime career. The system is said also to establish "the ability of the Government to provide continuing careers." [18]

The salary of a career executive under the Classification Act, which covers 88 percent of nonscience employees, is determined from a review of his duties and responsibilities. Naturally the way he does his work affects the job itself and hence his pay level. In government a man is paid for what he does and not according to his rank (as in the military system) or his academic degrees (as in some educational institutions). The Salary Reform Act of 1962 provides for the following rates in the higher grades:

| | |
|---|---|
| GS-18 | $20,000 |
| GS-17 | 18,000 to 20,000 |
| GS-16 | 16,000 to 18,000 |
| GS-15 | 14,565 to 17,925 |

In January 1964, substantial pay increases in the lower grades of the General Schedule went into effect.

Salary increases, including increases in grade for outstanding work, are granted at stated intervals until the top step in the pay scale is reached. Special plans are in effect for such groups as executives in the Foreign Service, the Atomic Energy Commission, the Central Intelligence Agency, the Tennessee Valley Authority, and for certain medically trained administrators in the Veterans Administration. In addition, a special salary scale is authorized for about a thousand scientists and engineers.

That Congress is becoming aware of the shortage of top executives in the GS-16 to GS-18 classifications is shown by the fact that it recently increased the number of these jobs, which is limited by statute, by 411 to make a total of 2985, and removed numerical restrictions entirely on several especially critical positions in engineering, medicine, and the physical and natural sciences.

---

[18] U. S. Civil Service Commission, *Federal Career Directory*, A Guide for College Students (Washington, D.C.: Government Printing Office, 1962), p. 5.

Each career executive commonly stays in a particular occupation and moves to higher levels in the same line of work, a fact that is reflected in federal classification practice. In most occupational series, for example, official standards start with entrance-level positions and extend through supervisory and management jobs to executive posts. Since 1955, however, the Civil Service Commission has encouraged employees to move from one specialty to another so as to develop general managerial abilities. The means is the creation of a new class series called program managers, for which no subject matter background is required.

Career executives receive the same legal protections against arbitrary removal for political or other reasons as do other public employees. Nevertheless, some of the higher career executives have resigned or retired when they found themselves in serious disagreement with their political superiors on political or policy issues.

A career executive may transfer to another position under the coverage of the merit system. In addition, his superior can order his transfer to another job or location. His superior can also promote him; if another government agency desires his services, it may employ him at a promotion. Moreover, a career executive may and sometimes does accept a promotion to an important political post, but he must then leave the career service and its protections against arbitrary removal. The career executive also has the same rights as other government employees to annual and sick leave, health insurance, life insurance, pension, and retirement annuities. As in the matter of entrance examinations, veterans receive certain preferences in some employee rights and protections.

Finally, as with all government employees, the federal career executive is subject to a number of special conditions and limitations that do not apply at all, or to the same degree, in private employment. Thus his political activities are restricted. His personal life is limited to the extent that he must avoid a conflict of interest, real or apparent. His decisions are subject to review not only by his political superiors, congressional committees, and the public, but also by the courts. And finally, his actions are hedged in by laws, regulations, and controls imposed by central management agencies such as the Bureau of the Budget, the General Accounting Office, and the Civil Service Commission itself.

Despite the structural faults in public personnel administration, such as jealousy between Congress and the executive branch, and a sometimes ill-defined scope for federal career executives, much recent progress has been made in the government's handling of human relations. An early important landmark in federal personnel administration was the Pendleton Act of 1883 which established the principle of equal pay for equal work throughout the government.

In the 1930s came the beginnings of a Personnel Council and special examinations, as we have seen, and also apprenticeship programs for college graduates. A major advance occurred about 1938 when personnel administration was largely decentralized, being transferred from the Civil Service Commission to the operating federal departments and agencies, with the Commission itself laying down the rules and standards and thereafter acting only as encourager and judge. From that time, personnel administration has been improved throughout the government. The Classification Act of 1949 exemplified this progress and was followed by the Federal Employees Group Life Insurance Act of 1954 and the Civil Service Retirement Act of 1956, both of which broadened and liberalized older laws. Then a Bureau of Programs Standards was set up within the Civil Service Commission to devise and coordinate a program of policy development, planning, and the setting of standards. In 1958 another major step forward occurred when Congress, for the first time in its history, provided for on-the-job training under the Government Employees Training Act, declaring as its purpose that the "self-education, self-improvement and self-training" of federal employees should be "supplemented and extended" by continuous, government-sponsored training to develop skills, knowledge, and abilities. This program is carried on jointly by the Civil Service Commission and the operating departments and agencies.

Yet another major landmark was the result of a reform program offered by the President in 1962. As already noted, in that year the Federal Salary Reform Act raised salaries for and added to the number of supergrade positions, GS-16 through GS-18. Even more important, however, this law enunciated for the first time the so-called comparability principle, according to which federal salary rates shall be comparable with rates in private enterprise for the same level of work. Then it reaffirmed and broadened the so-called alignment principle which provides equal pay for substantially equal work within the public service, plus pay differentials in keeping with work and performance distinctions. This latter principle had already been in force, but the new law facilitates annual salary reviews, the payment of special rates to meet special needs, the liberalization of rates in grade, and in cooperation with the Bureau of Labor Statistics the gearing of federal salaries to living costs and to changes in prevailing rates in private industry.

Only one major feature of the President's 1962 reform program failed of enactment: the rationalization of salary scales for top career executives so as to make them reasonably equivalent to salaries in private employment at corresponding levels of responsibility. The Senate Committee on Post Office and Civil Service, which considered the measure, acknowledged that the comparability principle enacted for the benefit of most federal employees stopped short of full reform at career executive levels, but promised to take the matter up in the following year.

Each inching step forward is to be welcomed, of course, but progress has not been noted for its speed. Perhaps the most that can be said

so far is that the morale of supergrade officials in Washington is remarkably good despite the disappointments they have experienced.
Current hurdles are mainly political and structural, including cooperation between Congress and the executive branch and between political
officials and career executives. For years the civil service has been a
bone of contention over which pressure groups, Congress, and the
White House have fought. Nevertheless, structural and organizational
lines must be further improved because "Political responsibility . . .
depends on having a responsive and well-trained professional corps, and
cannot be achieved by keeping it in a state of fragmentation and anarchy." [19]

## The Pros and Cons of a Career in Government

The foregoing is a picture of the federal executive and the conditions
under which he works. How good is he? And is this an attractive prospect for a young person of ambition?

A study of the qualifications of the 219 career executives who entered grades GS-16 and higher in the competitive service for the first
time in 1960 showed that 190 of them (nearly 87 percent) were rated as
having excellent experience records, 22 were rated as good, and only 7
were seen to be minimally qualified.[20] Along the same line, David Mc-
Clelland, head of the Psychology Department at Harvard University,
reported in *The Achieving Society* that in a comparison of top career
officials in Washington with a similar group in American industry, the
incentive to achieve was as high as or even higher among the government group than among the businessmen.[21]

Nevertheless, much remains to be done before the leadership needs
of the federal civil service are satisfactorily met. A major difficulty is
that top officials are ordinarily so specialized that the resulting bureaucracy is a patchwork of fragments, and an uncoordinated system is
neither efficient nor responsive to people's needs. More generalist executives must be recruited and trained.

At least equally serious is the failure to accord career public officials
the responsibility that modern conditions require. The career service
should have more support from Congress and the public in order fully
to develop the human potential that is at hand. Many European governments guarantee a career for permanent civil servants, but in the
United States only the first steps have been taken in this direction. Con-

19 Price, *loc cit.*, p. 755.
20 Pollock, *loc cit.*, p. 6.
21 David C. McClelland, *The Achieving Society* (Princeton, N.J.: D. Van Nostrand
    & Company, Inc., 1961), p. 295.

sequently the American career executive sometimes finds that government jobs and promotions are affected by shifting appropriations, variations in domestic policy, the pressure of international crises, changes in technologies, and an expanding population.

Promotion for an able public official may be very rapid in an expanding organization, and static or declining in another where advancement depends on the retirement or death of those ahead of him. In the United States we have failed to realize that the primary asset in public employment is the person, not the position, and that to do his best the gifted administrator must have more mobility and scope than is ordinarily accorded him. It must also be admitted, however, that none of these uncertainties nor those that stem from a change of political administration have so far prevented most of those who have reached top jobs in government from achieving a record of continuous employment.[22]

Under the British system both politics and the civil service are careers and hence little affected by political instability; in the United States the political heads of departments, Secretaries or Assistant Secretaries, hold the job so briefly that soon after learning it they leave it. There is little time to cement right relations between the political neophyte who is the boss and the experienced career man who is his subordinate. The vacuum of leadership that is created may be and often is close to dangerous.

The figures are eloquent. In the nearly twenty years between 1933 and 1952, the average tenure of presidentially appointed department heads (Secretaries) was forty-two months; for the next in command (Undersecretaries) it was twenty-three months; and for Assistant Secretaries it was thirty-two months. By contrast, during the fifteen years between 1933 and 1948, average tenure among bureau chiefs in seventy bureaus was eight and one-half years. In 1954, in six departments the sixty-three bureaus not headed by military men or Assistant Secretaries, were directed by chiefs whose average length of service was just under five years; their average federal experience was sixteen years, although fifteen of them were new and had been less than fifteen months in office at the time.[23]

Jay Walz, writing in *The New York Times,* put his finger on the core of the trouble: In the forward echelons of government, including Cabinet and sub-Cabinet positions, there are 750 offices of exceptional political and executive responsibility, dealing with continuing long-range problems such as national defense, foreign aid, atomic energy, space exploration, and the like. These jobs demand men of high talent, ingenuity, and determination in order to foster and administer the pro-

22 Pollock, *loc. cit.,* pp. 10-11.
23 Bernstein, *op. cit.,* p. 85.

grams by which an administration in office is judged. Yet in Washington, as recently as 1957, it was an accepted fact of life that fully one third of the men and women holding these crucial positions would be gone a year later and their places filled by new and inexperienced officials. In some agencies the proportion of departures is often higher. In two or three years, or even in an administration's four-year term in office, the cumulative effect of this turnover is startling.[24]

Despite the hazards of discontinuity that stem from this rapid turnover among top officials, in 1955 a Task Force report of the second Hoover Commission recommended not more but less influence for the career civil servant; that most positions held by career men be turned over to political appointees; and that career executives be barred from concern with policy questions because these are "political" matters to be dealt with exclusively by party appointees.[25] That this was obviously a wrong policy was the conclusion of a group of former top federal officials meeting under the auspices of The Brookings Institution to discuss *The Job of the Federal Executive.* Here it was pointed out that the career executive acquires a reservoir of knowledge, a degree of managerial competence based on experience, and an understanding of the peculiarities of government administration that help to keep the government operating despite the instability that customarily prevails.[26]

The real distinction, said these executives, is that the career man takes the lead in recommending action and the political appointee takes full political responsibility for the decision. Speaking of the career official, one executive remarked that it would be impossible to recruit top executives for a strictly nonpolitical job because that kind of work has no flavor, is not what "a man with spunk would live with, and he couldn't even if he wanted to." [27]

Moreover, it is pretty generally agreed that career men not only are more experienced in government administration but often have more political sense as well. One participant at this conference suggested that career executives often have even greater political skill than political executives, noting that top grade government jobs, whatever their nature, have much in common, and if there is a distinction it is in the degree of political experience possessed by the incumbent, whether career man or political appointee. Indeed, in political skill the long-time career executive easily outranks the transient political executive of limited tenure. A career man in Washington who has been on the job for

---

24 Jay Walz, "Help Wanted: Top Men for Washington," *The New York Times Magazine* (October 13, 1957), p. 24.

25 Commission on Organization of the Executive Branch of the Government, *Task Force Report on Personnel and Civil Service* (Washington, D.C.: Government Printing Office, 1955), pp. 1-4.

26 Bernstein, *op. cit.,* pp. 40-48.

27 *Ibid.,* p. 43.

twenty-five years or so is a master where most others would be rank am-
ateurs.[28]

What is needed, says Dean Price, is better general staff work, better
coordination at all levels, more scope for the expert career executive on
whom continuity rests:[29]

> I am not proposing that career administrators have any more authority
> —but only an opportunity to help bring up the issues that political
> authority must resolve. Nor am I advocating additional governmental
> controls—I am only asking whether the extensive controls we already
> have are being used in a rationally related manner.

The progress there has been is thanks largely to the policies of the
Civil Service Commission headed by men such as John Macy, former
president of the American Society for Public Administration. The very
existence of highly qualified career executives in the supergrades is a
case in point. As an executive at the Brookings round table remarked,
federal executives are more ingenious and more sophisticated than they
were twenty years ago, and many of them assert their independence of
Congress to a degree undreamed of in the past.[30]

Although salary scales have improved and are now on a flexible
footing that will make further improvement possible, it is doubtful
whether monetary compensation in the public service will ever reach
the heights achieved in some parts of private industry where a top man
may receive $200,000 or more a year. As noted in the Brookings study,
". . . existing wide discrepancies in executive salary levels deter promising men and women from pursuing careers in government, and obstruct
the interchange of executive personnel between private life and public
service." [31]

Much depends on the aspirations and values of the would-be public
official, how he balances financial compensation against the satisfactions
open to him in a career in government. Some aspects of public employment cannot be equaled elsewhere: a feeling of patriotism, work more
interesting and satisfying than is usually found in industry, friendly and
enjoyable human associations in which personal competitions are less,
and the greater challenge of a hard-hitting job. One former government executive at the Brookings round table told how, when he re-
turned to the clubs he had formerly frequented, he found people talking
about the same things that had concerned them four years previously.
"They seemed to have no conception," he said, "of what the govern-

28 *Ibid.*, p. 57.
29 Price, *loc. cit.*, p. 755.
30 Bernstein, *op. cit.*, p. 112.
31 *Ibid.*, p. 208.

ment was or how it worked. I felt like I was back in a little boy's game, despite the fact that I was making five times as much money as I did in Washington." Another participant at the same meeting underscored the challenge of public employment in these words: "The privilege of executive experience in the federal government is strongly affirmative. The daily involvement in critical programs affecting large numbers of people offers a stimulation that cannot be equalled in other types of executive positions." [32]

---

[32] *Ibid.*, p. 216.

## BIBLIOGRAPHY AND CASES

### Annotated Reading Suggestions

A number of books and articles have tried to give the "feel" of the rounded experience of operating officials. Donald S. Stone, who served in Washington for a number of years, has written "Notes on the Government Executive: His Role and Methods," in the symposium, *New Horizons in Public Administration* (University of Alabama Press, 1945). Case narratives on significant programs are found in Arthur W. Macmahon, John D. Millett, and Gladys Ogden, *The Administration of Work Relief* (Chicago: Public Administration Service, 1941), and in John M. Gaus and Leon Wolcott, *Public Administration and the United States Department of Agriculture* (Chicago: Public Administration Service, 1941). Paul H. Appleby in *Big Democracy* (Knopf, 1945) studies the growth of the United States Department of Agriculture, and in "Organizing Around a Department Head," *Public Administration Review,* 6 (Summer 1946), deals with executive functions at the departmental level.

Other books on the role of the administrator are Melvin T. Copeland, *The Executive at Work* (Harvard University Press, 1952); E. P. Learned, D. N. Ulrich, and D. R. Booz, *Executive Action* (Harvard Business School, 1951); Marver Bernstein, *The Job of the Federal Executive* (The Brookings Institution, 1958); Ordway Tead, *The Art of Administration* (McGraw-Hill, 1951); Leslie Lipson, *The American Governor: From Figurehead to Leader* (University of Chicago Press, 1939); Melvin Dalton, *Men Who Manage* (Wiley, 1959); American Management Association, *Defining the Manager's Job* (American Management Association, 1958); and Marshall E. Dimock, *The Executive in Action* (Harper & Row, 1945).

Special emphasis is on middle management in a book by Arthur W. Macmahon and John D. Millett, *Federal Administrators* (Columbia University Press, 1939), and one by Mary Cushing Niles, *Middle Management, The Job of the Junior Administrator* (rev. ed., Harper & Row, 1949).

## Case Studies

One of the best cases in Harold Stein, *Public Administration and Policy Development: A Case Book,* is called *The Defense Plant Corporation.* It was written in 1950 by Clifford J. Durr, one of the actors in the drama, and tells the story of decision making at a crucial time in American history: reconversion to peacetime activity at the end of World War II. It illustrates the range of executive interests, emphasizing the making of policy and deals with politics, interests, and personalities.

A second case in the Stein collection, *Cancellation of the Ration Stamps,* written by Martin Kriesberg, is shorter. It also illustrates decision making during World War II and in addition throws a good deal of light on the matter of public relations.

Other cases in the ICP program worth reading are No. 53, *Martial Law in East Texas,* by W. E. Mills, forty-one pages; and No. 74, *Coming of Age of the Langley Porter Clinic: The Reorganization of a Mental Health Clinic,* by M. Robinson, forty-one pages. Each of these illustrates other areas of administrative concern.

Two additional cases, both British, may be of interest. These are found in a compendium entitled *Administrators in Action: British Case Studies, Volume I,* edited by F. M. G. Willson (University of Toronto Press, 1961). These cases were reviewed by Harold Stein, "The British Administrator's World," *Public Administration Review,* 22 (December 1962). Two cases dealing with central-local relationships are "Coventry Moves a Market," and "The Administrative Consequences of Jim and Vera Fardell," the latter being concerned with seven long frustrating years during which public administrators tried to salvage a semidelinquent family.

Finally, William Alanson White in *The Autobiography of a Purpose* (Doubleday, 1938) tells the story of how, as the head of a federal hospital and through his own administrative methods, this famous doctor was able to convert into reality his vision of the way mentally ill people should be treated, thus helping to usher in a new era in the treatment of mental sickness.

# 4

---

# What
# the Administrator
# Does

---

An ADMINISTRATOR is both analyzer and synthesizer; consequently he must be the kind of person who can break a problem down into its parts and then put them together again in a rational design. This chapter examines the administrator's role in an effort to create a central image or construct to which the separate ingredients of administration may later be related.

## The Administrator Is Two People

Administration is substantive and it is also procedural. There is always a *what* of administration that involves a substantive specialization such as medicine, agronomy, utility regulation, or some other such body of knowledge; and in addition, there is the *how* of administration that everywhere involves knowing how to plan, organize, delegate, supervise, and accomplish all the other process aspects of a group effort.

Young people considering administration as a career often ask, Shall I study administration or a substantive field like engineering? In most cases, both are necessary. Many train primarily in administration and only later become familiar with the substantive field for which they have administrative responsibility. Others train initially in engineering or the law or a science and then find that as they climb the promotion ladder their work becomes increasingly administrative; in such cases, some acquaintance with the art of administration gained early in life becomes a considerable asset, the lack of which may handicap performance and even promotions throughout the latter part of a career.

The best rule, therefore, is to secure some knowledge of the concepts and principles of administration at the outset. Even if one never becomes an administrator, some knowledge of the discipline is helpful no matter what substantive field one enters. And if at some later time a more thorough knowledge of administration becomes important, one need only "bone up" through excutive development courses that are now widely available, in order to recognize and refresh the qualities needed in the new situation. Everyone has a number of different facets to his nature and, depending on what is required of him in different situations, stresses certain combinations and tempos at one time and a different set at another.

Is there no advantage, then, in becoming an administrator per se? Yes, of course. An individual may wish to become a specialist in a particular area of administration, such as organization, planning, personnel, budgeting, public relations—any one of the so-called staff specialities. Many people have found a challenging and profitable career in these occupations. But in every case these administrative specialists must also study the substantive field with which they are associated, just as those who have a substantive specialization but lack previous knowledge or experience in administration must learn something of that art when circumstances place them in positions of administrative responsibility. Consequently, if they are to be effective, most people need a dual competence.

Furthermore, in our highly organized society the higher the individual goes the more he finds not only the need for a knowledge of administration but also a greater number of variables to be mastered and synthesized. Thus a research scientist may have little contact with other people for the first ten or twenty years of his life, but if he then becomes a supervisor, which generally though not invariably increases his earnings, he will need to develop a new set of skills having to do with planning, organizing, supervising, deciding, coordinating, and energizing, all of which involve human relations. At this point his knowledge of a particular science becomes less relevant while a knowledge of society and economics becomes essential, as does an understanding of human relations, leadership, motivation, and similar factors involved in high-level administration. The accompanying chart, developed by John Corson, clearly shows how these understandings develop along with promotions in any field.

The best administrator is the one whose personality is best integrated. This is not the same thing, however, as being merely a generalist, if by this is meant one who has a little knowledge about many things but is unable to concentrate his skills to coincide with what varying situations require in terms of analysis and integration.

The higher one goes in administration the more important it is that one be able to think conceptually, that is, in terms of intricate relationships and how they add up; of values and needs and what people want and are willing to pay for; of the structure of society, the economy, and government in order that decisions may promote the long-range interest; and of human relations and psychological concepts so that the enterprise may be spirited and enduring.

There are three levels of need with which the administrator must deal. The first is the social need that involves the demands of consumers and the good of the country. The second is the enterprise's own need involving the means by which it may become profitable and efficient, spirited and responsive. Third is the needs of the people within the organization, involving performance at full potential accompanied by rewarding personal satisfactions. The administrative fulfilment of these three kinds of need requires a rather broad competence and a lifetime of study and reflection. No administrator ever reaches his full potential of power, for there is always a higher level of each of these needs to be met.

## The Administrative Generalist

A generalist may be a jack-of-all-trades and master of none, but as applied in administration the term has another and more useful meaning. Thus, an administrative generalist is a person who can think conceptually and hence is able to see the different aspects of a situation in relationship. He understands distant objectives as well as those that are close at hand. He is generally skilled in both administration and in a substantive field. This sort of person is needed for the top jobs that involve planning, policy, public policy, and decision making.

Administration is sometimes defined as the ability to coordinate the work of specialists in such a way as to secure a spirited and smoothly working enterprise capable of making the greatest impact on the problems at hand and on those who benefit from their solution. This definition is especially applicable to a society that, like ours, is characterized by intricate technology and specialization, since the complexity of administration grows as much out of these basic causes as it does out of human needs.

Administration is a fusion of opposites: ends and means, rationality and sentiment, specialization and coordination, individual and group effort, discipline and reward. The gist of administration is to secure coordination through the spirited work of individuals aimed at targets that are definite and compelling. If the administrator's personality is integrated and if he understands cause-and-effect relationships,

## REQUISITE UNDERSTANDINGS OF THE PUBLIC SERVANT

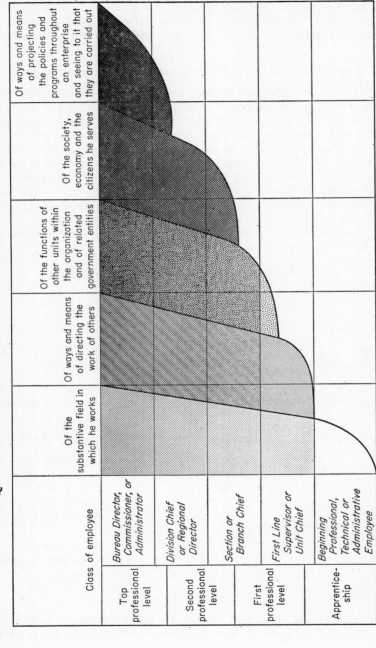

| Class of employee | | Of the substantive field in which he works | Of ways and means of directing the work of others | Of the functions of other units within the organization and of related government entities | Of the society, economy and the citizens he serves | Of ways and means of projecting the policies and programs throughout an enterprise and seeing to it that they are carried out |
|---|---|---|---|---|---|---|
| Top professional level | Bureau Director, Commissioner, or Administrator | | | | | |
| Second professional level | Division Chief or Regional Director | | | | | |
| First professional level | Section or Branch Chief | | | | | |
| | First Line Supervisor or Unit Chief | | | | | |
| Apprentice-ship | Beginning Professional, Technical or Administrative Employee | | | | | |

SOURCE: John J. Carson, "Equipping Men for Career Growth in the Public Service," *Public Administration Review* (March 1963). Reprinted by permission of the American Society for Public Administration.

he will find it easier to foster the larger integrations that group effort requires. Hence the need for generalists: balanced, well-organized administrators capable of constant growth in wisdom and understanding.

## *The Flow and Interdependencies of Administration*

There is a certain flow and logical progression in the administrative process that is not revealed in a simple description of the daily activities of the administrator, although everything he does is part of it. The day of the administrator may be taken up with a few concerns or many, but their relationship to the core of the process is sometimes not clear unless the central process itself is clear. Thus, each step in this process leads to the next and relates in some way to all the others. An understanding of this flow should become second nature to the practicing administrator because it is the basis of his ability to integrate, to conduct his daily work with a flair and a sense of artistry.

In outline, the elements of administration and the steps in the administrative process are these:

### THE INTERRELATIONSHIPS OF ADMINISTRATION

| *Planning* | *Ingredients* | *Dynamics* |
|---|---|---|
| Objectives (need plus law) | Organization (anatomy of the program) | Leadership (the signals) |
| Mandate (scope and authority) | Personnel (the people) | Direction (instructions) |
| Planning (refinement of goals) | Finance (buying power) | Delegation (energizing others) |
| Policies (the guidelines) | Material (goods and services) | Supervision (seeing that it is done) |
| Targets (accomplishment in a given time) | Incentives (what makes people work effectively) | Coordination (making a mesh) |
| Budgeting (the program in financial terms) | | Control (hitting the targets) |
| | | Public relations (explaining the program) |

In other words, the social need to be filled becomes a program; it is first defined in terms of legal authority and then in terms of the agency's mandate; this is further delineated by planning, policies, targets, and budgeting. Common vehicles to carry any program are organization, personnel, finance, material, and incentives. The dynamics of the enterprise are leadership through communication, giving to others their mandate, instructing and supervising them, coordinating their efforts to produce a unified result, establishing control devices so that targets will be hit on time, and finally, educating employees and other interested parties in the policies and objectives of the enterprise so that they may have a favorable view of it.

But administration is not only a series of related steps; it is also a circle. Note, for example, that the first step is to define a human need and that the last one is public relations, which is a further clarification of that need.

Note also that every part of the administrative process affects all the others. For example, every aspect of the program requires planning: its organization, its finances, its control, even the incentives by which people are encouraged to work at their best. Note, too, the close connection between targets and control: it is impossible to know whether objectives are being achieved without well-developed time schedules and criteria for evaluating performance.

Thus, no single factor is the whole of administration. All the steps in the process are so interrelated that each must succeed if the whole is to succeed, and a significant failure at any point may spell failure for the whole effort. If time-and-motion studies are emphasized to the point where all waste motion is eliminated, for example, a clocklike efficiency may be achieved but may eventually result in a strike or slowdown because the human element has been overlooked. It is sometimes easier to analyze a situation than it is to maintain the Golden Mean that Confucius and the Greek philosophers held in such high regard. The philosopher-king may be more useful in administration than the efficiency expert, although the latter has his place.

The best way to unify administration is always to keep in mind the human need and how best to serve it. For, all of administration is merely the filling of social and individual needs by various forms of service produced by means of orderly steps in a process. Administration is never something apart from people and their needs; rather, it is the means by which these needs are met. What the foregoing chart really says, therefore, is that a social need is fulfilled by a program built with universal ingredients and brought to life by wise and skillful leadership.

Philip Selznick, the sociologist, makes this matter of response to the outside world and to human need the center of his philosophy of administration. When it is a matter of determining what to do, providing motivation, deciding how to organize, developing a proper public relations program, or trying to make sure that the enterprise will survive and be profitable, what is more important than constantly keeping in mind the clientele to be served?

A recently popular approach to administration emphasizes decision making. Taking the factors set forth above it says, in effect, here is the problem, now let us gather the facts, set forth the alternative possible solutions, pick the most likely one, and then work out the steps in the administrative process that will contribute most to the result to be achieved. This is another way of providing a unifying theme. Instead of concentrating on externals like clientele, as Selznick's cooptation does, the decision maker concerns himself with logical processes. Obviously both procedures are useful. One might be used by a responsive salesman, the other by a normally more objective judge. The administrator should be both.

## Qualifying Factors

When administration is viewed as a process, certain of its elements appear to be universal; the administrator should know what these are, how they are interrelated, and how to deal with them. Much of this will become clear in subsequent chapters. For the present, some of the important qualifying factors that determine the character of administration may be mentioned, for these will help the administrator to get his bearings.

1. Administration operates in a social setting such as a nation-state, taking on its coloration, and becoming an important part of its thought and leadership apparatus, and hence contributing to its organization or disorganization. Nevertheless, though limited by the social environment, administration also may play an important role in changing that environment when change is due.

2. The character of administration varies with the type of work involved. Work related to technology, for example, tends to emphasize things, while work concerned with a social institution such as a hospital or a school is more concerned with people. It should not be supposed, however, that one type of work may properly be inhuman while the other is as human as possible, because to deny the human element in work related to technology would create a nightmare.

3. Administrative systems are frequently scalar, that is, they consist of a series of levels. Thus, the social security program is administered from local, state, regional, and national offices. This arrangement creates two new dimensions. The first is that of intergovernmental relations between these offices and the sovereign levels of government in question. The second is that of headquarters-field relationships within the agency itself. Such dimensions have important repercussions, one of which is on the administrative process. Work in a staff agency in

Washington differs considerably from work in an operating post in the field, as there will be occasion to see in a later chapter.

4. In some degree all administration is bureaucratic and this also affects its character. A bureaucracy arises in any public or private undertaking where specialization, hierarchy, and long lines of communication cause rules and regulations to supplant face-to-face relationships, and where, as a result, the whole setting of administration tends to become impersonal. These are the internal factors of bureaucracy. There are also external factors, including an insistence on strict legalism, a reverence for tradition, a reluctance to institute change, and a consequent tendency to rigidity. In the best and legitimate sense of the term, bureaucracy is a necessary and desirable characteristic of large, complicated organizations because it is logical, precise, orderly, rational, and efficient. But these qualities can be carried so far as to create difficulties in another direction: coordination is hampered, people tend to avoid responsibility if they can; irrational aggrandizements (Parkinson's Law) occur; human relations are neglected; and the quality of enterprise becomes conspicuous by its absence. Hence, bureaucracy is an asset to administration, but if it is not controlled it becomes a threat. To make its greatest contribution, bureaucracy must be complemented by the factors of enterprise and human relations.

5. Also, in all administration there is a distinction, much relied upon in sociology, between the formal and the informal aspects of organization. Nor is the formal one—mainly concerned with clear process —the more important, for the influence of the informal, relying on more casual personal relationships, is very strong indeed. These two systems supplement each other as bureaucracy and enterprise complement each other in the same organization. As a corrective to any formalistic notion gained from a consideration of the separate factors entering into the administrative process, the influence of informal organization must be given considerable weight.

6. Finally comes the political factor itself. On the American scene administrators increasingly initiate not only policy but also legislation. Indeed, most important laws are now drafted in the executive branch as a result of initiative developed by a pressure group, by a member of the legislature, by the chief executive, or because of firsthand knowledge gained by a particular department as a result of practical experience in that policy area. This does not mean that legislatures have abdicated. It does mean that under the American governmental system the chief executive's traditional legislative function is becoming more important every day. Here is another reason why, in the modern world of administration, the executive must be a political economist and statesman as well as an administrator in the strict sense; increasingly the weight of the problems of the nation is upon his shoulders.

What does the public administrator do? He analyzes society and the economy. He recommends legislation. He deals with other political elements in government. He defines his objectives and his targets. He clarifies his mandate. He plans. He directs the work of others. He makes decisions. He tries to create a stimulating atmosphere by means of tested incentives. He balances many factors and tries to achieve a unified operation. Further he should be expert in a substantive field or he will not be respected and his judgments will be faulty. He must stress personnel policy and public relations. He evaluates accomplishment. He develops the abilities of his colleagues and subordinates. He is interested in survival, in human needs, in the vitality of his enterprise.

Just how much of all this he does depends, of course, on where he stands in the hierarchy of the organization. He may have all of these responsibilities or only some of them. But one thing is certain: the nearer he gets to the top, the greater is the range of his responsibilities, the broader must be his vision, and the greater is the need to respond quickly and with sound judgment.

## BIBLIOGRAPHY AND CASES

### Annotated Reading Suggestions

The best single article on preparation for a career in the public service is John Corson, "Equipping Men for Career Growth in the Public Service," *Public Administration Review,* 23 (March 1963). Other stimulating articles are Paul Van Riper, "The Senior Civil Service and the Career System," *Public Administration Review,* 18 (Summer 1958); William C. Thomas, Jr., "Generalist Versus Specialist," *Public Administration Review,* 21 (Winter 1961); Arthur S. Flemming, "The Civil Servant in a Period of Transition," *Public Administration Review,* 13 (Spring 1953); H. Struve Hensel, "Ways and Means for Recruiting Capable Federal Executives," *Public Administration Review,* 13 (Spring 1953); Herbert Emmerich and C. Lyle Belsley, "The Federal Career Service—What Next?" *Public Administration Review,* 14 (Winter 1954); and York Wilbern, "Professionalization in the Public Service: Too Little or Too Much?" *Public Administration Review,* 14 (Winter 1954). For comparative purposes see International City Managers Association, *Post-Entry Training in the Public Service in Western Europe* (Chicago: International City Managers Association, 1962).

There are also a number of other good books and articles dealing with government service. For example, John J. Corson, "To Get Better Men for a Better Government," *The New York Times Magazine* (March 27, 1949), and

*Executives for the Federal Service: A Program for Action in Time of Crisis* (Columbia University Press, 1952). At about the same time, Robert A. Lovett wrote "A Business Executive Looks at Government," in Joseph E. McLean, ed., *The Public Service and University Education* (Princeton University Press, 1949); Paul David contributed "The Development and Recruitment of Administrative Leadership in National and International Programs," in Robert A. Walker, ed., *America's Manpower Crisis* (Chicago: Public Administration Service, 1952); Harvey C. Mansfield contributed "Political Parties, Patronage, and the Federal Government Service" in The American Assembly, *The Federal Government Service: Its Character, Prestige, and Problems* (Columbia University Press, 1954); and *Fortune* came out with "The Little Oscars and Civil Service" (January 1953).

After the publication in 1955 of the Hoover Commission *Task Force Report on Personnel and Civil Service,* a number of good books and articles appeared in rapid sequence: Paul T. David and Ross Pollock, *Executives for Government* (The Brookings Institution, 1957); Marver Bernstein, *The Job of the Federal Executive* (The Brookings Institution, 1958); and Stephen B. Sweeney, ed., *Education for Administrative Careers in Government Service* (University of Pennsylvania Press, 1958), this last dealing with all levels of government. Finally, the whole area of local government was intensively treated by the Municipal Manpower Commission in *Governmental Manpower for Tomorrow's Cities* (McGraw-Hill, 1962) and reviewed in *Public Administration Review,* 23 (June 1963).

The American public service has some way to go, however, before it will be wholly adequate to the expectations of a new age. For a comparison with developments in Europe, see Brian Chapman, *The Profession of Government: The Public Service in Europe* (Macmillan, 1959). The historical evolution of the American public service is dealt with by Paul Van Riper in *History of the United States Civil Service* (Harper & Row, 1958).

## Case Studies

A major case in Stein's *Public Administration and Policy Development: A Case Book,* is *The Foreign Service Act of 1946,* by Stein himself, told in sixty-eight pages. This case involved the State Department, the Bureau of the Budget, Congress, the President, and of course the Foreign Service itself. It provides a good cross section of how a government operates in a situation where many elements are involved.

Another ICP case that merits attention is No. 7, *The Rural Electrification Administration Personnel Report,* by Winifred McCulloch.

The best of the five cases appearing in F. M. G. Willson, ed., *Administrators in Action: British Case Studies, Volume I* (University of Toronto Press, 1961), is *A Clearing With Spain,* in which practically the whole narrative revolves about the activities of members of the Administrative Class of the Civil Service.

This was a national policy problem of such dimensions that permanent secretaries and their ministers were closely involved; it is reviewed in *Public Administration Review,* 22 (December 1962).

Biography is another useful source of case materials. The following are especially recommended and all appear in *Public Administration Review,* issues noted: Harold D. Smith, 7:77; William E. Mosher, 6:99; W. W. Stockberger, 1:50; William A. Jump, 9:64; Ferdinand A. Silcox, 2:240; Ellen C. Potter, 1:351; General Dawes, 11:167; and Joseph B. Eastman, 5:34.

# 5

## The Fields
## of Public Administration

THOSE WHO APPROACH the study of public administration for the first time are likely to experience bewilderment at the range of governmental activities and issues of public policy that somehow must be managed by mere mortals. To compound the bewilderment, until recently public administration was often defined so narrowly as to create the impression that techniques and procedures were all that were necessary to effective performance, and that substantive questions of what government should or should not do were beyond the scope of the subject, to be reserved for the attention of other specialists. Fortunately, as shown in an earlier chapter, the content of public administration has expanded far beyond mere techniques and procedures and is, in fact, capable of meeting the challenges posed by the size and complexity of the agenda of modern government.

For the student of public administration the following discussion of the substantive fields in which the discipline operates—what may be called the anatomy and physiology of the subject—will help to reduce the understandable sense of confusion that often exists.

Public administration relates to the whole of society and the political economy. Even economists and sociologists have trouble dealing with these complicated structures except in a taxonomic sense, that is, by means of formal categories just as biologists classify the varieties of animal and vegetable life. Nevertheless, we shall try to suggest the main lines of the structure of public administration, the fields in which it operates, the interrelationships of its components, the overlappings, and the areas in which growth and change are most evident today. This analysis will provide the base for a more detailed study of some of the essential areas most prominent in public administration today.

## *A Taxonomic Experiment*

Some idea of the major fields of public administration may be gained by using a number of different classifications, many of which overlap, because the feel of the subject comes from an over-all analysis and not from a given segment of it. The discussion that follows is subdivided under seven headings, each covering all or part of the subject and each from a different angle. If all seven could be separately charted on a transparency and all the transparencies laid on top of each other, the result would be an accurate picture in depth of what public administration is all about.

1. The first field of public administration is classified under the heading of *vocation*. As noted in an earlier chapter, every human vocation is put to use in government, oftentimes in great numbers. Technology draws scientists and specialists of all kinds to top administrative positions. In some areas businessmen are indispensable. Clerical workers and technicians are needed in vast numbers. Teachers are the single largest nonmilitary group. White-collar work predominates.

2. The second field comes under the heading of *area*, of which, in relation to sovereign governments, there are five in the United States: local, state, regional, federal, and international. At some of these, certain skill concentrations are more needed than others. City administration, for example, is primarily concerned with business matters and engineering; the public school system is a part of it, but set a little to the side in an attempt to protect it from politics. At the federal level there are political functions, such as the conduct of foreign relations, and technical functions, such as the operation of the mint, with which no other level of government is concerned.

It is also true, however, that since the 1920s a prominent and now accelerating trend is for most levels of government to be concerned with the same matters. As the economic and political problems of the nation become increasingly continental in scope, the federal government has progressively entered fields such as welfare, banking and investment, and utility regulation that formerly were reserved to state and local jurisdictions. The result is the concurrent handling of major programs and problems at every level of government.

3. The third classification is by *sovereign functions*. This is a group of activities at all governmental levels having to do with law and order

and constituting the main purpose for which the political state was created in the first place. Thus, the police and the courts secure the safety of person and property, protect the sanctity of contracts, maintain a stable environment for the operations of business and commerce, and deal with one of the principal ends of government, the dispensing of justice. At the local level fire protection and sanitation are among the chief functions.

At the national level defense is the single largest function in terms of expenditure, and employs nearly half of all top civilian federal administrators in addition to administrators in the military service itself. Also at the federal level is the conduct of foreign relations, the oldest executive department in the federal government and since World War II one of the fastest growing.

Finally, at all levels taxation feeds the engines of government, employs a large working force, and is a factor in strengthening the private sector of the economy. For these reasons, taxation is the matrix of some of the most difficult problems of public administration.

4. The fourth classification is by types of *organization* by means of which public administration operates. There are three main types and each requires special skills.

First are the regular operating departments of the executive branch, each consisting of a number (sometimes a great number) of bureaus. In the federal government every bureau chief reports to the Cabinet officer (the Secretary) who heads his department, and he in turn reports to the President. These agencies are supposedly the main vehicles not only for the conduct of government operations but also for the formulation of programs and policy and the securing of over-all coordination at the top. With variations this system operates also at the state and, in the case of the larger cities, at the municipal level as well.

The second main type of organization is the numerous independent agencies and regulatory commissions, for the most part at the federal but also at the state and local levels. As the functions of government began rapidly to expand under the impact of the Great Depression of the 1930s, new programs were commonly created outside and independently of the existing operating departments whose chief executives are members of the President's Cabinet. Some of these independent agencies are concerned only with administration, as in the case of the Housing and Home Finance Agency, but most of them are commissions that deal with regulation in some private field or other—transportation, communications, power, oil and natural gas, labor relations, securities and exchange, and the like—and now constitute what has come to be referred to as the fourth branch of government. Moreover, these commissions have created a new dimension in administration because they combine rather than separate the legislative, judicial, and administrative functions of government. And since they report directly to Congress rather than to the President, they effectively thwart his efforts to develop a coordinated executive branch under a unified command.

As a peculiarity of American government, these commissions have constant and direct contact with the business community, and have been under repeated scrutiny in recent years because the degree of expertness brought to their operations has much to do with the future of our private enterprise economy, on the one hand strengthening it and on the other greatly weakening it and thus opening the way to socialization.

The third main type of organization consists of public corporations and what is sometimes called authorities. These many legal and administrative entities, modeled after the private corporation and enjoying various degrees of financial autonomy and administrative flexibility, exist at all levels of government. There are over half a hundred in the federal government alone, including such large ones as the Tennessee Valley Authority and the Commodity Credit Corporation as well as smaller ones for agricultural and cooperative banking, home loan operations, and the like. This type of corporate organization is becoming especially popular among state and local governments, for as appropriated funds become harder to secure, the tendency is to create bodies similar to the Port of New York Authority and toll road and bridge authorities to administer a service that produces revenue. The administration of these agencies offers many lucrative employment opportunities to people trained in the right substantive skills.

5. The fifth classification is by particular *human groups* within the population. Certain bureaus and agencies at one or more levels of government deal with certain groups such as women, children, veterans, the aged, prisoners, the handicapped, merchant seamen, railway labor, and many more. Here again is the opportunity for the employment of substantive specialists. In such a career, administrators are clientele as well as functional specialists.

6. The sixth classification is by *classes* in the economy. In the federal and many state and local governments, the three main classes —business, labor, and agriculture—have their own executive departments to represent and foster their interests. In addition, government puts its arm around the professions, setting standards, administering qualifying examinations, and issuing licenses. Lawyers, doctors, psychiatrists, osteopaths, veterinarians, beauticians, morticians, family counselors, barbers, and real estate brokers are among the groups subject to this kind of control in order to protect the standards of the profession. Most of this activity occurs at the state level and to a lesser degree at the local level of government.

7. Finally, the fields of public administration may be classified according to the needs of the *national economy*. This is the largest and

most important category of all because it covers the whole productive, distributive, and consuming network of relationships in the economic life of the nation. Economists recognize that in an affluent society such as ours, it is nearly impossible to set forth all the intricacies of process and organization in sufficient detail to convey a true impression of what takes place. Nevertheless, we shall give it a try, sacrificing detail for the sake of the over-all picture.

According to the main areas in the national economy, public administration is concerned with the following activities and subject matter:

*a.* Certain government agencies at all levels, but primarily at the national, are especially concerned with the *resources* of the nation. This is a wide category, for even human beings may be so classified. Agencies to protect material resources are, among others, the U. S. Forest Service, the Bureau of Reclamation, the Fish and Wildlife Service, the Atomic Energy Commission, and the Soil Conservation Service. Counterparts of some of these federal units are also found among state and the larger municipal governments.

*b.* In the area of *production,* certain federal and state agencies regulate electric power, gas, oil, communications, and the like. In addition, many bureaus in the U. S. Department of Agriculture foster and regulate the production of food and fiber. This department is one of the oldest and largest of the federal executive departments whose frame of reference is chiefly economic.

*c.* With regard to *distribution,* there are agencies at all levels of government that try to police the competitive system to keep it from becoming monopolistic, and to prevent false and misleading advertising and other undesirable business practices. Most recently, new and tighter laws attempt to control the labeling of food, fiber, and other products so as to inform the consumer as to the content of his purchase.

For the Department of Agriculture, the major problem of control is not in the matter of production so much as it is the management of farm surpluses and securing for the farmer a larger share of the consumer dollar. For the Federal Communications Commission the problem of distribution relates to the use of the airwaves: what share of time shall go to advertisers, educational programs, and public service features? In the matter of oil and natural gas, there is the problem not only of distribution but also of conservation, for these are prime natural resources.

*d.* Then there are programs for the protection of *consumers.* As technology tends to concentrate social and economic power, consumers are presented with increasingly less choice in what they may buy and hence lose their bargaining power as to quality and price. Consequently government must provide the protections that once inhered in the free operation of the competitive market. In Britain, which has extensive public ownership, consumer councils have become a standard feature of the administrative services. In the United States, New Deal experiments in this area died out during World War II. Since then, however, consumers have become more conscious of their vulnerability, and there are now attempts at all levels of government to revive and extend special agencies for their protection.

In addition, the Department of Agriculture assists and promotes consumer cooperatives and the Food and Drug Administration seeks to control matters such as harmful additives in food, dirty and adulterated food produced under insanitary conditions, mislabeling, insufficiently tested drugs, injurious drugs, harmful cosmetics, and the like.

*e.* The area of *finance* is sometimes called the nerve center of capitalism. The Federal Reserve System was created in 1913. Since the 1930s Congress has established federal agencies to deal with stock market transactions, holding companies, the insurance of bank deposits, and has the legal right (as yet unexercised) to regulate insurance companies doing business in interstate commerce. Branch banking and bank mergers are among the most controversial issues of federal and state government. Controls over money, interest rates, and tax administration are important tools by which administrators in both the public and the private sectors, working together, may safeguard the health and stability of the economy. Few people realize that the work of even the federal Bureau of the Budget is more concerned with economic issues than it is with administration in the narrow sense.

*f.* Then there is the field of *transportation*. Outside of the United States most of the means of transportation are government-owned and operated; here this is only occasionally so, the concern of government being largely with regulation in the public interest.

The federal government entered the field of transportation in a major way shortly after the Civil War, fostering the continental expansion of the railroads. Later it similarly aided airlines, paying subsidies (often in the form of lucrative mail contracts); now it regulates all forms of transportation. The Interstate Commerce Commission, created in 1887, is the main federal transportation regulatory agency, dealing as it does with the railroads, waterways, and the trucking industry. Other federal agencies regulate aviation and ocean shipping.

At the municipal level, local transit and commuter services are among the main areas of activity, but in a large city such as Chicago or New York, almost every form of transportation must be dealt with. Finally, government itself also sometimes provides transportation services, especially at the municipal level where local transit systems may be government-owned and operated.

*g. Communication* is another prime government responsibility. At the federal level a single commission now regulates radio, television, telephone, telegraph, and cable communications. As in the case of transportation, communication in other nations is characteristically government-owned and operated and is a main avenue in the spread of public enterprise. In this country private ownership under public regulation is the rule. The 1962 legislation covering the ownership and operation of outer-space communication satellites, involving the private-public issue, was one of the hardest fought congressional battles of recent years.

*h. Public works* is one of the largest areas of government responsibility. Next only to education, which occupies more civilian public employees than any other single function of nonfederal government, is municipal government's concern with engineering and public works: streets, roads, bridges, sewers, public buildings, transportation, major urban renewal programs, and the like.

At the federal level the Tennessee Valley Authority and the atomic installations at Oak Ridge, Los Alamos, and elsewhere are spectacular illustrations of a similar concern. The long-standing and continuing rivalry between the Army's Corps of Engineers and the Interior Department's Bureau of Reclamation over the engineering and public works functions in the federal government is a classic case in the conduct of public administration. If urban renewal and land-use problems are to be solved, it will be partly because engineering has become and for years will remain a major activity in public administration.

*i.* Finally, there is the field of *welfare* in a broad sense (the largest part of which is public education), partly a federal and state function but predominantly a local one. Everywhere the attempt is to keep it semiautonomous and divorced from politics. At the federal level Congress created the combined Department of Health, Education, and Welfare in 1953, which quickly became one of the largest agencies in Washington. It is also one of the most controversial, for it is faced with problems such as welfare payments to the hard core of the continuously, even permanently unemployed as well as to those who are temporarily on relief, and the issue of what is called socialized medicine. Concerns such as these were once the responsibility of the family, private charities, or local authorities; now increasingly they are matters of federal responsibility, making the field of welfare a growing area of politics and administration.

Broad as the foregoing coverage of the political economy seems to be, the full impact of government's role in the economy cannot be more than dimly sensed from so simple an outline. And yet some of the boundaries do stand out. Except for the Atomic Energy Commission, none of the agencies mentioned under this classification is directly concerned with national security and defense. When it is realized that more than half of all federal expenditures are for Defense Department programs, and that most of these have to do with the devising and manufacture of "hardware"—a task largely discharged by private corporations—one may gain some idea of the impact of government operations on the national economy.

In addition, government has become the prime encourager of technological research and, through the defense program, is now industry's largest customer for the products of that activity. It is interesting to note that now the relationship between private and public enterprise is shifting in a manner reminiscent of the change that began in the late nineteenth century in the relationship between the federal government and the states. Grants-in-aid have increasingly tied the states to Washington in one field after another, including highways, social security, public health, soil conservation, and the like. Similar links are currently being forged between Washington and large private corporations: Dupont in the atomic energy field, for example, and General Dynamics in the missile field, with the Massachusetts Institute of Technology and the California Institute of Technology occupied with studies ranging from physics to international relations.[1]

Consequently, instead of looking down their noses at government as they once did, the managers of giant corporations perforce have to take a more conciliatory view of government. And for their part, competent public administrators at the center of government must be equally circumspect in dealing with the holders of corporate power if spending from the public treasury and the making of policy is to be consistent with the public interest. The situation requires a high order of statesmanship on both sides.

The foregoing seven-part analysis shows that beneath the surface and behind the outer facade of government, the fields of administration are almost infinitely diverse, colorful, and distinctive. Indeed, the only common element in administration is the process itself. But even this proposition must be qualified by the special needs of special programs, lest it do violence to inherent differences that characterize the administration of programs in the many different fields in which governments at all levels must operate.

## BIBLIOGRAPHY AND CASES

### Annotated Reading Suggestions

Generally speaking, books on business and government or on government and the American economy deal with a larger area of government's activities than any others. Among the standard texts are those by Clair Wilcox, Harold

---

[1] Don K. Price, "Administrative Leadership," pp. 750-763.

Koontz and R. W. Gable, Marshall E. Dimock, Merle Fainsod and Lincoln Gordon, George A. Steiner, Donald S. Watson, Howard R. Smith, and others. Other books, such as Gerard J. Mangone, *A Short History of International Organization* (McGraw-Hill, 1954), Arthur W. Macmahon, *Administration in Foreign Affairs* (University of Alabama Press, 1953), and James L. McCamy, *The Administration of American Foreign Affairs* (Knopf, 1950), all deal with international administration.

The range of municipal activities is taken up in Municipal Finance Officers Association, *An Inventory of Government Activities in the United States* (Chicago, 1947), and in Lent D. Upson, *The Growth of a City Government* (Detroit, 1942). An offshoot of the International City Managers Association, the Institute for Training in Municipal Administration, publishes study monographs relating to a wide field: public works, fire protection, police administration, city planning, and the like. Latest developments in school administration are dealt with by York Wilbern in "Municipal Government and the Schools," *Public Management*, 45 (May 1962).

For anyone considering a career, however, in many ways the most convenient reference is to the reports, in 1949 and again in 1955, of the Commission on Organization of the Executive Branch of the Government (the first and second Hoover Commissions). These studies are separately printed by the Government Printing Office and in most cases consist of a Task Force (staff) report and a Commission report, the latter based on the former. The task force reports are full of interesting data.

The 1949 reports of the Hoover Commission deal with the following program subjects, among others: agriculture, labor, medicine, overseas' activities, national security, veterans, foreign affairs, commerce, treasury, public works, natural resources, statistics, water resources, lending agencies, regulatory commissions, general supply activities, and the business enterprises of the government.

The 1955 reports of the Hoover Commission deal with an even larger number of subjects, all in separate monographs: intelligence activities, business enterprises, post office, legal services, lending agencies, overseas' programs and economic operations, research, transportation, medical services, water resources, real property management, defense, surplus property, food and clothing, depot utilization, water resources and power, military procurement, lending, and the corporate undertakings of the government.

On the future widening or narrowing of government's activities, see Adolf Berle, *The American Economic Republic* (Harcourt, Brace & World, 1963), or Marshall E. Dimock, *The New American Political Economy* (Harper & Row, 1962), especially Part III.

## Case Studies

An excellent case study is found in the Stein *Case Book: The Sale of the Tankers*, written by Louis W. Koenig in 1950 and revised in 1952, seventy-one pages in length. The story involves the sale between 1947 and 1948 of eighty-three government-owned tankers to thirteen foreign nations. High-level agencies are involved: the Executive Office of the President, and the Cabinet; inter-agency negotiations take place, culminating in congressional investigations.

A second ICP case is (unnumbered) *The Latin American Proceeding*, prepared by W. Scott Payne in 1949. Like the preceding case, this one also deals with international activities, the licensing of competing airlines for service to Latin America. The report brings out the play of private competitive interests, the methods used by the Civil Aeronautics Board in considering applications, the intergovernmental machinery used, and the discreet methods employed by pressure groups in furthering their own causes. It also illustrates how questions of high policy occur in the proceedings of all regulatory agencies.

Additional ICP cases showing the infinite range of governmental activities are No. 12, *New York Farm Labor Camps, 1940-46,* by R. M. Stout, seventy-six pages, which involves itinerant labor; No. 42, *Commuters vs. the Black Ball Line: Washington Purchases the Puget Sound Ferries,* by W. J. Gore, thirty-five pages, involving the extension of governmental activities; and No. 51, *Hanover Builds a High School,* by L. Menand, in the field of education, which is government's largest peacetime activity.

# 6

# Administration
# and Society

THE RESPONSIBILITY OF the administrator is both external to society and internal to the organization of which he is a part. Many of the problems that plague us, especially those that have to do with the size and complexity of modern institutions, are due, in part at least, to the fact that administrators at all levels have been so intent on their own internal affairs that they have neglected the needs of the community in which they operate and on which they depend.

This chapter examines the relation of administration to society to show that in the modern world the old order that proceeded from the internal to the external should be just about reversed. The reason is that the external responsibilities of the administrator now constitute the center of reckoning for everything he does, including the discharge of his internal obligations to his organization.

## The Thesis of Interaction

Administration operates in the context of the society of which it is a part. Hence, as society is concerned with goals, values, belief systems, and the image of what it would become, so also must administration be concerned with these. When too great a discrepancy arises between a social belief system and behavior, the resulting tension forces behavior to conform to the belief system, or forces the belief system to conform to behavior. Failure to make this adjustment leads eventually to social disorganization.

The responsibility for making the adjustment lies with administrative leadership, for it is here that the internal and external responsibilities of administration meet. The purpose of administration is to build not merely an organization but an institution. The external aspect of administration creates and maintains the institution, while its internal aspect develops techniques to promote efficiency. When the internal responsibility is emphasized at the expense of the external, the organization loses contact with its social setting, becoming self-centered and bureaucratic. When, however, astute and imaginative leadership keeps bureaucratic factors within bounds so as to maintain a proper balance between order and enterprise, then the organization becomes an institution. Its orientation is to human need, it is flexible and responsive, it becomes spirited, and is more likely than a rigid bureaucracy to survive.

Hence, a two-way relationship: administration exists in a social setting and the pattern of administration is determined by society; but through sensitive administrative leadership, society itself may be changed. Thus the administrator is not merely an executive; he is also a social engineer, helping society to fulfill itself.

The higher the administrator rises in his institution, the more does he become concerned with external factors. Questions of internal technique are commonly settled at lower levels, leaving the top man free to concentrate on responsiveness to external needs, for it is this responsiveness that determines the success and survival of institutions and society alike.

Nevertheless, it is not only the leader in administration whose job it is to respond to the external. As the number and variety of structural changes in modern society increase, and our institutions become more pervasive and intricately connected with one another, a complex of linkages is created. Individuals and society alike seek values to be translated into goals and the programs by which to attain them. Response to this must come from the administrative corps as a whole and not merely from its top echelon. Indeed, unless everyone in the organization is externally oriented, the weight of bureaucracy may become so great that leaders are powerless to change it. Accordingly, the societal, or external approach must remain the dominant focus for every administrator in the organization, no matter what his rank.[1]

At every level, therefore, the administrator must understand many things about society. But, says C. Wright Mills, most bureaucrats are caught in the limited milieus of their everyday lives and cannot ade-

---

[1] C. Wright Mills, *The Sociological Imagination* (New York: Oxford University Press, 1959), p. 10.

quately comprehend the structures and roles of which they are subordinate parts. Too often they find themselves carrying out a series of apparently rational actions without having any idea of the ends they serve; moreover, there is a growing suspicion that even those at the top only pretend they do.[2] This limited viewpoint is perhaps the outstanding modern dilemma of administration.

## Institutions and Organizations

The societal view of public administration represents a major contribution by sociology, psychology, and even psychiatry to the general theory of the subject. It is an important corrective to a formerly too limited view. One of the first to recognize the external role of the administrator was the anthropologist and psychiatrist, Alexander H. Leighton. In his book *The Governing of Men,* a case study of a Japanese relocation camp during World War II, Leighton found much evidence to show that an administrative body is always part of the pattern of leadership and authority in the social organization of the community in which it operates.[3] The administrator who thinks of his organization as something apart from the community will fail to recognize significant problems and thereby will court disaster. If on the other hand he realizes that a first task is to make his organization an integral part of the community, he will have laid the foundation on which everything else may be built.

The most systematic presentation of the sociological theory of administration has been developed by Philip Selznick of the University of California.[4] In the past, says Selznick, theorists have too often seemed to suggest that administration is merely organization and decision making. But this is a wrong view because "The cult of efficiency in administrative theory and practice is a modern way of overstressing means and neglecting ends."[5]

Administration is more than a smooth-running machine; it is also an institution and must be attuned to human need. If the inner life of the bureaucracy becomes the dominant interest, then not only are goals neglected but, in addition, techniques tend to become so neutral as to lose color and vitality. Thus the power to adapt to a particular stage of

2 *Ibid.,* p. 168.
3 Alexander H. Leighton, *The Governing of Men* (Princeton, N.J.: Princeton University Press, 1946), p. 343.
4 The best single source is his *Leadership in Administration: A Sociological Interpretation* (New York: Harper & Row, Publishers, 1957); also worth investigating are his *The Organizational Weapon* (New York: McGraw-Hill, 1952), and *TVA and the Grass Roots* (Berkeley and Los Angeles: University of California Press, 1949).
5 *Leadership in Administration,* p. 135.

economic and social development with its accompanying problems is lost.

In the societal-institutional view of administration it is assumed that a responsibility of the administrative leader is to rework human and technological materials in order to develop an organism embodying new and enduring values, and hence the administrator must have a considerable sensitivity to the need for change, both internal and external. Like individuals, institutions also develop by this means a corporate personality and a spontaneous vitality. Thus,

> The study of institutions is in some ways comparable to the clinical study of personality. It requires a genetic and developmental stage, an emphasis on historical origins and growth stages. There is a need to see the enterprise as a whole and to see how it is transformed as new ways of dealing with a changing environment evolve.[6]

Hence a theory of administration is needed that keeps the concepts of efficiency and organization in their proper place.

Efficiency is a proximate goal of internal or administrative management. It is assumed that goals are fixed and that administration is merely a matter of joining available means to known ends. And this being so, decision making, like everything else, is routine and hence can be dealt with through formal logic alone. Among other things, this stilted and unrealistic view overlooks the need of leadership to make *critical* as contrasted with *routine* choices and to recognize that these choices concern survival, values, personality, growth, and self-realization.[7]

As contrasted with administrative management, institutional leadership guides an enterprise in finding its role and distinctive competence by studying the structure of society and the division of labor within it. From this assessment of the distinctive role of the enterprise comes its personality and integrity. Organization then becomes the means by which roles are internally distributed among those who have a part to play. Their motivation comes from being attuned to the objectives of the undertaking and to the potentialities of their personal self-development. Indeed, self-realization becomes one of the principal values that institutions and individuals seek to serve, a source of policy and program to secure unity. The main import of policy will be to secure spontaneous and reasoned support. The personality of the organization will be primarily outward-rather than inward-directed, meaning that it will never lose sight of the public and the public purposes to be served.

---

6 *Ibid.*, p. 141.
7 *Ibid.*, p. 135.

This is not a public relations function, for as that term is usually thought of it means trying to justify or defend. By contrast, outward-direction is a basic philosophy affecting every aspect of administration.

Values are of many kinds, such as freedom of speech, or of competition, and the like. For an enterprise, the ultimate value is to further the community's aspirations, its sense of identity. An organization, says Selznick, is "expendable," merely a means to an end. But an institution is not expendable because it develops deeper loyalties and attachments. The way to determine whether a particular undertaking serves or fails to serve society is to ask the question, Is it expendable? To institutionalize is to infuse with value, which means developing something more basic than mere technique. Hence the principle,

> Whenever individuals become attached to an organization or a way of doing things as persons rather than as technicians, the result is a prizing of the device for its own sake. From the standpoint of the committed person, the organization is changed from an expendable tool into a valued source of personal satisfaction.[8]

Thus Selznick agrees with David McClelland, author of *The Achieving Society* and both were influenced by Freud: as in the case of an individual, a group also must develop an image of itself—something it believes in and would become—if it is to have the kind of integrity that produces a pleasing service.

This outer-directedness or "cooptation" is interestingly documented in Selznick's study of TVA. This federal agency was originally considered as a threat to state and local governments as well as to private utility companies. It overcame this difficulty, so far as governments were concerned, and found strength and acceptance by working through others. Instead of developing its own agricultural program, for example, as it was legally authorized to do, it chose to work through agricultural county agents and the Extension Service whose employees were already highly respected and accepted in the community. By means of this seeming self-abnegation, TVA remained in the background and developed more good will and public approval than if it had been out front administering an agricultural program through its own officials.

This illustrates Selznick's main thesis: the administrator who keeps his eyes on the public and its needs and attunes his organization to these external values will find every other aspect of administration, including decision making, falling into its proper place. By contrast, he who stresses a particular internal technique or process, such as decision making, creates an organization that is mechanistic and uninspiring.

---

[8] *Ibid.*, p. 17.

The best practical approach is the organic, societal one. Efficiency is a useful yardstick, but either it must be applied in a more limited sense than usual, or be definded more broadly than ever before.

## Evaluation of the Institutional Approach

The foregoing view of administration is more than a "school" of thought. It is a philosophy that has much to recommend it, perhaps more than any alternative approach to the theory of administration. Nevertheless, it is not the whole of administration, as Selznick would probably be the first to admit.

In part, the institutional approach is a protest against two others, one old and the second fairly recent, that have been pushed too far. The first, of course, is the one that stresses internal techniques and relies on the yardstick of efficiency—scientific management, for instance. More recent is the positivist approach, illustrated in Herbert Simon's book, *Administrative Behavior,* in which the assumption is made that administration can be reduced to a science simply by applying logic to organization and decision making, causing the subject somewhat to resemble classical economics.

Both of these approaches have their value as ingredients in the theory of administration, but surely they should be subordinated to and must work within the general intellectual confines of the sociological approach.

The value of the older emphasis on internal techniques is to bring down to earth administrators who talk a good deal about crucial issues and serving society, but who seem unable to do the practical things that group effort requires. Indeed, many who are skilled in the techniques of administration may contribute more to its objectives than those who never get much beyond talking about it. Selznick realizes this and has no quarrel with so-called practical administrators. He simply argues that they should know their techniques and be institutionalizers as well. In fact, of course, both approaches are practical, one in the short-range and the other in the long-range view, and both are indispensable.

Selznick agrees with the older approach that administration is a process. The difference is that the older view, while not wholly neglecting ends and social relationships, is more interested in what the administrator does in the course of the internal administrative process. By contrast, Selznick puts the external factors first and pays relatively little attention to the internal aspects of the program. But he recognizes the process in this way:

> Institutionalization is a *process.* It is something that happens to an organization over time, reflecting the organization's own distinctive history, the people who have been in it, the groups it embodies and the

vested interests they have created, and the way it has adapted to the environment.[9]

Clearly, the organization concept must be subordinated to and controlled by the need to institutionalize if society's needs, rather than the bureaucracy's narrower interests, are to be the main focus of attention.

To describe the setting of administration, the concept of society, which is the institutions people are attached to in various areas of interest, is a more viable one than the term culture, which, as Mills says, is too "spongy" and imprecise to be useful.[10] Spongy words frequently becloud rather than sharpen thought. Consequently Mills discusses structure as a social concept, the relation being to tension areas that groups must face up to and resolve in terms of public policy and institutional method if human needs are to be met. Social structure is the combination of institutions classified according to function. The most comprehensive institution is the nation-state, which among other things is the parent of public administration.[11] But whether it is the nation-state, the city, the school, the family, or world government that is involved, there are always three main factors in structural change (and Mills might have added, in administration also): *biography,* meaning people; *history,* meaning the time dimension; and *social structure,* which is adjustment to change.

Another advantage of the sociological view is that it combines the rational and the ethical ingredients of administration, in contrast to the positivist's reliance on the rational. When people cherish ethical values such as truth, reason, freedom, and the like, says Mills, and when they act successfully on the three questions that social scientists must constantly keep in mind—What is the structure of society as a whole? Where do we stand in human history? What varieties of men prevail? —then and not until then are people likely to experience well-being. When they have no values and feel no threat, the result is *indifference.* And when there are no values and no threat, but nevertheless a certain uneasiness, this constitutes *anxiety,* which, if it becomes sufficiently widespread, ends as a deadly disease.[12] A main advantage of an outer-directed philosophy of administration is that it guards against indifference and is more likely to find the clues to anxiety than is a philosophy that is wholly turned inward.

Finally, an additional advantage of the societal point of view is to predispose administrators to think and act like political economists, and hence to give the proper amount of weight to economic considerations.

9 Selznick, *Leadership in Administration,* p. 16.
10 Mills, *op. cit.,* p. 160.
11 *Ibid.,* pp. 134-135.
12 *Ibid.,* pp. 11, 179.

From time immemorial economic statesmen in governmental administration have stressed the very factors emphasized here: the time dimension, the organic nature of society, circular causation, and the long view as contrasted with the short one. Since the affluent society seems to be ill provided with leader-statesmen for positions of great responsibility, the societal approach to administration can hardly be overemphasized.

## Bureaucracy and Enterprise

One of the implications of the foregoing analysis is the bearing it has on the problem of bureaucracy. Within proper bounds, bureaucracy is a desirable development that occurs in all institutions, private as well as public. Studies made in the 1930s, for example, show that top business leaders in corporations such as American Telephone and Telegraph, General Motors, U. S. Steel, and others, readily acknowledged bureaucracy to be inherent in large corporations. The problem is, how can the good that is in bureaucracy be accentuated and its harmful effects offset by positive remedies? [13]

Bureaucracy is another name for a large, complicated administrative organization where the focus is internalized rather than externalized. Technically, bureaucracy may be defined as any organization with the predominant characteristics of a hierarchical and formalized structure, division of labor among many kinds of specialists, long lines of communication militating against face-to-face relationships, a resulting reliance upon rules and regulations, and a consequent impersonality affecting individuals as well as processes. It was Max Weber, a sociologist, who first brought the concept of bureaucracy into prominence, arguing that the wave of the future is a bureaucracy that will and should become universal, and that compared with its advantages, both capitalism and socialism become relatively insignificant.

The tacit assumptions in Weber's optimistic prediction resemble those of the scientific management and positivist schools. The dictates of technology (most recently in the form of automation) must be followed to their logical conclusion, irrespective of their effect on the individual. The best system for society is one in which logic and order have been advanced to their ultimate degree. The system and the role are more important than the person. Man exists for the ends of the state and its subsidiaries, and not for his own ends. The goal of life is machine efficiency, essentially an engineering concept.

There is much truth, of course, in Weber's thesis. So-called rationalization makes possible large-scale production, the standardization of productive units and their ready replacement, and the substitution of

---

13 See Marshall E. Dimock, *Administrative Vitality, the Conflict with Bureaucracy* (New York: Harper & Row, Publishers, 1959).

system for guesswork, all of which constitute a competitive advantage for producers and businessmen as well as for those processes of administration where input-output is the test of accomplishment.

Max Weber's world is the universe of the efficiency engineer, the systems planner, the specialist in operations research, the specialist in automation and computer technology. And as William H. Whyte showed in *The Organization Man*, American society in midcentury has become largely the environment Weber envisaged. Like any system, however, this one also has drawbacks as well as advantages. Any good thing carried too far and not balanced by elements that guard against excesses develops weaknesses or pathologies of its own.

The chief pathologies of bureaucracy are first, that the specialists who largely make up the personnel of a bureaucracy tend to create private worlds of their own which makes coordination, a main ingredient of institutional efficiency, difficult. Second, in a system that relies overmuch on formal structure and carefully assigned roles, the participants tend to adhere strictly to their narrowly defined functions, thus militating against spontaneous cooperation and the assumption of responsibility for taking the initiative in problem solving; and both of these are necessary to over-all institutional effectiveness. Finally, individuals in bureaucracies are deprived of normal ego satisfactions and tend to lose their personalities; to compensate, they try to aggrandize themselves by petty encroachments on the jurisdiction of others. Since in the long run there is no greater institutional efficiency than individuals who are spontaneously motivated, these three pathologies of bureaucracy are a hazard to any institution.

It is now generally admitted, therefore, that bureaucracy is a mixed blessing. Left to its own devices it tends to splinter and segment the life of the institution, to put a premium on routine administration, and to be lacking in humanness and consumer appeal. In short, this aspect of bureaucracy emphasizes the internalized, routine view of management that Selznick and others protest against. Such a system has everything in it that is useful except the most important one of all, which is man himself: man the producer, man the consumer, man the unified personality capable of resourcefulness, spontaneity, and growth. If bureaucracy is not to become an albatross around the neck of enterprise, therefore, the effective administrator must give as much of his attention to the human nature factors of his organization as he does to the system, to the outer as to the inner world of bureaucracy.

To accomplish this objective, the administrator must know something about psychology, about personality and motivation, about what constitutes integrity, and what makes man creative. At the same time he needs a better knowledge of how to build a total environment in which the weaknesses of bureaucracy are countered by a positive force producing spontaneity, creativity, and the other qualities that bureaucracy is powerless to produce. This complementary need is described by the term enterprise. Enterprise expresses itself in a number of ways: through the innovative individual, the entrepreneur in business, the inventor in technology, the creative person in art or literature. An enterprising society is one that has positive values and goals and is capable of making the adjustments needed to release tensions and accept change when required.

In a later part of this book more will be said about what makes men creative, spontaneously motivated, resourceful and ingenious. Here it need only be noted that administrators have a responsibility for creating such an environment of vitality not only in the organization they manage but also in society as a whole.

Vitality takes many forms: energy; resourcefulness in problem solving; initiative and self-confidence; willingness to take calculated risks; inventiveness. It is the creative spirit in all fields of endeavor. It is a knowledge of how to link the creativity of the person with the social process of utilization; here it ties in to the bureaucratic system.

The four main ingredients of enterprise are person, motive, idea, and process. It is always an individual who initiates; the group forms later. He needs an achievement motive. To be original he must have a distinctive idea. And if his idea is to become a reality, it must be tied into a larger process, the production line of bureaucratic administration. The end product of enterprise is spirit, an *esprit de corps* which bureaucracy finds it hard if not impossible to create. Bureaucracy is wooden; enterprise is responsive. And people dislike woodenness and appreciate service.

Nevertheless, enterprise also has its defects. Carried to extremes, it may produce disorder, duplicating and overlapping jurisdictions, objectives obscured by passing enthusiasms, and lack of follow-through. Consequently the best system is a combination of bureaucracy and enterprise, the first being logical and the second human. Even in bolt factories human considerations help make better bolts because, like every other enterprise, these factories are made up of workers and supervisors and depend on customers.

Even the USSR, which sought to become a huge efficient bureaucracy, is in process of learning this lesson. As David Granick remarks, the two things that Soviet administration has learned the hard way in recent years is that flexibility of management decision is necessary to effective production, and that incentives are needed at all levels if men and women are to put forth their best creative efforts.[14]

---

14 *The Red Executive* (New York: Doubleday & Company, 1960).

## BIBLIOGRAPHY AND CASES

### Annotated Reading Suggestions

The influence of organization and management on all phases of American life is nowhere more lucidly dealt with than in Adolf Berle, *The American Economic Republic* (Harcourt, Brace & World, 1963). Related books are Gerhard Colm and Theodore Geiger, *The Economy of the American People: Progress, Problems, and Prospects,* Planning Pamphlet 115 (National Planning Association, 1958; 2d ed. October 1961); and Robert L. Heilbroner, *The Making of Economic Society* (Prentice-Hall, 1962). The impact of change on government is dealt with in the symposium, "The City Manager in an Era of Change," *Public Management,* 44 (December 1962).

Among the outstanding contributions of sociologists, high rank should be given to Robert MacIver, *The Web of Government* (Macmillan, 1947). See also Talcott Parsons and E. Shils, *Toward a General Theory of Action* (Harvard University Press, 1944); William H. Whyte, Jr., *The Organization Man* (Simon and Schuster, 1956); Joseph A. Schumpeter, *Capitalism, Socialism, and Democracy* (Harper & Row, 1942, 1946); James Burnham, *The Managerial Revolution* (John Day, 1941); and Max Weber, *The Protestant Ethic and the Spirit of Capitalism,* tr. Talcott Parsons (London: George Allen & Unwin, 1930, 1948). In addition to the books by Philip Selznick mentioned in the text, one may consult with benefit his article, "Foundation of the Theory of Organization," *American Sociological Review,* 13 (February 1948).

The Swedish economist, Gunnar Myrdal, in *Beyond the Welfare State* (Yale University Press, 1960) argues that already in the "mature" economies, insufficient attention is being given to international policies for growth and expansion. And finally, the distinguished dean of the Yale Law School, Engene V. Rostow, in *Planning For Freedom: The Public Law of American Capitalism* (Yale University Press, 1960), correlates economics, law, and political science to project the societal problems that appear to lie ahead.

### Case Studies

The ICP collection is rich in cases that have broad societal implications. In the Stein *Case Book,* some already mentioned qualify in this respect: *The Defense Plant Corporation* and *The Sale of the Tankers* are representative. Others that will be mentioned in later chapters also are pertinent: *The Reconversion Controversy* and *The TVA Ammonia Plant,* for example.

Those especially recommended for this chapter are (unnumbered) *The Consumers' Counsel,* by Kathryn Smul Arnow (1949, rev. 1950), a study dealing with the representation of consumer interests in administration. Others are No.

34, *From Forest to Front Page,* by Roscoe C. Martin, sixty-six pages, dealing with the location of a paper company in Tennessee; No. 27, *Closing of Newark Airport,* by P. C. Tillett, fifty-two pages, the story of a celebrated dispute that shows the influence of public opinion on administration; No. 37, *Flagstaff Federal Sustaining Yield Unit,* by P. W. Bedard, twenty-four pages, dealing with the organization of a local industry (similar to the Tennessee case); and No. 65, *Battle of Soldier Creek,* by P. O. Foss, sixteen pages, having to do with grazing rights on public lands; No. 73, *District School Supervisor vs. Teachers and Parents,* by T. Firmalino, eighteen pages, concerning public pressures on educational administration; and No. 29, *Michigan Athletic Awards Rule,* by G. A. Schubert, also dealing with public opinion.

# 7

# Administration
# and the
# Political Economy

BECAUSE OF THE organic nature of society, every move of the policy
administrator should be consciously related to the good of the political
economy, which may best be described as the juxtaposition of government and the private economy in a joint quest for prosperity, a high
standard of living, and the good life. Political economy is another
name for economics that emphasizes policy and institutional relationships more than formal economics ordinarily does. It is a much older
concept, still widely employed in many parts of the world. Further,
it is being reemphasized in all modern countries, including the United
States, because economics without policy or policy without economics
has become virutally unthinkable in the modern world.[1]

## The Resurgence of Political Economy

It would be easier to train the new managerial elite for top positions in
business and government if it were unnecessary for them to know very
much about both sociology and economics. But considering the nature
of planning and decision making today, such a course would be reckless
and might even be nearly fatal.

---

[1] Marshall E. Dimock, *The New American Political Economy* (New York: Harper
& Row, Publishers, 1962).

Everything the public administrator does is related to the economic well-being of the nation. Unnecessary burdens of taxation and regulation on the private economy tend to blunt its competitive edge; conversely, right policies convey a competitive advantage. The policies of government go far to determine, over long periods of time, whether America's goods and services can be sold advantageously in the world market and whether the balance of trade between this country and the rest of the world will remain favorable. Too great a burden of debt, or too heavy an accumulation of taxes for unwise economic purposes act as sand in the gears of international trade. If the GNP (gross national product) and the country's rate of economic growth are to remain satisfactory, government policies, in part determined by its administrators, are crucial. Thus, policy relating to the supply of money, interest rates, investment incentives, inflation and deflation, the incidence of taxes, and the business community's confidence in the domestic and foreign policies of the government will determine whether the country regresses, stands still, or moves steadily forward. In the twentieth century, when the interdependence of public and private enterprise is so close, the free enterprise system is not likely to remain viable unless government policies are congruent.

No major problem confronting the United States today can be solved by a single entity working alone. It usually takes not merely a dual alliance but a triple entente, or even a more involved grouping to master the difficulty. And in all this, government is increasingly the middleman. If, for example, labor and management were to become so evenly matched in power that protracted strikes occurred on a number of fronts and the ordinary processes of collective bargaining became increasingly ineffectual, what range of alternatives could remedy this situation in the long run? More deconcentration of power in both management and unions? It is a possibility unlikely to occur without considerable governmental intervention. Alternatively, the use of strong-arm methods by government to suppress the strikes? But what does this do to freedom, to labor morale and efficiency, and to the likelihood that the unions will demand equally objectionable restrictions on management? The third alternative—a long-range one, to be sure— is for government to use its good offices to develop more statesmanship on the part of leaders in both business and the unions so that both learn to think as men responsible for the welfare of the country. This means finding a common interest above the selfish interest of each party which will stimulate voluntary agreements favorable to both sides and to the public good as well. If compulsion is to be avoided, this course would appear to be the only way out. But clearly it requires a highly sophisticated and effective type of government.

Similarly in almost every other area of national concern: the farm problem, dwindling natural resources, national transportation, urban renewal, tariffs and the European Common Market, featherbedding in labor and management, improvements in public education, the nation's health, unemployment and recessions. For no major problem is there a simple answer; and at the center of each is government, which will have to become more effective if it is to find the necessary solutions.

The moves are intricate. Take, for example, the farm problem, or how to improve the quality of public education. If the government administrators who recommend policy to the legislature are not sufficiently skilled in economics, it is doubtful whether they will know enough to make their complicated moves in the first place and it is almost certain that over a period of years they will do so many wrong things that countries having better economic statesmanship (and this includes Socialist as well as free enterprise countries) will eventually reduce the margin of advantage that we have enjoyed for almost a hundred years. As a result, and because the influence of economic wisdom in decision making is so great, we could conceivably become a second-rate power.

All this our economic powerholders are rapidly learning, though somewhat belatedly. Public administrators in many cases have been no less at fault, for too often their minds stop at the boundary of government and do not penetrate the complexities of economic structure and its resulting policy implications.

The further need is for government to give immediate attention to its economic priorities. What is more important than foreign affairs and defense? But can they be adequately handled if government tries to do too much and its machinery is obsolete? How about unemployment and recurring recessions, the failure of the economy to grow as fast as it should, and the widespread unemployment growing out of automation and other technological advances? Is this not the second priority and are not the two areas, foreign and domestic, inextricably interdependent?

In America's fifth state of growth—using Rostow's fivefold classification[2]—government's top policy administrators have an unequaled opportunity to perform economic miracles. The national debt, now over $300 billion, is not necessarily a liability. Under skillful over-all management it can be used to stabilize the economy and encourage a desirable rate of growth, and still avoid the shoals of inflation. The national debt, the national budget, and the banking system are probably the best combination we have for keeping the country growing and prosperous, but what a challenge it is to achieve the organization and the individual competence needed to make the system work!

Moreover, economic well-being is not merely effected by one big decision at the top of the pyramid. It is a series of thousands of decisions,

[2] Discussed in Chapter 1, *supra*.

private as well as public, all of them related to the principles of political economy. It is in this area more than any other that countries will rise or fall in the tense days ahead. The sixth stage of American development, if we are to hold our place in the world, should be the political economy stage, superseding the affluent stage, which has notable weak points.

It is not enough that whenever a crisis threatens—war, the possibility of war, or depression—business leaders should transfer in droves to Washington. They know too little about government and stay too briefly to supply the leadership that is needed. Consequently, this leadership must come from the career service itself. A certain traffic back and forth and a vast amount of common training in the principles of political economy would make it possible, of course, for policy administrators in both camps to work together toward common goals while playing independent roles. Indeed, this is a "must" for the survival of American institutions and the managerial elite that has been catapulted into leadership.

To the argument here advanced, two objections are sometimes made. First, it is contended that since any interference with the free forces of the market is to be avoided, a closer working partnership between government and the economy is likely to undermine free choice and supply and demand. The answer is that if government and the economy were to share a clearer perception of common principle, there would be a much better chance that the market system would be allowed to operate unimpeded. The market system is the best of all systems, but it will not operate effectively if government allows pressure groups to dominate, so that it tries to do too much, interferes too much, and at too high a price to enable us to hold our position in world competition. For government can be either the worst enemy of the free enterprise system, or its mainstay. For government to become a mainstay, however, top leadership in both private enterprise and public administration must manage and decide in accordance with the same mutually understood body of economic principle.

The second objection is that political economy sounds authoritarian while the market system does not. In fact, there is nothing authoritarian or Socialistic about the principles of political economy unless one argues, as few any longer do, that government should have no part at all in determining the climate of enterprise and in making crucial decisions. But so long as government handles foreign relations, reflects the demands of pressure groups of all kinds, and determines tax and money policy (the latter in part only), it cannot help entering into the development of high economic policy even if those in charge of government were determined to prevent it. To the degree, therefore, that government does help to mold economic policy, to that degree also must there be consonance between the advocates of free enterprise in both the private and the public sectors if the private sector is not gradually and irresistibly to erode.

There is nothing antidemocratic or anti-free enterprise about the statement that the political economy must operate on the basis of principle, with a clear idea of its objectives and constant consideration of the values to be nurtured and protected. In the lingo of the social sciences, this is model building. In the present instance, it means giving thought to the principles and methods according to which the market system may operate at its optimum in the fifth stage of economic development in which the nation finds itself today. Only if decision makers see and voluntarily do the things they must in the interest of a viable economy, can any country be spared the alternative of regimented planning and coercion. Advanced technology, the use of government by pressure groups for the wrong reasons, and the advanced governing skills of competitor nations make this conclusion inescapable, even if the situation is much less acute in the simpler stages of economic development.

### From Mercantilism to Political Economy

As already shown, except in the nineteenth century when laissez faire enjoyed a brief period of glory, government in most Western European countries has always made the most important economic decisions for the nation. This concern of government was called cameralism in Germany and mercantilism elsewhere, and was opposed only in France where the ideas of the Physiocrats, who regarded agriculture as the source of all wealth, gained a wide influence.[3] Some of Jefferson's theories were influenced by those of the Physiocrats.

When Adam Smith published *The Wealth of Nations* in 1776 he accorded the highest place in the formation of economic policy to government, especially to the moralist and the lawmaker. Smith also set forth the principles that businessmen should observe if they followed the dictates of natural law and its servant, the market system. Government and business were not independent of each other. Indeed, the success of the business community, said Smith, depended on the success with which government did its part. Consequently, businessmen and government officials alike had to understand moral law and legislation, as well as the nature of the self-regulating market.

With the first industrial revolution, government became even more active than before, legislating in the area of slums, industrial accidents, and the like, thus laying the foundation for what is now called the welfare state. Meantime, Smith's classical economics divided, the economic branch coming down through David Ricardo and the politi-

---

3 See Chapter 2, *supra.*

cal branch through John Stuart Mill and the Utilitarians. Thereafter economics became increasingly theoretical, and political science and public administration increasingly less interested in economics.

When the American Economic Association was formed toward the end of the nineteenth century, leaders from many fields, including sociology and political science, realized that public policy was being neglected because of the artificial separation of politics and economics, and tried to draw the two branches together again. Because the effort was only partially successful, political economy has come down to us through the institutional economists such as John R. Commons, Wesley Mitchell, and others, and through political scientists who were economically oriented, men such as Woodrow Wilson and Charles A. Beard. Today political economy is growing, but so also are separatist tendencies among some economic and political specialists. Nevertheless, the political economy area receives increasing attention because our very survival as a nation depends upon the understanding and application of its principles.

### *Evolution of the Economic-Political Relationship in the United States*

Until fairly recently an antigovernment feeling in the business community was strong in the United States, partly because we misconstrued the purport of Adam Smith's teaching. Moreover, as colonists, we had revolted against a government that taxed us and restricted our trade with the West Indies, with the result that we turned not only against the king but also against government itself. There was a continent to develop, and pioneers are notoriously independent and resourceful. Hence as individualists Americans developed the habit of using government whenever it helped their economic interests and talking against it when it did not.

During the first century after the adoption of the federal Constitution the federal commerce and taxing powers were used very little. For the most part Americans subscribed to Jefferson's physiocratic ideas and emphasized farming, small business, states' rights, and a limited national government. Centralization and bigness, which Hamilton favored along with a plan for manufactures, a national bank, and a strong Presidency, did not come into their own until after the Civil War. Then the industrial East became dominant in the nation, railroads spanned the continent, and business followed in their wake; America became a businessman's civilization.

An end to laissez faire came with the passage of the Interstate Commerce Commission Act of 1887, followed three years later by the Sherman Antitrust Act. Nevertheless, in the age of the "robber barons" business continued to get bigger and more centralized, as did government and labor, which by this time had formed the American Federation of Labor. The Federal Reserve Act was passed in 1913 and the Federal Trade Commission Act in 1914.

A second revolution in the business-government relationship occurred during the New Deal. It was then that the stock market, holding companies, and insurance companies became subject to federal control. The Social Security Act was passed. All forms of communication, including telephones and television, were put under commission regulation. Powerful agencies were set up to regulate labor relations. All major public utilities, such as electric power and natural gas, were made subject to state and federal regulation. America rapidly became notable for its independent regulatory commissions and their wide-reaching bureaucracies, such as the Interstate Commerce Commission, which by now regulated all forms of transportation except aviation and shipping, these being under the control of separate commissions.

With the outbreak of World War II, government's economic role was extended even further. The Reconstruction Finance Corporation and its subsidiaries built most of the new plant needed during the war. At the end of the war there were 101 federally owned corporations covering large segments of the economy such as housing, banking, and area development (TVA). Only gradually was the number of these business organizations reduced.

After the war also, defense and foreign aid became big business with the federal government supplying the initiative and the money. With a peacetime budget which by 1962 amounted to nearly $100 billion, defense was more than 60 percent of the total, and foreign aid accounted for some $3 billion more. Business was not only closely regulated by government but government was now its biggest customer and, in the sense that the income tax took 52 percent of all corporate earnings, its biggest shareholder as well.

In short, during the seventy-five years between 1887 and 1962, government has expanded from a modest collection of federal agencies to the point where it is now the biggest regulatory bureaucracy in the world, and most of its work deals with the economy: regulating, stimulating, fostering, subsidizing, planning, organizing, exhorting, cajoling, even scolding. In addition, government is the biggest buyer, the biggest seller, and the biggest banker in the nation.

Little wonder, then, that businessmen increasingly have come to believe that since an antigovernment attitude had failed to keep government in check, the wiser policy is to try to improve government's organization, personnel, and administrative processes. Once businessmen accept this idea, as many of them already have, then knowingly or unknowingly the decision is reached to return to the political economy tradition, which is as old as mercantilism and as new as high-level planning.

## Some Principles of Political Economy

Simply because it is not doctrinaire nor authoritarian, the study of political economy requires a lifetime of application by the interested administrator. It is not something that can be fed out in capsule form and in small doses. In the following analysis, therefore, necessarily in capsule form, there is the risk of oversimplifying a subject that is infinitely various. Consequently the discussion is merely suggestive, attempting to show interrelationships in an over-all view.

**1. The Economic Organism.** The economic structure, like the rest of society, is an organism that at each stage of its development exhibits needs and tendencies requiring special attention if balance is to be maintained. The importance of this principle is that it affirms the dynamic, sociological nature of economic study. Consequently, to study the economy under the impression that it is static will yield results that are bound to be incomplete and even misleading.

**2. Relating Government to the Economy.** Like economics, government also is concerned with human needs and the promotion of a better life. Thus the structure of government, especially on the administrative side, must be adjusted to the structure of the economy in a skillful blend, so that government's policies and practices may be more easily evaluated by reference to their effect on economic behavior. This sounds a bit like economic determinism, and in a way it is. But it does not go so far as to suggest that government has no independent existence or that it does not differ in important respects from business administration. It is simply to suggest that the economy produces wealth and well-being and that therefore an important criterion in governmental policy and administration is·the establishment of a congruence between the two that will make measurement and evaluation more effective for government and the economy alike.

**3. The Market System.** If natural forces relating to demand and supply and freedom of choice are allowed to operate freely, the end results usually give all parties of interest what they want, with a greater degree of freedom and self-determination than if all decisions were made by higher authority (that is, human authority) in economic or political offices.

Thus the market system has several advantages. First, it gives people what they want instead of setting someone up as an arbiter of what it is thought they should want. Secondly, it establishes a self-regulating mechanism that is more effective in determining prices, profits, wages, and "shares" than are manmade decisions in these areas. Third, it increases rather than decreases the areas of social freedom because the consumer decides what he wants produced, the worker decides whom he wishes to work for, the manager may choose among prospective employees, and the investor may risk his money where he pleases; the result is more freedom of will and less concentration of authority in supermen. Fourth, the market system reduces the amount of governing that is needed on both the economic and the political side of the ledger. Indeed, modern economies such as the American and the Soviet are so complicated that without the assistance of the self-regulating forces of the market, the fixing of supply, demand, and prices becomes a well-nigh insuperable managerial problem. Fifth, freedom of choice makes for flexibility in the growth and expansion of the economic system and hence, as suggested in the first principle enunciated above, the system is more likely to keep pace with society than if arbitrary decisions are relied upon for the same results. Freedom to allocate scarce resources on the basis of consumer sovereignty is one of the best ways to stimulate invention and enterprise in the hope of reaping profits therefrom.

**4. Built-in Incentives.**  Freedom of choice involves risk and risk justifies profit, although it also sometimes results in loss. The profit and loss system is the best one so far conceived for stimulating effective production and sales and for weeding out the incompetent. And because through competition society is relieved of its dead wood, the danger that society will become stagnant and noncompetitive is greatly reduced. Socialist economies are finding that they cannot eliminate profit and get the results they want from economic processes.

In a free economy profit depends upon excellence, and excellence depends upon keeping ahead of one's competitors. To keep the edge, new products must constantly be devised and old processes constantly improved. This encourages enterprise and tends to increase the number of entrepreneurs in many areas including scientific and social invention. Only by keeping ahead of competition and avoiding the tendency to become complacent and sluggish is society enabled to raise its standard of living and hold its own in world trade.

**5. A Unified Process.**  Like administration and society generally, the economy also depends for success on a combination of elements maintained in working accord. In addition, there is a cause and effect relationship that may be established in this process. Freedom allows choice, choice requires competition, competition involves risk, risk encourages enterprise, enterprise justifies profit, profit tends to establish a level of prices. One role of government, therefore, is to see that no stage in this series of steps becomes blocked. If competition is allowed to disappear, for example, the inevitable result is that monopoly of one kind or another, the private-corporate or the public-governmental, will have to take over the function once performed by the automatic market mechanism.

**6. Diminishing Returns.**   Where choice is free, the cut-off point between demand and supply and between price and no sale is the point at which the last unit sold continues to be profitable and the next unit sold would become unprofitable.[4] In some ways the law of diminishing returns is the most important principle of political economy because it avoids too much of a good thing and yet provides a sufficiency of the things people want. If it is assumed that people buy because of a utility involved, the cut-off point for both supply and price is the point at which one's margin disappears—hence the term, marginal utility. Similarly, if any enterprise, private or public, becomes so large that size affects efficiency and efficiency affects profit and service, at the point where this occurs the optimum may be said to exist. If a company has a high production that it sells at a profitable price, it tends to go on producing. But at a certain point any increase tends to be less profitable, and if production continues all production may become unprofitable. At the proper point, therefore, if management has sufficient intelligence, it will allow the law of diminishing returns to operate.

Because it is a universal, this same principle applies also to the functions of government. Because the span of human attention is limited and specialization is necessary to superior performance, government can do a certain number of things well, but beyond that point other things are done less well, and if the growth of government functions continues, nothing may be done as well as if the span of attention had been kept within reasonable bounds. The same principle applies, of course, to business corporations.

**7. High-level Capitalism.**   As the economic organism grows, inevitably it acquires more components, more layers of organization, more subprocesses, and an increasing number of intricate interconnections. Thus another impediment is added to the internal forces that tends to restrict, rather than encourage, what should be the free working of supply and demand and the price levels that result. It is almost as though a new element had been added: power, the power of decision. For the greater the number of variables in the situation, the less are they able to operate without human intervention. Consequently the more does power increase at crucial points in the structure.

This principle applies equally to both the economic and the politi-

---

4 This is meant to include the idea that it might be more profitable to divert any additional productive units elsewhere.

cal structure of the nation. What some German writers have called high-level capitalism therefore tends to increase the human decision-making power of key men: bankers, lawyers, top corporate executives, trade union executives, and certain government officials. These are the cream of the new elite we have mentioned so often. If these key people make too many mistakes or fail to realize what they are doing, over a period of time they may contribute to the demise of the self-regulating system and the substitution of Socialist planning and decision making.

**8. The Long View.**   At all stages of economic growth it is necessary to take the long view as well as the short, and the need increases as the economic mechanism becomes larger and more complicated. The economy is more like a space rocket than like the Wright Brothers' airplane; today it travels faster and has more parts to be kept in unison than ever before in history. The result is a greater speed potential but also a greater crash potential if something vital goes wrong with either the human or the nonhuman mechanisms on which it depends. This fact alone justifies the contention that management's greatest current need in both the private and the public realm is administrative statesmanship.

**9. Foreign Trade.**   With every increase in the speed and facility with which transportation and communication eliminate distance, the difference between domestic and foreign trade tends also to diminish. By the same token the political economy, which once was nationalistic, has rapidly become a combination of both the domestic and the international, a blend to which common principles must be applied. This has caused the eminent Swedish economist, Gunnar Myrdal, in his book *Beyond the Welfare State,* to argue that even if all the problems of high-level capitalism could be solved, there would still be a need to rethink institutional economics (political economy) in order to reflect the realities of international interdependence.

Here again it is almost as though a totally new dimension had been added to planning and decision making in economics and government alike. Small wonder, then, that one of the federal government's greatest organizational and administrative headaches is just at this point. It is possible that these problems will not be adequately solved until a new crop of administrators is recruited who are accustomed to thinking in terms of the dynamics of administration in the spirit of the space age.

**10. The Public Interest.**   The public interest is at least two things: First, it is justice or fairness, meaning equal freedom, objectivity, tolerance—in the vernacular, an even break. Second, it is part of an over-all value system. It is anything that makes it possible for the individual to develop himself toward higher goals: a chance to work, to become educated, to enjoy higher tastes and enjoyments, the things that make people human in the ideal sense.

The importance of the public interest is directly related to the complexity and interdependence of the economic organism. Theoretically, if man were in total isolation or if there were perfect competition (neither of which is so), there would be no problem of public interest. But the development of high-level capitalism changes the situation so that even seemingly unimportant details of economic behavior that once were left wholly to the individual now cause a wide circle of repercussions and are no longer merely an individual matter. Similar considerations apply to government: the more it has to do, the wider is the number of its concerns, and the more intensified are some of them bound to become; hence the more must the public interest become the main criterion in decision making.

But government is inherently different from business in the matter of public responsibility, or accountability. Government is *supposed* to operate in a goldfish bowl; it is *supposed* to serve all and not only some; it is *supposed* to be regulated by laws and constitutional provisions, it *must* be a government of laws and not of men. Of course, these differences can easily be exaggerated and doubtless they are. The point is that as economic administrative empires grow in size, complexity, and power, to the point where they resemble government, they must take increasing account of the public interest and become increasingly subject to the demands of public accountability. From this it may easily be deduced that the smaller and less important the unit, the greater is its privacy likely to be.

Hence the principle: the more developed the economic organism becomes and the greater its power, the closer is the public scrutiny to which it is properly subject and the higher are the ethical standards it is expected to observe. Only the insignificant may enjoy full freedom; the big, like government, are publically accountable.

**11. Private and Public.**   The more complex the economic organism becomes, the greater is the need to reconcile the kind of private and public gain that has nothing to do with financial reward. A main problem of the administrator, therefore, is to keep constantly in mind the need of individuals in the organization to find opportunities that will help them to develop their private ambitions, fulfill the image they have of themselves, and contribute their share to the total public good, with resulting approbations and rewards. During the nineteenth century this was a problem dealt with by the Utilitarians; it remains today a problem of modern character building to be dealt with by psychology and even psychiatry as well as by the administrator.

**12. Government's Role.**  Finally, since government needs to adjust to stages in the growth of the national economy, it must also change and adjust within itself. Values and constitutions may be fixed for all time (though this is arguable), but certainly the organization and methods of government must be constantly reexamined and changed if need be so that government may keep pace with social and economic development. The more the economic structure accumulates power, the more must government become rational and competent. A primitive society may make do with a weak government but a space age society must have the advantages of a government able to handle increasingly complex problems that affect not only individuals and nations, but the world.

If the market system is to be maintained, the first requirement is that public administrators understand it, sympathize with its objectives, and know what to do about it when it is in trouble. Second, they must know when and when not to intercede. Third, they must be enterprising in order to keep the economy progressive. Fourth, they must act on the basis of principle and the long view. And finally, they must act responsibly and with good effect.

This last requirement may call for a number of new developments in public administration: a more responsible party system; better legislative-executive cooperation; the organization of the office of the chief executive to attain a higher level of planning, coordination, and statesmanlike guidance. Public administration also needs more continuity. Politics, once thought of as a kind of game, is no longer a game but part of a complex system of political economy on which the needs of the people and the survival of the country's free institutions depend. The more intricate and power-laden the economy becomes, the more skillful must public administration also become or both will succumb together. To survive, therefore, government needs public administrators who are political economists and the economy needs leaders who also are political economists.

Where does one acquire such knowledge? In a lifetime of experience, reading, and reflection. By reading books such as Overton Taylor, *A History of Economic Thought,* John Stuart Mill's best works, or any and all of the suggestions made in the bibliography of one of the present author's *The New American Political Economy.* The work is never done, one never learns as much about political economy as should ideally be acquired, it is the work of a lifetime. But this challenge is one of the things that makes the life of the administrator the satisfaction that it is. In addition, if a knowledge of political economy was ever merely a luxury, today it is a necessity dictated by survival itself.

## BIBLIOGRAPHY AND CASES

### Annotated Reading Suggestions

Some of the reading suggestions in the previous chapter are pertinent also to this one.

Among books by professors of public administration who have emphasized the economic aspects of the subject, the following should be noted: Emmette S. Redford, *Administration of National Economic Control* (Macmillan, 1952); Robert A. Dahl and Charles A. Lindblom, *Politics, Economics, and Welfare* (Harper & Row, 1953); and Marshall E. Dimock, *Business and Government* (4th ed., Holt, Rinehart and Winston, 1961).

On the administrator's need to qualify in the realm of economic policy, see Donald Watson, *Economic Policy* (Houghton Mifflin, 1960); John Maurice Clark, *Economic Institutions and Human Welfare* (Knopf, 1957); Kenneth E. Boulding, *Principles of Economic Policy* (Prentice-Hall, 1958); William D. Grampp and Emanuel T. Weiler, eds., *Economic Policy* (rev. ed., Irwin, 1956); E. Ronald Walker, *From Economic Theory to Policy* (University of Chicago Press, 1943); and Marshall E. Dimock, *The New American Political Economy* (Harper & Row, 1962).

Business leaders need as firm a grounding in government as public administrators do in economics. On the connection between the two, with special attention to the new demands on leadership, see Robert A. Gordon and James E. Howell, *Higher Education for Business* (Columbia University Press, 1959), and Frank C. Pierson, *The Education of Businessmen* (McGraw-Hill, 1959).

The head of the world's largest corporation, Frederick A. Kappel of American Telephone and Telegraph Company, in his book, *Vitality in a Business Enterprise* (McGraw-Hill, 1960), stresses that two main factors account for vitality: long-range planning and outstanding leaders with ethical motivations.

### Case Studies

Two excellent cases are included in the Stein *Case Book.* The first, *The Reconversion Controversy,* written by Jack W. Peltason in 1950, tells the story of what went on in the government as a whole and in the War Production Board in particular at the close of World War II, when the country converted from war to peace. The second is *The Disposal of the Aluminum Plants,* written by Harold Stein in 1948 and revised in 1952. This is the story of a spectacular struggle with the Aluminum Company of America, coinciding in time with the Supreme Court's decision in the *Alcoa* case, March 12, 1945.

A third outstanding ICP narrative is No. 48, *President's Economic Advisers,* by C. Silverman, eighteen pages in length. This case involves the administration of the Employment Act of 1946, the key to economic stabilization. Another case is No. 24, *Army Flies the Mail*, by P. Tillitt, sixty-nine pages, dealing with the Army and the Post Office in the determination of a subsidy policy to commercial aviation. Another pertinent case is No. 30, *Public Advisory Board and the Tariff Study*, by D. S. Brown.

# PART TWO

# Administration
# and Public Policy

# 8

## The Politics
## of Administration

ALL GOVERNMENTAL ADMINISTRATION operates in a political milieu. No matter what position is involved, from the least discretionary job in the civil service to the highest policy posts in appointive office, the political setting is a central fact of administrative life for the government official.

There are, of course, many fine shadings in the degree to which the influence of politics on administration is felt. Although politics cannot be defined in a single simple statement, the various connotations of the term must nevertheless be identified and finally integrated to show how, through the influence of politics on administration, governmental operations serve society's larger interests.

### What Is Politics?

As to any high-level abstraction such as state, society, economics, democracy, government, and public administration itself, so also to the term politics many definitions may be applied. The main problem is how to avoid a rigid dogmatism on the one hand and fuzzy thinking on the other. If it is impossible to formulate a precise definition—and often the attempt beclouds rather than elucidates practical connotations—it is possible at least to analyze and describe what actually occurs in various areas and at different levels of institutional operation.

As a start, let us say that politics is problem solving in an attempt to meet human needs. Politics is also choosing among alternatives, making decisions where a choice is involved. Politics is deciding on the content of policy and the values to be promoted; this is like saying that politics is policy, which may and usually does involve philosophies, value systems, and other high-level abstractions. Politics is also partisanship, of course, meaning taking an active part in the work of political parties, pressure groups, and other groups that would influence public opinion for partisan purposes. As part of the power struggle for preferment, access to dominance, and control, politics is also competition for influence and position. And finally, politics is a process involving a division of labor between legislation, execution, and adjudication; but even so, in the large sense, discretion and law making occur in all three of these branches of the political process.

The foregoing rather impressionistic analysis shows that the range of possible connotations of the term politics covers a spectrum extending all the way from personal partisan manipulation on the one hand, to the ideas of political philosophers concerned with the public good on the other.

In public administration, politics is a process that affects every aspect of governmental operations, and because policy is a continuum, each aspect has an appropriate role to play that is interrelated with all the others. What these roles are depends partly on the form of government in question. Thus, a monistic type of government (one-party rule or a dictatorship) tends to concentrate power in one place, whereas a democratic government widely distributes power and decision making, creating fairly distinct roles in a system of checks and balances. The democratic pattern is harder to describe realistically than the monistic, the reason being that freedom is emphasized and hence citizens, public opinion, constitutions, law making, and popular control have a wider and more varied scope and influence. The broad distribution of roles and authority makes possible a degree of freedom that allows public opinion to be the arbiter of policy.

Consequently, the problem of government and its administration is to define roles precisely enough to avoid confusion and institutional ineffectuality, but with enough flexibility to make it possible for freedom and public opinion to pervade and control the whole of the governmental machinery.

This proposition has been well stated by Paul Appleby, former dean of the Maxwell Graduate School of public administration at Syracuse University and a long-time federal official. "Public administration," said Appleby, "is policy-making." If this statement seems to exalt administration, the impression is false because an emphasis on politics actually subordinates the administrator, for it exalts the politician and thereby exalts the citizen as well. Thus, continued Appleby, "Public administration is policy-making. *But it is not autonomous, exclusive or isolated policy-making.* It is policy-making on a field where mighty forces contend, forces engendered in and by the society. It is policy-making subject to still other and various policy-makers." Indeed, public administration is one of several basic political processes by which a people achieves and controls governance.[1] This statement comes only after Appleby has clearly shown that career and appointive officials alike share essentially the same responsibility for policy and leadership. Consequently, he is inclined to accentuate the policy role that professional administrators must play.

The best way to understand policy is to start with Appleby's statement that mighty forces contend. From that point, here is the way politics unfolds in a step by step progression: Society has certain needs. Government is the only modern social institution with sufficient scope to serve these needs. Some governmental functions, like the collection of taxes, are performed in order to maintain itself, but most of the others are the result of pressure from interested citizens and groups. Since people differ as to what government should and should not do, it is always the scene of active political controversy. Hence politics is the means by which society faces up to issues and decides how to resolve them. Politics involves a choice among alternatives that involve values, philosophies, ethical considerations. Politics is a quest for human betterment by public means. It is also, as Bismarck once noted, the art of the possible. In the ideal sense, politics is the purposeful activity by which men seek to live a better life.[2]

Needs, pressures, policies: these eventually become law. Law takes many forms including constitutions, legislative enactments, administrative determinations, and judicial decisions. Administrators occupy the midway station in this process, often suggesting legislation in the first place and interpreting and adding to it once it is passed. In addition, administrators have a good deal more to do with the execution and enforcement of the law than the judicial branch itself. From this point of view, administration is the application of policy formulated by law in a constantly unfolding process, making the laws of legislatures and the courts increasingly more specific by means of policy formulations and determinations applied to particular publics, to smaller publics, and finally to individual cases.[3] It has been rightly said that public

---

[1] Paul H. Appleby, *Policy and Administration* (University, Ala.: University of Alabama Press, 1949), pp. 169-170.

[2] This argument is presented in Leslie Lipson, *The Great Issues of Politics* (2d ed., Englewood Cliffs, N.J.: Prentice-Hall, 1960).

[3] Appleby, *op. cit.*, pp. 89-90.

administration is the intermingling of policy making and management that occurs between the levels of legislative, judicial, and popular-electoral policy determinations.

Where does partisan politics come in? So far, the discussion has centered on policy rather than partisanship. Although the question will be dealt with more fully at a later point, some reference to the role of political parties in administration is needed here. Much depends upon the form of government involved. In Britain, for example, where the party in power is responsible for carrying out the program promised the electorate, party policy is always government policy. By contrast, in the United States this responsibility is so much less that Appleby calls it marginal: "All administration and all policy-making within the government are political, being governmental, but only a small part of either, by mass, has identifiable partisan character." Moreover, he continues, not all partisan activity is concerned with policy and administration, for much is merely auxiliary, being concerned with keeping party machinery in readiness for the periodic selection and election of candidates for public office.[4]

In summary, it must be understood that public administrators are always and inevitably concerned with politics in the sense of policy, but the extent to which they are affected by partisan political activity depends largely on whether political parties attempt to unify all of government through their policies and programs, as is the case in Britain, or whether their role is largely confined to electing candidates and winning elections, as is more characteristic of party activity in the United States.

There is, however, yet another aspect of politics with which every administrator must be concerned. This is what may be called political sense, and it depends on the personality and character of the individual. The qualities involved are intuition, tact, the ability quickly to size up a situation, the ability to get things done despite opposition, the skill to get people to cooperate and to make them content in their work.

As noted in an earlier chapter, government differs from business in certain aspects, but a high degree of political sense is a universal requirement in both cases. A group of Harvard professors, for example, made case studies of large corporations, and concluded that a main requirement of executive leadership in business is political sense.[5] The reason, of course, is that as corporations become large they also become involved in competitions for power similar to those in government, and hence the same skills are needed in both cases. Again like

---

4 *Ibid.*, pp. 26, 64.

5 Edmund P. Learned, David N. Ulrich, and Donald R. Booz, *Executive Action* (Cambridge, Mass.: Harvard University Graduate School of Business Administration, 1951).

government, corporations also have policy problems that have to do with survival, an area that continually grows in importance. The chairman of the board of a large public utility once remarked, for example, that he could see little difference between his company and Tammany Hall.[6] Politics in this sense is a personal skill indispensable to administrative effectiveness. Indeed, the politician (in the best sense of that designation) and the administrator have certain skills that are interchangeable.

## Changing Attitudes toward Politics

Why is it then that during most of American political history, administration and politics have been considered as opposites rather than as two parts of a common experience?[7] The reasons are various. For one thing, both before and after the passage of the Pendleton Act of 1883, civil service reform developed a fight-the-spoilsman psychology in which the foe was politics and politicians. For a long time the ideal goal set for administrators was political neutrality, until it was gradually recognized that to neglect policy, which inevitably involves politics, is to dull incentive and defeat the public good; that it is not policy that is objectionable but only certain kinds of partisan activity. Then, too, certain crass forms of political activity such as bossism and spoils were condemned by conscientious citizens who saw in them a threat to democratic survival. In addition, at a later point, more was expected of political parties in the form of leadership and responsibility than they have so far been able to supply.

Equally important, in its extreme form the theory of the separation of powers seemed to suggest that there should be watertight compartments in government, leading to the notion—now recognized as naïve —that administrators should be excluded from the making and interpretation of the law. Government itself was regarded with suspicion and "politics" was a smear word. There was a failure sufficiently to differentiate between policy, which was the cornerstone of Greek philosophy, and partisanship, by which the authors of The Federalist papers meant faction.

Early in the present century Congress and the President were still fighting over who should run the administrative branch (as they still are, of course) and the civil service was timid and demoralized. The role of Congress was ill defined and the Presidency not yet sufficiently institutionalized to make administration as effective as needed.

---

6 Quoted in Eli Ginzberg, "Man and His Work," California Management Review (Winter 1962), p. 24.

7 See Appleby, op. cit.; Lepawsky, Administration; and Dwight Waldo, The Administrative State (New York: The Ronald Press Company, 1948).

Congress might have created a distinct career service, such as already existed in many western European nations, but decisive action was lacking. As a result, the administrative corps lacked the self-esteem, the self-confidence, and the freedom of scope that its duties required. As big government grew bigger, its structure became increasingly amorphous and confused. The original symmetry of a number of executive departments headed in each case by a Secretary as a member of the President's Cabinet was blurred when independent regulatory commissions and government corporations were created by Congress outside of the main lines of authority and responsibility leading up to the chief executive.

Fortunately, since the 1930s the situation has been changing: politics, which some blasé intellectuals regarded as merely a game, is now recognized as serious business. Government's role, once labeled by these same intellectuals as domination, is now seen as primarily a service to citizens and consumers. Administrators have always seen it this way, of course, but only recently have American political scientists generally begun to define politics broadly enough to include the service role of government and its organic relation to the rest of society.

It is irrelevant to speculate on which of the three branches of government is the most important, because all make and administer policy, as they should. Nevertheless, it has come gradually to be recognized that in practice the administrative branch is now relatively more influential than the other two and that its influence on policy is greater than was once supposed. Consequently there is a changing view as to the role of politics in administration and an attempt to make public administration a more effective instrument for the betterment of American society. Public opinion has come to see the need for more expertness, more sophisticated leadership, and more continuity for career officials in government employment.

The extent to which this change has occurred is reflected in a conference of former political and career executives sponsored by The Brookings Institution in Washington in 1957. There was general agreement among the members of the group, for example, that politically appointed officials could not provide the leadership needed in the federal government. Some of the findings and opinions expressed were these:

> The real difference between career and politically appointive jobs is not their nature, but the degree of political experience on the part of the incumbent. On this score, the career executive easily outranks the transient political executive of limited tenure. Career executives supply not only managerial competence, and expert knowledge of government administration, and a detailed understanding of the programs and

issues, but also a degree of political skill that political executives some-times lack.

Few bureau chiefs can avoid making policy or carrying political responsibility. Their role is conscientiously to promote the policies of the party in office, on the assumption that both seek the public interest.

Actually, the area in which the political executive can make any real impact on policy is relatively small compared with the area oc-cupied by Congress on the one side and by career executives on the other.

The best course for a political executive "is to work closely with his career executives, appreciate them fully, and thank God every night for having them around."

Moreover, career officials generally have more influence with Con-gress than political executives do, especially when a new administration takes office.

And again, "All of us career executives have testified on the Hill, and will continue to do so. When a clear line of policy has been laid down, and you are sent to the Hill to defend it, you do it. . . . It is a derogatory commentary on career executives to assume that they do not have the capacity, desire, or willingness to defend programs."

When, therefore, the second Hoover Commission tried to draw a sharp line between the two sets of public officials, and to call one strictly political and the other strictly nonpolitical, the logic of their recommendations may have been clear, said the members of the Brook-ings conference, but they did not square with the facts of administra-tive life in Washington.[8]

## Pressure Groups, Political Parties, and Public Opinion

Every government agency has a constituency for which it was largely created and whose interest and support are essential to its continued existence. In some cases the interest group involved is more obvious and tangible than in others. In the federal government, for example, the Departments of Commerce, Agriculture, and Labor reflect the existence of three major segments of the economy, although these agencies are also charged with serving the larger public interest as well. In each case the enabling legislation charges the department in question to "foster and promote the interest of" the particular economic interest involved. A similar link exists between educators and the Office of Educa-

---

[8] Marver H. Bernstein, *The Job of the Federal Executive* (Washington, D.C.: The Brookings Institution, 1958), pp. 46-69, *passim.*

tion, physicians and the United States Public Health Service, and lawyers and the Department of Justice.

Depending on the program in question, however, agencies differ in the kind of interest evoked from special groups. Thus, a government agency may provide a special service (to farmers), wider economic service (in handling the mails), or a service to a particular group in the population (veterans, for example). Or the agency may offer a subsidy (to the aviation industry), or discharge a regulatory function (for television). Or it may attack some particular social problem (such as juvenile delinquency). Thus not all agencies directly serve a particular interest group, for many offer a more diffused public service to society as a whole, as in public health or public assistance.

But irrespective of the category or, as sometimes happens, the combination of categories under which an agency may be classified, the support of some portion of effective public opinion is always necessary —at least in a democracy—before its program can be created and remain in existence. Every agency has not only its supporters but in many cases also its opponents who for one reason or another would like to put it out of business or greatly reduce its role, a situation faced by even the largest and most powerful government bodies. Many conservative businessmen and an occasional farmer would like to see the Department of Agriculture's $5 billion budget reduced by abolishing price support and food storage programs, the two items that account for the largest single chunk of that agency's expenditures. Consequently every administrator is in politics, so to speak, for two good reasons: he needs the support of his clientele in order to promote his agency, and second, in many cases to protect it from its natural enemies.

The government agencies that cannot be classified under the foregoing are those with sovereign functions inherent in the very survival of government: the collection of taxes, the maintenance of police and military forces, the operation of the foreign office, the control of immigration and naturalization, the coining of money, the control of currency, and the operation of the courts, to mention only the most obvious ones. Such programs must rely on the interest of all citizens and lawmakers in protecting the life, liberty, and property of the entire population. Generally speaking, these agencies receive a wide popular support rather than a narrow interest group support, although many specific problems do arise especially in connection with civil liberties, fear of a police state, the incidence of taxes, and the like.

Because most public programs have a specific clientele, an administrator has a strong incentive to stay close to his interest group and reciprocally the interest group will stay close to the agency. For the administrator the relationship is sometimes a divided pleasure, however. Although it constitutes an opportunity to gain support for his program and to expand budget and services, unless he is careful he will be accused of being dominated by the interest group and thus of failing to serve the larger public interest, which also is his responsibility. The difficulty is especially present, of course, in the case of agencies concerned with labor, agriculture, commerce, regulation, subsidies, and tax policies, areas in which millions and even billions of dollars are often at stake. In such instances, therefore, the administrator needs not only a keen political sense but also a sense of ethics so as to avoid violation of the law, conflict of interest, or breach of the public sense of moral decency.

In American government, interest groups have a greater influence on legislation (and hence on policy) than do formal political parties, even though parties are more often brokers for interest groups than tight little oligarchies with ideas of their own. With the possible exception of an occasional lawmaker, an interest group feels closer to "its" agency than to any other aspect of government; hence it is only natural that administrators should have much to do with the inception of legislation. In the field of immigration prior to World War II, for example, there were some fifty private organized groups that singly or in concert pushed a liberal kind of legislation, while a half dozen or so favored more restrictive laws. Those on the liberal side were usually religious, nationality, welfare, or civil liberties groups, whereas those opposing were patriotic or labor organizations trying to keep "cheap" labor out of the country. For both the target was the executives of the Immigration and Naturalization Service, which, like most agencies in Washington, consequently had an internal committee on future legislation to sift the many proposals coming to it.

The procedure is usually like this: In most government agencies legislation emanating from an interest group or from the agency itself is constantly to the forefront of the attention of top officials. Some of these proposals would amend existing law and some express new programs and policies. Once the agency has decided what it favors, the proposal is reviewed by the Secretary of the department, then by a division in the Bureau of the Budget *where all proposals emanating from government agencies are required by presidential order to be cleared.*

At this point, if it has not already been done, the interest groups concerned will prevail upon some congressman to introduce a bill which then becomes either a private member or an administration bill. An administration bill bears the mark of the chief executive's prestige and reputation which makes it a part of "his" program. Something similar to the procedure in Washington occurs at the municipal level where a mayor or city manager, working through councilmen, pushes the adoption of ordinances and programs worked out in the executive department.

When a bill is introduced in Congress it is assigned to the appropriate committee which then holds hearings on it. The usual procedure is for spokesmen from the interested executive department to appear first, followed by representatives of interest groups and the public. If the bill is an important one a Cabinet officer may make the opening statement; if less so, a bureau chief or an assistant secretary (sub-Cabinet level) will testify. In either case, permanent career officials also are present, and committee members are generally at least as interested in their presentations as in those of the political executives. Indeed, career officials will often be asked to give independent testimony either in addition to or as a substitute for the testimony of political officials.

This confirms what was said earlier about the career legislator being closer to the career executive, as a rule, than to the political executive. One reason is the obvious fact of friendship: longtime legislators and career administrators each have something the other needs. Second, both feel that they have become tested veterans and that most political officials are neophytes. Third, the members of the legislature believe they understand the motivations of career executives while they are less certain—at least until some time has elapsed—about political executives.

What is the motivation of the career executive? Generally speaking it is his and his agency's mature view of what constitutes the good of the service. The good of the service is that which will make it stand high in public approbation, is best for the country, and is practical.

The legislator respects the judgment of the career man who must live with whatever proposal is offered, whereas he is less sure about political executives who are often here today and gone tomorrow. Consequently, if the political executive is wise, he will make certain where the career men in his department stand before he launches a campaign for new legislation. A private word from a career official to a seasoned veteran of the legislative process will often finish the chances of a bill before it gets started. In theory, perhaps, this should not be so but in fact it happens so often that the reality of it must be recognized.

The upshot is that administrators have much to do with the determination of public policy, whether it is conservative, traditional, progressive, liberal, or a compromise. If the tone of a particular bureau is lethargic its chief will usually follow the path of least resistance, which means that new policies and departures are discouraged. For this reason among others, career executives should be even better grounded in sociology and political economy—in recognizing the public interest—than in how to get along with political officials, which more often than not is something they learn very early.

In earlier chapters where reference was made to the new elite of government career executives, the financial and quantitative aspects of public programs were noted. Even more important is *the influence of career officials on public policy and decisions governing the fate of the nation.* The reason is that although career officials do not often appear in the political limelight, they do constitute the second level of organization where most of the work of the world is accomplished. Indeed, whether it be in large corporations, labor unions, universities, or some other institution, it is generally the practical man experienced in getting things done who guides the destiny of the enterprise and who therefore has the greatest influence on it. This is due partly to his continuity in office, partly to his objectivity, partly to his skill as an administrator who can produce results. In most organizations there is usually a man out front who meets the public and a second man who is the operator and on whom the enterprise depends.

This is not meant to depreciate the role of the political executive in government. On the contrary, in all decisions of any consequence his must always be the last word, for anything less would constitute a subversion of democracy and popular control. Unfortunately the American political official is not as professionalized as he should be, nor do he and his political party provide the continuity in policy and personnel needed for strong, responsible leadership. So long as this is true the relation of career official and career legislator will remain the dominant force in American politics, aided and abetted by the pressure groups that focus upon both of them.

One of the countervailing influences against a tendency to oligarchy, of course, is public opinion. Public opinion is a much stronger force than is usually recognized, even under dictatorships or one-party rule. In a democracy much more is expected of it. A number of years ago, for example, when federal officials were losing a fight to protect the national forests against the efforts of stockmen to secure more grazing land, Bernard de Voto—an influential journalist—was able to arouse the supporters of conservation and recreation to the peril. When the natural gas industry was found to be influencing appointments to regulatory commissions so that the intent of the law was being disregarded, a fearless and independent press called it to the attention of consumers. Because consumers are typically unorganized in their own behalf, there is urgent need for alertness and independence on the part of newspaper, radio, television, magazine, and other purveyors of information and opinion. Indeed, since the time of de Tocqueville and before, the media of mass communication have been regarded as the best hope of democracy, champions of men and women unrepresented by strongly organized and well-financed pressure groups. In this respect the motivation of the career administrator and the professional journalist should be similar.

## Relations with the Legislature

Public administrators generally consider pressure group support to be more an advantage than a handicap and wish they could secure the same kind of support from the legislature. While the current fashion is to castigate legislatures, expecially Congress, those who believe in representative government realize that the legislature, being directly chosen by and speaking for the people, is the fulcrum by which government moves society.

Most of the difficulties encountered by legislatures are similar to those of administrators everywhere. As W. F. Willoughby so persuasively argued in his *Principles of Public Administration,* the work of a legislature differs from that of the executive or the judicial branches; nevertheless it is an organization and hence subject to the same principles and tools of analysis as they are. Few legislatures have ever done a proper job analysis inventory of themselves; even more rarely have they followed through with good effect. Like any organization, a legislature also must get the facts when there is a problem to be solved, analyze alternatives, organize so as to do its job effectively and responsibly, and concentrate on first things first. It must secure able personnel, arrange and oversee their responsibilities, and coordinate the whole effort to emphasize policy and accomplishment.

This is easy to say, harder to do. Legislatures make fundamental policy in the form of statute law. This law becomes the administrator's mandate, the legal basis on which he operates. Hence the quality of administration depends in no small part upon the quality of legislation. The main difficulty is that in terms of job analysis, legislators have so many other demands on their time that they have increasingly less to give to issues of high policy.

The Legislative Reorganization Act of 1946 made some improvements in the organization of Congress but for the obvious reason of vested institutional interests, failed to go far enough. There are still too many committees and not enough joint committees of the House and Senate. There are still too many congressional investigations, which sometimes turn out to be fishing expeditions, and not all of them are conducted by major standing committees. Although each major political party now has an internal policy committee, and although the major standing committees are sufficiently well staffed to be able to develop information independently and are no longer exclusively dependent in this matter on the executive departments, and although joint conferences between congressional leaders and the President are increasingly frequent, nevertheless Congress is still unable to develop reasonable priorities and timetables so as to take prompt and effective action in the solution of its own problems, to say nothing of problems relating to the needs of the nation. Legislatures should, of course, take time to air public issues and educate as well as heed public opinion in the process. But even for this function there seems to be less time each year.

There have been a number of proposals to remedy legislative weaknesses in the United States but since these go beyond the legitimate scope of public administration, only some of the more important ones will be mentioned here: Should there be further experimentation with unicameralism, which theoretically is more efficient than the two-chamber system? Are many legislatures too large to be effective? Should the majority political party, when it also controls the executive, be required to guarantee its program, in addition to trying to win the next election? Should there be a question period during which top administrators might regularly appear to explain and justify their policies and actions? Might not this procedure reduce the number of fishing expeditions? If a legislative-executive stalemate occurs, or if the legislative majority votes a lack of confidence in the chief executive, should new elections be held forthwith? Should the seniority system which currently thwarts the majority will be modified or even abolished so as more easily to secure key committee chairmen who favor the policies of the party in power? Should filibusters be controlled by changes in legislative rules? Should the power of the Rules Committee, which may refuse to allow a bill to be considered on the floor of the chamber, be modified so as to allow bills to be called up by a simple majority vote?

Such questions lie at the center of the average administrator's customary feeling of frustration at the hand of the legislature.

The basic conflict in the American system of government is the result of institutional jealousy between the legislative and executive branches. Institutions are naturally competitive. It is not the people in them that make it so; people are merely pawns in a kind of game. This fact becomes clear if one has served at different times as legislator and as administrator. In each case, one's psychology changes quite rapidly. The lawmaker finds himself thinking, How easy administrators have it. They are appointed but I must win an election. Their jobs are permanent but mine ends in two or four years unless I can be re-elected. Their jobs are definite; mine is ambiguous and confusing. They have all the help they need; I feel powerless. They don't know who is boss. It is we who should be initiating legislation, but it is they who do it and ask us to serve as their agents. Their main interest is to spend more money and build new empires; I must stop them. They seem to think that they should automatically get whatever they need. They will not recognize that we are the boss.

As a result of this jealousy, even former legislators elected to executive office have as much trouble securing the legislation they want as one who has never had legislative experience at all,

Structural remedies must eventually be found to overcome these jealousies, but in the meantime there is much the administrator can do if he has the right understanding and attitude. He must recognize that the legislature is in fact the boss, and that if an administrator respects the members of the legislature, they will respect him. It must not be assumed that because they are politicians they are somehow different from him. He must act in a friendly manner toward the members of his committee. He must tell them of his difficulties and failures as well as of his triumphs, never try to cover up, hide behind a superior, or blow his own horn. And he must give credit where credit is due. When he is to appear before his legislative committee or the appropriations committee, he must anticipate their questions, make his statement logical and complete, be as specific as possible about statistics and figures, let them know that he would like, if possible, to accomplish the same work with less money and personnel. To make his committee management-minded he must first become legislative-minded. And finally, he must recognize that every legislative committee wants above all to make its independent judgment.

Although the foregoing admonitions do not constitute a sure formula for success, they will go a long way toward establishing a comfortable relationship between the administrator and his legislative boss. Handled with a sophisticated understanding of the situation, an appearance before a legislative committee can be a pleasure instead of an ordeal.

Finally, since for the administrator politics is primarily policy and only secondarily political parties, it is an advantage to have consciously thought about what constitutes the public interest in his own field of activity. The public interest is always broader than group interest, although that is the usual starting point. The public interest involves a series of questions familiar to philosophers and political economists in particular: What is the effect of a given course of action on people? On national strength? On economic well-being? On self-determination? On respect for the law? On equality of opportunity? On opportunity for self-growth? On long-range interests? On the reconciliation of public and private interest?

On any legislative committee the majority will sit up and take notice when an administrator talks sense about such issues. To talk this kind of sense, the administrator must start early in life to think about and study fundamental questions that have to do with political economy, and then profit from experience and reading. The administrator who keeps abreast of the issues and developments in his field will find most politicians not only challenging but compatible.

In the final analysis, what the administrator thinks of politics and how well he fares in it greatly depends on his attitudes toward the subject. Consequently the recent change in administrative thinking about politics is likely to push the solution of the still unresolved issues relating to better intragovernmental operation. Just as any administrative program is effective only when the parts combine smoothly, so in the wider reaches of government the cooperative relationship of legislature and administration is the key to the fostering of the public interest.

## BIBLIOGRAPHY AND CASES

### Annotated Reading Suggestions

The main theme of Marver Bernstein's book, *The Job of the Federal Executive* (Brookings Institution, 1958) is the policy-political atmosphere in which high-level executive work in Washington is carried on; the book is based on the testimony of the main actors themselves. See also former Governor David L. Lawrence, "Balancing Good Politics and Good Administration," *Public Administration Review*, 14 (Spring 1954); and C. A. Harrell and D. G. Weiford, "The City Manager and the Policy Process," *Public Administration Review*, 19 (Spring 1959).

The best rationale of this whole subject is found in Paul H. Appleby, *Policy and Administration* (University of Alabama Press, 1949), a book that should certainly be read during the period of this course. The history of the relationship between politics and administration is in Albert Lepawsky, *Administration, The Art and Science of Organization and Management* (Knopf, 1949), Chap. 3, "Administration and Policy." The modern emphasis was anticipated as early as 1933 by Luther H. Gulick in his essay "Politics, Administration and the 'New Deal'," *Annals of the American Academy of Political and Social Science*, 169 (September 1933).

The shortage of adequate political leadership is underscored in John A. Perkins, "Staffing Democracy's Top Side," *Public Administration Review*, 17 (Winter 1957).

On the relative merits of the presidential and the parliamentary systems of government, see a debate between Harold J. Laski and Don K. Price in *Public Administration Review*, 3:317, 4:347, and 4:360.

The influence of interest groups is dealt with by Avery Leiserson, "Interest Groups in Administration," in F. Morstein Marx, ed., *Elements of Public Administration* (2d ed., Prentice-Hall, 1959).

On the methods used to develop policy, consult Donald S. Watson, *Economic Policy* (Houghton Mifflin, 1960), pp. 12-94. Several of the books in the two preceding chapter bibliographies also deal with policies and their formation. On policy making in general, see Daniel Lerner and Harold D. Lasswell, eds., *The Policy Sciences: Recent Development in Scope and Method* (Stanford University Press, 1952). And on decision making in administration, see Herbert

Simon, *Administrative Behavior: A Study of Decision-Making* (Macmillan, 1957); this volume is reviewed by F. Morstein Marx in *Public Administration Review,* 8:60.

## Case Studies

The case in the Stein *Case Book* that relates directly to politics and policy is *The Cambridge City Manager,* written by Frank C. Abbott in 1951. Involved are executive-legislative relations, personnel policy, and the skills of the administrator. Getting along with the legislative boss is the toughest job of the city manager; this case deals with that problem.

An equally interesting case is described by Emmette S. Redford, No. 62, *Congress Passes the Federal Aviation Act of 1958,* thirty-five pages long. This one deals with powerful interests, pressure groups, high national policy, and legislative-executive relationships. Another case, this one illustrative of pressure group activity, is No. 72, *Lobbying and the Natural Gas Bill,* by E. T. Carper, thirty-nine pages, written in 1962.

Others include No. 57, *The Grazing Fee Dilemma,* by P. O. Foss, ten pages, relating to pressure groups; No. 58, *The Florida Flood Control District,* by J. DeGrove, twenty-four pages, which involves legislative-executive relations; No. 59, *The Defense Appropriations Rider,* by E. T. Carper, twenty-eight pages, also concerned with institutional politics; No. 66, *Question of Religion,* by C. R. Foster, sixteen pages, which grew out of a census questionnaire; No. 67, *California Democratic Delegation of 1960,* by J. H. Bunzel, thirty-two pages, straight politics; No. 71, *Illinois Goes to Congress For Army Land,* by E. T. Carper, thirty-one pages, illustrative of intergovernmental relations and political influence; and No. 23, *Michigan State Director of Elections,* by G. A. Schubert, the subject being obvious from the title.

# 9

# The Law
# of Administration

IT IS FROM law that the administrator gets his mandate, that is, his jurisdiction and authority. Law is a body of rules of human conduct that is backed by the authority of government. Since the authority of government is sovereign, law is binding on everyone within government's jurisdiction. From this point of view, every administrator is *ipso facto* an enforcer of the law.

Because the administrator must know what his mandate is, must withstand constant public and official scrutiny, and hold himself accountable to legal authority, he must be familiar with the rudiments of law even though he may not be expert in any branch of it. Moreover, if he has not learned to think realistically and cogently about the legal network within which he operates, he will not appreciate the full extent to which administrators cooperate with the other two branches of government that also are concerned with law: the legislature and the judiciary.

## The Pattern of Law

Being a part of human activity, law is subject to the same cultural and change factors that cause administration to grow in complexity. The more people there are and the more complicated and technical the situations in which they exist, the more must human conduct be subjected to rules and regulations. Although in general law is more conservative than administration, it is roughly correct that as administration becomes more complex, law also becomes more complex. And with this tendency there seems also to be another for administrators to share in the functions of both legislation and adjudication. Consequently, most administrators either consciously (formally) or unconsciously share in making the law and on occasion deciding cases, much as judges do.

This administrative function is one of the connotations of the term judgment, which is a sterling characteristic of an outstanding top executive. The need for judgment is inherent in the administrative process: administrators at all levels must make decisions on the basis of a judgment; so must legislators; and judges themselves, of course, specialize in the making of decisions.

There are many forms of law, some of which go back to ancient origins. To begin with, law is custom, a conservatizing influence in its growth for it is thus based upon human attitudes, habits, thought patterns, and values backed by the force of public opinion. Some theorists believe that law and custom are the same thing, others that at a certain point custom becomes formalized into law in the technical sense. In either case law that is *not* backed by public opinion not only has difficulty in surviving but may even bring the whole network of law and government into disrepute.

The American system of law is the common law or Anglo-American law. It has developed gradually from case to case and precedent to precedent so that when a new case arises the problem of the administrator or the judge is to find the case or cases that on the principle of analogy will constitute a guide to the decision to be made.

The common law is not written law in the sense that the other main body of Western law—Roman law—is. The civil law of Rome predominates throughout most of Europe, Latin America, and some other parts of the world. Under this system, criminal law, civil law, and administrative law are formalized under a code, or lexicon of law, much as though all legal principles and rules had been legislated at one time and since been kept current. Under the common-law system the law is "found" in ruling cases, whereas under the civil law of Rome it is found in the appropriate code. The common-law system is more flexible than the civil-law system (Europeans would say less precise), and hence American administrators enjoy greater freedom than do their European counterparts. A paradoxical result of this situation, however, is to make the influence of lawyers on administration much greater than if our law were fully codified and administrators could simply look to the codes instead of to leading precedents in deciding common-law cases.

The second major form of law is constitutions, which determine the powers and limitations of government, its structure, and its principal operating methods. Constitutions rather than common law are the main sources of law for the administrator because generally speaking, and although there is no sharp line of demarcation, common law relates to private matters such as contracts while constitutions regulate public law. Public law deals with the organization and powers of government and relations between government and the individual. A specialized branch of public law is administrative law, which covers the organization and powers of the administrative branch and, again, with relations between government and the individual. Administrative law overlaps constitutional law to a considerable extent; in general, however, constitutional law relates to government *as a whole,* whereas administrative law is concerned with the administrative *process.*

So important has administrative law become in the United States that it is now the one subject consistently taught in all accredited law schools. The reason is that the administration of most government activities affects private interests of some sort. This is especially true of the departments and regulatory commissions that have economic powers, as in the regulation of public utilities or labor relations. One result is to make this a lucrative area for private law practice.

Other branches of public law relate to municipal corporations and international law; hence administrators in the municipal and international fields must know something about these areas as well. The main common need, however, is for an understanding first of administrative law, and second of constitutional law, because these two are basic and closely connected.

In addition to the common law and public law, the third main category is statutory law, or law enacted by legislatures. The main sources are Congress and the state legislatures. In a technical sense municipal councils do not make law but only ordinances, because municipalities are nonsovereign corporate bodies subject to control by the state legislature. Nevertheless in the eyes of the average citizen the ordinances of municipal councils are as binding as the laws of sovereign bodies.

Most of law encountered by the citizen today is statutory law and its linkage to the constitution and to constitutional law seems remote indeed. All legislatures including Congress pass literally thousands of laws in every session and some of them are longer than the federal Constitution itself. But every statutory law must be based on constitutional authority even though much of this derives from broad and not easily defined words and phrases such as general welfare, necessary and proper, the police power, and due process of law.

Increasingly, statutory law is enacted in skeletal form: the main purposes and provisions of the statute are set forth and the chief executive or some designated official under him is given the authority to spell out the details of enforcement. By this means does the administrator receive his mandate. And because life today is so complex and government is called upon to deal with so many aspects of it, the aggregate of administrative rule making (quasi legislation) and decision making (quasi adjudication) is a good deal greater than the output of either of the other branches, the legislature and the courts.

Perhaps the derivation of the administrative mandate may be shown graphically:

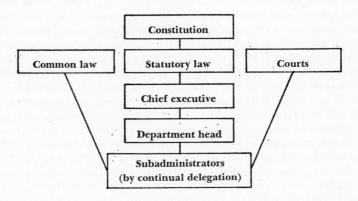

In other words, every public administrator receives his authority from the federal (or state) Constitution, the common law, and the courts. Congress delegates authority to participate in sublegislation and subadjudication to the chief executive and under him to the administrative branch. The chief executive has some constitutional authority of his own, of course, for he is charged with seeing that the laws are faithfully executed, and in dealing with foreign nations he may make executive agreements that, unlike treaties, need not be approved by the Senate. Most of his authority, however, comes from Congress.

Congress confers a legal mandate by two means. The first, which is indirect, is through a specific mandate to the President, who then promulgates executive orders or presidential orders affecting a particular government agency. On this authority, agency heads issue administrative orders that in turn also have the binding effect of law. These orders define organization and jurisdiction and delegate authority down the line, in the field as well as at headquarters. With every layer of organization the delegations are multiplied until eventually every administrator has some portion of authority on which he acts even if some of it is very narrow.

Congress confers a legal mandate through the enactment of basic law by which it creates a government agency in the first place and then enlarges or controls it by subsequent legislative amendments as needed. Accordingly almost every public program, whether it be a regular department, an independent agency, or a regulatory commission, can speak proudly and somewhat affectionately of its basic mandate. Actually, the vision of many public employees never extends beyond that point; to some this basic law seems like the original act of creation by which the world itself came into being.

Looking at the matter from a different angle—from the bottom up —where does the public adminstrator find his authority? Partly in his job description, which is a civil service matter. Partly in the agency's administrative manual if there is one. Partly in specific instructions from his supervisor. Usually in being a member of a group and sharing in a common assignment. But no matter what the immediate source of his mandate, it must be capable of being tied in with and justified by reference to a higher source of authority in the organization, which eventually traces back through the legislature to the constitution.

Just how familiar nonlawyers must become with statutory law depends a good deal on the nature of the agency. Immediately prior to World War II, for example, an administrator in the Immigration and Naturalization Service needed to understand the provisions of some sixteen basic laws, many of them dealing with the same subject such as the likelihood that a prospective immigrant might become a public charge or engage in subversive activity. Fortunately, in this field and in others such as income tax administration, railroad regulation, and the work of the FBI, commercially prepared codes draw together all the law on the subject for ready reference.[1]

## Delegation and the Separation of Powers

How far can the government go in delegating authority so that at last a particular administrator deals with a particular citizen on a particular matter at a given time? Much depends on the answer to this question because, as will later be seen, a goal of public administration is to administer by objectives, a system in which subadministrators receive assignments from higher authority and are then free to use their brains and their initiative in getting the work done. By this means it is possible to avoid being caught in a vise of inflexible rules and regulations. But so generous a delegation of authority is not possible, of course, unless the law permits it.

At one time the Supreme Court took a conservative view of the separation of powers doctrine and in consequence looked askance upon

---

[1] A convenient way to get some of the feel of the relation between law and public administration would be to examine a study of the Immigration Service made during this period by Dimock, McIntire, and Hart entitled *Report of the Secretary of Labor's Committee on Administrative Procedure* (Immigration and Naturalization Service, 1939).

delegations of quasi-legislative and quasi-judicial authority to administrators. The high point of this strict interpretation of the Constitution occurred in 1881 in the case of *Kilbourne v. Thompson*[2] which had to do with the investigatory powers of Congress. All powers of government, said the Supreme Court, are divided into executive, legislative, and judicial, and it is "essential to the successful working of this system that the persons intrusted with power in any one of these branches shall not be permitted to encroach upon the powers confided to the others, but that each shall by the law of its own creation be limited to the exercise of the powers *appropriate* to its own department *and no other* . . ." The italics are ours, the purpose being to emphasize that at this time the Court apparently assumed the presence of innate or inherent qualities capable of clearly differentiating administration from legislation and adjudication.

So greatly has the situation changed during the past generation or so, however, that as one authority on administrative law phrases it, the idea that the legislative power of Congress cannot be delegated is now "obsolete." [3] There may still be some limits to such delegations but *if* there are and *what* they are is uncertain because no recent leading case deals with the matter. The *Schechter*[4] case which in 1935 invalidated the National Industrial Recovery Act is distinguishable, says Davis, on the ground of *quantity* of power delegated, in this instance the power to approve detailed codes governing all businesses subject to federal authority.

The change in thinking has occurred in part because Congress would be literally swamped if it tried to operate without delegating power and attempted to spell out in detail every aspect of every enactment. The question for Congress therefore becomes: Which agency is best qualified to do particular parts of the total job of government? There are no neat divisions of power because operations in most major areas of law and public policy require cooperative arrangements in which all three branches may be involved at one time or another. Moreover, since skeleton legislation is now so widely used, administrative agencies must necessarily add to and amplify the basic policies contained in the statute. The result is that the concern of Congress is usually the simple one of deciding whether the delegations should or should not be required to run the legislative gauntlet. Emphasis has therefore shifted from a stand on nondelegability to seeking the means

---

2 103 U.S. 168, 191, 26 L.Ed. 377 (1881).

3 Kenneth C. Davis, *Administrative Law* (St. Paul, Minn.: West Publishing Company, 1951), p. 86.

4 *Schechter Poultry Corp. v. United States*, 295 U.S. 495, 55 S. Ct. 837, 79 L. Ed. 1570 (1935).

whereby exercises of delegated power may be reviewed and kept in check by Congress, the President, and the courts.[5]

The result of this change is that much administrative activity is now based on standards that are broad and general indeed, giving top administrators an almost limitless range of discretion. The rule of the Supreme Court is that so long as Congress lays down some "standard" (meaning words and phrases stating under what circumstances administrators may exercise a discretion), the separation of powers requirement of the Constitution has been met.

Literally hundreds of illustrations of these broad standards might be offered, but a few will suffice. Thus, in the original Renegotiation Act having to do with the recapture of excess profits from wartime contracts, the administrators involved were required to determine, by trial and error, the meaning of the broad standard created by the term "excess profits," because Congress felt that any further elaboration of it would be impractical. In some cases, delegations have been upheld where there seemed to be no real prescription of a standard at all, in the technical sense. A congressional statute, for example, provided that the American Railway Association should certify to the Interstate Commerce Commission a standard height for drawbars on freight cars and that after a specified date no car should be used in interstate commerce that did not comply with the height requirement. In another case the Secretary of War was required by congressional statute to "do everything by him deemed necessary to suppress . . . houses of ill fame . . . within such distance as he may deem needful to any military camp . . .", and violation of the regulation was made a misdemeanor. The Supreme Court dismissed the issue of delegation and appropriateness of standards with the statement, "Congress . . . may leave details of the regulation to the head of an executive department." [6]

This is not to argue that standards are unimportant or that in the past there may not have been some laxity on the part of Congress and the courts. The point is that the current volume of government work makes it a practical necessity for the courts to hold that delegation is a means, not an end; that if the work of government is not to be frustrated, someone must be trusted. In many cases the real question is whether administration can in fact do the job that needs doing; whether the procedural safeguards afforded interested parties are adequate; and whether review procedures are provided for to the extent needed. It is possible that improvements in the quality and content of public administration in the United States during the past thirty years or so have played some part in causing Congress and the Supreme Court to regard

---

5 Davis, *op. cit.,* pp. 54-55.
6 *Ibid.,* p. 51.

delegation with increasing favor. All of which makes administration even more challenging and interesting than formerly, as well as more in need of a sympathetic understanding of quasi-legislative and quasi-judicial procedures.

The foregoing has dealt with the delegation of authority primarily from Congress. Subdelegation, as the term is, describes the transmission of authority from an agency head to his subordinates. The need for this type of delegation was well stated by Joseph Eastman, commissioner of the Interstate Commerce Commission and a pioneer in public administration. "Sound principles of organization," said Eastman, "demand that those at the top be able to concentrate their attention upon the larger and more important questions of policy and practice, and that their time be freed, so far as possible, from the consideration of the smaller and less important matters of detail." [7] As early as 1839 the Supreme Court held that "The President speaks and acts through the heads of the several departments." [8] For obvious reasons the Secretaries of State and Defense have the widest powers of subdelegation, but in recent years the climate of opinion has favored even wider subdelegations across the board. Both the Hoover Commission on administrative organization and the Attorney General's Committee on Administrative Procedure, for example, have strongly recommended this course.

## Quasi-Legislative and Quasi-Judicial Powers

Because administrators share legislative and judicial powers with the other two branches of government, their influence on public policy is far more important than it used to be, and public administration itself has grown in importance.

Administration is quasi-legislative when it involves rule making, a shorthand expression for spelling out the law, giving specific expression to policy as the administrative process unfolds. Rule making, says Professor Fuchs, is "the issuance of regulations or the making of determinations which are addressed to indicated but unnamed and unspecified persons or situations." [9] Rule making is that part of the administrative process that most resembles the legislature's enactment of a statute; in a sense it is like a statute but more specific.

In quasi legislation the two kinds of rule are legislative, which makes new law, and interpretive, which theoretically should not make

---

[7] Hearing before House Committee on Interstate and Foreign Commerce, 1933; reported in Davis, *op. cit.,* p. 73.

[8] *Wilcox v. Jackson,* 38 U.S. 13 Pet. 498, 10 L. Ed. (1839).

[9] Ralph Fuchs, "Procedure in Administrative Rule-Making," *Harvard Law Review,* 52 (1938).

new law but which in practice often does. Legislative drafters some-times try to anticipate the interpretive rules that administrators will need, but for the most part these details are left to the administrator to formulate. In fact, therefore, if not in legal theory, an interpretive rule does make new law in the sense of policy that has binding legal effect.

In the illustration already given of the Renegotiation Act, for ex-ample, some of the issues that might have to be administratively decided are these: What is a reasonable profit? How is profit to be de-fined? What weight is to be given to depreciation? To what extent may the managerial services of a holding company be charged to operating costs? Where the same plant is used for governmental and nongovernmental contracts, how are joint costs to be allocated? And to what extent should bonuses be instituted to stimulate a more efficient operation? All that Congress said initially on these matters was that "excessive profits" should be ferreted out and recaptured.

As indicated earlier, the volume of quasi legislation in the federal government is now so great that for some time it has exceeded the volume of congressional legislation many times over. How are affected interests to know what the law is, therefore, and where they stand? What is to prevent a sudden administrative ruling that could jeopardize their business? Largely because of these concerns, the Administrative Procedure Act of 1946 provided that rules and regulations having the effect of law should be published in *The Federal Register,* an official periodical published five days a week and containing statements of general policy, descriptions of organization, and other matters that the public is interested in and should understand in order to know who does what and how to proceed. The volume for 1950, although in-complete, contained more than 9000 triple-column pages, which gives some idea of the extent of administrative legislation even then.

As a result of the Administrative Procedure Act of 1946 and the prior studies of the American Bar Association and the Attorney General's Committee on Administrative Procedure, federal agencies are encouraged (in some cases required) to allow interested parties to make suggestions or to comment upon proposed rules and pro-cedures. This consultation is through conferences, industry committees, questionnaires, and informal procedures and publicity. It is one reason that pressure groups and industry representation thrive in Washington to the extent they do, constituting a prominent feature of the American system of government.

Turning now to the hearing, deciding, and quasi-judicial aspect of public administration, the first thing to be noted is that the volume of decision far exceeds that of all the courts. This quasi-judicial activity is carried on not only by the many regulatory commissions that deal with issues of great economic and financial importance, but also by depart-ments and bureaus. In some areas, such as internal revenue, these agencies perform even more quasi-judicial work than the commissions themselves.

All administration involves decision, of course, and historically, in both the common-law and civil-law systems, the judiciary itself grew out of administration. As a matter of fact, in England it was not until the seventeenth century that a clear line between administration and adjudication, as we now know it, came to be officially recognized. This is not to minimize the importance of adjudication nor to magnify that of administrative justice, but to call attention to the fact that since both are concerned with enforcement, they are not so different as might appear. The main differences are that the courts hear fewer cases; that before there can be a court proceeding there must be a case or controversy giving jurisdiction to the tribunal; and that court procedures and rules are usually more strict than those of an administrative agency, especially in such matters as hearsay evidence and the role of opposing counsel. The result is that the courts frequently take a long time to complete their work and accordingly turn out much less volume.

By contrast, most of the volume in administrative cases is accounted for by informal proceedings, though in certain instances there may also be formal proceedings more nearly resembling the decorum and rules of a court of law. Were it not for the informal proceedings, however, there would be no possibility of getting the work of government done. The result is that administrative adjudication occurs throughout the length and breadth of government.

The arguments in favor of administrative justice are these: There is such a volume of work that the courts could not possibly add it to their already crowded dockets. In some areas, administrators are more expert and no less objective than judges. Justice is within easy reach when it is reasonably fast and inexpensive, neither of which is possible in the ordinary courts. There is no reason why administrative agencies should try to imitate a formal court procedure in every respect because the work of agencies differs so markedly that variety and flexibility are both desirable and inevitable. If public administrators are competent and there is provision for review through administrative channels, as well as ultimate recourse to the courts on matters of law, then safeguards to the individual are adequate on all scores.

The arguments against administrative justice are numerous; the principal ones are these: If administration continues to encroach upon the judiciary it will undermine the law, the courts, and the legal profession. All legal questions should be dealt with exclusively by lawyers. The courts set the highest possible standards of procedural fairness and these should be followed whenever important interests, such as those relating to property, are to be decided. The personnel of administrative agencies tend to be politically biased and even zealots (as in the administration of labor laws, for example) and should not be allowed to hear cases; or if they do hear them, then their decisions should be regarded as tentative and subject to review by the courts.

These issues came to a climax in 1946 when Congress passed the Walter-Logan Bill sponsored by the American Bar Association but vetoed by President Truman. In the same year, however, the Attorney General's Committee on Administrative Procedure published a study in several volumes that is a goldmine of information. As a result of this report the President and the American Bar Association compromised their differences and Congress passed the Administrative Procedure Act of that year. Something like it has also been adopted in many of the state governments. As indicated above, this legislation dealt with the judicial review of administrative action, procedural requirements in quasi legislation and quasi adjudication, and created a class of officials called hearing examiners for certain agencies and types of cases involving administrative justice. During and shortly after the passage of this law there was concern in public administration circles that the new statute might too greatly judicialize the administrative process and make it less effective, in an over-all sense, than it would be if the lawyers' influence were less. In practice, however, most of these extreme fears have failed to materialize.

Some of the more important rules and policies that apply to administrative hearings and adjudication are these: Within the framework of the Administrative Procedure Act, individual agencies may still make their own rules and procedures, and there is a considerable variation among them. Agencies, especially regulatory commissions, customarily delegate the power to conduct hearings to hearing examiners. There are still exceptions to the rule that every party to a controversy has a right to be heard, although often this right is provided. It is increasingly customary for agencies deciding cases after a hearing to provide a record and to state in writing its reasons for deciding as it does. An agency's failure to provide for a hearing is not a deprivation of due process of law so long as an aggrieved party has recourse to administrative or judicial review; except in the regulatory commissions, administrative review is frequently provided for. Reviewing courts generally accept the findings of the administrative tribunal as to facts and confine themselves to matters of law and procedure; but the line between law and fact is frequently arguable. In order to avoid a progression of stalemates, no appeal to a court is allowed until the interested party has exhausted all administrative remedies as provided by law.

Further, rules of evidence and proof are not so strictly enforced in administrative hearings as in the regular courts. In order to assure equality of treatment, bias on the part of a hearing officer is ground for review. In administrative procedure, decisions are increasingly institutional or collegial, a method that has been widely upheld. It is not imperative in all cases that he who hears shall decide, for the decision may be by a commissioner on the basis of a hearing held by an examiner. Nor is it imperative that the deciding officer be able to prove that he has examined the record in detail, so long as he shows reasonable familiarity with the case. On the other hand, there is a separation of certain kinds of function: a prosecutor shall not judge, and an appeal shall be heard by someone other than the official who heard the case in the first instance.

Most of these rules and policies are no more than common sense and fair dealing, but often they are of the utmost importance to the government and to aggrieved citizens. They are important to the citizen because he may have his life, liberty, or property at stake. They are important to government because if the rules of procedure were to become too onerous they might precipitate a breakdown of administration in crucial areas that could endanger the security of the nation.

There are many proposals for improving the quality of administrative justice. The American Bar Association originally intended to propose the creation of administrative courts, such as those in civil-law countries, but changed its mind. At present the two kinds of courts in the United States are first, so-called constitutional courts where the decision is final and cannot be overturned by the legislature or the chief executive; and second, legislative courts such as the U. S. Court of Tax Appeals or the U. S. Court of Claims, where in neither case is finality complete. The United States once had a special commerce court, but it was abolished. Other countries also have experimented with special courts for special purposes and the temptation is strong to try something similar in the case of regulatory commissions instead of having appeals from their decisions channeled through the regular court system. But at the last moment there is always a doubt because as a nation we pride ourselves on "the rule of law": one law enforced by a unified legal system and no one, including public officials, above it. If administrative legislation and adjudication are to continue their increase in volume, as seems likely, and if people are to retain confidence in them, then the quality of public administration itself must also be continually improved.

An advantage claimed by Europeans for their system of administrative courts paralleling the ordinary courts, is its better protection of the citizen against illegal acts, negligence, excess of power, and other offenses on the part of public officials. In France, for example, the government may be sued and so may officials. In the United States the general policy, deriving from the common law of Britain, is otherwise. We started with the dictum that "the king can do no wrong," which interpreted means that government cannot do wrong and hence cannot be sued.

Consequently, although Congress passed the Federal Tort Claims Act in 1946, and most legal scholars since the time of Dean Pound have thought that governments and public officials alike should be more available to suit than they are, there has not been much improvement. So long as government acts in its sovereign capacity as contrasted with its proprietary capacity (discharging an economic function or running a business, such as an electrical utility) it is immune from suit in tort. A tort is an action by an injured party claiming a right to damages for some illegal act or wrong. The proceeding may be against the government or against an officer but in neither event is the protection as great as in countries where tort liability is wider and special administrative courts hear such cases, among others. Here, then, is another reason why public administration in the United States must be principled and hold the confidence of the public and the legislature.

## Public Policy and Decision Making

The foregoing discussion of law and decision making has been primarily from the lawyer's standpoint. There is, however, another use of the term decision making that is currently much emphasized in the literature of public administration and which also has to do with public policy.

Public policy is government's long-range plans and values, and the principles and practices that should be adopted in various fields of national life. This factor in administration was explained in a preceding chapter and will be further dealt with in the chapter that follows. As already noted, one school of thought in public administration considers decision making as the hub around which every other aspect of administration revolves.

Is there any basic difference between decision making in this sense and as applied in the field of law? It is an interesting question. A minority answer would be, Yes, of course. Others would reply, No, not really. To those who see a basic difference, decision making is a rigorous logical procedure that reaches a climax in a choice among alternatives. Public administration thus becomes a series of climaxes.

To most students of the subject, however, decision making is part of a much larger operation. Administrators are continually laying down rules for the future, says Appleby; they decide what the law is, what it means in terms of action, what the rights of parties are. Thus, "Administrators make thousands of such decisions to one made by the courts." [10] Policy is developed in the course of normal administration; decision making is essential to the process but by no means the whole of it. The central point of reference is policy; decision is only a means.

To the same effect is the judgment of Harold Stein who, in his casebook, *Public Administration and Policy Development,* makes these

---

[10] Paul H. Appleby, *Policy and Administration*, pp. 6-7.

points: Decision is essentially a process rather than an isolated act without continuity in time. Decision involves a before and an after, not just a particular moment. Every act is part of a whole course of conduct; every decision is part of a psychological and social process and its consequences may stretch far into the future. What this means, says Stein, is that decision making is essentially an institutional, not merely a personal matter. Hence a main problem, especially in a large organization, "is how to bring to bear on the decision all the relevant intellectual resources in or available to the agency." [11]

It is well to remember the factors of time and institution, of continuity and the need for teamwork. Otherwise, under the influence of the legal mind whose natural habitat is categories and fine shadings of meanings, it might be erroneously supposed that there is little difference between the lawyer, the administrator, and the judge. Such, of course, is not the case. The administrator knows no time dimension; his work goes on forever, he is part of an institution that has clients and needs that carry far into the future.

## BIBLIOGRAPHY AND CASES

### Annotated Reading Suggestions

A step by step account of how administrators proceed from the elaboration of directives to administrative adjudication is found in Emmette S. Redford, *Administration of National Economic Control* (Macmillan, 1952), Chapters 4-8. See also Kenneth C. Davis, *Administrative Law and Government* (West Publishing Company, 1960), and a review, "Realities of Regulation," *Public Administration Review*, 20 (Autumn 1960).

A feature of the Brownlow Committee's work in 1937 was the inclusion of an essay entitled "The Exercise of Rule-Making Power," by James Hart, in the committee's *Report with Special Studies* (Government Printing Office, 1937), pp. 315-357.

Two law school professors who have written treatises on administrative law that are readily understood by administrators are Kenneth C. Davis and Walter Gellhorn, respectively; both served on the Attorney General's Committee on Administrative Procedure and have the administrator's viewpoint. Anyone wishing to go more fully into the subject should read the Attorney General's Committee on Administrative Procedure, *Final Report* (Government Printing Office, 1941), and accompanying monographs: *Administrative Procedure in Government Agencies* (2 vols., 27 parts, Government Printing Office, 1940, 1941).

---

[11] Harold Stein, ed., *Public Administration and Policy Development* (New York: Harcourt, Brace & World, 1948), p. xiii.

There is also a wealth of material in Robert M. Benjamin, *Administrative Adjudication in the State of New York* (6 vols., Albany, 1942).

On the relation between public administration and administrative law, see John A. Fairlie, "Public Administration and Administrative Law," in Charles G. Haines and Marshall E. Dimock, eds., *Essays on the Law and Practice of Governmental Administration* (Johns Hopkins University Press, 1935).

On the separation of policy, operations, and adjudication in the regulatory commissions, the best source is Robert E. Cushman, "The Problem of the Independent Regulatory Commissions," in the Brownlow Committee's *Report with Special Studies* cited above. Other useful references are James W. Fesler, "Independent Regulatory Agencies" in F. Morstein Marx, ed., *Elements of Public Administration* (2d ed., Prentice-Hall, 1959), Chapter 10; and E. Blythe Stason, *The Law of Administrative Tribunals* (2d ed., Callaghan, 1957).

## Case Studies

Two cases in the Stein *Case Book* may be suggested: *The National Labor Relations Board Field Examiner,* written by William H. Riker in 1951, ten pages, has to do with administrative procedure in the labor relations field, one of the most controversial since the early days of the New Deal. The second case, *The TVA Ammonia Plant,* was prepared by Ellen St. Sure in 1950, fifty-one pages, and concerns the National Defense Advisory Commission and the influences that were brought to bear in the decision on policy in the public-private realm.

Other cases in the ICP series illustrate the wide range of questions involving policy and decision. No. 56, *The General Passenger Fare Investigation,* by Emmette S. Redford, fifty-four pages, was written in 1960 and has to do with regulatory administration. No. 18, *Taxing the Southern Railroad in Alabama,* by V. A. and C. B. Earle, fifty-five pages, involves the assessment of a railroad for taxing purposes. No. 64, *Miracle Case: The Supreme Court and the Movies,* prepared by A. F. Westin in 1961, thirty-eight pages, has to do with a celebrated movie and censorship. No. 50, *The Trenton Milk Contract,* as told by R. Golembiewski, nineteen pages, illustrates yet another type of administrative proceeding. And finally, No. 13, *Wilderness Sanctuary,* by R. P. Andrews, twelve pages, concerns the conflict between wildlife conservation and the needs of modern aviation.

# 10

## Planning Objectives
## and Programs

A KEY WORD in the vocabulary of public administration is planning.
Planning is looking and thinking ahead. Until recently government
planning has carried the unfortunate implication that what government
plans, government will enforce. Today, however, governing institutions
are so large and their relationships to society, to the political economy,
and to cultural change are so numerous and important that planning is
now seen for what it is—a neutral function that may be applied
under many different circumstances; consequently it is no longer a
fighting word.

Planning describes a function that will probably be more widely
discussed during the coming decades than any other in public administration, for so much depends on it. Every aspect of governmental
administration must be planned; objectives, policies, organization,
finances, allocation of supervisory responsibility, work methods, incentive
systems, and public relations. All of which makes planning a more
comprehensive term than decision making, for it flows through the
length and breadth of administration in much the same manner as
law or finance or human relations.

In this range of activities, the planning of objectives and work
methods for carrying them out need special attention. The first of these
two major aspects of planning is the subject of the present chapter.

## What Is Planning?

Like law, planning also has many connotations and at the outset it will be helpful to mention some of them.

Planning is the French word, *prévoyance,* meaning looking ahead. It is an organized attempt to anticipate and to make rational arrangements for dealing with future problems by projecting trends. It is an attempt to cope with change, now the most common element in institutional as in social life, by anticipating and influencing it to prevent the organization from being overwhelmed with new problems and to promote its ability to cash in on opportunities. Planning seeks to avoid discontinuities that result in blind action, "muddling through," or making decisions on a day-to-day, crash basis. It is an attempt to improve present performance by relating it to future problems and desired results.

As a function, planning is something more than prediction. Leaving aside the moot question of whether social scientists will some day be able to predict the future more accurately than they can today, it must be recognized as a practical proposition that because administrative organizations are complicated and diverse, precise and complete prediction is hardly possible. Nevertheless, it is possible to plan for change itself. If alternative courses of action are carefully analyzed there will be fewer surprises than would otherwise be the case. It is true, of course, that a plan is not in itself a guarantee that the wished-for results will be achieved because planning is only one element of success and there are many others including follow-through. But the administrator who plans for change will be mentally conditioned and alert to make adjustments when the time comes.

Planning is a wholly practical matter, a step-by-step analysis of how objectives are to be made realities. As good a definition as any, therefore, is this one: Planning is clarifying one's objectives and then determining what action shall be taken by whom, when, by what methods, and at what costs in order to achieve the desired goals. Charles E. Merriam, who helped to organize the National Resources Planning Board, called planning the systematic, continuous, forward-looking application of the best intelligence available to programs of common affairs; it is a means, not an end.[1] Planning cannot be separated from management because plans must be put into effect or they remain in the realm of intention, not action.

Planning had been emphasized by American business corporations long before it became a matter of political controversy in the

---

[1] National Resources Planning Board, *A Report on National Planning and Public Works* (Washington, D.C., December 1, 1934), pp. 83-84.

1930s and 1940s. As early as 1912 Frederick W. Taylor, founder of the scientific management movement, staked out the proposition that planning is essential to all managerial advance. Textbook writers on business management such as Richard L. Lansburgh have for years devoted roughly a third of their discussion to the planning of objectives, so important do they regard the subject. More recently, an American Management Association study showed that planning is now taken for granted in all except a few business enterprises.[2]

Except for a flurry of studies in the 1930s, the planning function in government is still a relatively neglected subject in the literature of public administration. John D. Millett's *The Process and Organization of Government Planning* was advertised in 1947 as "the first attempt at a systematic presentation of planning as a vital phase of government administration." However, the National Resources Planning Board had published between 1934 and 1943, when it went out of existence, a series of planning studies that are perhaps unequaled in any country before or since. In addition, in 1941 George B. Galloway, one of the nation's top experts on Congress said, "Planning is the opposite of improvising. In simple terms it is organized foresight plus corrective hindsight." [3] And in 1945 Edward H. Hempel of Columbia University wrote that planning is merely the thinking process that should precede *any* action; further, that it invariably consists of three steps by which the best idea or scheme is selected: (1) determining what action should be taken; (2) ascertaining what the aim or goal of the action should be; and (3) deciding how the action should be carried out.[4]

Generally speaking there are three types of planning: (1) national economic planning covering the whole of the economy or only part of it; (2) top-level administrative planning for the government as a whole, especially for its principal departments and agencies; and (3) work or operational planning, primarily concerned with the carrying out of objectives.[5] At one point or another in this book planning will be discussed on all three of these planes, but in the present chapter the main interest is in top-level administrative planning for the development of objectives and programs.

---

[2] American Management Association, *How Companies Plan* (Research Study 54, New York, 1962), p. 24. This is perhaps the best single volume on the subject.

[3] George B. Galloway, ed., *Planning for America* (New York: Holt, Rinehart and Winston, 1941).

[4] Edward H. Hempel, *Top-Management Planning* (New York: Harper & Row, Publishers, 1945), p. 6.

[5] In addition, of course, there is planning in the physical sense, such as city or regional planning, an aspect only indirectly related to the present discussion.

## What Is Involved in Planning

Before planning can become the asset it should be in democratic administration, there are a number of issues to be carefully considered:

In *Planning for America,* Galloway described five main steps in the planning process. First is the determination of objectives; second, fact-gathering, research to understand the problem; third, setting forth alternative solutions; fourth, policy making or choosing among alternatives so as to spell out the law and the guidelines that underlie it; and fifth, the detailed execution of the chosen alternative, or what is called work or operational planning.[6]

Another way of viewing the administrator's job is to recognize that planning involves three time dimensions: The first is of current business, basic to everything else. The second is of long-range objectives for five to twenty years or more, covering the needs of the undertaking and its market. The third is of such matters as the survival of the program, its vitality, and its orientation to the consumer. While these distinctions have formal existence, in practice each type of planning is related to the others. Present and future planning, for example, are inextricably connected because every policy and decision, whether called short- or long-range, is immediately both.

The administrator should plan as far as he can visualize end results. Here a number of distinctions become important:

Planning is more than *forecasting,* which is an effort to discover the probable course of events and the choice of alternatives that will become available. One then plans in order to prepare for them and to have decisions ready when the time comes.

Every plan is based upon carefully thought out *assumptions.* How much risk may be rationally accepted? What is likely to be the effect on the needs of the clientele one serves, on the technology of the program, and on the societal changes relating to politics, economics, and the habits and expectations of the employees of the program? Increasingly in the modern world the societal factor requires management to make certain highly speculative assumptions, such as how long the cold war may last and where it is heading, how much economic expansion may be anticipated, and what the growth factors are likely to be in the program's own field of activity. In this last area, the very least the administrator can content himself with is the range of probabilities, which is one reason for the modern emphasis of management on probability theory and game theory.

*Objectives* are clearly formulated goals, targets that give the enter-

---

[6] Galloway, *op. cit.,* pp. 5-6.

prise something tangible to shoot at. Nothing is more important in administration, because when targets are clear literally every other factor in the administrative process falls into its proper place, and an incentive is engendered that probably does more over-all to vitalize administration than any other top-management function. Nevertheless, it must not be supposed that the setting of objectives exhausts planning. Objectives are the outgrowth or end result of a plan after everything else, including feasibility, has been considered. What one does, in effect, is to say: This is the objective I really favor; all things considered, is it possible of achievement or shall I have to modify it in the light of all other factors involved? But at some point the objective must lose its tentativeness and become agreed upon for a given period of time,—always subject to later modification, because otherwise clear targets are lost.

The setting of objectives applies to a large area of concern. Some of the major questions are these: Should the enterprise be a paying, a break-even, or a deficit operation? How much growth is desirable, of the enterprise as a whole and of major activities? What new lines of activity, if any, should be in the hopper? What is the optimum size for effective operation and results? How shall balance be maintained between quantity and quality in production? What new forms of competition should be anticipated and acted upon? What kind of special skills are available or must be created if the enterprise is to respond to its potential market? Should certain older lines of activity be discontinued or minimized as more urgent and progressive ones are initiated? And should management try to perpetuate the undertaking, or does the handwriting on the wall indicate that it should be liquidated and its assets reallocated to some objective more in demand?

Planning invariably involves a time element without which the function cannot be performed. Once the decision on alternatives has been made, the next step is *scheduling,* by means of which the feasibility of the plan is tested. Suppose, for example, that the National Aeronautics and Space Administration (NASA) decides that one of its major objectives requires a certain kind of hardware within a year. If what it needs will not be available before three years, clearly this is the end of that particular plan; the timing factor has upset the applecart and a new plan will have to be made.

Scheduling starts with the desired end result and works backward. Questions to be asked are these: What are the priorities if all elements are synchronized so that the plan can come out on time? How many parts can be started simultaneously? Where should each subsection be at various points in time, every three months, say, or six months? Is there any part that can be accelerated without injury to other parts? In other words, an acid test of the practical administrator is his ability to establish target dates, adhere to them, and then discover in advance if they are not being achieved and why not. Here, methods of control and evaluation, to be discussed in a later chapter, come into play. But methods of control are useless without clear objectives and subobjectives.

Finally under the heading of scheduling is the indispensable concept of lead time. This is the length of time required between the decision that new products, services, or methods are needed and the date they become available. Thus it determines whether their design, production, and practical utilization can serve the larger plan. The term is customarily applied to what has been called hardware or saleable products. In nearly every administrative undertaking, however, there are always key elements to be thought up and put into the works well in advance of other steps in the process lest the whole plan collapse. In many areas of defense and advanced technology the lead time is not uncommonly as much as twenty to thirty years.[7]

*Operating plans* relate to the production line, to internal administrative arrangements revolving around the line or productive process. In this area objectives, targets, and schedules are put into production step by step, and most of the actual work is done.

A number of terms describe this function: production planning, work planning, organization and methods (O&M), work detail, operations research, program execution, and line operations. These terms are not all synonymous, but all are related to the final stage of an unfolding planning process, which occupies most employees.

In operations, questions of quality and quantity become important, control devices must be developed, and appropriate organization and methods must be tailor-made for the program. Careful recruiting and training of specialists is essential, and leadership, supervision, and coordination are involved every hour of the day. Here budgets translate plans into financial sinews. This is what, in a narrow sense, used to be called administration but is actually only the production stage in planning, requiring, of course, a great deal of prior work planning if the whole process is not to be stillborn. It is necessary to realize that planning is *not* something engaged in solely by a few top people, with other members of the bureaucracy excluded from this interesting and exciting process. Such, in fact, is not the case except in highly authoritarian regimes, and even there it is more theoretical than likely. In the centralized and concentrated regime of the USSR, for example, planning is a gigantic web extending into every level and minute agency of administration.[8]

---

7 *How Companies Plan*, pp. 24-25.
8 See for example Granick, *The Red Executive*.

## Who Does What?

In 1912 Frederick W. Taylor thought that the planning and execution functions of management ought to be kept pretty much apart from each other, at least in thinking about what is involved in scientific management. One group in the organization would plan and work out efficiency methods; another would see that the plans were carried into effect. It was not long, however, before most of Taylor's followers began to modify this aspect of his theories. They came to see that administration of any kind must be a unified process with hand and brain working together, and hence they sought methods of securing coordination between planning and production so as to weld each part of the process into a smoothly operating program.

It is not that they deemphasized planning. On the contrary, Harlow Person has shown, for example, that the concept of planning is applicable to all levels and stages of institutional evolution and that the elements and thought processes of planning are everywhere the same. There is a progression from shop planning to business planning, to government planning, and even to international planning. Sooner or later, said Person, the need for rationality in large enterprises would make planning the key element in administration.[9]

By and large, however, there are still two views of how the planning function should fit into administrative organization. In the USSR, which was greatly influenced by the earlier stages of the scientific management movement, planning is kept separate from execution and parallels the line activity from the top down. Some American firms have created separate planning units, usually under the direction of a vice president, to engage in long-range planning, a pattern that is becoming increasingly common. This type of planning, however, is a staff activity and hence lies outside the main links of command from the president down. The staff officer in charge does report to the president and sometimes even to the board of directors, and before any of his recommendations can be adopted, the chief executive and the board must make the decision and take responsibility for it.

Also there is a long history of city planning in the United States, with a separately organized and independently authorized planning commission commonly located outside the integrated network of action agencies. The organization of professional planners in government, the American Society of Planning Officials, located in Chicago along with other major professional public administration agencies, has always subscribed to the notion of a separate planning function.

---

9 Harlow S. Person, "Planned Execution—The Issue of Scientific Management," *Advanced Management* (December 1945).

In general, however, the predominance of American opinion in business as in government favors the close integration of planning with the rest of the administrative process. In this view the important thing is to give planning the weight and attention it deserves. In the Pentagon, for example, the work of the Joint Chiefs of Staff is almost wholly a planning function, especially in peacetime. Most businessmen and governmental leaders realize how much there is to learn from military planning and that with minor exceptions, mostly among large corporations, civilian planning still falls a good deal short of that record.

There are, of course, some steps in the planning process that could hardly be administered except by a separate staff agency equipped to study, sift, and recommend possible alternative courses of action. This is especially true of the research function, sometimes called information gathering in order not to sound too impractical. The purpose of research is to secure the facts and prepare the analyses that will enable line executives to make up their minds on the external and internal work of the enterprise. Both business and government now function in such complicated technical areas that research has become a major career in administration for great numbers of trained men and women.

Most of this staff activity is delegated to the appropriate functional departments, however, rather than being brought together in one place. In scientific and engineering research as carried on by Bell Laboratories or General Electric, for example, the concern is also with planning, but it would hardly be feasible or desirable to combine this kind of technical research with other company planning functions. Accordingly, the vice-president in charge of finance often conducts a study program in economic and financial policy, the personnel department explores the frontiers of human relations, and the production department employs experts in operations research and improved methods of organization and procedure. Consequently there is no issue as to whether planning should be organized widely as a staff activity or confined to one place. The validity of both viewpoints is now almost universally recognized.

Most administrators object to a separately organized planning function because, tending to become isolated from the main stream of line operations, it is often neglected by the chief executive and other line officials, all of whom would doubtless put more steam behind it if they were directly responsible for it. The arguments in favor of an integrated planning function are impressive. Thus, planning in the modern world is increasingly the basis of institutional health, profits, even survival—all the factors with which the top executive is most concerned. Hence he must take a personal hand in planning, cooperating with his board of directors. Planning cannot be abandoned somewhere out in left field. Moreover, in any organization of any size, nothing gets done with vigor and drive unless everyone in it knows that the big boss is keen about the program and is giving it his active support.

Then, too, as suggested in an earlier chapter, policy today is multi-dimensional. The test of its effectiveness is the degree to which interconnections and continuities are recognized and provided for by the synthesizers who are the program's top executives. When the planning function is isolated, the top line officials whose job it is to make the most difficult syntheses find that responsibility shunted off onto someone else. In the average business or government agency, for example, at least four areas of knowledge must be studied for fact finding and policy formation: the social, the economic, the political, and the scientific and technological; the last probably belonging in first place. How is it possible to coordinate all these data in terms of objectives, policies, decisions, and action unless the synthesis is tied in with the line organization that alone can decide and get things done?

In most areas of administration, therefore, planning is a top-level responsibility second not even to personnel matters or public relations. If there is a separate planning function it should be of the long-range variety, relatively small, and closely tied in with the office of the chief executive and his board. Planning is so widely involved in every aspect of administration that staff activities dealing with it are normal accouterment to almost every function of administration. And if integration is not achieved, planning is likely to fail because not being meant to be acted upon, it becomes daydreaming.

Before accepting all of these conclusions, however, a caveat must be registered, an amendment that in effect largely resolves most of the differences between the two points of view. How much planning occurs and how it is organized depend in the first instance on the nature of the undertaking. This is not to imply that some administrative agencies can get along without any planning at all. It is simply that some programs can do with much less planning than others, while some areas of activity—such as the military in wartime, the development of new technologies like atomic energy and space exploration, or the responsibility of the State Department for long-range foreign policy—must make planning a central motif.

Much the same applies in business. A corporation decides to merge and expand, for example, or to discontinue an old line of product and start new ones. In all such cases, top management will develop teams of executives, possibly with some outside professional help, before any such program involving a major shift of policy or activity can be launched. This type of undertaking is always a main concern of the top executive because the future profits and even the survival of the program depend on what must always be a gamble in some degree.

Similarly, city planning involves so many factors and cuts across the work of so many departments that if the responsibility for long-range planning (as contrasted with zoning and immediate planning decisions) were not centered in one place, it seems unlikely that it would ever be a useful municipal function. Although a case is therefore made for a separate city planning commission, the matter does not end there. The accompanying question is: How much or how little assurance is there that the findings and recommendations of the planning commission will be put to good and immediate use? If a satisfactory answer cannot be found, then the validity of a separate operation is negated. Plans are not made to be filed away in handsome steel filing cabinets and the drawer closed.

Is there such a thing as too much planning? Clearly there is. If all procedures and decisions are reduced to writing to be slavishly followed, this militates against adaptation and change when needed. But here it is not the objective that is at fault but the method. Another common error is to assume that every aspect of the program can safely be predicted. On the contrary, alternatives must be provided in the program or the gamble will not pay off. Still another difficulty arises when management sometimes agrees to try a plan despite serious reservations about its practicability and ultimate success. The consequence is to diminish their own and everyone else's enthusiasm for and confidence in the plan, which may have been an ambitious one requiring more than usual dedication. Finally, there is the difficulty that long- and short-range planning are sometimes not sufficiently differentiated, with the result that roles are confused, the present is neglected, too much effort on useless coordination is wasted, and frustration breeds a general debility in the organization.

On balance, however, there is usually far more loss deriving from underplanning than from overplanning in the United States. In underplanning, the administrator ignores significant predictable problems and events that are within his working purview; he fails to foresee the range of contingencies and problems that *could* overtake his enterprise.[10]

The practical approach to planning, therefore, is always to think in terms of major problems but never to allow a preoccupation with present difficulties to cause the neglect of foreseeable problems that may become increasingly serious if not recognized in time. A good manager is problem-oriented. He learns to put first things first and to see how every factor bearing on the solution of major problems falls into place.

Once his scheduling has been worked out and he has a viable work plan, he has laid the foundation for administration by objectives: He can provide a clear mandate for every official with supervisory responsibility and then encourage him to develop all the resourcefulness and drive of which he is capable. Thus is planning the key to one of the administrator's main opportunities for making the enterprise energetic and spirited.

---

[10] *How Companies Plan*, p. 48.

## Program Formulation as Coordination

A main trial of the administrator is the need to keep synchronized too many parts of a going concern. Bureaucracy tends toward insularity and splintering, and the only effective answer is to use the program itself as the innate coordinator. No one likes program planning better than the expert who devotes his life to his specialty. Anyone deeply committed to his specialty will usually cooperate when he realizes that the success of his work depends on the equal success of the work of others. Thus, in the hands of skillful planners, the program itself becomes the vehicle by means of which cooperation and vitality are most likely to be assured. This assumes, of course, that every specialty will be allowed to take part in the planning process, encouraged to help form the over-all objectives of the program, consulted before policies become official, and recruited for cooperative effort well before time schedules and work methods are made final.

The goad to planning is change, the one common ingredient in every administrative situation. People tend to resist change, which interferes with their comfortable habits and set ways of doing things. If adjustment to change is to be taken in stride, therefore, and planning is to succeed, the planner must learn to think constantly about human reactions to change and what assurances must be supplied before everyone in the program will do his part to turn change from a liability into an advantage. No more than other actors in the administrative drama are planners supermen or dwellers in ivory towers; they are humanists with a special skill and a special mission that covers the whole enterprise.

## BIBLIOGRAPHY AND CASES

### Annotated Reading Suggestions

A long-time adviser in the U. S. Department of Agriculture and a leader in the scientific management movement, Harlow S. Person, probably understood the philosophy and techniques of planning better than any American to date. See especially his articles, "Planned Execution—the Issue of Scientific Management," *Advanced Management,* 10 (December 1945), reprinted in Albert Lepawsky, *Administration, The Art and Science of Organization and Management* (Knopf, 1949), and in C. Seckler-Hudson, *Processes of Organization and Management* (Washington, D.C.: American University Press, 1955). Another article by Person, "Research and Planning as Functions of Administration and Management," is found in *Public Administration Review,* 1 (Autumn 1940), found also in Lepawsky.

Lepawsky's own discussion of planning is Chapter 16, "Planning and Programming," in his book, *Administration;* he treats the subject historically and by major areas.

Another major contribution to the subject is E. J. Coil, "Administrative Organization for Policy Planning," *Advanced Management,* 4 (January 1939), also reprinted, in part, in Lepawsky.

One of the best discussions of the connection between objectives, policies, and decisions is Lawrence L. Durisch and Robert E. Lowry, "The Scope and Content of Administrative Decision—the TVA Illustration," *Public Administration Review,* 13 (Autumn 1953). See also Norman Wengert and John C. Honey, "Program Planning in the U. S. Department of the Interior, 1946-53," *Public Administration Review,* 14 (Summer 1954). On the international level, consult Richard C. Snyder, *et al.,* eds., *Foreign Policy Decision-Making* (Free Press, 1962).

Two contributions to the subject of planning by John D. Millet are *The Process and Organization of Government Planning* (Columbia University Press, 1947), and, showing his current thinking, "Planning," in F. Morstein Marx, ed., *Elements of Public Administration* (2d ed., Prentice-Hall, 1959).

One of the first and still one of the best full-length treatments of planning is Edward H. Hempel, *Top Management Planning* (Harper & Row, 1945). As stated in the text, however, the American literature on planning is still somewhat sketchy, but the indications are that this deficiency will soon be rectified, due to the clear need for it.

## Case Studies

In the Stein *Case Book,* the story of *The Emergency Rubber Project* is told by Martin Kriesberg, thirteen pages. This is an analysis of wartime planning, with the theme of emergency running throughout.

An early case prepared for the ICP (although not in the Stein *Case Book*) is that of *The Feasibility Dispute,* written by John Brigante in 1950. This tells of the work of the Planning Committee of the War Production Board; how President Roosevelt ordered vast production requirements, and how the planning unit had to determine the feasibility of the President's requests; and how finally, these goals were greatly exceeded.

Two additional ICP cases give variety to the selection. The first, No. 70, *U. S. City Planners in Iran,* twenty-five pages, was written by Frank Sherwood in 1962 and illustrates overseas administration as well as the subject under discussion. The second illustrates local administration, No. 61, *The County Buys Dunwoodie Golf Course,* seventeen pages. This account was undertaken by T. Flinn and was published in 1961. In this case, the county was not entering into a new activity—there were other public golf courses; the decision revolved around coordinated and long-range planning.

# 11

---

# Budgeting as Planning
# and Control

---

For today's complicated governing institutions the importance of budgeting is hard to overemphasize. Budgeting is plans converted into money availabilities. Without money, work would come to a stop or never would be undertaken in the first place. Hence in a real sense budgeting is at the heart of the administrative process.

## The Role of Public Finance

Budgeting is the control aspect of the larger subject of public finance. Public finance deals with government's income and expenditure policies and their effect on the growth and health of the economy. Traditionally in the United States the teaching of public finance has been oriented toward economic theory and only secondarily toward the political and administrative requirements of government. Since the onset of the depression of the 1930s, however, the control function of the budget is frequently a front-page issue of public policy. The stock market rises and falls and economic growth waxes and wanes as economic policies incorporated in the national budget arouse feelings of confidence or anxiety in the business and financial communities of the nation.

In contrast with an earlier emphasis on private investment and the market system, today public finance is more interested in budgeting and its effect on the national economy. Thus in common understanding, budgeting is public finance with a public, administrative orientation. Both emphases are useful, of course, in governmental as in business circles, for both are based on common principles and a common concern for national well-being.

A related development in the last generation, and especially since the end of World War II, is that public finance has been rapidly politicized and is now recognized as a central element in public administration—so much so, in fact, that the modern budget official must be an astute political economist as well. Budget policy, remarked the London *Economist* in 1955, has become "the Fourth Dimension" of economics, so central is it to production, distribution, consumption, and the whole issue of economic growth and stability. Thus,

> A budget is a political act, as well as a set of fiscal decisions. To apply to it the standards of criticism that would be proper if there were no political parties, elections and self-interested voters would be absurd. Strict economic reasoning of the fashionable arithmetic kind, finds little room in its system of notation for the Fourth Dimension of economics—for the degree of confidence and buoyancy, of incentive and initiative in the economy.

It is now clear, continued *The Economist,* that the Fourth Dimension can entirely upset any predictions based upon mere figuring; that whether economists "know what they are talking about or not," they should not be the only ones to sit in judgment on a budget; and that eventually budgetary policy must be judged "by the standards of political economy." [1]

These are fighting words with strong overtones of Keynesian economics, and many economists were infuriated by such strictures. *The Economist* is quoted here not to convey the impression that political judgment is superior to mathematical theory, but simply to illustrate the changed character and increased influence of public finance in the whole of the administrative process.

Public finance has, of course, always been central to statecraft because money is power: whoever controls money controls government and what it does. Today, therefore, as in the time of mercantilism, the public finance official is the molder of the political economy. His ideas go far to determine how the national income shall be distributed and whether equality or control by a financial and executive elite shall prevail.

Nowadays the chief aim of the budget official is to promote economic growth by encouraging the maximum degree of investment,

---

[1] *The Economist* (London), April 23, 1955; quoted by Edward H. Collins in "Economics and Finance," *The New York Times,* January 23, 1956.

production, and employment of which the economy is capable, but not so much as to induce shortages, excessive demand, and inflation. It is a delicate balancing act.

What should budget policy be, then? Must the budget always be in balance? Should a sinking fund be set aside to repay the national debt over a period of time? Keynes contended that the budget regulates the distribution of income and the pattern of spending. His followers frequently argue that the national debt and deficit financing, rather than being invariably evil as was once assumed, may be used as instruments of economic growth and stabilization. And underlying all such issues, of course, is the ancient political issue of equality. On one side it is argued that greater equality of income achieved through taxation policy will increase total happiness and at the same time create greater demand and hence greater profits. On the other, denying that such a course is possible it is held, first, that only the rich can accumulate the funds needed for saving, investment, and economic progress; and second, that overly progressive rates of taxation blunt incentive, reduce ambition, and retard economic progress.[2]

In a related area it has been generally agreed that in times of economic prosperity the tax rate should be raised in order to take care not only of current expenditures but also to reduce indebtedness and even to accumulate a financial cushion, on the ground that levies of this kind will be less felt and optimism and confidence less affected than in times of economic depression. Contrariwise, when the economy is depressed tax rates should be lowered and government expenditure reduced, so as to give people more to spend, thus stimulating the economy and getting it on a higher plane, after which taxes may again be raised. In simple words, take while the taking is good and lay off when the pickings are poor.

The proposition sounds simple enough, but in fact it is too simple. People riding high on cloud seven dislike heavy taxes almost more than when they are in dire need. Psychologically, therefore, the innate human disposition is the opposite of what economic policy assumes it should be. Since politicians are inclined to think as the majority of voters do, they are likely to vote that way and not in terms of economic statesmanship, more because of pressure and less because of principle. This is especially apt to be the case in a nation that like the United States lacks responsible government under responsible political parties.

The foregoing is perhaps enough to show that the issues of public finance relating to the budget are unusually difficult of solution and that those who decide economic policy by means of the budget must be exceptionally gifted. The finance officer must be first a political econo-

---

[2] Robert Neild, "The Budget: Social or Economic Weapon?" *The Listener* (London), April 25, 1957.

mist. No matter how high or low his position in the hierarchy, he makes economic policy that directly contributes to the strength or weakness of the economy. Second, he is a planner. He advises politicians, policy officials, and practical administrators in the matter of priorities, the interactions of different lines of activity, and the practicalities involved in the discharge of particular programs. As a specialist at the very heart of executive work, the finance officer must also be a generalist in order to grasp the over-all picture of what his job entails. Without this over-view, the whole of executive performance is divided and debilitated.

Seen in this perspective, public finance is far from the dull, technical, confused subject that some who have trouble in maintaining their own personal budgets would naturally suppose. Rather, public finance and budgeting is a lively subject containing much challenge and human appeal.

## Elements of the Financial Plan

Who is this financial planner who holds such power over the economic destiny of the nation? He is the man in the organization who deals not only with high-level policy but also with maintaining a reasonable balance between income and expenditure, deciding on the sums that particular programs may spend, making long-range studies of finance and organization, and controlling the actual expenditure of funds. He is located among the top echelons of government in the Office of the President (or the governor), in the Bureau of the Budget, the Treasury Department, or the General Accounting Office or state auditing agency. In any one of these spots the finance officer will need as wide a competence as demanded in any field of public administration.

At the lower levels of government the financial planner is the department head or bureau chief who is firmly grounded in finance because he knows it to be one of the half-dozen subjects he must blend if his administrative record is to be a distinguished one. Alternatively, on the chief executive's team he is a staff man with the title of budget officer, administrative assistant, special assistant, or some such designation. In yet another relationship he may be more like a corporation's financial vice president with duties that are primarily line (action) and not merely staff (advisory). In this case he may go by the title of finance officer, comptroller, treasurer, or something similar. Again, he may be a professional accountant who keeps the books, a specialist in facts and their meaning, a student of costs and efficiency. Or he may be an auditor, his job being to examine accounts to discover whether the money is being honestly and efficiently spent, and in accordance with the legal mandate.

As with the larger field of administration, the financial process also is made up of a progression of elements and steps.

First comes the legal mandate and the plan of each action agency. The plan takes money and money is administratively controlled. In the federal government (and the procedure is similar among the states and larger cities), the second step is for the action agency and the budget agency together to make an *analysis* (hence the title, budget analyst). They get the facts and translate them into organization, assignments, and money. In this process, the finance men in both agencies must understand the plan and work so closely together that each knows what the other knows.

Then there is a *hearing* before the budget agency acting in a semi-judicial capacity with the action agency as pleader. The budget agency expects the pleader to submit *estimates,* meaning tabulated figures for personnel, equipment, rent, materials and similar items constituting the total request for a given period of time, usually a year. At this hearing, the budget bureau will be interested not only in how much money is requested but also in how efficiently it will be spent. Consequently it will check on how the agency is organized and staffed and what the prospects are for the success of its program. After the hearing the budget bureau, since it speaks for the chief executive and is familiar with his over-all financial policies, analyzes, trims, works over all the estimates, and finally brings together the figures for all action agencies in a bulky volume called The Budget, which the chief executive then sends to the legislature.

The budget agency has now completed the first stage of its work: It has told each action agency what the chief executive—be he mayor, city manager, county commissioner, governor, or President—will allow, having determined the total in the light of the economic considerations mentioned above.

But behind the scenes of the entire process, although sometimes exposed to view, are the activities of *interest groups* that support the various action agencies and their plans. The approach of these groups to the budget agency is usually discreet enough, but in the legislative process following submission of the budget to the legislature, their representation at committee hearings, to individual lawmakers, and to the chief executive himself is for the most part open and above board.

The methods of pressure groups are many and various, ranging all the way from closed-door conferences and entertaining to large social functions and the distribution of literature (including "comic" books and strips that convey the desired message), and the stimulation of letters and telegrams from constituents to key legislators. Many of these activities are expensive, and in a battle over a major issue enormous sums may be spent in the hope of influencing the outcome of legislation. Where the budget is concerned the issues are commonly of a less spectacular nature than, say, health insurance for the elderly, and hence in the budget process pressure activities are less in the news. They are none the less active and influential, however, on behalf of most of the regular action programs of government.

Of the three main types of budget, the legislative budget, now rarely used but once dominant, is formulated by committees of the legislature on the basis of requests from the executive branch. More common is the executive budget which was instituted in the federal government as a result of the Budget and Accounting Act of 1921. Traditionally, the executive budget is organized under headings such as personnel, services of different kinds, equipment, rent, supplies, and the like. But these categories are merely means to an end and fail to supply an over-all financial picture of particular agencies and programs. Consequently, recent emphasis is on the so-called performance budget which concentrates on the service to be rendered and what it will cost. The executive budget and especially the performance budget increases the authority of the budget bureau and encourages advance study, planning, and executive leadership. When the chief executive sends this type of budget to the legislature with his budget message, it is thereafter referred to as "his" program.

In his budget message, the chief executive asks the *legislature* for a certain amount in appropriations and a certain amount in authorizations. During the legislative stage these two matters are handled by different committees. Authorizations decide whether a certain program should be undertaken at all; appropriations grant a specific amount of money in its behalf. The function of taxation (ways and means) also is handled separately. Each of these legislative functions is a gigantic undertaking and hence a division of labor is needed. Moreover, in a large government such as the federal or that of New York State, the appropriations committee will operate in several subsections, each dealing with different areas of public activity and the economy.

Authorizations may be either standing or special. When a program has been created by specific legislation setting a definite and continuing frame of reference, the authorization also will be continuous or "standing." In some cases, however, the legislature may reserve the right to pass a specific authorization bill each year, in which case the authorization is said to be "special." Under both types the money subsequently appropriated must not exceed the total specified in the authorization. Legislative committees handling authorizations usually take a sympathetic interest in the programs within their jurisdiction and consequently committee authorizations are likely to be more generous than the sums that Congress as a whole will support.

Two additional forms of authorization are by means of a kind of back-door device. In the first, legislation may empower a specified government agency to tap funds borrowed by the Treasury and spend or lend the money in the operation of its program. In the second, the legislature may empower authorized agencies to go ahead and contract for the expenditure of money in anticipation of subsequent appropriations.

After the legislative stage of the budget, the next is *expenditure*, which is the actual disbursement of funds. Here the matter goes back to the central budget bureau and also to the Treasury Department. The final step is *auditing* to test the legality and compliance of the expenditure with the original plans and legislation; it is like the evaluation of a plan that has been executed. This function also ties in with the legislature because by long practice and tradition, an outside auditor is considered more reliable than one supervised by management. Hence in government the auditor (in the federal government the General Accounting Office headed by the Comptroller General) reports directly to the legislature.

In the federal government only about two thirds of the money appropriated at each congressional session is spent in the fiscal year covered by the budget, the rest being reserved for later use. Theoretically, therefore, Congress could cut the President's requests by as much as a third (the sums withheld for future use) without affecting current expenditures. Nevertheless, it is actual expenditure that counts, and if in any given year it exceeds revenue, the budget is unbalanced and the government must borrow to make up the difference.

The trouble for impartial scorekeepers in this matter is the difficulty of determining the effect of authorizations and appropriations—contained in over a dozen separate bills—on government expenditures in the year in question. Consequently, until the year is ended the total for expenditures is little more than an estimate covering a considerable range of possibilities, by which time, of course, another battle of the budget is under way. For budgeting is a continuous process and plans must necessarily be made clear a year in advance.

In the executive type of budget the chief executive has a good deal of authority to determine how much money shall be requested. This, however, does not prevent the legislature from appropriating less, and sometimes even more than is asked for certain programs. By contrast, under the so-called responsible or Cabinet form of government the program formulated by the party in power remains unchanged unless dissidents wish to precipitate a parliamentary crisis as a result of which the party in power may be overthrown, elections held, and a new government formed.

One way to bring more party responsibility into the American system of government would be to allow the chief executive to veto individual items in appropriation bills, something that Presidents have sought for a long time but which Congress has not been willing to authorize. Some state governors, on the other hand, do enjoy this power.

In the expenditure of government funds, no action agency can draw on its own account without a *warrant* issued by the Treasury Department. In the federal government this authorization to transfer funds from the Treasury to the agency disbursing officer must be countersigned by the Comptroller General acting in his capacity as watchdog for Congress. In addition, as the President's representative, the Bureau of the Budget keeps a checkrein on agency expenditures, prorating annual withdrawals over fractions of the year and even refusing to release funds at all if for reasons of policy the President desires it.

In every government, and especially in a large one, these rather complicated arrangements are designed to assure honesty and accountability in the handling of enormous sums of money; accounting becomes an indispensable aspect of management. Every plan and action program must be analyzed into categories such as wages and salaries, equipment, supplies, and other requirements of the program so that finally the total amount of money allocated to each agency is clearly shown. Thereafter these categories are the chessmen to be used in executive planning and program execution. A certain degree of flexibility is provided for when, in case of convincing need, the transfer of sums from one category to another in the same department or agency is authorized. But such transfers must be approved by higher departmental officials, often by the Bureau of the Budget and the Comptroller General as well. Thus, the more competent the work of the planning and finance officers in the action agencies, the better is their access to funds when these are needed.

A main strategy of budget administration, as in administration generally, is to allow action agencies as much responsibility in the formulation and administration of budgets as the requirements of efficiency and flexibility demand. Consequently in most American governments, the federal included, a recent tendency is to accord departmental finance officers more authority over estimates, preauditing, and the control of expenditure. A preaudit is an internal audit within the spending agency, whereas a postaudit is made outside the agency by the Comptroller General (or his counterpart in state governments) acting as watchdog for Congress.

This more liberal policy represents a considerable gain for effective public administration, for it allows a certain degree of financial autonomy at the departmental and bureau levels, thus encouraging the initiatives and responsibilities required for effective planning and program execution. In passing it may be noted that the same tendency has appeared in government personnel administration, as will later be shown.

In this brief account of financial management, certain major steps have been noted: estimates (plans), budget defense (master plan), legislative authorization (mandate), appropriation (funds made available), warrants and accounts (disbursement authorized), expenditure (plan execution), and audit (evaluation). In this arrangement, financial administration appears as a combination of planning and control, the two functions being inextricably related. By simplifying these matters instead of dwelling upon the special aspects of the budget procedure that exist at various levels of government, there is the risk of glossing over differences that are interesting and in some cases important. In general, however, the main lines of financial policy and management are similar at all levels—local, state, and federal—and a trend at one level is apt to appear at others as well. More significant than detailed procedure, which may always be studied later if needed, is the role of finance in administrative planning and its relation to the political economy.

## Unresolved Issues of Public Finance

Much recent progress has been made in public finance administration due largely to the recommendations of the three major administrative surveys of the federal government that have been mentioned: those of the Brownlow Committee in 1937 and the two Hoover Commissions in 1949 and 1955 respectively. Considering that major budgetary reform in the United States is for the most part as recent as the passage of the Budget and Accounting Act of 1921, budgeting as a central vehicle for planning and control is still a relatively new field.

Consequently, much remains to be done. Some of the principal issues are these:

**Strengthening the Bureau of the Budget.**  As recently as the 1961 report of the Jackson Subcommittee on National Policy Machinery, the Senate Committee on Government Operations (of which the subcommittee was a part) recommended that the Bureau of the Budget be still further strengthened—a proposal in striking contrast to a common congressional complaint that the Bureau is already too strong. It is true that this agency, concerned not only with budgets but also with administrative management and organization and legislative clearance, is in fact a powerful one. Nevertheless, said the Jackson Committee, "The budget process can be the President's most powerful instrument for establishing a scale of national priorities and marshaling, through the Congress, the resources required on their behalf." The Committee conceded that the Bureau would "never win a bureaucratic popularity contest" but implied that its reputation as "the villain of the Executive Branch" was undeserved. The report stressed the Bureau's role as the "lengthened shadow" of the President, reaching over every agency of the government and working at "that most sensitive pressure point—

the pocketbook nerve." There was also a plea for less of the usual incomprehensible jargon in which budgets are customarily written.[3]

**Collaboration at the Top.**  Still another proposal would broaden the base of top planning. Admitting the Bureau of the Budget to be the center of top planning, what other agencies should be brought into active cooperation? Since the Employment Act of 1946 created the Council of Economic Advisors, this agency has become almost a full partner in budgetary planning. When the Director of the Budget consults with the President and his aides—as much as half of the Director's time is spent this way—the Chairman of the Council of Economic Advisors is frequently a party to the deliberations. The reason is that a responsibility of the Council is constantly to study and analyze economic trends in the nation and try to avoid recessions and promote economic growth. Consequently the Council's advice on the use of government controls in areas such as taxation, monetary policy, Federal Reserve discount rates, public works, and the like goes to the core of high-level planning for the health of the political economy. It is a needed supplement to the economic analyses of the Bureau of the Budget which, being so near the trees, has a more limited view of the forest than is possible from the vantage point of the Council of Economic Advisors. Both agencies cover the whole of the federal government, of course, but a function of the CEA is to establish liaison with the key public agencies whose activities impinge upon and influence major economic policy—the Federal Reserve System, for example—constituting scrutiny from a slightly different angle from that of the Bureau of the Budget.

In addition to bringing the Council of Economic Advisors into a top-planning position, there has also been an attempt to secure coordinated effort relative to accounting and other matters of joint fiscal policy and financial administration through a Joint Accounting Committee representing the Comptroller General, the Secretary of the Treasury, and the Director of the Bureau of the Budget. Informally created in 1947, this group was formally recognized in the Budget and Accounting Procedures Act of 1950 and since then has succeeded in simplifying financial administration, thus making it easier to tie in this function with planning at the top.

Is this enough? Should something akin to the National Resources Planning Board, which operated successfully between 1933 and 1943, be brought back into the picture? At present the Bureau of the Budget deals largely with operational administration. Should some other agency

---

3 This report was the last of a series of six staff studies based upon the subcommittee's two-year effort to conduct a searching nonpartisan examination of the machinery that makes national policy for the cold war. Quoted in *The New York Times,* October 23, 1961.

or a division of the Bureau itself give more attention to the substance of policy, especially the long-range variety? It seems likely that something of the sort will have to be devised.

**Long-range Planning.**    Increasingly the Bureau of the Budget tries to plan budgets for several years in advance—especially in areas such as national defense, mutual assistance, atomic energy, and space exploration, where major programs will most likely continue and expand. Considering that large corporations sometimes plan for some of their programs as far as twenty to thirty years ahead, it seems only reasonable that the federal government should do the same where similar technologies are concerned.

But Congress is slow to agree to long-range spending schedules, as illustrated by the Eisenhower Administration's unsuccessful attempts to secure a foreign aid program that would remain constant and continuous for as long, perhaps, as ten years. How can the strength of allies be built up if support runs in fits and starts? Economic growth is always a continuous, long-range development, not an on-again-off-again kind of undertaking. But Congress balked and will doubtless continue to do so. Elected for only two years, congressmen are loath to give even moral support to policy—especially where great sums are involved—that may be of dubious legal validity.

**Jealousy between the Two Branches.**    In addition to the foregoing, of course, is the institutional jealousy that makes congressmen in any case hesitate to increase the power of the President and the executive branch. Certain aspects of financial policy would no doubt be handled differently were it not for the problem of securing teamwork between the two branches, even when the same political party controls both. The item veto has been mentioned, and also what amounts almost to hostility on the part of Congress toward the Bureau of the Budget and the Council of Economic Advisors. Under a responsible government system such as exists in Canada, Congress would regard these staff agencies as partners serving The Government (that is, the party in power) and there would be no feeling of suspicion and downright resistance in the consideration of their recommendations. How to solve these difficulties short of converting to responsible government is still a roadblock in the determination of public policy, although the solution is possibly the greatest need for improved public administration.

**Location of the  Bureau of the Budget.**    When the Bureau of the Budget was created in 1921 it was placed in the Treasury Department, after the pattern of Great Britain and many American state and local governments. Nevertheless, the director of agencies so located is regarded as the chief executive's representative and reports directly to him. Both in Britain and frequently in the United States, this unified type of finance department has worked well.[4] A number of leading authorities on financial administration, including A. E. Buck, the National Municipal League, and the Fiscal Task Force of the Hoover Commission, favored retaining the Bureau of the Budget in the Treasury Department, but in 1939, in one of its reorganization orders, Congress moved it to its present location at the center of the Executive Office of the President. This was to strengthen its position as a presidential agency, placing it above any department and even the Cabinet, and increasing its power and stature to the point where its privileged position would make it the most influential agency in the White House establishment. This situation is not likely to change unless there is developed a modified view of how best to institutionalize the work of the Presidency, a subject to be dealt with more fully in later chapters.

**Tax Policy.**    Even more controversial than any of the foregoing issues is the matter of tax policy. There are two aspects of the matter. First, should the balance between federal and state-local taxation be altered so as to reduce the federal government's dominant position and increase the tax resources of state and local governments? At present state and local governments find it increasingly difficult to secure new sources of revenue to finance their expanding activities; at the same time the federal government, because of its widespread use of the federal aid formula, is increasingly influential in areas that formerly were state-local responsibilities.

In some countries, especially in Europe, all taxes are collected by the local tax collector, who then passes along agreed-upon shares to the equivalents of our state and federal governments. This decentralized tax collection system assures local and state governments of their fair portion of tax revenue and avoids what sometimes amounts to financial starvation at the local level. Is such a method too novel for Americans to consider seriously?

The second issue is the incidence of taxation and the kind of taxes most favored. So great is the scramble for revenue that tax policy has become something of a crazy quilt. The income tax may be levied at all three levels, even the municipal. The sales tax, usually state or local, is a big producer but its effects are regressive, meaning that it falls proportionately most heavily on those in the lower income brackets. There are few areas of American government where careful study and rationalization are more needed than in the duplicating, overlapping,

4 See, for example, Frederick C. Mosher, "The Executive Budget, Empire State Style," *Public Administration Review* (Spring 1952), pp. 73-84.

hit-or-miss tax policies that now prevail. The danger is that confused and short-sighted policies may depress the very activities on which incentive for growth is most likely to be found under the capitalist system.

## A New Approach to Budgeting, Accounting, and Auditing

By now it should be clear that there is no royal road to perfection or even improvement in financial administration. As a subsection of the administrative process, financial policy is closely related to planning and control. What is needed, therefore, is an integrated system, not a piecemeal one; a continuously growing technique, not sporadic improvisations. Sometimes, however, a real innovation appears, one of which is the so-called performance or project budget, already alluded to, which began to be emphasized a couple of decades ago.

As described earlier in this chapter, conventional budgetary categories in the executive classification budget deal with amounts under specific headings: so many employees in certain wage brackets; so many tons of cement for highway construction; so many buildings to be rented or owned; so many dollars for maintenance and repair; so many millions or billions to be paid in subsidies to farmers or to businesses, such as the airlines.

This quantitative method appeals to legislative appropriations committees because it makes possible a comparison with figures for the preceding budget period and shows whether there has been an increase or a decrease. Is the agency holding the line, reducing costs, or asking for more money? If the request constitutes an increase over the past year, how is that to be justified? In other words, it is assumed (not always wisely) that if a certain quantitative base has been approved in the past, only an increase needs careful scrutiny.

Similarly, if the committee knows that the cost of a certain item differs in other agencies, it wants to find out why. The Veterans Administration, for example, has established an average cost for maintaining a patient in its hospitals for a day or a week. How does this figure compare with the cost of similar care in the U. S. Public Health Service or the armed forces? The method is not always reliable, to be sure, but when undertaken by a skilled budget examiner or an experienced member of an appropriations subcommittee, he can bring out some revealing facts as to the efficiency or inefficiency of the programs under review.

By contrast to the preference of the legislator, the average line official in an operating bureau finds the performance budget more appealing because it is more useful as a tool of administrative control. In the course of his duties he asks himself, What is my objective? What is my plan for attaining it? He must have a clear idea of what he wants eventually to accomplish and an equally clear picture of how far along his plan stands at various given stages. He must have the proper tools of administration in order to follow through with his plan. So, as in the case of the more conventional type of budget, he creates categories. Then he determines unit costs, in the manner of scientific management. Finally he combines all of these factors in order to make his pictured objective stand out clearly and he can see where he is in relation to it.

Many illustrations of this technique could be given. A city department plans to raze a slum area, for example, and build a park. It prepares a photograph of the slum area and an architect's drawing of the park as it would look when completed. Then through newspapers and other communications media, it gets out publicity to its own employees and to the public to show what is envisaged, what the major cost units will be, and what the time schedule is. In other words, project budgeting is almost interchangeable with the planning procedure, as discussed in the preceding chapter.

It is easier, of course, to use this technique in some areas than in others. The Tennessee Valley Authority, for example, can picture its completed dams, explain how a proposed new dam fits into the total plan, and show on a map the recreation area that will become available. Though in several parts, this also is a complete project. On the other hand, the Immigration and Naturalization Service, say, finds it harder to show how many aliens will be educated in American institutions or how many are likely to become citizens in a given time.

But the advantages of the performance budget far outweigh the difficulties. For one thing, it supplies powerful incentives to the management team of the agency that uses it. It is also one of the best of methods by which to convince legislators and the public that something specific should be done about a particular problem, or in order to seize a social opportunity. It also makes planning necessary, especially time planning according to a prearranged schedule. In addition, because it relies on analytical tools it facilitates the administrative evaluation of results. Under conventional budgetary methods, it may be said, for example, the park cost $500,000, or, we employed fifty men on the average and it took 100 tons of cement to do the job. While possibly interesting, these data do not evoke a picture of the completed project nor do they make it possible for the taxpayer or his legislative representative to answer the question, at least to their own satisfaction, Was it worth it?

Because legislators find the older classification system useful for certain purposes while operating officials get different things out of both systems, it is not surprising that in budget hearings before legislative bodies a combination of both approaches is frequently employed. As every mathematician and administrator knows, the use made of figures depends upon the purposes to be served; as an old saying has it, There are lies, damned lies, and statistics.

Similar considerations apply to the choice of governmental versus business methods of accounting. A concrete result of the Hoover Commission survey of 1949 is that the federal government has gradually been converting to a business-type accounting system. The old method emphasized a detailed audit in order to assure honesty and accountability. The result was an enormous expenditure, with hordes of employees relentlessly plowing through tons of paperwork, but except for the satisfaction of detailed scrutiny, the method left much to be desired.

Under the newer system, the General Accounting Office uses a sampling technique to check honesty and faithfulness to the law; the operating agencies are allowed to do much of their own accounting, again reducing the burden on the General Accounting Office. The result is a decentralization of accounting procedures to departmental and agency finance officers both at headquarters and in the field.

Perhaps the most notable feature of the new system, however, is its growing emphasis on accrual accounting as commonly used in business, instead of cash accounting which is the method traditionally favored in government. Under accrual accounting, obligated funds appear on the ledger as soon as they are committed, instead of when they are actually paid out, as is the case under the cash method. The innovation facilitates accurate planning and control because the administrator is always up to date. Also, as part of this conversion to business accounting methods, the emphasis on honesty has been supplemented by an increased emphasis on efficiency by means of cost accounting where this may be applied. As cost accounting is increasingly used, for the first time government is in a position to evaluate, control, and identify the administrative situations that need attention. Accountants (CPA's) are now being trained for government work in which they deal with matters formerly reserved to management consultants: If costs are out of line, what is wrong with organization, with planning, with work methods, or even with the qualifications of key executives? The development is a rational one because while accounting deals with responsibility, which involves honesty and probity, it also deals with cost, which involves efficiency.

So a new day in accounting and auditing in government has caused the accounting profession to become management-minded, and the whole administrative process has benefited. Budget and finance is therefore not a field set aside for a few experts who happen to be mathematically minded. These are useful, to be sure, but financial management is so much more than figures. Rather, it is the area for planners, economists, cost analysts, statisticians, people who are careful, logical thinkers and who also have vision and imagination. A good finance man, in the modern world, is no different from the ideal executive.

## BIBLIOGRAPHY AND CASES

Annotated Reading Suggestions

The material on budgeting is much more adequate than that on planning in general. Many of the best articles are found in *Public Administration Review*. Top priority should be given to V. O. Key, "The Lack of a Budgetary Theory," *American Political Science Review*, 34 (December 1940); Harold D. Smith, "The Budget as an Instrument of Legislative Control and Executive Management," *Public Administration Review*, 4 (Summer 1944); Verne B. Lewis, "Toward a Theory of Budgeting," *Public Administration Review*, 12 (Winter 1952); Aaron Wildavsky, "Political Implications of Budgetary Reform," *Public Administration Review*, 21 (Autumn 1961); Paul Appleby, "The Role of the Budget Division," *Public Administration Review*, 17 (Summer 1957); Pendleton Herring, "The Politics of Fiscal Policy," *Yale Law Journal*, 47 (March 1938); Arthur N. Holcome, "Over-All Planning through the Bureau of the Budget," *Public Administration Review*, 1 (Spring 1941); Edward C. Banfield, "Congress and the Budget: A Planner's Criticism," *American Political Science Review*, 43 (December 1949); Frederick J. Lawton, "Legislative-Executive Relationships in Budgeting as Viewed by the Executive," *Public Administration Review*, 13 (Summer 1953); Symposium, "Symposium on Budget Theory," *Public Administration Review*, 10 (Winter 1950); and Symposium, "Performance Budgeting: Has the Theory Worked?" *Public Administration Review*, 20 (Spring 1960).

Among the best books and monographs are these: Harold M. Groves, *Financing Government* (6th ed., Holt, Rinehart and Winston, 1964), deals with fiscal policy in general. Harold D. Smith, *The Management of Your Government* (McGraw-Hill, 1945). President's Committee on Administrative Management, *Report with Special Studies* (Government Printing Office, 1937), pp. 139-206. Lucius Wilmerding, Jr., *The Spending Power: A History of the Efforts of Congress to Control Expenditures* (Yale University Press, 1943). Jesse Burkhead, *Government Budgeting* (Wiley, 1956). Arthur W. Buck, *The Budget in Governments of Today* (Macmillan, 1934). Daniel Selko, *The Administration of Federal Finances* (Brookings Institution, 1937). Commission on Organization of the Executive Branch of the Government (first Hoover Commission), *Budgeting and Accounting, Treasury Department, Fiscal, Budgeting, and Accounting Activities*, and *Office of General Services: Supply Activities* (all by Government Printing Office, 1949).

Notable studies relating to departmental budgeting are these: Norman M. Pearson, "The Budgeting Function in the Department of Agriculture," *Public Administration Review*, 3 (Winter 1943); Donald C. Kull, "Decentralized Budget Administration in the Tennessee Valley Authority," *Public Administration*

*Review,* 9 (Winter 1949); Robert A. Walker, "The Relation of Budgeting to Program Planning," *Public Administration Review,* 4 (Spring 1944); and Jesse V. Burkhead, "Budget Classification and Fiscal Planning," *Public Administration Review,* 7 (Autumn 1947).

Budgeting at the state and local levels is considered by Frederick C. Mosher in "The Executive Budget, Empire State Style," *Public Administration Review,* 12 (Spring 1952); Glendon A. Schubert and Donald F. McIntyre, "Preparing the Michigan State Budget," *Public Administration Review,* 13 (Autumn 1953); Lyman S. Moore, "The City Manager Looks at the Budget," *Public Administration Review,* 12 (Summer 1952); International City Managers Association, *Municipal Finance Administration* (Chicago, 1949); and John A. McMahon, *Municipal Budget Making and Administration* (University of North Carolina Press, 1952).

Outstanding books on government accounting are these; Lloyd Morey and Robert P. Hackett, *Fundamentals of Governmental Accounting* (2d ed., Wiley, 1951); and Eric L. Kohler and Howard W. Wright, *Accounting in the Federal Government* (Prentice-Hall, 1956).

## Case Studies

The role of the budget bureau in legislation as well as in administration is dealt with in one of the Stein cases, *The FBI Retirement Bill.* This case was written by Joseph F. Marsh, Jr., in 1949. The Bureau of the Budget lost this battle, but then the FBI is no mean adversary.

Another important facet of a budget bureau's work is dealt with in ICP case No. 28, *Impounding of Funds by the Bureau of the Budget,* by J. D. Williams, thirty-three pages. An interesting state level case in the ICP series is No. 69, *Budget for New York State,* 1956-57, by D. G. Herzberg and Paul Tillett, thirty-one pages.

# PART THREE

# Executive Performance

# 12

---

# Executive
# Responsibilities

---

IN SUCCESSFUL ADMINISTRATION, every individual with supervisory responsibility must think like an executive, from the top man down to the lowest grade supervisor. It was once supposed that leadership resided only in the chief executive, a charismatic personality, and that those below him in the administrative hierarchy were mainly routine, bureaucratic employees taking their orders from on high and carrying them out without question. It is true, of course, that the outstanding chief executive will have certain special leadership qualities and that if he is dynamic and understanding, he will set the tone of the whole enterprise. Nevertheless, his over-all success depends also on the degree to which he takes a team view of leadership, allowing his subordinates a wide discretion in this respect.

The reason that leadership is a pervasive element in administration is that administration itself is an organic act. Many specialties and subprocesses are involved, and over-all effectiveness depends on the skill with which these factors are synthesized in a proper time schedule. Leadership energy flowing at these subordinate levels produces a far greater effect and accomplishment than it does when it is confined to the office of the chief executive. Energy and vitality are generated from the sum total of all segments in a hierarchy and, as in an interconnected grid, flow continuously through all of them.

Consequently, a test of an effective administrative organism is the degree to which every employee with supervisory responsibility acquires an executive point of view and motivation, no matter what his position in the organization. An additional advantage, of course, is the creation by this means of a source of trained top leadership from which the institution may replenish itself in the future.

In essence, therefore, an executive at whatever level of organization is a leader. This vital and necessary philosophy is the secret of why in the long run democratic administration is more successful, both in immediate accomplishment and in long-range staying power, than the older aristocratic tradition that is now vanishing.

## Executive Leaders, Administrators, and Managers

The most common lack in public administration is leadership. A sufficient supply of specialists and technicians is pretty well guaranteed by modern technology, the educational system, and the administrative bureaucracy. But none of these aspects of modern society seem able to assure a sufficient supply of executives with the ability to plan, to make policy, to delegate and coordinate, and to provide the motivation that produces teamwork and energy. The highest aim of the future public administrator, therefore, should be to become an operational, production-minded executive, capable of organizing and motivating the staff he directs to efforts that produce measurable results for the public benefit. Administration is not a game nor a speciality; rather, it is production on a broad front for social accomplishment.

Consequently, this introductory chapter in Part III, which deals with how the operating official makes a success of his program, is in many ways the most important one in the book. In a mass-production society where government is called upon to do so much, the public bureaucracy would soon become dispirited and inert without adequate leadership widely and strategically deployed so as to produce viable solutions to the myriad problems with which government is confronted.

In order to get this point of view across, therefore, the term "executive leadership" is preferable to either administrator or manager. The term "administrator" has come to connote routine and orderly procedures but not necessarily an imaginative, creative approach, and the term "manager" suggests someone who from an overhead position manipulates and directs the enterprise single-handedly. Hence, in combination, the term "administrative management." But although both terms and their respective connotations are useful, something more is needed to include these qualities and also a more dynamic approach to administration. The terms "executive," or "executive leadership" seem to supply this requirement.

Leadership shows others, by example and a knowledge of human motivation and administrative technique, how to do a better cooperative job than the members of the group could do if left to their own devices. Leadership is influence *with* people, not power *over* them.[1] Hence leadership is not power, nor dominance, nor social superiority, nor anything suggestive of snobbery—connotations of the term that in the past have caused people in the democracies generally to be suspicious of the word.

Leadership responds to the needs and desires of one's administrative constituency in order to satisfy its wants and relieve its tensions. There is also a time factor involved in that leadership supplies what is needed when it is needed. In addition, leadership encourages workers so that their motivation is continuing and self-induced, causing them to grow in ability and work satisfaction. It martials the competence of the work group in such a way that individual and group effectiveness grow with the challenge of the job.

An executive leader supplies dynamism to his program. He does not play an instrument, he leads an orchestra. He has the feel of all the parts that must be blended into a unified operation; he has the sense of timing and rhythm that goes with this quality, and a drive to get on with the job.

What does the executive do? In the first place, he must have a clear conception of plans and strategy, as dealt with in Parts I and II. Then he must have people he can rely upon to do the job. He must also have a streamlined organization where a direct flow of responsibility will make possible a hard-hitting and effective program. And finally, he must be on guard against a cumbersome superstructure of staff and advisory personnel who merely get in his way and take up his time.

After he has the plans, the personnel, and the straight line of organization, program effectiveness becomes a matter of timing and synchronization. Every aspect of the organization is interrelated. Every move affects many other parts of the program, no matter how distant. If the executive concentrates upon one area to the neglect of others, the machine becomes deranged, and unless the imbalance is recognized and straightened out, he loses control of his organization. In short, an executive is the man or woman at any level of organization who has the feel of what must be done and how to do it, making that part of the program for which they are responsible mesh with energy.

To this end, executive work is partly a matter of taking routine

---

[1] A point argued by Mary Parker Follett in her article, "The Illusion of Final Authority," which originally appeared in the *Bulletin of the Taylor Society*, XI (December 1926), pp. 243-246, and conveniently reprinted in part in Lepawsky, ed., *Administration*, pp. 326-327.

and periodic inventory, at least once a day and sometimes more often than that, of the current state of accomplishment in an unfolding program, in order that the head of the enterprise may secure a bird's-eye, integrated view of the program of the work as a whole. After a time this inventory, which is based on a logical sequence of the various phases of the activity, becomes more or less automatic. Such a checkup is an indispensable part of the executive's work because it gives him the feel of having a finger on everything that is going on, the feel of the completeness and integration of every component part of the common task.[2]

## *Varieties of Executive Responsibility*

The range and variety of executive responsibility is, of course, enormous, but in general they are determined by whether responsibility at the top of the organization is dual, plural, or single.

Widely in business and to some extent in government, there is now a system of *dual executives,* one being largely responsible for policy and the other for efficient execution. The board chairman in the large corporation, for example, presides over the board and reflects on long-range policy, while the president is responsible for execution and, jointly with the chairman of the board, recommends policy. The council-manager plan of municipal government gives the mayor the policy function but entrusts authority over execution to a paid professional manager.

A variation on the same theme is found also in business practice where the president of a corporation is often the ultimate authority in administration, but the day-to-day running of the enterprise is turned over to an executive vice president. Indeed, this arrangement is coming to be almost standard operating procedure in the largest American corporations, the reason being that external relations and policy areas now figure so prominently in business affairs and take so much of the time and thought of the chief executive.

There is much to be said for this division of responsibility. In the modern world the number and difficulty of executive tasks are frequently too much for one man to handle alone. This is especially true of the office of President of the United States, where the incumbent has at least six major functions, any one of which would be a full-time job for a man of even the greatest ability.[3] Because the burden is so heavy, directing the work of the executive agencies is either neglected, slowed

---

[2] For an illustration of how this may be done, see Marshall E. Dimock, *The Executive in Action*, pp. 85ff.

[3] These functions are party leader, legislative leader, ceremonial head, commander in chief of the armed forces, architect of foreign policy, and administrative leader.

down by one-man attention to too many details, or delegated to anonymous assistants.

In addition to dual executives, there is also a modern tendency to make use of *plural executives* in the running of a business enterprise. This arrangement is never, of course, carried to the point of no ultimate authority at all, for there is usually a president or chief executive officer, as he is sometimes called. The merit of the plan is that the thinking and acting of a group, all of whom know the score, is frequently more effective than entrusting all authority to one man, with all the inherent risks involved. In government the collegial method is successfully employed in the Pentagon's Joint Chiefs of Staff and also in the policy board of the State Department, although in neither case is the plan wholly analogous to the usual arrangement in the business corporation.

For the most part, however, the collegial executive plan in government has yielded poor results, the reason being that ultimate authority is often lacking, and work is parceled out among different persons and then never again brought into focus. Because regulatory commissions are notable offenders in this respect, a recent reform has been to encourage them to create the office of chief executive as a center of administrative responsibility. The commission form of municipal government, which started shortly after the turn of the century in Galveston, also has suffered from the fact that too many men go their separate ways, resulting in poor coordination and even conflicts of jurisdiction.

Generally speaking, then, a plural-headed organization is not designed to provide energy and leadership in the executive, and when the device is used, as it is in business, it should be in conjunction with a scalar or hierarchical type of organization in which final responsibility is always clear.

Because the dual and plural types of executive are useful for only limited purposes, therefore, most executive leadership consists of a *single responsible official* at each successive level of organization, from the top to the bottom of the pyramid. This is called line or the military type of organization and has the clear advantage of sharply defined authority and responsibility so that a particular official may act with energy if he has the other qualifications.

In a small municipal government the only executive may be the mayor or the town or city manager. In larger city governments there are department heads and even bureau and section chiefs. In county government there are commissioners or a county manager, often supported by department heads for schools, highways, police, and taxation. In state governments there is always a governor and many departments subdivided into bureaus, sections, and even divisions, and there may also be officers in charge of field (geographical) divisions of the central office operations. Thus the typical state government may include as many as four or more levels of executive work, and in the larger states, such as New York, California, Illinois, and Pennsylvania, there may be even more levels in scalar succession.

Finally, the federal government, being enormous in size and world-wide in extent, has a great many levels of executive performance: The President, the Cabinet, departmental Secretaries and independent agency heads, undersecretaries, assistant secretaries, bureau chiefs, assistant bureau chiefs, coordinate division heads, section heads, area office heads, area office department heads, regional coordinators, and office managers, to mention only the most obvious ones. From the President down to the section head in a field office having supervisory responsibility, therefore, the chain of executive command is continuous.

Alongside these various levels of operating organizations are the so-called staff or facilitative services, the work of which is often partially operational as well as primarily of a service nature to the line official at the appropriate level. These service functions have to do with house-keeping arrangements such as personnel administration, finance, supply, and sometimes research and planning.

With literally hundreds of thousands of executives in American governments at all levels, the ratio of public executive employment to total executive employment in the United States tends constantly to increase. Because of the technical nature of government's work and the constant need for planning, leadership, and coordination, it is in this crucial area that executive leadership must be strengthened and improved if public administration is to make significant advances.

## The Role of Authority in Administration

Executive work at all levels of organization has common needs and requirements. Every aspect of administration is important to the total result and must be meshed with every other aspect of it. Especially important, however, are policy determination, program planning, supervision, coordination, motivation, and communication. Leadership runs throughout this composite process, supplying incentives and motivation and providing the basis for delegation and its counterpoise, coordination.

What, in this complex, is the role of authority? It is not position, nor is it legal right, nor is it bossing people, nor issuing orders. Rather, authority is influence with people, a form of voluntary consensus. Thus, said Mary Parker Follett, leadership and authority are plural because many people are involved.[4] Chester Barnard, former head of the New Jersey Bell Telephone Company and later head of the Rockefeller

---

[4] Follett, *loc. cit.*

Foundation, confirmed this view when he remarked that a "superior" is not an "authority" nor does he have authority, strictly speaking, because authority lies in the "potentiality of assent" flowing from a widespread loyalty to the common goals of the organization.[5] In fact, in the accomplishment of the objectives of the program, officials among the lower ranks of the hierarchy may have even more actual power than those at the top. According to Ordway Tead,

> The real basis for authority is not in the person. It is not something for the executive properly to arrogate to himself and to become self-important about. This is what Miss Mary P. Follett meant when she said "authority belongs to the job and stands with the job." The authority lies not in any single source, including its prestige or status in the hierarchy. It lies rather in the capacity, understanding, judgment and imagination shown by the one "in authority." [6]

The authors of a study of actual business practice sponsored by the Harvard Business School, concluded that few large modern corporations are "dominated by a single man who deals with his subordinates one at a time. . . . The trend is obviously toward the development of some kind of team effort at the top management level." The concept of the leader as "one who helps the organization to do is in fact vastly broader in scope than the concept of the leader as one who holds the helm alone. . . . In most of the companies studied, we found that the task of top management was no longer a one-man job." And finally, showing the wide influence of the human relations approach in administration, in a more real sense than is commonly supposed, "the administrative leader is trying to integrate the needs of the organization with the requirements of the individual for growth and personal development." The greatest potential of administration, continue these authors, is the human potential, and the greatest expansion of resources to be anticipated in coming decades is the effective release of human talents and energies in ways that are both productive and personally satisfying.[7]

The conclusions of this study were based on case studies made over a two-year period in twelve companies of various sizes located in different parts of the country. Among the many cases reported is one concerning twenty plant managers and purchasing agents who reacted typically

---

5 Chester Barnard, *The Functions of the Executive* (Cambridge, Mass.: Harvard University Press, 1938), pp. 172-173.

6 Ordway Tead, *The Art of Administration* (New York: McGraw-Hill, 1951), pp. 126-127.

7 Learned, Ulrich, and Booz, *Executive Action,* pp. 202-212, *passim.*

when a newly installed purchasing vice president at headquarters failed to understand what is involved in authority and in human relations.[8] He was a new man whom the field people had never met. When he decided to make some immediate and drastic changes, his associates at headquarters advised him to discuss his plans with those affected before the written orders took final form, but he ignored the advice and sent out the formal order: "Hereafter, each of the purchasing executives in the several plants of the company will notify the vice-president in charge of purchasing of all contracts in excess of $10,000 which they are negotiating at least a week in advance of the date on which they are to be signed."

What followed is described as a sit-down strike. The plant purchasing agents did not protest the order, they simply ignored it. Doubtless supported by the plant managers, they considered this unilateral statement of new relationships as wholly inadequate to the needs of the plants. They realized that the new vice president could never do the job alone and that furthermore, he could not afford to fire them because he needed their knowledge of the company, their understanding of their jobs, and their experience of working together. Being a new man with a single intent, he had overlooked the fact that people have feelings, knowledge, and a set of informal relationships on the job that form the core of the organization and that even an official dare not disregard. Authority carries conviction only when backed by the assent of those on the receiving end; no one can beat the organization if it has made up its collective mind to resist.

### Winning Acceptance for Organization Goals

This case and many like it lead directly to the central problem of leadership: How does the administrator gain acceptance for the objectives of his program? By what means can he persuade his employees to want to do what he wants to do? How is loyalty assured? How can employees be stimulated to put loyalty to the program above their own self-interest?

The dream of every adimnistrator, says Tead, is total mobilization of total ability for total achievement of a unanimously accepted goal, but such a dream is seldom realized. Most people have a two-way interest, "in their integrity or selfhood, and in their effective relation to the total surroundings." If they can merge their personal interest and their job interest, a synthesis is largely achieved. Actually, most people would make this synthesis if they could because human nature "is never a fixed bundle of separately identifiable components"; people usually act as wholes in whole situations. In addition, people like "to go *all out*

---

[8] *Ibid.*, pp. 15-18.

for some socially justified project, if only the situation is deemed propitious." The difficulty is to shape the situation so as to make it an appealing one for everyone concerned.[9]

Following this line of reasoning, Tead concludes that there may in fact be "conditions and terms under which individuals might measurably 'lose themselves' in loyalty to the organization" for which they work. The question is whether modern executives, guided by the precepts of psychology and institutional dynamics, are willing to pay the price in reconstituted morale-building policies to make this loyalty possible. Chester Barnard describes this sense of dedication as "communion," a concept "related to social compatibility, but . . . essentially different. It is the feeling of personal comfort in social relations that is sometimes called solidarity, the gregarious instinct, or social security. . . . It is the opportunity for comradeship, for mutual support in personal attitudes." [10]

Tead identifies six aims of organization: the legal, functional, technical, profit-making, personal, and public. The legal aim is to conform to whatever laws affect the enterprise and is considerably less prominent in business than in government where the administrator's mandate is specifically defined by the legislature. The functional aim is the manner in which each employee's work fits into the over-all pattern of the undertaking. The technical aim is good workmanship, or pride of craftsmanship. Profit making is not always an aim in public administration, but its equivalent is an effective public program or service. The personal aim is the opportunity for individual development compatible with the goals of the enterprise. And finally, the public aim is to contribute to the public welfare or at least to operate in a manner that the public approves.

Are these aims proved sound simply because employees accept them? Certainly not, replies Tead; acceptance merely means that one test of fitness has been met. Furthermore, acceptance may be negative, as when accompanied by a shrug of the shoulders or considered the lesser evil. But when acceptance is positive, the result will be a dynamic attitude toward the program instead of a passive one, plus an increased self-respect on the part of all who participate in the program. When these two conditions have been met, the administrator has won a long step toward his objective, although the final test of policy, of course, is acceptance by the public for whom the program was designed in the first place.

A central truth of psychology, continues Tead, is that a person puts

9 Tead, *op. cit.*, pp. 34, 43, 45, 46.
10 Barnard, *op. cit.*, p. 148. In his use of the term "social security" he refers, of course, to a feeling of security and not to the system of insurance that goes under that name.

forth his best efforts under conditions that he has helped to determine
and that satisfy his need for self-expression and growth. It is for this
reason that democratic administration, in which all participate under
the kind of leadership that exists at all levels is patently superior to
authoritarian administration. In both cases the executive leader is concerned with getting the job done quickly and economically; the difference is that democratic administration is also concerned with *how* the
job is done on a long-run basis and whether it is done to the satisfaction
of all who are party to it.

## *Job Analysis*

Once the objectives of the program are set and accepted, the next step
is to assure teamwork within the organization so as to attain them. To
this end the functions of every employee must be analyzed so as to
apportion the work in a rational manner; then an effective communication system must be installed so that signals may flow easily throughout
the institution. When these steps are pushed to their conclusion they
lead to delegation, supervision, coordination, and control, the subjects
of later chapters.

It bears repeating that administration is partly a matter of carefully
dividing the work of an agency according to functions and specialties,
and then just as carefully bringing it all together again to form a balanced whole, a unity based on a rational pattern. The larger the organization, furthermore, the greater is the need for this kind of analysis and
synthesis. Lawrence A. Appley, a leader in the American management
movement, first came into prominence when as a young man he introduced a job-analysis method in one of the big oil companies. It was
once thought that while lower-paid routine jobs could be analyzed,
higher administrative positions could not, but Appley disagreed with
this view, advocated job analysis at all levels from the top down, and
argued that the difficulties involved were no reason for not making the
attempt.

Job analysis on this broad scale, said Appley, would clarify goals
and functions for every executive position, would uncover duplications
and gaps, and would show up the points of friction that always exist. It
would be a little like psychoanalysis: an attempt to make plain what
was little understood so that integration might take the place of confusion. At first, under the Appley plan, top executives were reluctant to
set forth exactly what they did with their time and who did what and
why, but once they got used to the idea they found the system paid off
with greater effectiveness and a tighter organization.[11]

---

11 Among Appley's articles, see especially: "Executive Practices in the Field of Human Resources," Bulletin No. 12, Industrial Relations Section, California Institute

Job analysis consists in carefully studying every job and then laying all job descriptions side by side to see how the flow of work really occurs. As a tool of executive leadership the function is a continuing, inside responsibility of management and should not be delegated to outside consultants. Its most effective use, furthermore, is in conjunction with other aspects of administration. Joined with planning and the determination of objectives, for example, job analysis is a tool of organization and reorganization, identifying jobs and making it possible to regroup them as desired. In the delegation of responsibility and authority, it shows where such devolutions may logically be made. In personnel administration it shows who is falling down on the job and why. It shows where official relationships within the organization are arbitrary and where they are rational, and may even help to resolve personality conflicts.

One thing that job analysis cannot do, however, is to describe the informal social situations that exist within, and are at least as important as, the framework of formal organization. To illustrate, Chester Barnard supposes that the entire top management of a corporation is wiped out, with the exception of the president who becomes the nucleus of a new organization. How long could such a newly installed team function? Not more than twelve hours, says Barnard, the reason being that despite their technical competence they would not be accustomed to working together as a team. They would be unfamiliar with the local situation, they would have difficulty in understanding each other and being understood by their employees. As a team they would lack the qualities of a smoothly working social group within the formal organization.[12]

The importance of these factors is one reason that drastic reorganizations—such as governments seem prone to make—may entail losses in teamwork and morale that are not immediately apparent and not easily measurable. When government agencies are shifted around and functions, along with their personnel, are pruned off or transplanted, the damage to morale and loyalty and dedication to the job may last a long time. Reorganization may be and often is desirable, and job analysis is essential to it, but job analysis can never show more than a part of what needs to be done. The social aspects of the situation are controlling and so far, at least, no useful technique for describing them has been developed.

of Technology, April 4, 1946; "Factors in Modern Organization Development," *Personnel*, XV (November 1938), p. 49; and "What's New in Training Technique?", Personnel Series No. 24, American Management Association, 1936.
[12] Chester Barnard, *Organization and Management* (Cambridge, Mass.: Harvard University Press, 1949), pp. 201-202.

## Communication in Leadership

Because communication is a dominant factor in the life of complex institutions, a main function of leadership is to remain at the center of a system of signals that run throughout the organizational structure. Signals going down the circuit are conventionally called instructions and those coming up are advice, but this formal description is not the whole of the matter. Certain informal systems of communication—notably the grapevine—may be even more useful than formal instructions and advice so far as the links between an executive and his employees and subordinates are concerned. What travels by the grapevine may be true or false, but the system itself touches nearly everyone in the organization. Indeed, ways are currently being developed by which it may be used by management to test employee reactions to a proposed policy, and as a kind of pulse by which to gauge employee morale in general.

Furthermore, it has been shown that authority springs more from particular functions than it does from particular positions in the hierarchy, the top position included. The authority of the top man depends a good deal on the degree to which he is functionally active in the organization, and he cannot be active without an effective communication system by which to make himself known. Such a system is the link between him and the various sites of delegated authority in the middle range of the organization where most managerial duties center; it is also the link to organized labor.

In addition, of course, a proper communication system is the basis for coordination within the organization. It also helps to neutralize the harmful effects of bureaucracy by mitigating somewhat the impersonal relationships that characterize large enterprise, for it is partly through communication that people may be kept human in an institutional setting. And finally, communication helps to determine the administrator's span of control. Span of control is the number of units or subordinates that an administrator can personally direct before the law of diminishing returns operates; that is, direction takes so much time that other responsibilities suffer. Where does this point arise? It depends in part, of course, on individual abilities and the nature of the work, but a properly sensitive communication system will make possible a larger span of control than a poor one will.

Public administrators have been slower to appreciate the importance of communication than businessmen and students of politics.[13]

---

[13] Herbert A. Simon et al., *Public Administration* (New York: Alfred A. Knopf, Inc., 1950), chap. 10, "Securing Teamwork: The Communication Process," with bibliography on pp. 572-574. See also John J. Corson, "The Role of Communication in the Process of Administration," *Public Administration Review*, IV (Winter

Possibly because he was in the communications industry for most of his life, Chester Barnard developed an interesting administrative theory centering on the concept of communication. More than anything else, said Barnard, communication determines how much authority a leader shall exercise. Consequently, communication must be effective and he suggests several rules to that end: The channels of communication must be definitely known; there must be a formal channel of communication to every member of the organization; it must be as direct and as short as possible; the lines of communication should generally be respected (procedure through channels); those who serve as communication centers (officers, supervisors) must be competent; lines of communication should not be interrupted during the operation of a distinct phase of work; and every communication must be authenticated.

These rules are based on the assumption that there are two kinds of equally influential authority in administration, one of position and the other of competence or leadership. "When the authority of leadership is combined with the authority of position," says Barnard, "men who have an established connection with an organization generally will grant [the existence of] authority, accepting orders from outside the zone of indifference. The confidence engendered may even make compliance an inducement in itself." [14] In this synthesis is found the reconciliation of the military type of leadership emphasizing position and structure, and the more democratic kind of leadership so effectively developed in the writings of Ordway Tead.

A final point on the subject of communication is the importance of language. Leadership becomes possible when a man's subordinates can say, He speaks our language, and it is not likely to be effective when the opposite is true. No matter what the reason for the appeal or the kind of group to which it is made, or whether the direction is upward or downward in the organization, the language must be a common one. Because most leaders have always known this, it is only the refinements of the theory that are new, together with the recognition that the influence of leadership is a two-way process. The language difficulty is more prevalent than many administrators realize. Other blocks to easy communication include a failure to recognize the existence of social relationships, the kind of emphasis on prestige that intimidates subordinates, confusion as to context, an atmosphere that is not free and open, and the administrator's failure to catch latent meanings, for these are the things that make the language a common one.

1944), pp. 7-15, and by the same author, "Weak Links in the Chain of Command," *Public Opinion Quarterly,* IX (Fall 1945), pp. 346-349. See also Marshall E. Dimock, *The Executive in Action,* chap. 13.

[14] *The Functions of the Executive,* p. 174.

## Functions and Skills of Executive Leadership

It has been emphasized here that leadership is not simply what comes from the front office; rather, leadership is the spirited and effective effort of every member of the organization according to the range of his authority and responsibility, and it extends clear down to the working level. Leadership is "something more than the personality and methods of individual leaders"; instead, "the patterns include the whole hierarchical system of leadership from top to bottom and all the collateral branches and they encompass leadership in work, recreation, religion and informal groups as well as local and national government. Also included are the acts and attitudes that the people expect the leaders to have and the forms of communication in both directions between the leaders and followers." [15]

In a small agency the framework of leadership may be a simple one, but with each addition to the size of the organization the setting rapidly becomes complicated. In business enterprise it is customary to distinguish top, middle, and shop management as three separate levels of administrative leadership and coordination. In government the anatomy is somewhat different, the levels being those of the chief executive, the department, the bureau, and the section. Disregarding the position of the chief executive in government, the departmental level is the equivalent of top management in industry, the bureau is comparable to middle management, and the section to the shop, with the section chief and the shop foreman being virtual equals as to rank. But this threefold classification is susceptible of even more subdivision because leadership appears also in every office, staff agency, and subunit all along the line. A distinction is also made between the central office at headquarters and offices in the field, and when government agencies or business concerns become large, most of their employees are located in the field. Like the living cell, institutions also multiply, and with every increase in size and complexity, additional levels of coordination and leadership commonly appear.

Are there any duties and traits shared at all the various levels of leadership? The function is so personal an art that no general classification of requisites is possible. Nevertheless, some authoritative descriptions have appeared and a comparison of them will help to round out an understanding of the role of the executive.

The requirements of executive leadership grow out of the situation in which the executive finds himself, and no two situations are exactly

---

15 Alexander Leighton, *The Governing of Men* (Princeton, N.J.: Princeton University Press, 1945), p. 335.

alike. In general, the higher a man's job in the hierarchy, the less is he concerned with detail, the more he delegates, and the more he deals with policies, groups, and public relations. The reverse also is true, so that the lower the position in the hierarchy, the more detailed is the administrator's work and the more he handles concrete situations and problems of direct operation.

Also, some factors and considerations are common at all levels of leadership. Some differences are merely in the degree of attention paid to the same elements of policy, organization, method, human relations, technical skills, and public relations. At the highest level of leadership, certain factors of personality and character also are usual. Thus a study of thirty-three of the nation's top executive leaders in business showed that as a group they had demonstrated future leadership qualities during their formative years, having been class presidents, fraternity officers, school paper editors, and the like; at the same time they were good students of better than average intelligence. Today these man enjoy outside activities in athletic, social, and literary fields, they like people and know how to get along with them, and they love their work.[16]

Not all successful executives possess these qualities, to be sure, nor are all of them fully conscious of the priorities of their job. For the most part, top business executives are preoccupied with keeping the business alive, meeting competition, and making a profit, and only thereafter do they think of relating the business to its environment, which is public relations. Consequently most businessmen have too little time for a third area, which is human relations and planning.[17] In many cases it would be better for the enterprise if the priorities were reversed, because top business leaders are wasting their time when they devote too much of it to detailed operations. With proper delegation and teamwork these could be taken care of and the administrator's time freed for the kind of work for which he is primarily responsible.

In Barnard's opinion the three main executive functions are to maintain communications in the organization, to secure essential services from individuals, and to formulate purposes and objectives.[18] The active qualities of the good leader, he says, are vitality and endurance, a sense of moral responsibility, intellectual capacity, persuasiveness, and an intuitive propensity. To these might be added the qualities of drive, a sense of strategy, political sense, a sense of composure, the ability to evaluate people, a sense of fairness, and good judgment. In the education of future executives, Barnard would include the stimulation

---

16 Robert M. Wald and R. A. Doty, "The Top Executive—A First Hand Profile," *Harvard Business Review*, XXXII (July 1954), pp. 45-55.
17 A conclusion confirmed by Learned, Ulrich, and Booz, *op. cit.*, pp. 8-9.
18 *Op. cit.*, pp. 217-234, 289.

of broad interests, the cultivation of a wide imagination and understanding, the training of superior intellectual capacities, a rigorous
training in subjects that are intellectually difficult but which require a
deep understanding of human relations, and finally, an appreciation
of the importance of persuasion in human affairs.[19]

Because of the nature of the situation in which the administrator is
involved, his primary tool must be "a skill of communication." Thus,
he must be able to deal "with many groups with different points of view,
with many unique individuals whose perceptions of the situation are
different, as he administers not only the situation as he sees it but the
many different perceptions of it." [20] This is the skill of human relations
which Elton Mayo called "the capacity of an individual to communicate his feelings and ideas to another as well as his capacity to respond
to the feelings and ideas of others in such fashion as to promote cooperation and congenial participation in a common task." [21] To Roethlisberger, this is the most important part of the executive's job because
"all the problems of securing the understanding and cooperation of
people depend upon it."

A synthesis of many of these functions and skills is offered by Robert L. Katz, who classifies the three basic administrative skills as technical, human, and conceptual. In this context, technical skill implies competence in an activity having to do with methods, processes, procedures,
and techniques, and relating generally to things rather than to people.
This kind of skill is more often important at the lower levels of administration and becomes less needed (provided subordinates have it, of
course) until, at the top, technical skill may be almost nonexistent and
the program will not be harmed.

Human skill, on the other hand, is the ability to work in and with
groups and "to build coordinative effort within the team" of which
the administrator is the leader. This skill is especially important at the
middle and lower levels of an enterprise where the contacts between
administrators and subordinates are greatest. In contrast to the technical skill, the human skill is needed at every level, but it becomes proportionately less necessary than the conceptual skill at the highest levels.

Conceptual skill is the ability to see the enterprise as a whole, to
recognize the interdependence of its functions and the fact that changes
in any part affect all the others, and to visualize the relationships of
the program "to the industry, the community, and the political, social,
and economic forces of the nation as a whole." Conceptual skills be-

19 Barnard, *Organization and Management,* pp. 92-96, 195-204.
20 F. J. Roethlisberger, "The Territory and Skill of the Administrator," *Michigan
Business Review,* VI (November 1954), pp. 1-9.
21 Elton Mayo, *The Social Problems of an Industrial Civilization* (Cambridge, Mass.:
Harvard University Press, 1945), pp. 13-22.

come increasingly important at the higher levels; at the top it "becomes the most important ability of all." [22]

Taking all kinds of administrative situations into account, probably there is no one type of personality that is best suited to positions of leadership, for it takes all kinds of people to do the work of the world. Some leaders are mean and others generous, some introverted and others extroverted, some Republicans and some Democrats.[23] Nevertheless, the requirements of most institutional situations make certain qualities indispensable. Because teamwork is replacing one-man rule, technology requiring specialization, and delegation superseding centralization, the qualities of leadership needed today have been modified from those of the general handing down orders to those of the chairman of a committee trying to get his group to work together with mutual tolerance and understanding. In this case success may be described in terms used by the late Bernard De Voto in recounting an experience he had when watching a group of firefighters about to jump from a plane into a burning forest area, according to a plan that had been worked out cooperatively among several organizations with great patience and skill: "Suddenly," said De Voto, "it was one of those moments charged with tension and a kind of beauty when the thinking, planning, and skill of many men come together for a single, irrevocable act. For that moment there are no individuals but a joint personality making a joint effort. Spotter, jumpers, pilot, training, equipment, experience—it was the instant of total commitment." [24]

------

[22] Robert L. Katz, "Executive Skills—What Makes a Good Administrator?", pamphlet (Hanover, N.H., 1954).

[23] For an amusing summary, see Learned, Ulrich, and Booz, *op. cit.*, p. 67.

[24] Bernard De Voto, "The Smokejumpers," *Harper's Magazine,* CCIII (November 1951), p. 59.

## BIBLIOGRAPHY AND CASES

### Annotated Reading Suggestions

One of the best of the monographs written for the first Hoover Commission was called **Departmental Management,** Task Force Report, Appendix E (Government Printing Office, January 1949), and although it is only fifty-nine pages long it packs a wealth of information. In this connection, see also the Commission's summary report, **General Management of the Executive Branch** (February 1949), the first half of which deals with the Executive Office of the President and the second half with departmental management. In briefer compass, consult Frederick J. Lawton, "The Role of the Administrator in the Federal Government," *Public Administration Review*, 14 (Spring 1954). Earlier, Arthur W. Macmahon and John D. Millett had dealt analytically and biographically with bureau leadership in *Federal Administrators* (Columbia University Press, 1939), and Macmahon had dealt with *Departmental Management* in the report of the Brownlow committee in 1937. Millett also has an article entitled, "Purpose and Organization of Departmental Management" in Dwight Waldo, ed., *Ideas and Issues in Public Administration* (McGraw-Hill, 1953).

Among the best articles on executive responsibilities, high place must be given to the following: Paul H. Appleby, "Organizing Around the Head of a Large Department," *Public Administration Review*, 6 (Summer 1946); C. Herman Pritchett, "The Postmaster General and Departmental Management," *Public Administration Review*, 6 (Spring 1946); Dwight Waldo and William Pincus, "The Statutory Obligations of the President: Executive Necessity and Administrative Burden," *Public Administration Review*, 6 (Autumn 1946); and John W. Masland, "The Secretariat of the United Nations," *Public Administration Review*, 5 (Autumn 1945).

In 1956 the editors of *Fortune* published a book called *The Executive Life*, which gives a good deal of interesting information about the characteristics of executives and what is expected of them. Ordway Tead, *The Art of Leadership* (McGraw-Hill, 1935), although written in 1932, has few peers even today.

## Case Studies

A book of cases on executive work in business is that of J. D. Glover and R. M. Hower, *The Administrator: Cases on Human Relations in Business* (rev. ed., Irwin, 1952).

In the Stein *Case Book, Gotham in the Air Age* is the story of the efforts made by the mayor and his administration over a period of years to solve the international airport problem in the New York metropolitan region. The study was written by Herbert Kaufman in 1950 and revised in 1952; it is a relatively long case, fifty-one pages, but a careful reading well repays the effort.

Other cases in the ICP series illustrate a variety of executive problems. No. 49, *Seattle Seeks a Tax,* by R. L. Peabody, twenty pages, is the familiar story of local governments' problem of finding sufficient sources of revenue. No. 77, *Florida Milk Commission Changes Minimum Prices,* contributed by H. Zeigler, thirty-one pages, is an interesting story of Governor Collins' attempt to regulate the milk business, which came to involve not only interests but also organization. And finally, No. 36, *Appointed by the Mayor,* by W. N. Kinnard, involves not only executive power but also personnel administration.

# 13

# Organization
# as a Tool
# of Management

ORGANIZATION IS THE basic tool by means of which the administrative process is kept operating, and hence everything done by the administrator involves a knowledge of organizational theory. In practice and theory alike, no element of administration is more essential than another to a smoothly functioning program. Organization is at least as essential as the other elements that have already been discussed: law, policy, planning, budgeting, and leadership, to mention only a few. Organization is equally central to other areas that have not yet been systematically taken up: the human element, motivation, coordination, control, and public relations among others.

Even with top quality leadership, administrators are frustrated and defeated if the organizational mechanism will not allow their energies to be freely given and coordinated. It is partly for these reasons that of all the elements of administration, organizational theory has been more intensively delved into than any other since the time of Frederick W. Taylor and the scientific management movement.

## The Scope of This Chapter

There are two principal ways in which organization is customarily considered. The first is to deal with it as a scientific study in the manner of

March and Simon, for example.[1] Here the attempt is to develop "models," or ideal types, along with hypotheses capable of some degree of verification. Like any cognitive or logical exercise for purposes of academic analysis, under this approach organization must be considered taxonomically and more or less in logical isolation. The second, more common method is to consider organization empirically, that is, as a practical matter closely related to everything the administrator does, to draw upon experience gained through trial and error plus accumulated insights and wisdom.

Since the present book deals with what the administrator needs to know, the latter approach is stressed more than the former, although it must be remembered that no sharp dividing line can be drawn between the theoretical and the practical aspects of the matter because all administration relies upon theory as well as on practice. Consequently both sources of knowledge must be drawn upon by the administrator who would improve his performance.

As the title of this chapter suggests, the tendency must be resisted to consider organization as an end instead of the means to an end, a clear and present danger if the logician's model building in isolation is taken too seriously. Being honest scientists, March and Simon are aware of this problem when they comment, "As is often the case, common sense appears to be more relevant to the real-world phenomena than do the models." [2]

Shall we speak here of principles or of hypotheses? It is a good question. What March and Simon refer to as "classical" theory has often used the term "principle" on the ground that vast amounts of practical experience are at least as reliable a guide to truth as academically isolated hypotheses. Hence a reference to "principles of organization" simply means that working hypotheses have been empirically tested for so long and in such a variety of situations that administrators now believe them to be valid. There is no claim to finality, of course, nor any denial of exceptions to the rule, nor of the need for further refinement. It is simply that practice, trial and error, and wide experience dispose practicing administrators to accept particular cause-and-effect propositions as valid.[3]

---

1 James G. March and Herbert A. Simon, *Organizations* (New York: John Wiley & Sons, Inc., 1958).

2 *Ibid.*, p. 26.

3 Anyone interested in the history of organizational theory can easily arrange his own excursus, starting perhaps with James D. Mooney and Alan C. Reiley, *The Principles of Organization* (New York: Harper & Row, Publishers, 1939), or Luther H. Gulick and L. Urwick, eds., *Papers on the Science of Administration* (New York: Institute of Public Administration, 1937), and including more recent treatments such as those of John M. Pfiffner and Frank P. Sherwood, *Administrative Organization* (Englewood Cliffs, N.J.: Prentice-Hall, 1960), or March and Simon, *Organizations*, where the sociological and behavioral aspects are brought out more than in the past.

Organization has so many uses that the concept is hard to define in a single statement. Basically, organization is structural arrangements developed for the purpose of achieving consciously held group objectives. But even this attempt at definition has at least three defects: first, it may define formal organization but it neglects the informal aspects of the matter which may be just as important, or at the very least, coordinate. Second, the definition suggests a static situation, whereas the practical administrator knows that organization is a dynamic, constantly changing process, and that furthermore it is only one of a number of variables that must be synchronized and coalesced. And finally, it gives insufficient weight to the role of the individual, to personality, and to human motivation and incentives.

It may be more fruitful to stress the purposes of organization in order to arrive at a proper definition, but even here there is the possibility that some important ones will be omitted. As a starter,

*The social utility test:* organization is the anatomy and physiology of administration through which behavior aimed at satisfying human needs is channeled.

*The sociological test:* organization is the means by which roles are assigned in an enterprise involving teamwork.

*The engineering test:* organization results from the need to arrange specialized skills and processes in logical order for purposes of planning, operations, and coordination.

*The political economy test:* organization is the structural means by which the work of the world gets done, through governing and serving institutions, in a society where technology brings continual change.

*The psychological, human relations test:* organization is group effort responding to the human needs and motivations of participants in a common enterprise in order that they may find release and self-fulfilment.

Additional tests might be mentioned,[4] but perhaps enough has been said to show the range and importance of the subject.

In what follows, organizational theory is viewed primarily from the standpoint of its dynamic qualities. Organization is a tool of many uses; it frequently becomes unrealistic when considered in isolation; the practical administrator considers it simultaneously with other crucial factors such as goals, plans, policies, budgets, programs, personnel, leadership, delegation, coordination, supervision, control, and external

---

[4] Herbert A. Simon mentions five main purposes of organization: to divide work among its members, establish standard practices, transmit authoritative decisions, provide a communication system, and train and indoctrinate its members.—*Administrative Behavior* (New York: The Macmillan Company, 1947), pp. 102-103.

relations. An organization that cannot adjust to change is threatened with extinction, so rapidly do custom and conditions alter. On the other side, an organization without stability or principle is in equally bad shape because it leads only to confusion and frustration. Although organization is no sacred cow, it can never be neglected. Few organization analysts, expert though they be in their own area, can be the judge of every factor the operating executive must weigh in the balance when he decides future organizational policy.

## Common Sense Rules of Organization

In organizational theory, a particular rule or generalization will sometimes run afoul of an equally legitimate rule if both are applied indiscriminately instead of in proper context. For example, division of labor is generally necessary and proper but when carried too far it can create a problem of coordination verging on anarchy. By the same token, coordination is necessary and proper but when carried too far it can stifle freedom and initiative. Hence a fundamental rule of organization is balance, which depends on the law of the situation, that is, what is required in the particular time, place, and dominant conditions.

Similarly, too little organization or the wrong kind of organization can actually create disorganization along with debilitation of effort. By the same token, too much organization may destroy freedom, initiative, and employee morale. In order to get a little closer to the matter, some of the major areas of policy and decision making in organizational theory may be examined. This will show the strengths and weaknesses of various assumptions.

**Specialization and Division of Labor.**   It has long been recognized in economics, engineering, and other areas that division of labor is a social asset, the means to competence and depth; that specialization is necessary to the survival of the species and the advancement of human skills in the mastery of the environment. Applying this concept in organizational theory, several rules appear:

Thus, other things being equal, a unifunctional, single-purpose organization is easier to run than a multifunctional one for several reasons: a greater concentration is possible; a wider visibility exists both as to workers and the public; and people identify more easily with a single purpose than with several, and hence cooperation and morale are higher.

However, government is notoriously multifunctional, and as industrial size and diversification increase, business also is becoming increasingly so. In both areas, therefore, a conflict of values and interests is steadily growing. Even when the principle of specialization is applied to a single enterprise—say, the Department of Health, Education, and Welfare—how is one to determine, except in the most general terms, what constitutes a distinct function? Despite every effort to build clear boundaries, even a major grouping of activities will have many fields of gray and overlappings among programs.

Organizational theorists generally agree that programs should be developed around major purposes, activities, and functions. The rule is doubtless a sound one but when carried too far and not balanced with other equally important considerations, many unfortunate side effects will inevitably appear.

**Functionalization of Roles.**  Another rule deriving from the principle of specialization holds that within a single-purpose program, roles should be divided in such a way as to safeguard specialization. For example, all planners, finance men, lawyers, engineers, and other such experts, if sufficiently numerous within the agency, should be separately grouped according to their functions in the vertical pattern of the organization. Thus, a finance man should report to another finance man, an engineer to another engineer, and so on up the line, the underlying idea being that if like is associated with like, the specialized results are better than if like is associated with unlike.

But when does a particular role become sufficiently important to be accorded a distinct status? There is the danger of winding up with so many vertical functions that the problem of coordinating and teaching them to work together becomes highly complicated. The problem is intensified when, especially in large organizations, too much specialization tends toward isolationism and resistance to voluntary cooperation. Here again, the principle of balance must keep within proper bounds the price paid for functionalization.

**Span of Control.**  Another limitation on functionalization is that the more units in an organization an administrator must supervise, the harder it becomes to give adequate attention to all or even to any of them. Because there are outside limits to the range of human attention, organizational theorists have developed span of control as a guiding principle, derived largely from the law of diminishing returns. Up to a certain point, any increase may be beneficial; beyond it, each additional unit may be harmful; and if the process is carried too far, every unit may have less value than it did at the optimum.

Thus it is possible for the principles of specialization and functionalization to run headlong into the principle of span of control, and the pertinent question becomes, What is the number of supervisory units to which effective attention can be given? The answer, of course, differs with the person, the type of undertaking, and possibly other factors as well, so that it is impossible to set an arbitrary figure except in concrete cases. Nevertheless, like other principles, the administrator disregards this one also at his peril.

**Optimum Size.**    Is there an identifiable point at which an undertaking reaches optimum size in terms of ease and efficiency of management, thereafter becoming increasingly hard to handle? Apologists for big business and big government deny that there is. Engineers, on the other hand, do see such a limit. It differs, of course, for various types of undertaking, and since not all the criteria of efficiency can be positively measured, empirical factors and trial and error must be relied upon to some extent.

Having the law of diminishing returns on their side, the engineers would appear to be right. There are instances, therefore, when it would seem better to start a new enterprise, to stop growing, or to encourage competition, rather than to continue to exceed the optimum point of size by too wide a margin.

**Hierarchy in Organization.**    The three dimensions in any organization are the vertical, the horizontal, and the lateral. Hierarchy in organization, or what is sometimes called the scalar principle, applies to the vertical dimension and develops from a combination of specialization and size, both of which are universal variables.

As specialization and size increase and an institution multiplies as to variety of work and number of workers, so also must the levels of organization multiply. At headquarters, for example, there may be a top executive, a second level of department heads and special assistants, a third level of bureau chiefs, even a fourth level of section heads; and in the field there may be regional offices as well as state and district offices. On top of the whole enterprise, in government and business alike, there may be something resembling a holding company apparatus headed by a board or a cabinet, and above that a chief executive.

As already noted, this tendency to proliferate levels of organization is a dominant phenomenon of the times, and the limit may not yet be in sight. For one thing, no natural law seems to limit scalar organization. Size is not inherent in nature but it is subject to human decision. Nevertheless, once size reaches a certain point, the adding of new levels of planning, coordination, and decision making is hard to stop. May this tendency be called a principle, or is it merely a phenomenon? If the former, it is hard to state in precise terms.

In any case, some administrative functions are better performed at one level than at another. Generally speaking, the higher the level, the more must external relations, policy, and long-range planning be emphasized; the lower the level, the more must detailed operations be accentuated. When hierarchy becomes overextended, the lines of communication stretch to the point where the current is lost, human relations are neglected, motivation and morale suffer, pride of craftsmanship and cooperation are harder to secure naturally, and power and bureaucracy create problems that test top managers to the limit.

**Centralization.** About the closest one can come to stating a principle of centralization is to say that those functions should be centralized that can best be handled at the top—planning, external relations, power relationships, research, the quest for consistency, access to large financings, and the like. Thus, centralization inclines toward power and domination.

Decentralization, on the other hand, inclines toward competition and self-determination. Decentralization permits of less standardization and hence allows more variation and experimentation, more freedom to innovate and choose, encourages more self-reliance and a wider scope for initiative, both of which stimulate leadership.

Institutions seem to fluctuate back and forth between centralization and decentralization depending partly on the influence of dominant personalities who incline toward one or the other policy. In any case, equilibrium is seldom reached nor long maintained, if ever it is.

Centralization and decentralization constitute the horizontal dimension of organization, a subject to be dealt with more fully in a later chapter.

**Lateral Relationships.** It should not be thought that the efficiency of an enterprise is determined simply by the vertical and the horizontal dimensions of organization. Indeed, a main source of management improvement is the sidewise or lateral organization that is based largely on informal relations among peers. So important is this aspect of organization that frequently the difference in efficiency between two competing institutions lies at the point where coordination occurs more or less informally within or among departments. A major role of middle management, as Mary Cushing Niles[5] argues, is to see that this kind of coordination takes place. The subject will be further discussed in the chapter dealing with coordination.

**Communications.** A basic requirement of a proper organizational structure is that it facilitate communications and decision making. Not that administration is by any means merely a thinking apparatus or similar to a court of law. Nevertheless, organizations make countless decisions, some large and many small, and everyone destined to become organizationally involved in the result must be brought into the act as early in the planning stage as possible.

---

[5] Mary Cushing Niles, *Middle Management* (New York: Harper & Row, Publishers, 1941).

What kind of organization makes this involvement possible? A committee? Boards of directors are essentially committees and generally speaking they have more to do with the determination of basic policy than any other component of the enterprise. But plainly, a board alone is not enough; administrators at perhaps several subordinate levels also must be consulted. In order that these may be identified, organization must be clear, showing where responsibility resides in specific matters.

In an attempt to be scientific, some positivists, including March and Simon, have assumed that "organization members, and particularly employees, are primarily *passive instruments,* capable of performing work and accepting directions, but not initiating action or exerting influence in any significant way." [6] Clearly, this is a mistaken assumption; organization is a dynamic process in which all key administrators are participants. In the real world, therefore, the only situation in which the *passive instrument* assumption would be valid is under an authoritarian regime where supposedly every decision is made on high and every subordinate is acquiescent. It bears repeating that to assume a static state of affairs in organizational theory is as wrong as a similar assumption in economics.

**Line and Staff.** In their pathbreaking work, *The Principles of Organization,* Mooney and Reiley identify four basic principles of organization, three of which—the functional, the coordinative, and the scalar—have already been dealt with in this chapter. The fourth principle has to do with line and staff relationships. This subject will be dealt with more comprehensively in a later chapter, but a word here will help to round out the present discussion.

As has already been shown, the line is the action, operational, authoritative side of the hierarchy. By contrast, the staff function is concerned with advice, research, ideas, facilitation, and in theory at least relates to the line organization through the endorsement of a line official at the appropriate level where staff work occurs. In other words, the staff official, being only an advisor, supposedly has no independent authority to decide or to act.

This, however, is an oversimplified view of what actually happens, as will later be shown. It need merely be noted here that in fact no sharp dichotomy exists between line and staff, each function is complementary to the other and they are mutually dependent; staff work tends to expand with the size of the undertaking and increased emphasis on rational decision, long-range planning, human relations, and the like; and in consequence, a test of organization is whether the line-staff relationship works as well as it should. It may also be noted that the

---

6 March and Simon, *op. cit.,* p. 6 (italics in the original).

outcome depends far more on attitude and general administrative excellence than on the more limited question of formal structure.

**Unity of Command.**    What does this dual line-staff relationship do to the military, hierarchical type of organization? Nothing injurious, necessarily. It used to be emphatically asserted as a fundamental rule of organization that every employee should have but one superior, that no man can serve two or more masters. But this belief has been modified. Although generally speaking an employee should know who his boss is, nevertheless in modern organization many strategically placed executives constantly deal with several equals or superiors. So long as it is accompanied by understanding and trust and no one is bypassed or undercut for political reasons, this system of collaboration works much better than adherence to formal channels in a rigid hierarchy.

To illustrate: a particular line executive in the field deals in most matters with his superior in the line, but on staff matters pertaining to law, personnel, finance, public relations, purchasing, accounting, and the like he may deal with a different staff official at a higher level than his in each case. The result is many upward lines of communication, all of them touching each other at each level of coordination so that every line official knows what the staff men are doing. This is sometimes called *dual hierarchy:* a man has only one line supervisor but he has a number of staff superiors whom he may consult directly. The arrangement saves time and keeps communication channels from becoming clogged.

**Persons and Organization.**    A final issue will complete this part of the analysis. Should organization and position be defined in the abstract, and individuals of differing experience and characteristics then forced into these preexisting spots, or should formal structure be adjusted to take account of special individual qualifications?

This subject has been endlessly argued by zealous organizational and personnel experts on one side and by operating officials on the other. There is merit, of course, on both sides. An objective of organizational practice is to create as rational a structure as possible. Nevertheless, the talents of key individuals are often so outstanding and distinctive that it pays to adjust organization to them, even if only temporarily, rather than to restrict their scope and effectiveness. As in a housewife, perfectionism in organization also is a dubious quality. In any absolute choice, the betting odds are on the superior individual rather than the perfectly rational organization.

## Forms of Organization

There were once thought to be four main types of organization: line, line and staff, functional, and committee-commission. There was also much debate as to which was best. It is now realized that each type has its special uses, frequently in some kind of combination, and especially in large undertakings.

Generally speaking, however, in both business and government the functional type is now preferred. More than any other, its success depends on subdividing the work of the enterprise, drawing definite lines of demarcation between each sphere of activity, and then just as carefully providing for their coordination. Although functional organization resembles the line and staff type in many ways, responsibility at all levels rests with line officials. For their part, the staff people, instead of remaining wholly outside the line of authority, are brought into the flow of operations and hence have a better chance to apply what they know. Thus, functional organization secures a better balance between specialization and coordination than do its competitors.

It must also be noted, however, that in the right time and place, there is a need in nearly every agency for almost every type of organization, and the most useful structure is therefore a composite one. A line organization, for example, may be enlarged by a staff group in one division, by committees in another, and by a purely functional unit in a third.

Closely related is the matter of the criteria according to which services or functions are grouped. In both business and government, four main bases for this purpose are generally accepted:[7]

1. According to *product* or service, such as water supply, education, highway administration, and so on.

2. According to *clientele*, such as immigrants, veterans, Indians, children, and the like.

3. According to place or *geography*, as in the case of a region, state, or local district.

4. According to *process*, as when a department organized for a particular purpose includes subgroupings for pooled management services such as clerical, finance, personnel, and supply.

As in many other aspects of administration, however, there is no single ideal criterion to suit all occasions and possible situations. The

---

[7] Based on a composite of Luther H. Gulick, "Notes on the Theory of Administration," in Gulick and Urwick, *op. cit.*, pp. 1-45; and William H. Newman, *Administrative Action: The Technique of Organization and Management* (Englewood Cliffs, N.J.: Prentice-Hall, Inc., 1951), pp. 125ff.

most usual pattern is some combination of these four bases, tailored to meet the needs of the particular organization, time, and place.

## Governmental Reorganization

As noted in earlier chapters, some of the main thrusts forward in public administration in the United States have stemmed from comprehensive surveys and reorganizations. There was the reform of municipal government after the turn of the century; then state reorganizations in the 1920s and 1930s; then the survey of the federal government by the Brownlow Committee in 1939; followed by the Hoover Commission studies of 1949 and 1955.

Why do governments—much more than large businesses—seem continually to be surveying and reorganizing themselves? Is it because government is so much in the public eye? Are reorganizations politically inspired? Are they an easier expedient than some alternative remedy, such as a thorough study of policies and planning? Are governments so much less efficient than other organizations that they need constant attention, ranging from mere tinkering to major structural adjustments?

Is it not equally true that constant reorganizations have an unsettling effect and are themselves sometimes the cause of the malaise they supposedly seek to overcome? This has been said, for example, about the State Department which over the last thirty years has many times been "Wristonized." Organizations cannot begin to operate effectively until they get into the groove with established ways of doing things and enjoy a certain degree of mental peace and composure. Then why so much reorganization?

Although these queries underline many truths in the complex matter of reorganization, certain deeper structural factors explain why reorganization is so much in view.

For one thing, the division of labor in government between legislatures and chief executives is not clear. Some areas, such as civil service, the creation of new agencies, budget control, and the like, are a constant battleground on which both sides contend. Some reorganizations seek to bring some order out of this confusion of responsibility.

For another thing, beginning in the 1920s it has come to be recognized that chief executives—especially governors and the President—must have a more rounded responsibility for running the executive branch, and that in order to achieve this the offices in question must be more highly institutionalized. This means the short ballot, appointment instead of election of department heads, the creation of a budget bureau in the office of the chief executive, and the like. Again, many reorganization plans would make these changes possible.

Third, American government is more variegated and illogical than most. At both the state and federal levels there are many virtually independent commissions of one kind or another, most of them dealing with economic matters. There are also many government corporations, modeled after the private corporation, to deal with programs resembling a business operation. Commissioners holding over from a previous regime and corporations run by boards of directors constitute a fourth or "headless" branch of government, sometimes so large and formidable as to create an empire within an empire. The result is to make it hard to integrate the overhead structure of government so as to allow the chief executive to formulate and carry out a policy he can call his own. As he is elected to do this very thing, many attempts at reorganization seek to make it possible.

Then, too, American governments are run largely by pressure groups rather than by political parties whose main concern is merely with candidates. Pressure groups require public programs to be created in the first place and fight to preserve them thereafter. The result is an irrational pattern that reorganizers would redraw in the name of logic and necessity.

In addition, people are increasingly concerned with the burden of taxation and hope that economy and efficiency in government operations might reduce it. Indeed, more reorganizations have been inspired by this objective than by any other.

Also, the second Hoover Commission study dealt largely with issues of *what* the federal government does rather than *how,* and whether certain activities—especially those that might compete with private enterprise in the same field—should continue. Some reorganization studies are favored in the hope that government will wind up doing less than formerly.

Finally, social change affects government more than it does most institutions because old functions expand or are discontinued and many new ones are added according to the social or economic needs of the times. Thus internal integration is a constant problem, and government's organization and methods must periodically be reviewed and restudied. Thomas Jefferson saw this need when he argued that the machinery of government, including the Constitution, should be reviewed at least once in every generation.

On the basis of the foregoing a good case can be made for the periodic reorganization of governments. At all levels the underlying ideas are pretty much alike and may be summarized as follows:

1. The position of the chief executive should be strengthened to enable him to make and enforce government-wide policies for his administration.
2. The chief executive should be provided with better planning and other staff assistance, especially a budget bureau and a department of general administration (although this last is debatable).

3. The load of the chief executive should be reduced by strengthening administration at the departmental level.

4. The number of separate units reporting to the chief executive should be reduced to the point where a workable span of control is achieved.

5. To this end, it becomes necessary to functionalize and integrate. Wrongly placed programs should be reassigned within a logical framework. Regulatory commissions should be made accountable. Detached, virtually independent government corporations should be affiliated with major departments (a move favored by the Brownlow Committee but not by the Hoover Commissions).

6. Personnel management should be strengthened and a career service promoted.

7. Accounting and auditing should be reconsidered: accounting and the preaudit should be made wholly executive functions, with only the postaudit a function of the legislative branch.

8. Archaic laws should be stricken from the books, and obsolete agencies and programs discontinued.

9. Government is the single largest purchaser of supplies and food in the nation and maintains an enormous physical plant scattered in many places; hence an office of general services to serve the entire government is usually recommended.

10. Finally, headquarters-field relationships need to be improved so as to promote decentralized administration while at the same time strengthening accountability.

It will be seen that these aims of reorganization favor a strong governor or President with the operations of government largely revolving around him and his staff apparatus, the main theme being unity and integration.

Some of the results of reorganization have been notable; in other cases progress is exasperatingly slow. Pressure groups and legislative-executive jealousy are obstacles. But because modern government costs so much and public support is increasingly forthcoming—due largely to the dual threat of atomic war and recurring depression—attempts at reorganization are likely to be regarded as more important than ever before. Hence further reform, some of it of a fundamental nature, does seem within the realm of possibility.

## BIBLIOGRAPHY AND CASES

### Annotated Reading Suggestions

One of the best discussions of organizational theory is still that of John M. Gaus in John M. Gaus, Leonard D. White, and Marshall E. Dimock, *The Frontiers of Public Administration* (University of Chicago Press, 1936). This may also be said of Luther H. Gulick's essay, "Notes on a Theory of Organization," in Luther H. Gulick and L. Urwick, eds., *Papers on the Science of Administration* (New York, Institute of Public Administration, 1937). A good chapter length analysis is that of John D. Millett, "Organization as a Technical Problem," in his book, *Management in the Public Service; The Quest for Effective Performance* (McGraw-Hill, 1954), Chapter 7.

Several recent books have attempted to be scientific. Among these may be mentioned John M. Pfiffner and Frank P. Sherwood, *Administrative Organization* (Prentice-Hall, 1960), and James G. March and Herbert A. Simon, *Organizations* (Wiley, 1958).

In his book of readings, *Administration: The Art and Science of Organization and Management* (Knopf, 1949), Albert Lepawsky devotes almost a third of his space to organization (Part II), in which he includes some of the "classics" in the field.

Among the better articles are those by Charles McKinley, "Some 'Principles' of Organization," *Public Administration Review,* 12 (Summer 1952); Philip Selznick, "Foundation of the Theory of Organization," *American Sociological Review,* 13 (February 1948); and articles by Harry A. Hopf and Lounsbury Fish in *Advanced Management,* 11 (June 1946).

Theories of organization and reorganization are dealt with by Louis Brownlow, *A Passion for Anonymity* (University of Chicago Press, 1958); Herbert Emmerich, *Essays on Federal Reorganization* (University of Alabama Press, 1950); President's Committee on Administrative Management, *Report with Special Studies* (Government Printing Office, 1937); Commission on Organization of the Executive Branch of the Government (first Hoover Commission), *General Management of the Executive Branch* (Government Printing Office, 1949); Council of State Governments, *Reorganizing State Governments* (Chicago, 1950); Leslie Lipson, "The Executive Branch in New State Constitutions," *Public Administration Review,* 9 (Winter 1949); Hubert R. Gallagher, "State Reorganization Surveys," *Public Administration Review,* 9 (Autumn 1949); Anonymous, "Summary of the Hoover Commission," *Public Administration Review,* 9 (Spring 1949); James Fesler, "Administrative Literature and the Second Hoover Report," *American Political Science Review,* 51 (March 1957); and William R. Divine, "The Second Hoover Commission Reports: An Analysis," *Public Administration Review,* 15 (Autumn 1955).

There are good chapters on the organizational problems of regulatory commissions and government corporations, by James W. Fesler and V. O. Key, respectively, in F. Morstein Marx, ed., *Elements of Public Administration* (2d ed., Prentice-Hall, 1959). On regulatory administration in particular, see Ferrel Heady, "The New Reform Movement in Regulatory Administration," *Public Administration Review*, 19 (Spring 1959); and on government corporations, Harold Seidman, "The Theory of the Autonomous Government Corporation— A Critical Appraisal," *Public Administration Review*, 12 (Spring 1952).

## Case Studies

One of the most interesting of the cases in the Stein *Case Book* is *The Transfer of the Children's Bureau.* A short case, only twelve pages, it was written by E. Drexel Godfrey, Jr., in 1949 and revised in 1952. Under the transfer order, the Children's Bureau, one of the best managed in Washington, was transferred to the Federal Security Agency (now part of the Department of Health, Education, and Welfare) because it was not "functional" but related, rather, to "clientele."

A second study in the Stein *Case Book* is *The Office of Education Library*, also a short case, eighteen pages. It was prepared by Corinne Silverman in 1950. Are special libraries ever justified, or should they be part of the larger organization of which the specialized unit is a part?

Several other ICP cases have appeared since then. One of the best is No. 14, *Reorganization of the Massachusetts Department of Conservation,* forty-eight pages, contributed by Thomas H. Eliot, now President of Washington University, St. Louis. Another case, No. 75, *Reorganization and Reassignment in the California Highway Patrol,* twenty-three pages, was written by P. O. Foss. A third, also a California case, is No. 32, *Reorganization of the California State Personnel Board,* fifty-six pages, supplied by Frederick C. Mosher. And a fourth, which relates to an intensely interesting subject, is No. 9, *New York City Health Center,* eighteen pages, contributed by H. Kaufman, revised in 1959.

# 14

## Personnel Administration

CHAPTER 3, "A Career in Government" dealt with employment opportunities in government at all levels, the preparation needed for this work, the conditions of employment offered, and the pros and cons of a career in the public service. To continue that discussion, the present chapter is concerned with personnel administration from the standpoint of the operating official.

Public personnel administration is the joint responsibility of line officials plus staff officials called personnel administrators. Ultimate responsibility rests with the line officials, but so important is human relations in the modern world that the job could hardly be done were it not for the special skills brought to it by personnel experts on the staff of the civil service commissions and in operating departments, commissions, corporations, and independent agencies of any size. In the federal government, personnel administration was formerly largely centered in the U. S. Civil Service Commission, but since 1938 it has been decentralized among the operating agencies so that today the personnel function is an integral part of over-all management. Consequently, not only is public personnel administration more effective than formerly, but in addition there are now increased opportunities for men and women who would specialize in this type of work.

It is not intended in this chapter to consider the detailed aspects of personnel administration, which can always be acquired by the future specialist. Rather, the present purpose is to try, from the vantage point of the operating official, to understand the psychology and philosophy of personnel administration as a foundation for dealing with the problems of human relations that are so large a factor in all administration, public and private alike.

## The Human Relations Emphasis

Since the passage of the Pendleton Act of 1883, in terms of prevailing ideas and emphases there have been three main periods in the development of civil service and personnel administration. The first was the fight-the-spoilsman psychology which emphasized purity and policing; the second, which began during the New Deal era of the 1930s, stressed efficiency, getting the most out of public employees; and the third, which began shortly after the end of World War II (from earlier beginnings, however), focused on human relations.[1]

The human relations movement is based on several assumptions: It is *people*, rather than organizations, machines, methods, or things, who are the ultimate source of efficiency. People are smothered and encumbered by an overemphasis on system, formal organization, and procedures. The chief incentive to human efficiency is a high level of motivation, and the condition of maximum motivation is the opportunity for self-growth and self-expression. Accordingly, if large-scale administration is to become both human and efficient there is a great need for research by social psychologists, sociologists, public administrators, and others, in the whole area of motivation and incentives and the psychology and behavior of large organizations. Practicing administrators should welcome these findings as an indispenable part of their resources. Some experts even hold that human relations should become the dominant emphasis, not merely one among many.

There has been adverse reaction to this creedal formulation. It is sometimes criticized as sentimental and softheaded, idealistic and impractical, and antipathetic to practical considerations such as profits, cost acounting, organization, and automation. In short, those who criticize on these grounds tend to regard human relations as the foe of machine progress. Nevertheless, after twenty years of heated debate, the human relations emphasis remains dominant in personnel administration, which indicates some degree of durability. The debate is gradually shifting, however, to the reconciliation of the mutually opposing human and efficiency approaches without either giving ground, a matter with which the operating official must necessarily be concerned.

Is organization the foe of human beings? Potentially, Yes; practically,

---

1 Felix A. Nigro, *Public Personnel Administration* (New York: Holt, Rinehart and Winston, 1959), pp. 1-36.

No, on condition that administrators are clear about what they are doing. But if automation and computers are not to displace personality and the human spirit as the symbols of modern civilization, administrators and personnel experts alike must work even harder at their task than many of them have.[2]

Felix Nigro believes that the human relations movement, growing out of earlier work by Mary Parker Follett, Ordway Tead, and others, has had at least a fivefold impact on personnel administration. Thus it has shown the need for employees to give of their best efforts; it has caused personnel programs to become people-centered; it has recognized the line supervisor rather than the more remote personnel officer as the key man in the equation, because it is the supervisor who deals most intimately with employees and must therefore be expert in human skills; it has given personnel administration a positive emphasis as contrasted with the negative fight-the-spoilsman approach; and finally, it has shown that personnel experts must have as broad a background and experience as the operational administrator, so as to provide the needed insights into human problems and motivation.[3]

The engineer is concerned with production, the personnel expert is more interested in morale, and it is the job of the operating administrator to make both of them possible. The overriding motive in modern personnel administration is morale, the creation of a healthy, dynamic atmosphere in which employees work with satisfaction. Morale, says Alexander Leighton, is "the capacity of a group of people to pull together persistently and consistently in pursuit of a common purpose."[4] As Lord Haldane once remarked—and he was one of Britain's great administrators—the test of all administration is "atmosphere"; you feel it as soon as you step inside an office.

Glenn Stahl, another leading writer on public personnel administration, quotes H. L. Mencken's quip to the effect that "There is always an easy solution to every human problem—neat, plausible, and wrong," which Stahl would apply to most pat ideas of mechanical efficiency and probably also to most notions of employee psychology. He concludes, however, that on the basis of current psychological research into human relations, most employees in large public agencies have certain definite needs if they are to remain satisfied and motivated. At a minimum they must have a sense of security, a sense of success (achievement and recog-

[2] See, for example, Chris Argyris, "The Individual and Organization: An Empirical Test," *Administrative Science Quarterly*, 4 (September 1959), pp. 145-167; E. D. Bakke, *The Fusion Process* (New Haven: Yale University Press, 1955); and Felix Nigro, "The Modern Concept of Personnel Administration," *Public Personnel Administration*, 18 (July 1957), pp. 160-166.

[3] Nigro, *Public Personnel Administration*, pp. 35-36.

[4] Alexander Leighton, "Applied Science in Human Relations," *Personnel Administration* (July 1947), pp. 4-6.

nition), and a sense of belongingness, all of which are probably mutually related in some way.[5] In later chapters these and other motivations are dealt with in more detail.

## The Role of a Personnel Agency

Because the approach to civil service has evolved from a negative to a positive one, the role of the personnel agency in government also has changed. There is no less emphasis on the underlying purpose of the civil service system, which is to make sure that the best qualified person is secured for each job and that he is protected from removal for any but a legitimate reason. But because of the insights into positive motivation, the attitude of personnel agencies has changed from one of watchful suspicion to one of active collaboration with supervisory officials at all levels. In other words, personnel administration has become management-minded to the point where in some governments, personnel officials are at the forefront of dynamic administrative thinking. What is more, they think almost as much about proper organizational practice as they do about personnel practice because in fact, of course, the two are inseparable. How is a particular position to be classified, for example? First, it must be known what the position is intended to accomplish and how it relates to surrounding positions and the mission of the whole enterprise. A skilled personnel official therefore must have the same outlooks, skills, and range of abilities as the operating official who is his opposite number. The only exceptional quality about a personnel administrator is his intense interest in people and what makes them tick.

Nigro defines personnel administration as "the art of selecting new employees and making use of old ones in such manner that the maximum quality and quantity of output and service are obtained from the working force." [6] This a rather "tough" definition of a skill that is people-directed, but perhaps that is just as well.

As early as 1942 Lawrence Appley remarked with prophetic vision that the three most important functions of the staff official in charge of personnel administration include first and foremost the development of *influence and understanding with operating officials* because without this rapport, useful ideas are never applied. His second function is to carry on *research into motivation,* policies, and techniques that will improve motivation and morale and make the work experience a more rewarding one. The third function goes beyond that of a staff official to include certain *operational responsibilities,* as for health, welfare, retirement, and related matters that usually cannot be as efficiently handled by

---

[5] O. Glenn Stahl, *Public Personnel Administration* (4th ed., New York: Harper & Row, Publishers, 1956), p. 248.

[6] *Op. cit.,* p. 36.

line officials or by other staff departments.[7] However, a danger arises just at this point: unless personnel administrators watch themselves, they become so busy with record keeping, social security, and similar detailed concerns that they tend to neglect their most important functions that involve research of a pioneering nature and the formulation of recommendations with regard to policy. When this occurs, however, it is usually the fault of top management because, like any specialist, a personnel man also is largely bounded by his job and needs to be reminded from time to time of the over-all pattern of administration of which that job is a part.

It is not necessary to explore in detail all of the duties of a personnel agency, but the following points are suggestive:[8]

1. *Organization:* Develop within the personnel agency an internal structure in which roles are assigned and high-level policies and recommendations are formulated.

2. *Influence:* Establish constructive programs to improve the human relations skills of supervisory personnel and raise the morale of the undertaking in general.

3. *Research:* Carry out a progressive program to deepen insights into motivation, personality, and manpower utilization.

4. *Recruitment:* Secure the best qualified individuals for every job by means of imaginative and original recruitment techniques in order to match individual skills with organizational needs.

5. *Placement:* Appoint the best fitted candidates to the jobs for which they are best qualified; oversee probationary arrangements; recommend new assignments in the career service.

6. *Positions and salaries:* Clearly describe the work of all positions, from the highest to the lowest; develop a positions classification plan that is broad, systematic, and yet flexible; recommend salary and incentive scales; assure equal pay for equal work.

7. *Training:* Recommend and carry out inservice training programs to improve skills and as a basis for promotions; counsel employees.

8. *Promotions:* Develop a comprehensive promotion plan based on merit and designed to foster a full-fledged career service.

9. *Rating:* Identify the most competent employees by a system that evaluates as accurately as possible individual effectiveness and

[7] Lawrence Appley, "Organizing for Personnel Administration," *Public Personnel Review,* 3 (April 1942), pp. 100-106.
[8] Adapted from Nigro, *op. cit.,* p. 37, and John F. Pfiffner and Robert V. Presthus, *Public Administration* (4th ed., New York: The Ronald Press Company, 1960), p. 266.

growth; utilize individual abilities to the best possible advantage.

10. *Labor relations:* Suggest and assist in the administration of policies and plans for dealing with employee organizations and unions.

11. *Discipline:* Develop policies and techniques for dealing with discipline, suspensions, removals, loyalty, and the like.

12. *Records:* Devise and maintain various kinds of necessary records showing time and payroll, vacation, sick leave, retirement, and similar data.

The difficulty with most personnel staff agencies is not that they have too little work to do but that they will try to do so many things that their highest priorities are neglected. Much of their responsibility is advisory only, of course, with the main burden of administration falling on general management; which makes it all the more important that personnel officials work closely with line officials at all levels.

As indicated in Chapter 3, a major turning point in public personnel administration occurred in 1938 when, on the recommendations of the Brownlow Committee, President Roosevelt provided by executive order for the appointment of personnel administrators in all federal departments and major agencies and as far down the line among subordinate units as the need required. These staff specialists, assisted where necessary by other specialists in the various distinct areas of personnel administration, were to work closely with the line administrators in each agency. The basic principles governing the proper division of personnel functions were these:[9]

Authority for action on matters of personnel administration should be delegated to operating agencies to a degree commensurate with the responsibility vested in them for the execution of their respective programs.

The major functions of a central personnel agency, such as the federal Civil Service Commission (and, it might be added, similar state agencies) should be to develop over-all policies and standards and to assist the operating agencies to apply them, imposing controls only when central review and the rigid maintenance of standards are more important than speed, economy, and the efficiency of the operating agency in getting program results.

The personnel function of an operating agency should be to deter-

---

9 Summarized from the Brownlow Committee's monograph, *Personnel Administration in the Federal Service* by Floyd Reeves and Paul David, in President's Committee on Administrative Management, *Report with Special Studies* (Washington, D.C., 1937).

mine the means of making over-all personnel policies and standards effective and to take final action in applying such standards to specific cases.

This major move toward decentralization stemmed from and in turn strengthened the new philosophy of personnel administration, as a result of which the whole personnel function in the federal government assumed a new prestige. Moreover, because innovation at the federal level often constitutes a model for the states, the influence of the decentralization policy adopted in Washington was eventually felt in the states as well.

Since 1938, therefore, the responsibility for personnel administration within the federal government has been divided between the Civil Service Commission, which sets the standards, and the personnel officers of the departments and agencies that administer them. Both sets of officials collaborate closely in all matters of common concern, with the Commission taking the lead in certain areas of research and policy such as internship programs, manpower utilization, training and executive development, and the like.

The keynote of modern personnel administration was again confirmed, in 1947, in the language of another executive order that stated, "Personnel management is a primary responsibility of all who plan, direct, or supervise the work of . . . employes." [10] In line with this proposition, two important developments took place. First, teams of high officials (undersecretaries and assistant secretaries of the departments) began meeting together to develop a grand strategy for the improvement of personnel administration and to put the whole weight of the executive branch behind it. Secondly, the chairman of the Civil Service Commission became the President's advisor on all personnel matters, an arrangement that was later replaced, however, by the direct appointment in the White House Office of a Special Assistant to the President for Personnel Management whose responsibility included not only civil service matters but also political appointments to policy positions in the government.

## The Training Act of 1958

Also symptomatic of the new approach to public personnel administration is yet another legislative landmark, the Government Employees Training Act of 1958, passed just twenty years after the 1938 decentralization program was initiated. In 1958 Congress declared that "self-education, self-improvement and self-training" by federal employees should be supplemented and extended by continuous government-spon-

---

[10] Executive Order No. 9893, operative May 1, 1947.

sored training, in order to develop skills, areas of knowledge, and abilities. The Civil Service Commission is responsible to the President for government-wide leadership in this area and the head of each department also is responsible to him for the conduct of training. Federal agencies administer their own training programs through the use of their own facilities so far as possible, but if these are inadequate, employees may be assigned for training at agency expense to a nonfederal institution. Areas of employment mentioned in the Act are wide, including personnel in the "scientific, professional, technical, trade, clerical, fiscal, administrative and other fields." However, the law specifically prohibits agencies from assisting an employee to secure an academic degree when it is needed to qualify for an appointment.

The Training Act had an immediate impact, for it obliged departments and agencies to review their training needs, encouraged interagency cooperation for training, increased the government's use of private training facilities, and secured the wide endorsement of training by top management.

An interesting by-product of this training function is that the Civil Service Commission felt obliged to develop a checklist of desirable executive traits in order to have some kind of goal to shoot at. While modestly admitting that no single list of requirements can adequately reflect the diversity of federal executive positions, the Commission finally printed the following:[11]

### GUIDE TO EXECUTIVE SELECTION COMMITTEES
### GENERAL CHECK LIST OF EXECUTIVE QUALIFICATIONS

*Effectiveness with People*

1. Ability to represent his organization effectively at all appropriate levels.
2. Ability to gain the confidence of his superiors.
3. Ability to handle human relations problems so that morale and productivity are improved.
4. Ability to assign employees to jobs so that optimal utilization of employee abilities results.
5. Willingness to accept subordinates who are not "yesmen."
6. Ability to get the full cooperation of other units.
7. Ability to deal effectively even with people who are opposed to him.
8. Ability to get people who work for him to want to do their best.

---

11 *The University-Federal Agency Conference on Career Development,* working papers for meetings held at Princeton University, November 2-4, 1961 (Washington, D.C.: Government Printing Office, 1961), pp. 17-18.

*Decision-Making Ability*

1. Ability to anticipate how people will react to his decisions and proposals.
2. Ability to absorb new data and concepts quickly.
3. Recognizes need to get the facts first before making a decision.
4. Ability to make decisions on the organization of his unit which promotes coordination and efficiency.
5. Willingness to change his program and methods in order to keep up with current needs and developments.
6. Ability to make decisions on technical problems which keep in mind the latest developments.
7. Ability to take a broad-gauged approach to problems.
8. Ability to spot the key parts of complex problems—not get lost on minor points.
9. Effectiveness in thinking of new approaches to problems.

*General Executive Abilities*

1. Ability to delegate effectively.
2. Effectiveness in checking results.
3. Ability to set priorities effectively.
4. Ability to use his manpower effectively.
5. Willingness to correct situations when they need improvement and not wait for an emergency.
6. Ability to plan carefully.
7. Ability to handle effectively the administrative details of day-by-day operations.
8. Effectiveness in presenting budget requests for his unit.
9. Ability to select highly capable subordinates.
10. Ability to relate his work to the work of the whole organization.
11. Ability to take into account the public relations implications of his actions.
12. Ability to handle many different problems at the same time.
13. Ability to work effectively under frustrating conditions.
14. Ability to properly balance interest in details and in broad problems.

*Personal Characteristics*

1. Objectivity in considering divergent and new points of view.
2. Flexibility in his approach to problems.
3. Reliability—you can depend on what he says.
4. Willingness to accept responsibility; doesn't pass the buck.
5. Ability to adjust easily to new situations, problems, and methods.
6. Ability to keep his head in an emergency.

7. Willingness to work to fix things that go wrong instead of making excuses.
8. Willingness to give an honest report on a problem even if it would hurt him personally.

The Civil Service Commission remarked that not only should the answers to these questions provide an interesting profile for self-analysis or for official scrutiny, but that in addition they might indicate certain fundamental, important attributes considered vital in executive jobs, qualities such as broad interests, courage, integrity, the ability to articulate ideas and to innovate.

One of the major long-run results of the training legislation of 1958 is to get executives at all levels to realize the need for continuous career training and to work closely with their professional personnel staff on this and other means to better management practices. Although there are still some sluggish areas where little or nothing has been done, a good deal of progress has been made. In 1961, for example—only three years after the Training Act was passed—some 40 percent of all federal agencies had provided inservice management training for their employees. The materials used were similar to those common in university courses, but in addition included subjects such as statutory authority and major programs, present or proposed new policies, current organizational structure or proposed changes in it, and relations with various publics.[12]

## Problems of Personnel Administration

In personnel administration, certain problems stand out as more vexing than others and, being chiefly of a human kind, cannot be solved merely by adopting a different rule or an alternative procedure. One of these, formerly more in the public eye than at present, is the matter of national security and loyalty. In the federal government, responsibility in this matter rests in the first instance with the Civil Service Commission which, since 1947, checks on the background of all applicants for jobs in certain sensitive federal agencies as well as in international organizations of which the United States is a member. The Commission also makes a continuing study of the administration of the whole employee security program to make sure that the national security is maintained—so far as public employees are concerned—and that all employees under question are treated fairly and their rights protected.

A second special problem relates to corruption and conflict of interest. Irregularities have turned up or been searched out in many places

12 *Ibid.*, p. 36.

at all levels of government. In the federal government, two major instances in 1951 were the Reconstruction Finance Corporation and the Bureau of Internal Revenue; there have been less spectacular examples in connection with the Securities and Exchange Commission, the Federal Power Commission, and others. In the case of the RFC, President Truman abolished the five-man board in favor of a single administrator and charged him with cleaning up the situation. The Bureau of Internal Revenue underwent a thorough housecleaning, more than a hundred employees were fired for unethical practices, and a reorganization of the agency took place in which even its name was changed—it has since been known as the Internal Revenue Service.

A third major problem is not necessarily, but may be related to the matter of corruption among employees in the public service. The problem of conflict of interest is one of long standing and a federal statute on the subject has been in effect for more than a century, although it is often disregarded, especially in time of war. The issue arises most often when businessmen become government executives, either as paid employees of the government or as so-called WOC's (without compensation). It is largely for this reason that during the first few years of the Eisenhower Administration, when many businessmen entered government service as much from a sense of duty as for any other reason, there were a number of cases in which conflict of interest was a factor. Men occupying positions such as consultant to the Bureau of the Budget, the Secretary of the Air Force, an official of the National Production Authority, the Assistant to the President himself, the chairman of the Interstate Commerce Commission, the chairman of the Federal Trade Commission, and the General Services Administrator—to cite only some of the more prominent cases—resigned because it was found that their official and their private interests had come into conflict by reason of being too closely associated in the same person. This problem also appears at all levels of government, especially in the larger cities.

The matter is a hard one to resolve because in most instances there is no intention of wrongdoing. According to William S. White, the general view of the matter seems to be that (1) Businessmen are as honest as any other group in the community, but no more so, and the longer they have been successful in business, the more likely are they to confuse business interest with public interest. (2) Few businessmen in government are out to "turn a fast buck," but nevertheless it is hard for a long-time businessman not to favor instinctively the interests of business over, say, the interests of labor. And (3) in business a man can do things that are considered perfectly proper; but if he did them in government they would be considered highly improper, although entirely within the law.[13] In addition, of course, nearly every aspect of modern government

---

13 *The New York Times,* July 31, 1955.

is woven into the fabric of society more tightly than ever before. Professional men and executives shift back and forth between business, the universities, and public employment, and more persons own stock or participate in small businesses as a sideline, often to supplement low governmental salaries.

By 1955 full-time government employees were required to divest themselves of all outside financial interests that might conflict with their official duties. Those working without compensation were allowed to continue to draw their salaries from their private employment while on loan to the government (generally for short periods only), but were required to file a full statement of their financial condition along with details as to their employers and the companies in which they held stock; in addition, they were prohibited from participating in actual policy decisions. On top of this, outside experts and consultants serving on a per diem basis also were prohibited from participating in policy decisions or from having anything to do in the line of public business with firms with which they had any connection or financial interest. Furthermore, when such men were appointed to government positions, the reasons for choosing them instead of a civil service employee had to be explained and published in the *Federal Register*, thus making the information available to the press and to the public. Finally, a man so appointed was required to publish in the *Federal Register* a full statement of all his business connections.[14] Indeed, so far had regulation gone by the end of 1956 that a group studying how to improve the political management of the federal government concluded that a reexamination of the rules of conflict of interest and the substitution of a code of conduct for the guidance of public employees were essential to assure an adequate supply of political executives to the federal government.[15]

In 1960 a special committee of the New York City Bar Association issued a report on *Conflict of Interest and Federal Service*[16] in which it sought partly to tighten federal regulations by bringing order out of a confusion of seven largely obsolete statutes, and partly to modify the rules in order to make it easier for government to recruit top quality personnel, especially for short-term assignments. The substance of this report was embodied in a bill and President Kennedy supported it with a special message to Congress, but it was not until late in 1962 that the measure passed.

Meanwhile the question of conflict of interest in the area of research

---

14 *Ibid.,* November 29, 1955.

15 A group directed by Stephen K. Bailey at Princeton University, sponsored by the Woodrow Wilson School of Public and International Affairs, reported in *The New York Times,* March 5, 1956.

16 Special Committee on the Federal Conflict of Interest Laws of the Association of the Bar of the City of New York, *Conflict of Interest and Federal Service* (Cambridge, Mass.: Harvard University Press, 1960).

became of special concern to the Pentagon, for potential conflict began to appear between the privileged advisory roles of some directors of government-sponsored corporations and their private business and financial interests. The Defense Department finally ruled that a company serving as a technical adviser in a research program could not later compete in the hardware phase of it.

Perhaps the best analysis of the problem of ethics in government is a study by a subcommittee of the Senate, under the chairmanship of Senator Paul Douglas. The forces that encourage corruption, said the Douglas report,[17] "center chiefly upon a limited area, the area in which government is heavily 'action-laden,' " so to speak. This is the area in which there are "big economic stakes, where the decisions of legislators and administrators directly affect the business, or the property, or the income of particular groups or individuals." Thus the abuses of discretion or the exploitation of power are most serious "where the government is dispensing valuable rights and privileges, constructing extensive public works, spending vast sums for military supplies and equipment, making loans, granting subsidies, levying taxes and regulating the activities of privileged monopolies or economic practices in which there is a public interest."

As for blame, the Douglas report placed it on the executive branch, on Congress, and on the public. "On the record," it said, "we in Congress must also seem unduly complacent. Neither house has acted vigorously to tighten its discipline in moral matters or to raise its ethical standards. In recent years some members have been convicted of crime and sent to prison, but they have not been expelled. Neither house has been particularly diligent in searching out and punishing questionable conduct on the part of its members."[18]

The fact is, continued the report, that no group in society "is in a position to point the finger of scorn at others." Influence peddlers can exist only as long as businessmen or others are willing to patronize them. Favoritism can be a problem only when individual men and women seek special treatment from the government. Gifts, improper pressure, and bribes come from outside the government, "from individuals, from organizations, and from groups which are part of what we call the 'public.' " The morals of officials, said the subcommittee, can be distinguished but "certainly not separated" from the public morals generally, because the moral standards of the country "provide the ethical environment which in turn conditions the standard of behavior of public officials."[19]

17 The substance of this report appears in Paul H. Douglas, *Ethics in Government* (Cambridge: Harvard University Press, 1952).
18 Quoted in *The New York Times,* October 18, 1951.
19 *Ibid.*

A final major problem of public personnel administration concerns political neutrality, if such a thing is possible, on the part of public employees. If civil servants are to administer programs that are political in origin, how can they help being concerned with politics? And if they are to dedicate themselves to the successful carrying out of these programs, why should either party have to tolerate an attitude of indifference as to its objectives? Indifference means listlessness and inefficiency and is partly responsible for the excessive drafts of manpower that government often seems to require.

This issue of neutrality has been debated for many years and the outcome is still unclear. For example, exasperation with all that political neutrality connotes led John Fischer, editor of *Harper's Magazine*, to publish a piece a few years ago entitled "Let's Go Back to the Spoils System." The tested rule of business, argued Fischer, must be more widely adopted in the public service: When you get a good man in a supervisory job he must be free to hire the members of his own staff, assign them the tasks they are best suited to do, and replace them when their work is no longer satisfactory; politics has nothing to do with it.[20]

Prompted by the recommendation of the Brownlow Committee that the civil service system be extended to include all but a few top policy posts reserved for executive appointment, Kenneth C. Cole remarked that advocates of the merit system should either explain how political appointments are to be reconciled with the American party system, or propose a different basis for the party system itself. Moreover, said Cole, if executive responsibility in government is to become a reality, then administrators must be allowed to hire and fire employees as they see fit, checked only by the oversight of the administrators' own official superiors.[21]

In the Hatch Acts of 1939 and 1940 Congress tried among other things to distinguish between public officials who have a political status and are entitled to participate in a political campaign and those who are merely public employees and should remain neutral. In either case, individuals are forbidden by these acts to use their power of office to influence elections; in addition, nonpolitical civil servants are denied "any active part in political management or in political campaigns" and the prohibition extends even to state and local officials paid in part from federal funds.

Prohibited activities include running for national or state office; urging others to become candidates for political office; campaigning; transporting voters to the polls; distributing campaign material; taking part in political parades; selling tickets for political events; signing

20 *Harper's Magazine*, XCCI (October 1945), pp. 362-368.
21 Kenneth C. Cole, "The 'Merit System' Again," *American Political Science Review*, XXI (August 1937), pp. 695-698.

petitions or other documents in favor of or against any party or candidates; and asking for or receiving a political contribution. A federal worker may, however, under certain circumstances, become an independent candidate for local office, but must resign his federal job if he is elected.

Both Hatch Acts have proved hard to enforce and Senator Hatch himself has proposed their repeal. A determination to elude the law is generally successful and the violations that are caught are usually minor ones. Thus, a state director of the Federal Crop Insurance Corporation was once ordered suspended for five months for having spoken in behalf of a certain candidate at a crop insurance meeting. In another instance, thirteen federal tax employees were suspended for periods ranging from three to six months for having sold tickets for the Democratic party's annual Jefferson Day dinner.

Many people think that the Hatch Acts go too far, but attempts to modify them have failed. Public servants constitute a large sector of the electorate and they are generally well informed on public issues. Their opinions as well as their votes are needed. On the other hand, it is clearly improper if they use their public position to coerce votes or contributions from subordinates. A better solution than the Hatch Acts has been developed in New York State where all civil service employees except police commissioners, police officers, members of a police force, and state and local employees covered by the second Hatch Act may legally engage in politics. "I believe that an employee of the state or of any political subdivision of the state," said New York's attorney general in issuing the ruling, "may be a member of a political committee, (1) if his activity in that connection does not occur during the hours in which he is required to perform his duties to the state or a political subdivision of the state, and (2) if he does not use his official connection with the state government in the course of such political activities." [22]

As noted in earlier chapters, politics and policy, interest groups and pressures, accompany public administration from the highest to the lowest offices. If government is to secure persons dedicated to their jobs there would seem to be a prima facie case in favor of appointing qualified supporters of the party in power who have a personal interest in achieving the programs endorsed by the voters. The most ardent reformer must admit that there are meritorious as well as hack supporters of political parties. Furthermore, as Alexander Leighton has pointed out, administrators at all levels, like people everywhere, operate effectively only when they have a belief system to guide and inspire them, and a political faith is part of such a system. Lacking this kind of incentive, the bureaucracy tends to narcissism, to lavish its affections on itself, on the interests of the guild to which it belongs—which, of course, only

[22] *The New York Times*, December 5, 1950.

creates another problem. How, then, is this question of political neutrality to be resolved?

J. Donald Kingsley contends that what may be termed the monastic view of the civil service is, indeed, an erroneous one. The British civil service has never been neutral, and even if it had been, it could hardly have remained so in a period of social change such as the British Labor party inaugurated in 1945. Kingsley argues that in contrast to the relative handful of political appointees at the top stand the 550,000 civil service employees who form the permanent administrative corps and reflect middle-class interests and outlooks. Two thirds of these employees are primarily engaged in operating the social services and enforcing the major regulations and controls of the nation's economic life. Kingsley sees all political institutions—including the structure and personnel of the executive agencies—as inescapably caught up in the struggle for power.[23]

## Leadership at the Top

These major problems of personnel administration lead directly into the question of the kind of leadership that is provided at the top of the governmental structure, because it is through these executives, appointed in part at least for political reasons, that the majority of government employees is directed and the vitality of public programs maintained. The federal government is often charged with wasting manpower, and to the extent that such charges are based on fact and not on prejudice, the reason is lack of adequate leadership to convert potential energy into accomplishment. The first Hoover Commission stressed the leadership factor and the second went even further in making concrete recommendations to fortify leadership in the top ranks of the federal government.

The fact is that the number of policy officials in the federal government is surprisingly small, indeed much smaller than it should be. In 1954 a task force of the second Hoover Commission found 313 federal officials who were agency heads or deputy or assistant heads. Assisted by permanent or career civil servants, these policy officials are supposed to direct the activities of an army of some 2.5 million men and women employed throughout the nation and in many foreign countries. It must also be remembered that so long as the top civil servants below the rank of appointed policy official are supposed to be politically neutral, not much in the way of initiative in the matter of public policy can be expected from them. Moreover, most top policy officials are replaced when party fortunes change, and as noted in the chapter on the career service, even when a party remains in office for two terms, there is much turnover in these positions.

---

23 J. Donald Kingsley, *Representative Bureaucracy: An Interpretation of the British Civil Service* (Yellow Springs, Ohio: The Antioch Press, 1944).

Thus, two pressing problems remain to be solved if leadership at the top is to be encouraged. First, how can politics be made a more acceptable career so that qualified persons will become increasingly available as heads of agencies and departments, undersecretaries, assistant secretaries, and other types of policy official? And second, how can the top positions in the executive career service below the rank of appointed official be made sufficiently attractive to appeal to men and women capable of providing policy leadership and executive initiative? As noted in Chapter 3, the so-called super grades program in the civil career service is an attempt to solve this second problem, and in the end it might help to solve the first one, too.

## BIBLIOGRAPHY AND CASES

### Annotated Reading Suggestions

Personnel administration is a dynamic and rapidly changing field. Unusual importance attaches, therefore, to Cecil E. Goode's book, *Personnel Research Frontiers* (Chicago: Public Personnel Association, 1958). On personnel management as an integral part of general administration, see William B. Parsons, "The Personnel Function in Public Management," *Public Administration Review,* 17 (Summer 1957). The challenge of the human factor to the nonhuman is nowhere better presented than in Chris Argyris, *Personality and Organization* (Harper & Row, 1957). See also Elton Mayo, *The Social Problems of an Industrial Civilization* (Harvard Business School, 1945); Schuyler D. Hoslett, ed., *Human Factors in Management* (Park College Press, 1946); Robert Dubin, ed., *Human Relations in Administration* (Prentice-Hall, 1951); and E. D. Bakke, *The Fusion Process* (Yale University Press, 1955).

Both the Brownlow and the Hoover studies produced some excellent materials on personnel administration. One should start with a provocative essay by Floyd Reeves, "Civil Service as Usual," *Public Administration Review,* 4 (Autumn 1944); it was Reeves who organized the personnel department in TVA. The study that he and Paul David wrote for the Brownlow Committee is called *Personnel Administration in the Federal Service* and is included in the Committee's *Report with Special Studies* (Government Printing Office, 1937).

Between the time that these two surveys were made, John Fischer, editor of *Harper's Magazine,* wrote "Let's Go Back to the Spoils System," which appeared in that magazine, 91 (October 1945); and Henry Hubbard, a prominent personnel administrator in Washington contributed "The Elements of a Comprehensive Personnel Program," *Public Personnel Review,* 1 (July 1940). See also Bernard L. Gladieux, "Civil Service versus Merit," *Public Administration Review,* 12 (Summer 1952); and Robert Ramspeck, "Administrative Flexibility in the Federal Civil Service," *Public Administration Review,* 12 (Autumn 1952).

The task force and Hoover Commission reports on personnel in 1949 and 1955 are outstanding, although the task force report of 1955 has since been widely criticized for not allowing career officials enough scope.

Paul Van Riper, *History of the U. S. Civil Service* (Harper & Row, 1958) has already been mentioned in an earlier chapter but should be consulted here also.

On the future of this interesting and vital field, see Felix Nigro, "The Modern Concept of Personnel Administration," *Public Personnel Administration,* 18 (July 1957); G. Lyle Belsley, *Federal Personnel Management and the Transition* (Chicago: Public Administration Clearing House, 1953); and a symposium on the Federal Service Entrance Examination by Philip Young, Henry Reining, and others in *Public Administration Review,* 16 (Winter 1956).

A complete bibliography on personnel administration is found in Felix Nigro, *Public Personnel Administration* (Holt, Rinehart, and Winston, 1959).

## Case Studies

Reference has already been made in previous chapters to three cases in the Stein collection that illustrate personnel practices: *The Cambridge City Manager, The Foreign Service Act of 1946,* and *The Rural Electrification Personnel Report.* There are a number of other good cases in the ICP series. One of these (unnumbered) is *Smith and the OPA,* which has to do with firing policy. The case was reported by Robert L. Gold in 1950.

Reference has also been made in an earlier chapter to No. 32, *Reorganization of the California State Personnel Board,* by Frederick C. Mosher, which is an outstanding case. Others that also are interesting and colorful are No. 20, *Promotion of Lem Merrill,* fifty-six pages, by C. B. and V. A. Earle, which has to do with a *cause celebre,* the superintendent of streets in Birmingham. See also No. 10, *Displaced Career Employee Program,* forty-two pages, by J. E. Drury, which relates to the cutback problem, one of the most difficult in personnel administration.

No. 31, *Transfer of the Kansas State Civil Service Department,* by P. Bart, illustrates both organizational and personnel problems. And finally, for comparative purposes, there is another British case, *The Posting of Captain Robinson,* in F. M. G. Willson, *Administrators in Action: British Case Studies, Volume 1* (University of Toronto Press, 1961); this has to do with executive officers in the field staff.

# 15

# Supervision
# and Delegation

THE HUMAN RELATIONS philosophy examined in the preceding chapter is the key to better supervision, which is simply another term to describe leadership in the directing function. Personnel administrators are well aware of this fact and make human relations a principal emphasis in their work.

Supervision is closely tied to the delegation of responsibility and the authority to go with it, the purpose being to relieve the executive of that which others can do as well, secure coordination, and strengthen tactical and strategic leadership. Thus in both supervision and delegation, leadership and the human factor are key ingredients.

In any program, supervisors are the closest to employees and, by the same token, closest to the personnel office. The main objective of the personnel officer, says Nigro, should be to train operating supervisors to be their own personnel officers. As a staff official, the personnel man should judge his success by the degree to which supervisors understand and support personnel administration.[1] Harry Case, former director of personnel for the Tennessee Valley Authority—where from the outset personnel administration was a model—goes even further. The supervisor, says Case, can be trusted to decide basic personnel policies and decisions; personnel administration in the federal government has not

---

[1] Felix A. Nigro, *Public Personnel Administration*, pp. 80-81.

been fully effective simply because the supervisor has been unduly restricted. Hence he is not free to apply his firsthand knowledge to the solution of personnel problems, including those relating to grievances and the motivation of the work force.[2]

The quality of personnel administration also affects the success of the directing function. The main interest of the top executive is to get a job done, but he soon finds that he can do relatively little of it himself. Hence he must delegate, he must have staff assistance, and he must have harmonious relationships between headquarters and the field offices. Then at each layer of coordination in the hierarchy of his program he must provide for the supervision of the work to be done.

In this sense, therefore, supervision is the extension of the leadership function applied to the direction of the work at all levels. It is telling people what to do and helping them to do it; it is a principal means by which coordination is achieved and employees trained and inspired to a high level of morale and performance. And finally, through supervision a basis is laid for controlling results: indeed, so close is supervision to the administrative control function that the two are sometimes confused one with the other. For all of these reasons, supervision within the enterprise is the central point of operational administration, converting policies and general plans into work plans and thence into units of production.

Moreover, supervision is political in the administrative sense because people who exercise power and influence (a category that includes supervisors) must understand enough about the objectives of the program to be able to communicate desirable attitudes to their subordinates, comprehend enough about motivation to evoke the best efforts of the men and women whose work they oversee, and be sufficiently diplomatic to get along well with people and agencies on whose cooperation they depend for results in their own program. Stemming from human relations, supervision is equally dynamic.

All supervisory jobs, says a civil service publication, are essentially the same, the differences that appear being in degree only. The common factors are dealing with subordinates, handling technical matters, coordinating with the work of other units in the enterprise, training employees, devising work improvement methods, and building morale.[3]

---

[2] Harry L. Case, *Personnel Policy in a Public Agency, The TVA Experience* (New York: Harper & Row, Publishers, 1955).

[3] Milton M. Mandell and Sally H. Greenbert, *Selecting Supervisors*, U. S. Civil Service Commission, Personnel Methods Series No. 2 (Washington, D.C., 1956), pp. 4-7.

## *Supervision and Supervisors*

Wherever an individual in an organization is responsible for the work of others, supervision is involved, from the chief executive down to any field office employing more than one person. Some supervisors are full-time managers and others are only part-time, combining with supervision a production job of their own.

The three usual levels of supervision are top management, middle management, and primary or first-line supervision. In government the situation is something like this:

1. Top management
      According to levels of government
         Federal—the President
         State—the governor
         County—commissioners or county manager
         Municipal—mayors, commissioners, and/or city manager
      According to type of agency
         Department—the Secretary (federal), or head
         Commission—chairman and commissioners
         Corporation—board of directors and general manager
         Administration or agency—administrator or head
2. Middle management
      At all levels and for all types of agency—division and bureau chiefs
3. First-line supervision
      At all levels and for all types of agency—section and unit heads

In the federal government it is estimated that some 85 percent of all employees report directly to primary unit supervisors.

This threefold pattern is repeated on a smaller scale in the subordinate units of any large program. At the regional level of a federal agency, for example, the regional director is top management, the directors of the functional divisions (finance, personnel, planning, and the like) are middle management, and so on down to the local offices until a point is reached where a unit is too small to justify more than one level of management.

Whatever their station in the hierarchy, all supervisors have certain responsibilities in common. They plan the work within their jurisdiction, issue orders as to how it shall be done, watch over and coordinate the work of their subordinates to see that the work is satisfactorily accomplished, and exercise the administrative control function discussed in Chapter 17.

Looking at the matter from the standpoint of a personnel administrator, Nigro identifies fifteen aspects of the supervisor's job. These are to satisfy their employees' desire for recognition, keep them informed, allow subordinates to make as many independent decisions as possible, avoid invading the specialist's bailiwick, keep the door open for conferences and consultations with subordinates, accept the probability of being unpopular with at least a few subordinates, avoid overoptimism, assure the proper interpretation and execution of orders, abolish useless regulations, recognize that assistants will sometimes be more intelligent than oneself, make no promises that cannot be fulfilled, expect loyalty and give it too, avoid discrimination even in favor of a friend, resist undue pressure, and fight for the interests of subordinates.[4]

## Levels of Management

Administrative supervision is worker-centered and in its highest development recognizes the indispensable role of leadership, training, example, and respect, plus the fact that management must secure employee response by means other than arbitrary threats of dismissal. Consequently, although supervision is involved at all levels of organization, it is especially important at the lower ones, occupied in government by the section chief and in industry by the foreman.

The main function of supervision in industry, say Roethlisberger and Dickson, is to maintain order and control. To maintain control requires, first, that orders be transmitted down the line to supervisors at the various levels, and second, that accurate information as to results be communicated back up the line by the supervisors. The second function is the harder, partly because even under the most favorable circumstances workers are apt to freeze up when foremen come around to check on results or for any other purpose, the reason being that in the eyes of workers, foremen represent authority, employers, the they-group in contrast to the workers themselves who are the we-group.[5]

The importance of the first-line supervisor lies in the fact, already noted, that he is the connecting link between authority and accomplishment, between management and workers. Furthermore, he usually has identifications with both groups and both compete for his loyalty and influence, which is one reason for the significance of recurring drives to organize foremen into national trade unions.

Top management must win the support of middle management and first-line supervisors so as to reach the workers and secure their support as well. The researches of the Harvard Business School show the psy-

4 *Op. cit.*, pp. 363-380.
5 F. J. Roethlisberger and William J. Dickson, *Management and the Worker* (Cambridge, Mass.: Harvard University Press, 1939), pp. 456-458.

chological aspects of this problem to be basic. Class and social groupings, group identifications, and group loyalties are all involved. Although not much has been written on the supervisory relationship in government, the basic principles are much the same as those that apply in industry.

In industry, studies of the attitudes and behavior of workers toward different ranks of supervisors revealed that most employees regarded the group chief "very much as one of themselves." They were not especially conscious of his authority and did not hesitate to disobey him.

> Although they recognized the section chief as possessing more authority, they did not always obey him either and they frequently argued with him. But toward the assistant foreman, their attitude was quite different. They never disobeyed him or argued about his orders. Their behavior when he was in the room was much more restrained than when any section chief was present. Toward the foreman they were still more apprehensive. They not only obeyed him with alacrity but also when he was present, refrained from doing anything that was not strictly according to the rules.[6]

In other words, the higher the supervisor, the more deference he was accorded, but also the more apprehensive and restrained the employees became. Similarly, the nearer the supervisor was to the workers, the less they feared him and the more they treated him like one of their own. Higher supervisors enjoyed the advantage of official position but the disability of social distance, while lower supervisors were deprived of the deference due to official position but enjoyed the advantages of social identification. Management must reckon with these two important variables in all supervisory work.

If management is to get close to the men, supervisors at the foremen's level must help to overcome the inherent difficulties of positional distance. This is made clear in the statement:

> . . . the foreman had little opportunity to find out what the situation was for himself. When he entered the room, the behavior of the men underwent a sudden change; they acted as they were supposed to while he was present. The group chief and section chief sided with the men and did not dare to give the foreman an objective account of the facts. It is even doubtful if they could have done so; their own hopes and fears were too much involved. The outcome was that the departmental performance records became distorted and the foreman remained ignorant of much that was going on. There was something in the relation

---

[6] *Ibid.*

between subordinate and supervisor which inhibited the free upward passage of facts necessary for intelligent control.[7]

The Department of the Air Force recognizes this difficulty as one rooted "in the autocratic type of family organization where accumulated experiences, skills, and worldly goods in the hands of the parental generation represented enforceable authority." So long as this pattern prevailed, communication *up* from the worker level was merely a means of complying with authority. How to fill the gap caused by authority and social distance and to open the channels of free communication that a relaxed situation makes possible comes close to being the central problem of supervision. In the words of the Air Force, "The field is wide open for application of creative managerial effort."[8]

The human relations approach to this problem will go a long way toward solving it. The need is that supervisors understand and take an interest in the people they work with. Says the Air Force, "People just naturally are happier and work better when they have a feeling that the 'boss' is interested in them and looking out for their interests." But effective human relations also means that the supervisor must know himself as well as his subordinates do. "For example, he cannot afford to let his personal conflicts, problems, and moods influence his relationships with people on the job; he must know them in order to curb them effectively. Neither can he afford the luxury of 'blowing his top' too often." People expect some stability of action toward them on the part of their superiors.[9]

Another reason that communications from the bottom up are distorted is that distortions have already occurred from the top down. Top management would direct, coordinate, and control the operations of a program in accordance with specific policies, but the guidance that filters down through the ranks of the hierarchy is amplified, interpreted, and "clarified" by a number of people with differing experiences, attitudes, habits, and ways of looking at things. Consequently a web of interpretations is substituted for the original version to the point where the web becomes gospel to the lower echelons. To the degree that interpretations differ from the original version, action at the lower levels also deviates; so also do communications back up the line, which, in their turn, are subjected to the same distortions that occurred on the way down. When top management becomes aware of results that were not anticipated, new instructions are issued and receive the same treatment

7 *Ibid.*, p. 458.
8 Department of the Air Force, *The Management Process*, AF Manual 25-1 (Washington, D.C., 1954), pp. 67-68.
9 *Ibid.*, p. 75.

as the previous ones. "It is surprising," comments the Air Force, "how many projects have been reported as successful when in reality actual performance had all the features of a distorted image."[10] The interpretive treatment is seldom a malicious one and often it is not even a conscious one, but the results are the same.

With regard to middle management, the area has best been described by Mary Cushing Niles, long active in the scientific management movement, who first brought the term "middle management" into prominence and gave practical insights that are indispensable to the future administrator.

A chief problem of administration, says Mrs. Niles, is coordination, the forces of which run upward, downward, and sideways in the organization. And since middle managers stand in the center of this flow, they are key people in the coordination process. The lines of communication also meet in middle managers, for it is they who transmit orders, decisions, and guidance from the top down, and problems, difficulties, and suggestions from the lower ranks up to the top. Middle managers share in the burdens of their superiors by working out policies and grand strategy, but they are also close enough to first-line supervisors to know their problems as well. Top management is too remote from most employees to be able to exercise much direct influence and hence in many respects middle management occupies the most strategic position in any organization.[11]

To his subordinates, says Mrs. Niles, the middle manager is leader as well as boss, thus confirming the view that leadership must occur at every rank in the hierarchy. In his capacity as leader, the middle manager is responsible for transmitting an accurate interpretation of policy and for inspiring his subordinates with a will to carry it loyally into effect. It is here that the problem of interpretation and "clarification," as noted by the Air Force, can best be solved. As a first step, of course, middle managers must be aware of the problem, and often they are not.

In addition to representing top management, the middle manager is also spokesman for his subordinates "in carrying upward suggestions, information, needs, and desires." This is a focal point in the meeting of minds that goes to make up a happy working group. Furthermore, says Mrs. Niles, "just as the senior officers see, hear and analyze problems outside the scope of internal administration, so do the junior administrators see, hear, and in the main deal with problems vital to internal operations."[12] Thus middle management may be called the spark plug of operational administration.

At the top of the organization, it has already been noted in a pre-

---

10 *Ibid.*, p. 67.
11 Niles, *Middle Management*, pp. ix, 217, 251.
12 *Ibid.*, pp. 217, 251.

vious chapter that supervision is more a matter of providing leadership, formulating policy, making plans, checking results, and setting the tone of the enterprise than it is one of actually overseeing the work of others. The higher in the scale one goes, the more does one deal with ideas and papers instead of with people.

The role of top management is illustrated by the Farm Credit Administration, a holding company type of federal agency created in 1933 through the merger of formerly independent agencies; since then others have been added. The three credit services are land bank, short-term credit, and cooperative bank, and each subordinate unit goes by its own name and is a separate, legal, self-financing corporation free to plan, organize, and supervise its own operations. On what basis, therefore, is responsibility divided between the FCA headquarters—the holding company—in Washington, and the member corporations in the field?

Following the merger, the head of the agency, called the governor, not only controlled the supervisory staff at headquarters, but also succeeded to the broad jurisdiction of the former boards of the member corporations to supervise the general operations and loan policies of the field units. His primary function, however, was "not administrative, nor even policy determination in the ordinary, impersonal sense, *but rather . . . to provide leadership, to determine the direction, to set the tone for the whole organization under his control.*" The occupant of such an office "must divine on what matters emphasis may be safely subordinated from time to time and what phase of the system requires the attention and the whole force and energy of himself and staff at any specific time."[13]

Another illustration of the application of supervision from the top comes from the field of library administration. Over a period of years the head of a large library in Michigan had acquired a reputation as an outstanding library administrator. Those who studied his methods concluded that his success was due to this philosophy: Choose good people; tell them the policies and what they are expected to do; give them their heads and don't interfere or try to run their business because if they are expert, they will know more about their respective fields than anyone else; go easy on supervision and stress coordination and teamwork.

One problem, however—and it is a fairly common one—perplexed this librarian. Although he recognized as a rational proposition that he should confine his relation with higher grade department heads to coordination and should not attempt very much in the way of supervision, he found that in the specialty in which he himself was trained, which

---

13 Reported by Herbert Emmerich, former executive officer of the Farm Credit Administration, in "Distinguishing Administrative Aspects of the Farm Credit Administration," *American Political Science Review*, XXX (December 1936), p. 1118. Italics added.

was cataloguing, he tended to interfere and that the head of the cataloguing department consulted him more than other department heads did.[14]

The tendency is a human one, of course, but for the good of a department and the personal development of its director, it should be resisted by the superior. If he fails in this, he is likely to have the department of his own specialty one of the weakest in the organization, because either the department head will be a weak man to begin with or he will lose his initiative. In that case the chief executive merely adds to his own burdens, exceeds his span of control, and neglects other duties including coordination. When a chief executive interferes with internal departmental administration "he runs the danger of getting in beyond his depth. One hour a day cannot possibly permit him to know as much as his subordinates do about details, but he will be tempted to use his judgment above theirs on matters where he has only partial knowledge." [15] When the chief executive finds it impossible to keep his hands off internal departmental administration, then something is wrong; either the department head is not qualified for his job or he needs further training.

## The Techniques of Supervision

The techniques of supervision include an understanding of the point of view, training, work plans, written procedures and instructions, and staff meetings. It is important to remember, however, that although these aspects of supervision may be separately identified for study, in everyday practice they are so interrelated as to constitute a kind of multiple instrument that the administrator applies as though it were a single one, only changing the emphasis a little here and there to meet the requirements of particular situations. It should also be remembered that among the techniques of supervision appear also the techniques of executive leadership, including clarification of objectives, the determination of administrative policy, the planning of the future of the program, stress on integration and coordination, and the like.

Subordinates commonly react to the instructions of a supervisor with the mental query, What does this mean to me? Not, What am I personally going to get out of it? but, How does this affect my work? In other words, instructions that are of general application become of individual personal application by the time they reach the employee. Consequently, the employee must be given a clear idea of the policies and techniques

---

[14] Carleton B. Joeckel, ed., *Current Issues in Library Administration* (Chicago: University of Chicago Press, 1939), p. 97.

[15] *Ibid.,* pp. 96-97.

in question and the supervisor must understand the psychology of his subordinate and know something of his learning aptitudes. Here again is the human approach to administration, stressing face-to-face relationships and converting impersonal policies into human goals through a meeting of minds.

Alexander Leighton makes the point that new policies should not be arbitrarily announced and that any proposed shifts in policy should be carefully communicated to those concerned so that they will recognize the need for the change.[16] The authors of *Executive Action* confirm the need for this approach when, in commenting on an interesting case, they remark that "the more closely we look at any given activity, the more we realize that the people performing it see it in terms of their past experience and their own direct firsthand awareness of what is going on around them. To be received easily, new information and ideas usually have to be fairly consistent and compatible with what is already known and understood." [17]

People in different parts of the same organization see a particular product, procedure, or program in different ways. Each has his own interests determining his point of view. In another example reported in the Harvard study, the president of a certain company thought of a new product in terms of profit and corporate strength; the sales vice president, in terms of a gleam in the eye of the wary buyer; the controller, as a variable in the game of figures; the manufacturing vice president, as triumph after a long and tense developmental period; the purchasing agent, as converted raw materials; the machine operator, as a victory for human skill over physical resistance; and the maintenance man, as a microscopic measure of wear on bearings. Because each individual sees through his own mental glasses, the task of the supervisor is to make sure that through a process of education and coordination, a more complete vision of the same object is secured through all stages of the administrative process, from production to profits.

To be effective, however, supervision must be based on authority adequately delegated within the internal operating structure of the enterprise. The rules that apply here have been summarized in these terms: select subordinate supervisors capable of shouldering responsibility; define the authority for which each is responsible; train subordinates to carry responsibilities; establish general policies and disseminate them throughout the organization; strive toward maximum standardization of both functional and housekeeping procedures (there could be some question about this one); establish internal checks that automatically flash danger signals; assure the flow of information up, down,

---

16 *The Governing of Men,* p. 357.
17 Learned, Ulrich, and Booz, *op. cit.,* p. 38. Italics added.

and across the hierarchy; and carry on planning as a perpetual function of management.[18]

Studies made at the University of Michigan's Survey Research Center confirm the belief that rather than artificial technique, it is emotional maturity and a human relations philosophy that are the keys to successful supervision. In a study of the Prudential Insurance Company, for example, it was found that the best supervisors enjoyed the widest degree of latitude from their own supervisors, placed less direct emphasis on production as the goal, and were employee-centered, spending less time on straight production work than on supervision. In addition, they had a considerable confidence in their own abilities as supervisors, and felt they knew where they stood with their employer.[19]

## Supervision as Employee Training

The foreman has always been a teacher, for he is constantly breaking in new men and showing experienced men how to do new work. As a result of experiments, training courses have been introduced to teach supervisors in industry, and to some extent also in government, how to teach employees how to do a better job. In this instruction, the supervisor must first learn to look at the job analytically, breaking it down into units to understand the flow of work. Then he must learn the technique of instruction, which means giving clear directions, allowing the employee to experiment, and patiently showing him where he has made mistakes or how he can improve his working methods.

There are four main rules under each of these two headings. In preparing to give job instruction, the supervisor must have a timetable to determine how soon to expect a particular degree of skill in a worker; he must break the job down into its components and identify the crucial operations; he must have everything at hand before he begins, including tools, equipment, and materials; and he must see that the work is properly laid out so as to encourage a basic habit to be acquired and maintained by the worker. Thereafter, the four rules of instruction are to prepare the worker by putting him at his ease and discovering what he knows; explain the technique clearly and not give the worker more than he can master at any one time; have him try out what he has learned; and finally, follow up by checking on him frequently, giving him personal attention, and praising him when he deserves it.

In line with the current human relations emphasis in administra-

---

[18] John M. Pfiffner, "How to Delegate Authority," *Public Management*, XXV (December 1943), pp. 351-353.

[19] University of Michigan, Survey Research Center, *Productivity, Supervision, and Employee Morale*, Human Relations Series 1, Report 1, (Ann Arbor, Mich., 1948),

tion, certain other rules also are important. Thus, the supervisor should anticipate what to expect of each worker, let him know how he is getting along, and show him ways to improve. Credit should also be given when deserved, extra or unusal performance should be recognized and the worker told of it while it is still fresh, not later. It is desirable also to tell employees in advance about a change that will affect them, if possible giving them the reasons and persuading them to accept the change both intellectually and emotionally. And finally, the supervisor should make the best possible use of every worker's ability, looking for neglected talents and encouraging rather than hampering progress.

Yet another requirement of effective training is that employees must have confidence in the fairness and impartiality of their supervisors. Difficult problems will be decided impartially if a supervisor is careful to get all the facts by consulting all who are involved in a given situation, if he then weighs and decides the issue without jumping to conclusions, if he acts promptly without trying to evade responsibility, and if he checks results by constant follow-up, a requirement that is most often neglected.

It is desirable to stress the one best method, so long as the possibility is admitted that an even better method might be found. In searching for the best method, the supervisor should break the job down into its separate elements, scrutinize and question each detail, develop a new method if there seems to be a better one, and finally, apply the new method. At this stage the supervisor must first secure the approval of his superior, then present the plan to the employees in such a way that all agree to it; and then he must be careful to give credit where credit is due. The more repetitive the operation in question, the more does it need this kind of analysis in order to provide a clear basis for instruction.

In the training function, certain skills are needed. A man who is an able workman himself is not necessarily an able teacher nor even an able supervisor; hence it has not been easy to devise tests to determine the qualities required of supervisory personnel. Written tests are of little use in selecting supervisors; intelligence tests are helpful, but only as one factor among several; and the testimony of fellow workers may be a reliable guide, but often is not. In the end it is generally necessary to fall back on actual performance in a previous job.

After careful study, the Civil Service Commission has drawn up a list of qualities and abilities that apply to the training function in administration, all of them skills basic to the human approach. They include:

1. Self-understanding and insight to permit one to see himself as others see him
2. Ability to work effectively as a member of a group

3. Awareness of the causes of group behavior and sensitiveness to the needs and motivations of subordinates

4. Ability to diagnose and treat human relations

5. Ability to create a proper working climate within which his subordinates feel free to express themselves and are encouraged to participate in cooperative team efforts

6. Ability to communicate successfully his ideas, decisions, and attitudes to subordinates and others

7. Ability to understand successfully what others by their actions and words (explicit and implicit) are trying to communicate to him

Training in the principles and methods of supervision, says Milton Hall, are not enough; there should also be some means by which supervisors may judge their own performance and see where they fall short. Too little is known about the effect of teaching and supervision on employees and about what goes on in their minds. Further, it seems likely that the most important employee problems are those the supervisor never hears about. Thus it is desirable to discover what employees think of the supervisor's performance and what constructive suggestions can be secured for improving it.[20]

Hall has formulated a plan that has been put to successful use. By prearrangement, an outside consultant meets with a particular supervisor and his employees. The supervisor proposes that they take stock of the supervisory job that is being done and suggests the consultant as the one to do it. The consultant explains frankly that he is trying to improve the effectiveness of the unit and to enable the supervisor to see himself as others see him. The supervisor withdraws and the consultant encourages the employees to talk freely, frankly, and constructively.

The employees fill out score cards, the questions being something like these: Are you much troubled or hindered because your supervisor fails to explain, sufficiently ahead of time, the changes that affect you? Do you know what your supervisor thinks of your work? Have you been given a clear understanding of what your duties and responsibilities are? Do you usually get recognition or praise for good work? Do you believe that anyone above your supervisor shows personal favoritism in making decisions that affect the people in your office? Do you feel that any work procedure you are required to follow is merely someone's pet idea and that it doesn't really help to get the work done? Suppose that you had a complaint or were dissatisfied and your supervisor could not solve the problem, do you think he would hold it against you if you talked it over with the people above him?

---

[20] Milton Hall, "Supervising People—Closing the Gap between What We Think and What We Do," *Advanced Management*, XII (September 1947), pp. 129-136.

When the questions on the score card have been filled out, the supervisor returns to the group and the consultant reviews the answers. At the end of the discussion the supervisor should have a much better idea of his own performance and of how it might be improved and his relationship with his employees strengthened.

Hall agrees that the procedure is a drastic one but he has observed its successful application. In one instance in which production was measurable, for example, average output per employee increased 50 percent. The procedure seems to break down tensions and to relieve pent-up fears and anxieties, proves to employees that the supervisor is not too aloof and proud to allow criticism, and encourages a feeling that the enterprise is a cooperative one. Hall admits that the method is potentially dangerous when handled by an inept consultant or when it involves a vain supervisor. Moreover, few consultants have the needed combination of skills; but when applied under the right conditions, the method has much to recommend it.

## Work Planning

The central mechanism of supervision is a comprehensive and practical work plan. As the *operating* aspect of the planning function in administration, the work plan is the final step in the broad over-all process discussed in Chapter 10. Work planning takes over after objectives and policies have been determined and broad plans involving outside factors have been formulated. The work plan is the vehicle of administrative direction and supervision and more adaptable, of course, to certain types of program such as social security than to others such as foreign affairs.

Work planning has been accepted procedure in large business concerns ever since the onset of the scientific management movement in the early part of this century.[21] Its application in government is more recent, but already enough experience has accumulated in that area to prove the need for this step in the administrative process.

Concretely, a work plan is a step-by-step detailing of what every employee is expected to do.[22] Thus, in the hands of a supervisor a work

---

[21] How work planning is used in industry is explained by J. K. Louden in "Work Planning in Industry," *Advanced Management*, VII (July-September 1942), pp. 98-101, 116.

[22] The following analysis is based on an article in two parts by Arnie Solem, a student of scientific management and a former official of the Social Security Board in Washington—"Work Planning in Government," *Advanced Management*, VII (July-September, October-December 1942), pp. 131-142, 180-184. This two-part study is the outgrowth of a round table on work planning in government, carried on over a period of time by the Washington Chapter of the Society for the Advancement of Management.

plan is similar to a musical score in the hands of an orchestra conductor; in both cases, the playing of the parts in unison is no small aspect of the matter. A work plan is a realistic operating schedule in that every note can and must be played. A proper plan rests on a broad base of fact and analysis; past experience and performance and trends in adjacent fields are reviewed and tested as guides to determining present priorities and future action. In other words, careful fact finding, analysis, and a precise blueprint for action are substituted for the whims and guesses of executives that provide only a vague indication of the work to be done.

A work plan somewhat resembles the control aspect of the budget, but it is even more comprehensive and dynamic. The main factors in its development are these: First, the executive is the key to the matter; if he fails to see the need for work planning and to push it, nothing useful will come off. Second, headquarters and the field units must be persuaded to work together; consequently, once a plan has been developed it must be sent to the field for suggestions and proposed changes. Third, coordination of the work plan should reside in the hands of a staff assistant in the chief executive's office, because line supervisors responsible for their own share of the total plan are ordinarily too busy to see it as a whole. Fourth, staff and line officials must actively cooperate not only in the formulation of the plan but also in its execution. Fifth, a proper work plan invariably provides for the what, the how much, the when, and the who of a detailed program. Sixth, the work plan should not be projected too far into the future because facts and figures must be timely and current. Seventh, when the plan is in final form, every employee should have a copy of it so as to see his role in its execution and to judge the extent to which his suggestions, if any, were used. Eighth, there must be provision for modifications when unforeseen developments occur. And finally, a work plan is a major instrument of executive control, an aspect of the subject to be explored in Chapter 17.

It has been said that a work plan specifies the what, the how much, the when, and the who of a program. The *what* is the objective sought over a period of time; for convenience, it may be broken down into subobjectives spaced along the way. The first step is to assemble data from all units of the organization, as in formulating a budget. With this information, the administrator then weighs the needs of each part of the program, one against the other, to determine individual goals to be aimed for during a specified period ahead. Administrators at every level of the hierarchy go through this same procedure, but the farther down the line they are, the more restricted is their area of decision. Nevertheless, because there is always some leeway in decision making, each administrator has a chance to contribute toward the building of the work plan structure.

SUPERVISION AND DELEGATION

Once the what has been determined, the next question is *how much* shall be accomplished under each heading or in terms of each subobjective in the work plan. Work units must be devised so as to project the total load into a reasonable future and to measure accomplishment. Consequently, measuring devices must also be developed even for activities traditionally supposed to be nonmeasurable. The available funds, man-hours, and materials will buy only so many units of production, and these factors must be expressed in terms of a common denominator.

In all administration, time is a major factor, the *when* factor of the work plan. A test of a skillful executive is his keen sense of timing. Although this quality is sometimes at least partially based on intuition, its instrumentation must always be deliberately accomplished through teamwork. The timing of a work plan must be fixed over a period of six months, a year, or longer, but always the limits must be definite and all parts of the plan must move forward in synchronization so as to meet the deadline on schedule.

Timing involves scheduling, which is the selection of significant control points along the course of the plan, the deadline dates for which will give the administrator the means of checking on the progress that is being made. The logical sequence is something like this:

> When the substance—the *what* and *how much*—of a work plan is agreed upon, the control points should be selected and the control system designed around them. In the case of revision of the work plan, or the adoption of a new plan, new control points should be determined where necessary. The objective is always to have an immediate summarizing of the progress of the program in terms of the best indicators of progress.[23]

The final element of a work plan, the *who,* means the assignment of specific responsibilities all along the line among both operating and staff personnel and at headquarters and in the field. The plan must show who is responsible at each point and each stage in the process. Moreover, where several units share in the same function, the degree of responsibility of each must be clearly defined. This parceling out of duties is supervision in the literal sense because unless the *who* is clearly determined there can be no adequate follow-up of assigned duties.

Here now is a word of caution: "One thing that should *not* go into the work plan is a listing of projects and work, the money, facilities and personnel for the accomplishment of which do *not* exist. If this is done your 'plan' becomes a research document, a job load analysis of work desirable to accomplish rather than a plan of work which actually *can*

---

[23] *Ibid.,* p. 139.

228 Executive Performance

be accomplished." [24] It becomes a wish plan, useful in the formulation of long-range projections but useless as a tool of operations. A detailed work plan applies to the immediate present and projects the future only in terms of what has been specifically arranged for.

The essential respect in which administration according to a work plan is superior to administration without one is that the whole procedure is clear in advance, giving greater assurance to a supervisor that no factor has been overlooked and that all are ready when needed. So long as flexibility is maintained and quick revisions can be made as needed, overrigidity is avoided. Properly constituted, the work plan is a main feature of the grand strategy by which programs are carried forward. All supervisors must sometimes play by ear, so to speak, but with a work plan in the desk drawer they have the score available when they find it necessary to consult it.

A proper work plan comes close to being the essence of scientific management, including as it does all of the eight steps recognized as basic to that process: Define your purpose, analyze your problem, seek the facts, devise the one best method, find the one best person, teach him the one best method, plan carefully, and win cooperation.[25]

## Written Procedures and Instructions

Written procedures and instructions may or may not be incorporated into an administrative manual. Such a volume is usually a looseleaf binder containing not only procedures and instructions but also standards, orders, statutes, and other guides to action; its use is becoming increasingly common. The Visa Division of the State Department has had a manual of policy and procedure for many years, and so have the armed forces. The Resettlement Administration rather overdid the idea in the 1930s when it produced something like fifteen large volumes covering everything from policies and procedures to organization charts, flow charts (showing how different kinds of material were to be routed among officials and divisions), maps, and other information, and employed a runner to take new insertions around Washington every other day or so to its more than a dozen scattered offices. Many temporary agencies during World War II had certain common characteristics in that they operated over a wide geographical area and the subjects dealt with were complicated, were often covered by court decisions or opinions by the general counsel's office of the operating agency, or included technical questions of procedure. Quick decisions had to be made by remote officials in the field and a manual was indispensable.

---

24 *Ibid.*, p. 139.
25 Statement by William H. Leffingwell in 1921 and reproduced in *Advanced Management*, VI (January-March 1942), p. 31.

The administrative manual of the Immigration and Naturalization Service is an illustration of a useful government manual. Although some statutory consolidations have since occurred, when the manual was created in 1940 the law relating to entry, deportation, citizenship, alien registration, and the like was complicated and scattered over many statutes. Court decisions by the hundreds bore on difficult problems arising in the course of enforcement. And yet some 6500 civilian immigration inspectors needed to know what the law and regulations were when they boarded a vessel in New York harbor or picked up an illegal entrant in the desert on the Mexican border. The solution was to provide a concise "bible," divided according to topics, which could be quickly consulted. As finally developed, this particular manual set forth policies and procedures, directions for action under given circumstances, explanations of substantive and adjective law, and brief references to decided court cases and opinions of the chief counsel.

The development and maintenance of an administrative manual is usually the responsibility of a staff unit attached to the office of the top operating official. In Immigration, such a unit dealt also with information, citizenship education, and inservice training. When the manual was initiated, a by-product of the study it required was the clarification of policy and procedure throughout the agency and the use of field as well as central office personnel in a mutually beneficial cooperative effort.

A manual is worthless, of course, if it is not both current and brief. It is kept current by being looseleaf, thus facilitating the insertion of new pages and the disposal of obsolete ones. It is kept brief by a careful consideration of policies and procedures so that only what is pertinent will be included. Indeed, this fact in itself may go a long way to correct one of the most serious faults of bureaucratic administration, namely, the tendency to multiply orders, rules, regulations, and written instructions of all kinds to the point where first-line supervisors are bewildered and confused.

## Staff Meetings

As a tool of supervision, the staff meeting may be employed at any point in the organization where its application is pertinent, to secure teamwork and mutual understanding. The top-level staff meeting of functional heads presided over by the chief executive is a familiar device in both industry and government, but there is a growing tendency to rely on the conference technique at all levels as a means of securing the benefits of face-to-face relationships, as a method of coordinating the functional aspects of an enterprise into a unified program, and as a follow-up procedure for the supervisory executive.

The conference technique is closely related to group dynamics and other forms of human relations procedures. Because it is increasingly prominent as an administrative technique, students of public administration are paying it more attention than formerly. Thus in a preliminary study of the use of conferences in the administrative process, it is suggested that three major purposes served are to stimulate an awareness of problems, to help in their solution, and to gain the acceptance and promote the execution of the solutions that have been determined.[26] These are all aspects of the supervisory function.

A staff meeting may be held at regular intervals or only from time to time as needed. In either case, as any experienced administrator knows, such a conference can be pretty bad or highly useful, and between the two extremes is a wide range of possibilities. A staff conference will not succeed unless certain conditions are present: The chairman must never be arrogant and overbearing, speaking mainly to hear himself talk; rather, he must be a good listener and show by his attitude that he welcomes helpful ideas.

Second, the agenda must be planned, the main outline being known in advance if possible, because scattered talk off the subject will discourage an exchange of ideas faster than almost anything else. But if the participants know what is to be discussed, and if they are kept to the subject and still made to feel that they are not being pressed to reach a particular decision, there will usually be a meeting of minds, which is the objective of the conference.

Third, a staff conference should be conducted in an atmosphere that will dissolve barriers due to vocational specialization and that will encourage functional heads to show an interest in matters of concern to the whole agency, and not confine themselves (as often happens) to those that relate only to their own departments.

A well-conducted staff meeting in a relaxed atmosphere will generally attain the three practical objectives of stimulating an awareness of problems, helping in their solution, and promoting the execution of the solutions that have been adopted. But if the meeting is used merely as window dressing, the participants will unerringly sense its hollowness and it will accomplish little beyond irritating busy men who feel that their time is being wasted for the benefit of the top man's ego.

A weak executive may rely too heavily on conferences because he cannot make decisions himself. At the other extreme, an overbearing executive may think it unnecessary to consult anyone at any time and under any circumstances. Thus the key to the situation is the presiding officer. The desirable balance is a man capable of making his own decisions but who also wants everyone in his supervisory relationship to go through the same intellectual process that he does in deciding current

26 Martin Kriesberg and Harold Guetzkow, "The Use of Conferences in the Administrative Process," *Public Administration Review* X (Spring 1950), pp. 93-98.

issues, and hence to share in the sense of importance, teamwork, and self-interest that comes from joint decision. It is a truism, already noted, that people cooperate better when they have had a part in making the decisions that later they will have a hand in carrying out.

## Delegation of Authority

By delegating a portion of his authority to subordinates, the administrator multiplies himself, so to speak, so as to be able to take care of all the needs of his enterprise, whereas if he tried to do all these things himself he would never get them done.

This is what is meant by the concept of "management by objectives" as contrasted with "management by authority." Management by objectives is so important as almost to be called a philosophy of administration. Instead of relying on authority, orders, coercion, hierarchy, and other formal concepts, let the manager secure willing and superior responses from his subordinates by making the objectives clear to them, by laying out plainly what each part of the program is to do, and then let each subordinate work out his own methods by which to meet the objectives for which he is responsible.

The success of management by objectives depends on several basic factors:

1. All parts of the program must be integrated under the executive direction of a single person, who then delegates authority and responsibility as needed.

2. On the basis of a thorough job analysis that has systematized the flow of work and enabled the executive to know where authority and responsibility should be located and in what amounts, a delegation of authority is made that involves the partition of a larger responsibility accompanied by an appropriate portion of authority, all of which is to be passed along to an official or series of officials down the line in order that they may adequately carry their part of the work load. By "authority" is meant the freedom within prescribed limits to make independent decisions affecting the conduct of the work of the enterprise.

3. The degree of authority must coincide with the degree of responsibility to which it is allied.

4. The person to whom the delegation is made must clearly understand his mandate.

5. He must be given sufficient freedom and independence of action to prove what he can do.

6. Occasional mistakes of judgment must be expected if delegation is used as generously as it should be. This is part of the price that must be paid to unlock energies that would otherwise be wasted,

and it is a small price, compared with the disadvantages of monopolized authority that overburden the time and energies of the top executive.

7. The executive making the delegation must check up periodically on his subordinates to see that the work is going forward and that specific plans fit in with larger ones.

8. Organization and chance cannot be relied on to keep all the forces and relationships within an agency in balance; the active agent is the intelligence of unified leadership.

In any enterprise, says Drucker, there are always three jobs for top management: managing the business as a whole, managing the managers (subordinate executives), and managing the workers and the work to be done. But what is often overlooked, he remarks, is that, realistically, the executive cannot divide his work in this fashion at all, because not only does a decision in one area affect the other two; in addition, most decisions of immediate concern also affect the long-range interests of the organization.[27] Today, any management decision is likely to have a long-term influence; indeed, ten years is getting to be a short time. Moreover, in making such decisions, it should be remembered that managerial enterprise is created and maintained by individuals, and that it is not the product of immutable "forces." A manager is one who by definition makes destiny instead of being swept along by it. Since individuals are fallible, their decisions are not invariably the correct ones, and since influence is long-range, the effect of error may be serious. The right kind of leadership will detect some of these errors before they are made and will be able to neutralize many others.

The second point to remember is that management by objectives involves clarity of understanding at three levels: the enterprise as a whole, the department, and the job assignment of every individual. This threefold division of work involves careful organizational analysis, position classification, work planning, and scheduling. But it also involves the realization that planning and doing are not separate jobs; rather, they are parts of the same job and neither can be done well without the other.

To what extent should authority be delegated? The answer is that decision making and action must be devolved as far down the line as possible so that men may act confidently as close as possible to the problem with which they are dealing. Jobs should be organized from the bottom up, not from the top down, because it is on the front line of operations that customers are served and the reputation of the organization is won or lost. The work of higher supervisors, important

---

27 Peter F. Drucker, *The Practice of Management* (New York: Harper & Row, Publishers, 1954), p. 16.

though it is, may be considered as deriving from the lower ranks; the top exists to serve those who wait on the public. Since this is so, a first rule of management is that administrators in the lower ranks should be granted all the authority and responsibility they can handle. When authority is delegated in this manner, each administrator passes up the line to higher authority only what he cannot decide for himself. A good rule would be that "all authority not expressly reserved to higher management is granted to lower management."

Two additional rules governing delegation may be suggested. Decisions may be classified as to kind and character, and Drucker distinguishes four types: those that depend on the length of time to which the enterprise is committed; those that affect the internal relationships of the enterprise; those of a qualitative nature dealing with simple or complex political, economic, or moral questions, for example; and those that are recurrent, rare, or unique. The rule is that to the extent that decisions are long-range, multirelational, qualitative, and rare or unique, they should generally be referred upward.

The second rule of devolution is that as authority is pushed downward, top management must exercise a restraining hand so as to be sure that the interests of the program are not jeopardized by conflicting policies. Thus where one rule is that decisions should always be made at the lowest possible level and as close to the scene of action as possible, another is that decisions should be made at a level that will assure top management that all activities and objectives affected by the decisions are fully considered. The first determines, in theory, how far down the decision *should* be made; the second controls the question of how far down it *may* be made with safety to the program. When the limitations of safety have been reached, then either top management must itself make the decision, or it must involve others who have a stake in the outcome.[28]

The five phases of decision making are to define the problem, analyze the problem, identify alternative solutions, decide on the best one, and then implement it.[29] A point often overlooked is that whereas most decision making is primarily problem solving, or asking the right questions, important decision making deals with strategy. It is decisions of this kind that really matter, not the tactical ones that are merely routine. Decisions on strategy deal with questions such as how to meet goals, keep friends, survive, and grow. Furthermore, decision making is a function that must constantly be exercised, often on conflicting and incomplete evidence. "Courage," says an English expert, "is needed to make decisions at all, and hunch to make them right." It used to be said, he continues, "that the most important thing was to make deci-

28 *Ibid.*, p. 199.
29 *Ibid.*, p. 353.

sions quickly," but today it is much more important "to be able to reverse a wrong decision quickly, which is harder to do." [30] The chances of wrong decisions are greater than formerly because the context in which they are made is more complicated. The more strategic the decision, the higher in the hierarchy it should be made, which is one reason that experienced top executives devolve authority as far down the line as they safely can: it gives them more time to look ahead, to reexamine goals, to check on progress, and to plan strategy in that 5 percent area of any organization on which survival depends.

A successful executive is often described as one who knows how to get other people to work for him. But delegation is not an easy task. Many large organizations limp along because there are men in top positions who cannot learn to delegate, who have an almost visceral revulsion to the suggestion that they unload part of their work, and who in consequence try to do everything themselves, thus creating an overload and a bottleneck at the top and frustration everywhere else.

## *Administrative Follow-up*

Important as the instruments of supervision are, there is no substitute for administrative follow-up if the program is to proceed as the administrator would have it do. Supervision is hard, sustained work and requires constant attention to duty. It bears repeating that the more delegation there is, the more of follow-up must there be if the administrator is to assure himself that the delegation is merited. Such assurance can be secured only by keeping in daily touch with what is going on, through personal observation and by utilizing the control devices to be discussed in Chapter 17.

An administrator should fix in his mind a check list of his responsibilities and run through them daily by a quick mental calculation to make sure that everything is being taken care of.[31] Such an exercise also gives him a feeling for the wholeness of his duties because the pieces fall more readily into place. Moreover, by checking off his areas of responsibility he gains a sense of strategy that he can achieve in no other way. If he is a busy man he may have to keep a dozen to a hundred balls in the air at a time, and if he stops to give too much attention to one of them, or if he has a one-track mind, the balls will begin to drop all around him.

If an executive is attentive to the problems of those who report to

---

30 Bosworth Monck, "How to Make a Captain of Industry," *The Listener* (London: January 1955), p. 57.

31 See the checklist of responsibilities mentioned in Marshall E. Dimock, *The Executive in Action*, pp. 85-86.

him, he will enlist interest and appreciation. A capable supervisor does not "ride" his people; he handles them as gently and as knowingly as a conductor handles the members of his orchestra during a concert. The higher an executive rises, the greater is his need to go to the heart of problems rapidly and skillfully. He must be intuitive or he simply will not have time for everything he is expected to do. This power of penetration is something that can be developed early in life, especially through the right kind of academic training. Education also helps a person to become sensitive to people and to situations, although here education must be defined broadly enough to include experience in all kinds of situations involving struggle and conflict.

With all the devices at his command, therefore, including training, work planning, instructions, and staff meetings, the administrator at every level must still do much patient follow-up if he is to remain fully informed, keep his finger on the pulse of his program, and maintain his personal contacts within the organization. In other words, the administrator must develop the art of composing a connected picture of his supervisory task, enabling him quickly to tell whether every part of it is in its proper perspective and nothing out of focus.

## BIBLIOGRAPHY AND CASES

### Annotated Reading Suggestions

The most comprehensive book on supervision is that of John M. Pfiffner, *The Supervision of Personnel* (3d ed., Prentice-Hall, 1958). The methods of operating administration are dealt with in Marshall E. Dimock, *The Executive in Action* (Harper & Row, 1945), Chapters 16 and 19. The TWI (Training Within Industry) experience, which was a turning point in both business and government, is dealt with in *War Manpower Commission, The Training Within Industry Report, 1940-45* (Government Printing Office, 1945). This may be compared with U. S. Air Force, *Management Course for Air Force Supervisors* (Government Printing Office, 1955); and with British experience in F. J. Tickner, *Modern Staff Training* (University of London Press, 1952).

Perhaps the best single research monograph is one published in 1948 by the University of Michigan's Survey Research Center, *Productivity, Supervision, and Employee Morale.*

As stated in an earlier chapter, planning is a process that is found at all levels in administration. On planning at the work level, see Arnie Solem, "Work Planning in Government," *Advanced Management,* 7 (July-September, and October-December 1942).

The U. S. Bureau of the Budget has assumed a leadership role in this area.

See especially its 1945 publications: *Trainer's Guide to the Work Simplification Training Sessions; Specifications for Agency Work Simplification; Supervisor's Guide to the Work Distribution Chart; Supervisor's Guide to the Process Chart;* and *Supervisor's Guide to the Work Count* (Goverment Printing Office, 1945).

A good short article on communication is by John Corson, "The Role of Communication in the Process of Administration," *Public Administration Review,* 4 (Winter 1944). For a booklength treatment of the subject, see Charles Redfield, *Communication in Management* (University of Chicago Press, 1953).

Evaluation also is important and is dealt with by Floyd Mann and James Dent, *Appraisal of Supervisors* (University of Michigan Survey Research Center, 1954).

On administering by objectives, a good source is Robert S. Avery, *Experiment in Management: Personnel Decentralization in the Tennessee Valley Authority* (Knoxville, 1954). See also Frederick N. Cleaveland, "Administrative Decentralization in the U. S. Bureau of Reclamation," *Public Administration Review,* 13 (Winter 1953); and Herbert Kaufman, *The Forest Ranger* (Johns Hopkins University Press, 1960).

The classic work on attitudes is Mary Parker Follett, *Dynamic Administration,* her papers collected and edited by Henry C. Metcalf and L. Urwick (Harper & Row, 1941), especially Chapters 2 (on giving orders), 4 (on power), 5 (on professionalization), and 7 (on employee participation). See also Fred E. Fiedler, *Leader Attitudes and Group Effectiveness* (University of Illinois Press, 1958).

In an important sense, supervision is a branch of human relations. Many references have already been given to studies in this area. Two of special relevance to this chapter are Lawrence A. Appley, *The Human Element in Personnel Management* (Washington, D.C.: Society for Personnel Administration, 1941), and *Management in Action: The Art of Getting Things Done Through People* (New York: American Management Association, 1956). Appley, who now heads the American Management Association, was once executive officer of the War Manpower Commission.

## Case Studies

In the Stein *Case Book,* there are two cases that clearly illustrate the problem of supervision. The first, *Production Planning in the Patent Office,* was written by Arch Dotson in 1952 and is only ten pages long. It deals with work flow and similar practical concerns. The second, called *Indonesian Assignment,* has to do with the foreign service and relationships between supervisor and subordinate that became strained. This case was prepared by Charles Wolf, Jr., in 1950 and the story is told in only six printed pages.

Two more recent cases in the ICP series are equally good. No. 43, *Mayor and the Fire Chief,* twenty-four pages, was written by Frank P. Sherwood. No. 76, *City Manager Tries to Fire His Police Chief,* is also a Sherwood report.

Mechanization is increasingly a problem in human relations. The question is dealt with in one of the British cases, *Machine Accounting Comes to the West Country,* in F. M. G. Willson, *Administrators in Action: British Case Studies, Volume 1* (University of Toronto Press, 1961).

# 16

---

# Incentives

---

THE POTENTIALITIES FOR individual and social accomplishment are constantly expanding as psychologists increasingly learn more about incentives. An incentive is that which arouses a feeling, kindles an incitement to action. A motive is similar, being that which prompts action, initiates movement, or guides behavior. As institutions become progressively large and bureaucratized, requiring an ever more careful planning of all the steps in the operational process, it is evident that nothing is more important than motivation. This is true even of whole economic and political systems; in the last analysis, superiority depends on incentive.

In the present chapter, what is known about incentives in managing systems, especially in large-scale business and government, is explored and any differences or peculiarities attaching to government are noted. Because incentive depends on institutional method as well as on inherent human responses, the discussion here is less psychological than it is motivational-administrative.

The possibilities relative to incentive may be briefly indicated. Psychologists such as L. L. Thurstone find that most people perform at only a fraction of their potential and that a release of underutilized energies usually creates enhanced individual job satisfactions and a heightened institutional morale. Sociologists and students of management have shown that new programs generally excite more enthusiasm than old ones do. But the fact is that in a mass-production society such as ours, most programs are old and already bureaucratic. It is necessary, therefore, to face up to individual and group expectations and satisfactions within a less than exciting preexisting institutional milieu. Most of every individual life is spent in this kind of working situation so that if administration is to be kept spirited and dynamic, capable of drawing forth more of the unused potential that exists everywhere, more must be known and applied in the area of psychological and institutional research. This chapter indicates some of the discoveries that have been made thus far and suggests a few working hypotheses that look promising for the future.

## The Old and the New View

An older view of motivation assumed that in a routine, specialized performance of the machine, any standardized fragment of a person could be fitted into the operation; that as units of production, employees were to be standardized, counted, and passed out like any other material or equipment needed in production. This conception of what is important, says one writer, "either left human beings out of the picture completely or substituted for the complex personality a simplified mechanical model of man." [1]

In the American environment, four different managerial emphases relative to incentives and morale have overlapped and succeeded each other in a kind of evolution. At the outset, because they were intent on organization and quantity production and knew next to nothing about human nature, administrators chiefly relied on *fear and punishment* to get results. Workers could be docked severely if they punched in a minute late. They could be fined for work spoilage. They could be fired by their foremen for infractions of rules. The philosophy was authoritarian and military in tone, and the individual either toed the line or faced the prospect of looking for another job.

Later, the emphasis shifted somewhat to *reward and concessions;* later still, as organized labor gained influence, as business organizations became larger, and as complexity spread, there was a search for some *magic formula* that would somehow solve the problem of how to get the best out of the human element in production. But there are no magic formulas and no short cuts. The current emphasis, therefore, is on *human relations,* on an adequate social psychology based on empirical research; on positive incentives. As noted in a previous chapter, what has so far been discovered in this area is little short of revolutionary in its effect on established viewpoints.

---

[1] Daniel Katz, "Morale and Motivation in Industry," Survey Research Center, University of Michigan (mimeo., Ann Arbor, Mich., 1949), p. 1.

Two pioneers in the field of motivation are Chester Barnard and Ordway Tead. As an experienced executive Barnard maintained that the alert manager will use positive incentives to bring out the best efforts of his employees and will apply sanctions only when he must for the sake of discipline.[2] There are several types of inducement to superior effort, including the material, the personal nonmaterial (the opportunity to advance, for example), desirable physical surroundings and conditions, and ideal benefactions (the satisfaction of personal ideals such as good workmanship). Among strictly institutional or administrative incentives, Barnard mentions attractive personal associations, the easy adaptation of conditions in the organization to habitual methods and attitudes of employees, an opportunity for enlarged participation in the organization, and the condition of communion, which is a sense of belonging to a group or an enterprise to which one is, in turn, both loyal and dedicated.

Barnard believes that financial rewards are low on the list of incentives, having reached the limit of usefulness, except in the case of a few men, when the "subsistence" level is attained. By subsistence, however, Barnard means a level of remuneration necessary to sustain family life at a degree of comfort that is expected in a particular vocational stratum, which is not the usual connotation of the term "subsistence." Most men work no harder for the sake of additional increments to material rewards, nor can they be induced thereby to devote more than a fraction more of their time to institutional effort. Successful administration has almost invariably been built on incentives that were either low or lacking in materialistic elements. Recent tests seem to confirm Barnard's position in this respect.

The personal, nonmaterial factors that so successfully stimulate human effort are the chance to acquire distinction, prestige, and personal power; the right to be considered successful and to be respected; and an opportunity for self-development. These are the incentives that count most. Others are pride of craftsmanship, opportunities for altruistic service, associational compatibility, and this thing called communion, or a sense of dedication to the group. This part of the analysis also has been confirmed by recent studies.

More than a decade after Barnard's views were published, Ordway Tead wrote *The Art of Administration,* in many respects an analysis coinciding with Barnard's. Every human personality, says Tead, is unique because, like the administrative situation itself, each is a different combination of common elements. Human beings have two kinds of interest: the internal, which is integrity or selfhood; and the external, which is the successful relation of this self to its surroundings. The basic principle is that every individual "wishes to stand well in his own

---

2 *The Functions of the Executive,* chapter entitled "The Economy of Incentives."

eyes and also in the eyes of those whose approval he values. Satisfactions are thus being sought in two directions at once—inner and outer. And the choices and balance of these two will differ from person to person." [3]

The inner and outer interests are interdependent and the skill with which the individual combines them determines both his personal integrity and the integration of his personality. In effecting this combination, furthermore, the individual seeks and is guided by values, which are influences or things held in sufficiently high regard by the individual so that he uses them to determine his choice of behavior. People are also what may be called other-minded, or altruistic, being happiest when they are devoted to something worthwhile outside themselves.

Although both Barnard and Tead have had some experience in government and their analyses apply inferentially to public administration as well as to business management, their thinking is primarily oriented toward business. In the field of government it is interesting to note the views of John Hobson, Lord Haldane, Sir Arthur Salter, and other British leaders, most of them economists, who at one time or another had seen government service.[4] Salter, for example, noted that among the highest type of men, financial gain is a less powerful incentive than dedication to nation and to humanity, and that, hence, although government salaries are not as high in the upper ranges as corresponding positions command in private business, there is an enormous appeal in the feelings of patriotism, power, and altruism that are engendered by identification with the government of one's country. This analysis coincides in most respects with those of Barnard and Tead, suggesting that the net differences in motivation in business and government are perhaps not as great as might be supposed.

One of the present authors has developed a scale of incentives beginning with financial gain at the bottom, followed by power, prestige, and public service at the top. Such a scale is, of course, an oversimplification because no one stops wanting financial security, power, and prestige simply because he craves most of all a chance to be acknowledged a public benefactor. But it does point to a truth recognized by many businessmen, that government has an advantage over business in that the public-service incentive may be so widely experienced by all its employees. Consequently, if the other desires can be met, service in government can be made widely appealing.[5]

---

[3] Ordway Tead, *The Art of Administration*, p. 45.
[4] Reported in Marshall E. Dimock, "The Potential Incentives of Public Employment," *American Political Science Review*, XXVII (August 1933), pp. 628-636. The five incentives dealt with in this article are financial rewards, security, prestige, pride of craftsmanship, and the public service philosophy (altruism).
[5] Marshall E. Dimock, *The Executive in Action*, pp. 252-253.

## Confirmation of Earlier Assumptions

As interest in the human aspects of administration has increased, some first-rate studies have been made in a number of business and manufacturing establishments, in public utilities, and in government. One of the first of these was the so-called Hawthorne experiment, conducted by Elton Mayo and F. J. Roethlisberger as early as 1933, and now a classic in the literature of personnel management.[6] According to this study, the principal things people desire in work situations is attention, solicitude, and due praise. Attention centered on employees raised morale and hence also production, irrespective of whether through that attention working conditions were improved or made worse. The manner in which people are supervised affects output more than do their surroundings, hours of work, or even rate of pay. In other words, people respond more favorably to attention than they do to physical factors or to other material inducements.

Most of the other studies cited here were made under the direction of the Survey Research Center at the University of Michigan, the concentration being on two main questions: What causal factors make for a high level of group performance? What causal factors make for a high level of group morale and individual satisfaction?

In the testimony of most workers, monetary rewards are apparently not the most important ones, *once a certain level of income has been attained.* "The central fact about the outcome of the studies of worker morale is that they do not corroborate the general philosophy of management that emphasizes the importance of external rewards." [7] This conclusion is substantiated by a nationwide poll of 3000 employees and several hundred employers, also reported by the Survey Research Center, in which it was sought to discover the relative position of eight morale factors by asking the employees to rate them in order of importance to them and asking the employers to rate them according to what they thought would be the choice of the employees. Although employers placed remuneration first on the list, employees placed it third. This does not mean, of course, that wages can be ignored as an incentive, but rather that if workers are at a wage scale in keeping with "the expectations of their industry and their community, there are many other aspects of the job which affect their satisfaction and enthusiasm for the job." [8]

---

6 Described in F. J. Roethlisberger and William J. Dickson, *Management and the Worker* (Cambridge, Mass.: Harvard University Press, 1939).

7 Katz, *loc. cit.*, p. 7.

8 *Ibid.*, p. 5. *Cf.* R. S. Urbrock, "Attitudes of 4430 Employees," *Journal of Social Psychology*, V (July 1934), pp. 365-377.

Security is another factor that employees apparently do not rate as highly as employers think they do. In the poll referred to, for example, the employers thought that job security would come second, but the employees put it eighth, at the end of the list. Clearly this was a subjective judgment subject to change in hard times. But the times were prosperous and many employees had never faced insecurity; hence other values were more in favor. As with remuneration, this does not mean that employees do not value security; merely that they rank other things higher if security is not in question.

Highest on the list in this particular poll, a majority of the employees put receiving credit for work done, whereas the employers put it in seventh place. Interesting work was the second choice among employees, again showing that for many people the work situation itself is usually more important than financial compensation. In a similar test among a group of manual and clerical workers, the three top factors were a congenial work group, being treated like human beings, and appreciation for good work done. According to the Michigan group, workers like jobs that give them a chance "to display their skill and to show their work [pride of craftsmanship], and they place considerable value on being a member of a congenial work group. They are favorably affected by a supervisor or boss who treats them as human beings; they are motivated to work for a company where there is confidence in the fairness of the top management." [9] In yet another study it was found that in a small group the factors most often mentioned for liking the job, in descending order of importance, were one's associates, the work itself, the boss, variety, freedom in work, hours, and earnings. The reasons for disliking the work were the work itself, low earnings, and long hours.[10]

An authority on labor relations has found that institutional workers usually rate their personal goals in this order: respect for their fellows (a combination of pride of craftsmanship and prestige), creature comforts, increasing control over one's own affairs, "knowing the score," the full utilization of one's capacities, the desire to experience consistence within one's self and among the parts of one's world, and a significant relationship to that world.[11]

Allowing for differences of vocabulary, there is a good deal of agreement among the results of these studies: morale and output both increase when the policy of management is employee-centered, findings that confirm the analyses of both Barnard and Tead. If employees are

---

9 Katz, loc. cit., p. 7.

10 R. Hoppock and S. Spiegler, "Job Satisfaction," Research of 1935-37, Occupations, National Vocational Guidance Association, No. 16 (Washington, D.C., 1938), pp. 636-639.

11 Cited in Neil W. Chamberlain, The Union Challenge to Management Control (New York: Harper & Row, Publishers, 1948), p. 247.

more interested in congenial working relationships than in material rewards above a certain level, the challenge to operating management is obvious: the way to improve morale and increase output is to improve internal administration and executive leadership.

## The Achievement Motive

When all is said and done, however, the fact remains that the strongest motivation is an individual matter and often it is a built-in quality, a factor that management also must take into careful consideration. The most interesting and significant research on this subject was pioneered by David McClelland and revolves around the concept of the so-called achievement motive.[12]

The achievement motive is apparently a built-in incentive to accomplishment, a need of the individual comparable to the other needs that actuate behavior. The quality is inborn as well as environmental, for it appears early in the life of the individual and cannot be explained on the basis of environment alone. It has been detected in children of both sexes and all races, nationalities, and conditions. The evidence of its presence is a strong early interest in self-expression, at about the time that formal schooling begins. When this need to achieve does not depend on social stimulation, approval, or disapproval, but is as persistent as appetite, then the achievement motive may be said to be built-in. People who have it are independent, persistent, not easily deterred; they think up tasks for themselves instead of having them suggested; they possess initiative early in life; they may have a passion for a particular field such as art, music, mathematics, science, reading—a wide range of knowledge. They tend to be somewhat lopsided in their interests; they resent interference and authority; they are self-disciplined and hence to some extent resist external discipline. Although most of them escape this extreme, they have the stuff of genius.

Similar factors relating to achievement may be found in whole societies. An achieving society is one in which relatively large numbers of people have the characteristics just mentioned. The primary unit is always the individual, enough individuals with the need to achieve constitute an achieving group, and enough achieving groups produce an achieving society.

In addition, however, McClelland's research suggests the importance of a factor not previously emphasized: the concept of the image. An intensely motivated individual, group, or society invariably has an image of what he or it dreams of becoming. Without such an image, there is

---

12 David C. McClelland *et. al.*, *The Achievement Motive* (New York: Appleton-Century-Crofts, 1953), and David C. McClelland, *The Achieving Society* (Princeton, N.J.; D. Van Nostrand & Company, Inc., 1961).

no appetite to achieve. With a workable image, there may be great and sustained accomplishment. McClelland found his clues in the Freudian idea of fantasy in which imagination and conceptualization created a vivid image.

This idea of imagery ties in closely with some of the results of empirical research in administration. Thus, the most effective executives are those who are able to conceptualize, to see things whole, to integrate, to use their constructive imagination, to convey to others their vision of the desirable and the practicable. There are many intervening steps, of course, between image and accomplishment, including planning, scheduling, organizing, leading, coordinating, and all the rest. Nevertheless, there is a striking resemblance between what McClelland has posited as a basic theory of a progressive society, and the conditions of progressive management.

McClelland's findings constitute an exciting challenge to the administrator. The need to achieve and actual achievement may both be measured, thus making periodic comparisons possible. Comparative studies in business and government show that career executives in Washington are equal, if not slightly superior, in achievement motivation, to a comparable group in private industry.[13] In the United States the achievement motive of the nation as a whole apparently reached its peak around 1898 and has since been declining. With the current acceleration of the need to achieve in certain other countries, including the USSR, the trends show that we also must now accelerate or be overtaken.

If theories of the achievement motive and the achieving society are valid—and so they appear, although some factors need additional testing—then the possibilities are significant in several directions. Growth is built-in, not confined to the period of formal education for the individual, but measured by a lifetime. Like people, societies also must have goals or they lose their drive. Most juvenile delinquency may be caused more than anything else by boredom and the lack of achievement motivation. In most governmental administration, the individual is the key factor, the group only a secondary one. Perhaps what most bureaucracies need is more room to innovate and to dream, with less emphasis on systems that tend in the opposite direction.

## Special Challenges to the Public Administrator

Although the factors that influence morale and motivation are generally alike in the same society, it has already been shown that government service has some distinctive advantages as well as some serious inequities in comparison with employment in commerce and industry. Government's greatest advantage is the patriotic, altruistic nature of most of

[13] McClelland, *The Achieving Society*, p. 295.

the work done. In public employment, the public service appeal is quickly felt, instead of developing later, as is the usual pattern in large corporations. Generally speaking, too, the merit system in government offers a greater security of employment than is usual in industry, and hence there is less fear of what may happen when one reaches fifty or sixty years.

As Theodore Roosevelt once remarked, government service appeals only to the red-blooded individual, not to those whose skins are thin. Some of the findings of the Brookings conference discussed in Chapter 3 bear this out. Political executives lead a much less sheltered life than do their business counterparts. Accountability in government is infinitely greater than it is in the private sector. Little that government does is immune from public debate, scrutiny, and inquiry, and disputes are argued in the open, not silenced by executive fiat. Thus the government executive must have a keen sensitivity to public desires along with a capacity to absorb abuse. The businessman's job usually stops at his portal, but to the government executive's job there are no limits, for it can lead to 1600 Pennsylvania Avenue, to Capitol Hill, and to the offices of pressure groups. Many able executives either refuse a government job or leave it after a short time because of the lower pay than for comparable work in industry, interruption of a career if the government job is a temporary one, the unsettling of family relationships, and the conflict of interest laws. Clearly the long-range solution, therefore, is to find tough-minded executives who will welcome the challenge of a lifetime career in government.

There are many advantages in government employment that tend, of course, to offset the adverse factors. Above all, there is the feeling of patriotism, already noted in several connections. In a survey of business executives who had held high-level posts in the federal government, for example, patriotism and the pull of the public service were found to lead the list of satisfactions gained through governmental employment. Confirming this, another poll of 180 businessmen with government experience showed that 70 percent reported patriotism as a significant incentive in times of war and international tension; but 30 percent thought that in normal times, patriotism was an insufficient incentive. Other influences mentioned were prestige, requests by high officials, the urgings of friends and colleagues, the example of others, and the opportunity to broaden one's contacts. Then there were the opportunities for self-development or self-fulfillment, a chance to pursue political objectives, to do more interesting and stimulating work, a desire to be influential in public affairs, to occupy a position of power, and a wish for prestige, esteem, and deference.[14]

The respect in which public and private employment differ most

---

[14] Bernstein, *The Job of the Federal Executive*, pp. 139, 141.

is in the matter of compensation. The findings of the Survey Research Center, it will be recalled, placed compensation third in importance rather than first, in the judgment of industrial workers. The same judgment might also prevail in government relative to salary ranges up to $15,000 or so a year, but thereafter the rates are generally lower than in the private sector. The principal reason given by many executives for quitting the federal service since World War II, for example—a period of steady inflation—has been the inadequacy of salaries compared with certain other areas of employment, especially in business and the professions. Income is relative, not absolute, the relation being to "the expectations of a skill group" or to "a degree of comfort that is expected in a particular vocational stratum." Consequently, when compensation in the higher ranks of government falls considerably below the level for men and women of similar education and skill in industry, the result is lowered morale in government accompanied by a greater desire on the part of public servants for income than for any other benefit in the work situation.

This question of compensation and of other perquisites of government employment has already been discussed in Chapter 3 and need not be pursued here. However, to round out the comparison with private employment and to indicate wherein public employment must be improved if it is to fulfill its crucial role and maintain a high level of morale, some of the areas that need attention are higher levels of compensation, protection of the prestige of the public service, and enhanced opportunities for leadership.

A task force of the second Hoover Commission studying the problem of morale in government found that some factors, such as material rewards, employee relations, working conditions, and the like, are within the administrator's immediate control and determination. But one of the most important elements of morale—the prestige of the government itself—is less susceptible of administrative control because it is influenced by the attitudes and traditions of business, agriculture, labor, and other areas of American society. "Each instance of an abuse of power or position for private ends," says the task force, "even though such instances are relatively rare, lowers the prestige of the government and damages the standing of the public service as a whole." Others who have the good name of the government in their keeping are members of Congress and other political leaders, and also the general public in that "there is a gossipy tendency to believe the worst about public officials on very slight evidence." [15] Having a direct bearing on the matter is the question of politics in the merit system, including the granting of

15 Commission on Organization of the Executive Branch of the Government, *Task Force Report on Personnel and Civil Service* (Washington, D.C.: Government Printing Office, 1955), pp. 117-118.

improper exemptions from the competitive service, entry into the service
without genuine competition, and the political clearance (approval by
a member of Congress or other politician) of appointments and promotions.

There is reason for encouragement, however, because there is evidence of a new vigor and a more imaginative approach to the whole
morale problem since the late 1930s. Personnel administration has
adopted the human relations approach. Leadership is being emphasized
as never before. The Civil Service Commission administers an incentive
awards system to secure better employee performance and to attract
suggestions for improving services and achieving economy and efficiency.
The Commission also helps the operating agencies to establish such
programs of their own, keeps them informed on new developments in
the subject in both government and industry, and circulates employee
suggestions to all agencies that might benefit from them. In 1962 suggestions were being received at the rate of 155 for every 1000 employees
on the federal payroll, nearly $65 million was saved in the first year,
and nearly $3 million was paid out in cash awards. In the same year
more than 75,000 superior performance awards were made at the rate
of 33 for every 1000 employees, and honor awards for distinguished or
meritorious service were made to 1633 employees. Since 1957 the highest
award in the federal government has been the President's Award for
Distinguished Federal Civilian Service.

Another source of encouragement, this time from a private source,
was the establishment in 1952 of the Rockefeller Public Service Awards
for outstanding service by civilians in the federal government, to be
administered by the Woodrow Wilson School of Public and International Affairs at Princeton University. Under this program, recipients
nominated by government officials receive grants to enable them to
spend from six to twelve months at any college or university, in this
country or abroad, or in educational travel, or in a comparable form
of study, the grant amounting to the equivalent of federal compensation
plus tuition, moving, and other expenses. An additional objective of the
program, adopted in 1961, is to enable officials of long service, if they
wish, to make their experience available to others. The immediate popularity of this program among federal employees not only demonstrates
the appeal of such an incentive but in addition, as a task force of the
second Hoover Commission noted, indicates "a substantial demand for
off-duty training" and emphasizes the great potential value of such
training.[16]

---

16 *Ibid.*, p. 73.

## Program Factors in Motivation

A consideration of the psychological and comparative aspects of the incentive problem leads directly to the matter of what program policies will help to determine a high level of employee morale. There are some important rules to keep in mind:

1. If a program has a compelling social purpose, such as child welfare or soil conservation, with a strong appeal to many people, it enjoys an advantage that other programs, however necessary, may not enjoy. Employees willingly accept a good deal of frustration and disappointment if they are spurred on by a cause.

2. If the work in question is interesting in itself, even though the program may not be an especially urgent one, its employees may gain much individual satisfaction from it and hence will demonstrate a high level of morale.

3. If the management of a program utilizes nonmonetary as well as monetary incentives, all employees will be favorably affected, irrespective of what may be done in connection with other factors.

4. Good working conditions, including physical surroundings, contribute to high morale because most people are ordinarily far more sensitive to environmental and temperamental influences than is usually supposed.

5. The more attention the group receives, the more it produces, a factor brought out in the so-called Hawthorne experiment.

6. Morale is higher among employees who are treated as human beings than among those who are treated as so many machines to get the work done. Thus, morale is significantly related to supervision and is highest among the employees of the supervisor who has a genuine insight into motivations and especially one who openly recognizes good work well done. Morale is also high when supervisors are reasonable in what they expect, when they stand up in behalf of their employees, and when they welcome their ideas and suggestions.

7. The size of the work group affects morale in that a small group stimulates morale and a large one lowers it.

8. The centralization and pulling upward of all decision making chokes off the contributions of the work group and negates morale and motivation. But when work groups themselves are allowed to share in the setting of the bogey, or quota, output is usually effectively increased.

9. People do better work when they are allowed a certain amount of discretion and freedom of choice than when all decisions are made for them. When the individual can *voluntarily* identify himself with his job and with the work of his group, his potentialities may be fully utilized in the production process. Supervisors who use a tight rein are seldom as effective as those who use a looser one.

10. If the individual is able to "internalize" the goals and tasks of the group, in the sense of making them a part of himself, his stimulation will come from within himself instead of from outside sources that are more artificial. Further, such internalized drive is more effective in the long run because it is cumulative and does not easily cause undue fatigue. As in the acquisition of knowledge, incentives in employment are wholly effective only when they have become part of the working equipment of the individual.

11. Employees seem to bestow their primary loyalty on the primary group, which in most cases is the work group; higher loyalties, such as those to the employer, are derived or secondary. Consequently, morale must be won, for it can seldom be bought; it grows naturally from the bottom up and cannot, as a rule, be artificially manipulated from the top. As one interesting study has shown, "company men," meaning those who make the greatest show of loyalty to symbols, are not the most highly motivated nor are they the most productive workers.[17]

12. And finally, morale does not develop by chance; on the contrary, to develop it is a central responsibility of the supervisor. Moreover, studies indicate that it is line officials rather than staff officials who must be mainly responsible for building morale, for it is the job of line management to get the facts, interpret them, and make the decisions that directly affect morale.

F. Morstein Marx and Wallace Sayre note that the kind of motivation that produces morale is both individual and group, psychological and managerial, and involves commitment to desirable purposes, persistence against adversity, and a capacity for constant renewal.[18] Some of the important factors are these:

*Individual*

1. The institutional climate should allow for self-expression and self-accommodation.
2. There should be outlets for the individual's pride of workmanship.
3. To encourage a sense of identity and belonging, the individual must be able to see the relation between his own purposes and values with those of the group.

*Group*

1. The prestige of the group is important, especially when it relates to what the public considers to be important values.

---

17 Katz, *loc. cit.*, p. 7.
18 Fritz Morstein Marx and Wallace S. Sayre, "Morale and Discipline," in Fritz Morstein Marx, ed., *Elements of Public Administration* (Englewood Cliffs, N.J.: Prentice-Hall, Inc., 1959), pp. 435-439.

2. Motivation is sparked by the opportunity for personal participation in the formulation and execution of group objectives.

3. Since high morale is both emotional and intellectual, the decisions of leadership must inspire approval.

4. Serious inconsistencies in group purposes create stresses and strains that endanger group identity.

5. Morale is promoted by an adequate flow of information and the opportunity to share in institutional thinking.

6. A feeling of security is a by-product, an effect, not an objective, and can be easily overemphasized resulting in complacency, smugness, and exclusiveness.

There are other factors in this complex that are occasionally mentioned in the literature of public administration, but some of them are ambiguous and debatable. Thus, unity is said to be relatively more important in relation to ends than to means. Homogeneity is not necessarily as effective as balance. A group feeling of success is a by-product rather than an objective. And indoctrination is a mixed blessing when deception is involved, although unquestionably indoctrination in the best sense is necessary when the objective is educational.

Motivation is such a highly personal matter that generalization is precarious. Moreover, problems of motivation vary along with the nature of the organization, the attitudes prevailing among people who have been associated with it for a long time, with different periods in the organization's history, and with different stages in the individual employee's career. And in addition, *" 'bigness' in modern organizations, which tends to separate management from the worker, does not make an individualized approach an easy one."* [19]

## Employee Counseling

One way to give this individualized attention is through employee counseling, the purpose being to give personal as contrasted with group advice to employees who seek it because of some difficulty arising either at work or at home and in such a manner as to affect his work. On the basis of a survey made in the early 1940s, the counselor's focus of attention is in four main areas: effective job performance, satisfactory working conditions, personal adjustments within the plant, and community and domestic difficulties that affect the employee's ability to deliver a full day's work.

Under the systems currently in use, counseling is done either by the

---

19 U. S. Civil Service Commission, *Recognizing Employees Through Incentive Awards* (Washington, D.C.: Government Printing Office, September 1954), p. 2. Italics added.

supervisor or by specially trained experts attached to the personnel office and acting as roving consultants at various levels of line activity. In the latter case there is the familiar problem of a specialist having to secure the cooperation of the department head, supervisor, or foreman, because without such cooperation there can be no effective counseling. But the responsibility of securing good employee adjustments to work, says Ordway Tead, is basically a line one and hence should be located in the line units instead of in the personnel office. If the supervisor is too busy for the job himself, then the number of workers under one foreman should be reduced and each foreman should be "so trained, so guided, and so compensated that he is truly competent to be the over-all head of personnel as well as [to] process problems in his department. Ideally, at the point of day-to-day operation the foreman should be his own personnel officer. He has heretofore and he will again draw substantial staff aid from the personnel officer; and he can always refer complicated personal difficulties of individual workers to the personnel office." [20]

The best system, therefore, is to make it possible for the foreman and his workers to have the time, the skill, and the desire "to work out their problems together without benefit of another functionary who has to be integrated into the picture." In suggesting fifteen principles to guide employee counseling, the one concerning relationships within the organization is probably the best that can be devised in this area: "The responsibility of the foreman for the competent conduct of his department," says Tead, "is a unitary one. All efforts of employe counselors to help facilitate the work within a department are subject to the agreement of the foreman. Within the department the employe counselor is subordinate to (and helpful to) a foreman. For his basic effort, status and competence, the employe counselor is responsible to the Personnel Manager." [21]

The employee counselor must be guided by facts and by a mutually arrived at sense of justice; he cannot rely on tricks and techniques. He must be personally amiable and yet not too soft. And he must be in a position to guarantee the employee complete secrecy in discussing personal problems when disclosure might be prejudicial to the employee's status in the organization.

---

[20] Ordway Tead, "Employe Counseling: A New Personnel Assignment—Its Status and Its Standards," *Advanced Management*, VIII (July-September 1943), pp. 97-103.

[21] *Ibid.*, pp. 101-102.

## Balancing Incentives and Sanctions

The pleasure-pain formula made famous by Utilitarian philosophers assumes that rewards and punishments, positive incentives and the negative fear of retribution, are the chief regulators of human conduct. In concluding this discussion of motivation and morale, some word should be said about this central issue.

It has been said that a former point of view in management, dominant less than fifty years ago, stressed an either/or proposition based on fear: Either you do as I say or I will fire you. Although the right to fire or to demote an employee under certain circumstances remains a tool of management for disciplinary purposes, as a dominant point of view it has been replaced by a positive emphasis on incentives and morale. This change of attitude is due partly to the growing strength of organized labor, which protects its members from arbitrary action, partly to the increasing social consciousness of management, and partly to the growing realization that positive incentives are more conducive to the welfare of the enterprise than negative sanctions based on fear of demotion or dismissal. The changed approach is so widespread that it now applies not only to the work situation but also to child raising, education, and many other human activities. The question arises, therefore, whether there is any longer a need for the concept of sanctions.

It is believed that there is. Chester Barnard points out that there are many forms of persuasion.[22] Although the most effective are positive motives having self-propulsive powers, these alone are not enough; if they were, the millennium would have arrived. Consequently, other forms of persuasion must also be used, the idea being to provide a balance of methods that will achieve the results desired. Among these methods, Barnard believes that the fear motivation has a necessary and proper place. For his part, Millett mentions five types of sanctions in decreasing order of severity: the power of dismissal, suspension without compensation for a given period, withholding promotion or a pay increase, reassignment to another job or another place, and official reprimand.[23]

Exclusion is the means of separating undesirable individuals from the organization in the interest of efficiency and the morale of those who are doing a proper job. A second and related purpose of exclusion, a corollary of the first, is its use "as a means of persuasion *by example,* to create fear among those not directly affected, so that they will be disposed to render to an organization certain contributions. It presents

---

22 *Op. cit.,* p. 149.
23 John D. Millett, *Management in the Public Service* (New York: McGraw-Hill Book Company, Inc., 1954), p. 15.

realistically the alternative either of making these contributions or of foregoing the advantages of association." [24] Contributions secured by force, concludes Barnard, seem often to be a necessary form of cooperation.

So far has the pendulum swung from the earlier fear psychology, however, that there are now many writers who would take issue with Barnard and contend that fear per se has no place in the methods of management. The use of example they would agree to, but the use of fear, as such, they would reject. They believe that although dismissal may sometimes be necessary to maintain the efficiency and morale of the organization, in most cases dismissal does more harm than good, especially if opinion within the institution fails to support the decision. Here again is the proposition that the key factor is the morale of the work group. If the group believes the dismissal to be "for the good of the order," the action will reinforce confidence in the justice and predictability of management. This does not mean that the right to fire should be left to democratic decision; it means only that a wise management will consider employee opinion and take pains to inform it when borderline cases arise involving severance of employment.

Rather than argue that sanctions can be entirely eliminated, however, it seems nearer the truth to say that as positive incentives are made effective there is less need to apply negative sanctions, and that in any case a sanction should be reserved for individual cases and rarely if ever used on a group. Care must be taken, of course, not to tip the balance too far in either direction. The complete elimination of sanctions would represent so soft a policy that it would quickly get the administrator into trouble. In any over-all formula, inspiration and discipline in proper amounts are still complementary ingredients.

---

[24] Barnard, *op. cit.*, p. 149.

## BIBLIOGRAPHY AND CASES

### Annotated Reading Suggestions

Before the role of incentives could be fully appreciated, certain traditional assumptions of civil service had to be changed. On this, see David M. Levitan, "The Neutrality of the Civil Service," **Public Administration Review**, 2 (Autumn 1942), and Leon Epstein, "Political Sterilization of Civil Servants: The United States and Great Britain," **Public Administration Review**, 10 (Autumn 1950). An early anticipation of positive incentives is found in Marshall E. Dimock, "The Potential Incentives of Public Employment," **American Political Science Review**, 27 (August 1933).

Bureaucracy and its tendency to dehumanize tends to weaken incentives. On this, see Reinhard Bendix, "Bureaucracy and the Problem of Power," *Public Administration Review*, 5 (Summer 1945), or Marshall E. Dimock, "Bureaucracy Self-Examined," *Public Administration Review*, 4 (Summer 1944).

Perhaps nowhere is the choice between routine and motivated behavior more forcefully stated than in E. N. Gladden, *Civil Service or Bureaucracy?* (London: Staples, 1956). Some of the basic challenges are also dealt with in Everett Reimer's review, "Magic and Science in Human Relations," *Public Administration Review*, 12 (Summer 1952).

A discussion of the positive incentives that should supplement bureaucracy are found in Marshall E. Dimock, *Administrative Vitality; The Conflict with Bureaucracy* (Harper & Row, 1959), Part III. On the significance of a public service philosophy, see H. C. Nixon, "Ethics and Politics," *Public Administration Review*, 12 (Autumn 1952).

*Advanced Management* is a good source of articles on monetary and non-monetary incentives. See especially Robert Wolf, "Non-Financial Incentives," 5 (1940); H. B. Maynard, "Some Aspects of Non-Financial and Financial Incentives," 7 (1942); and Donald MacKenzie, "Wage Incentives," 9 (1944).

On the new, positive approach to motivation, see the following: Chris Argyris, *Personality Fundamentals for Administrators* (Yale University Labor and Management Center, 1953); Robert L. Katz, "Skills of an Effective Administrator," *Harvard Business Review*, 33 (January-February 1955), and "Human Relations Can be Sharpened," *ibid.*, 34 (July-August 1956); Edward C. Bursk, ed., *Human Relations For Management: The Newer Perspective* (Harper & Row, 1956); Robert Dubin, *Human Relations in Administration* (Prentice-Hall, 1951); Morton Grodzins, "Public Administration and the Science of Human Relations," *Public Administration Review*, 11 (Spring 1951); Connie C. Frost, "Supplementing Pay with Recognition," *Personnel Administration*, 19 (November-December 1956); Department of the Army, *Promoting the Will to Work* (Government Printing Office, 1954); U. S. Civil Service Commission, *Recognizing Employees Through Incentive Awards* (Government Printing Office, 1954); and William B. Parsons, "The Personnel Function in Public Management," *Public Administration Review*, 17 (Summer 1957).

Finally, as suggested in the text, two indispensable sources are David McClelland, *The Achievement Motive* (Appleton-Century-Crofts, 1953), and *The Achieving Society* (Van Nostrand, 1961), for these are the new frontiers of a technological age.

## Case Studies

Most to the point in the Stein *Case Book* is *The Attack on the Cost of Living Index*, that involved the integrity of the Bureau of Labor Statistics, an important economic agency of the federal government. The story was written in 1951 by Kathryn Smul Arnow and is seventy pages long.

Another interesting and colorful case is No. 1 in the ICP series, *The Firing of Pat Jackson,* reported by W. H. Riker, seventeen pages. The account is by the disputants themselves and involves policies as well as personalities.

Another case on the subject of integrity (also pressure groups) is No. 68, **Battery Additive Controversy,** thirty-three pages, prepared by S. A. Lawrence in 1962. The controversy took place in the Bureau of Standards.

In many ways, however, the most appealing case is No. 22, **Van Waters Case,** by T. H. Eliot, fifty pages. This is the story of a highly respected social worker in Massachusetts who became involved in a dispute with her superior because of differences in ideas and values. At the time, the case received national publicity because of its concern with professional standards.

Finally, there is an ICP case similar to one mentioned in the preceding chapter from the British collection; this is No. 44, **Personnel Problems in Converting to Automation,** by J. R. Bell, fourteen pages.

# 17

# Coordination
# and Control

THE MORE CAREFULLY a program is planned, the more meticulously organization and roles are delineated, and the more stress placed on supervision along functional lines, the more important it becomes that these aspects of an ongoing enterprise be brought together again into a commensurate unity, and the progress of the program checked to assure adherence to schedule in the attainment of goals. Hence the importance of coordination and control. On the American scene, and especially in the larger governing units, coordination is probably the greatest single weakness of public administration.

Why is coordination seemingly so difficult? Is it because the more freedom there is, the harder it is to coordinate? Is it because pressure groups work to avoid coordination? Is it because the machinery of government is creaky? Is it because human intelligence and imagination have not kept pace with the accelerating subdivision of specialization and organization? Or is there a simpler explanation: that the principles of coordination are less well understood than those of planning, delegation, and supervision?

Above everything, administration is an attempt to bring diverse units into a working relationship so that together they may produce a socially desirable result.[1] *Coordination* is placing the many aspects of an enter-

---

[1] Nowhere has this been better expressed than in an essay entitled "Making Sense Out of Things in General," by Paul H. Appleby, a former newspaperman who

prise in proper position relative to each other and to the program of which they are a part; it is harmoniously combining agents and functions toward the achievement of a desired goal. *Control* is checking the speed and direction of action, regulating steps in a larger process aimed at a particular objective; it is synchronization, accountability, and the evaluation of accomplishment.

Once the goals of the program have been set, its plans and policies determined, money provided, organization tailored to the need, personnel assigned, directions given, delegations determined, and supervision provided for, then coordination is the means of bringing all of these factors together in an interlocking relationship, and control is the technique whereby all are checked and kept on the track toward the goals that were set in the first place. Coordination is the active means by which a blend is secured; control is the analytical method by which the blend is regularly tested and evaluated. Thus coordination and control close the circle in the administrative process.

## *Some Rules of Coordination*

Empirically speaking, the following generalizations relative to coordination appear to be valid:

1. The more the work of a bureaucracy is subdivided, the more important it is that the components be assembled in a unified relationship if the social purpose of the program is to be furthered.

2. In the sense of social accomplishment, specialization is inherently efficient, but much of this efficiency is lost unless integration and teamwork can also be secured. Consequently, the area of overlap is often more efficient than any of the ingredients operating in isolation.

3. The integration of diverse functions occurs in individuals and in groups, and the better the individual integrations, the better the group integration is likely to be.

4. Coordination relies on the authority that accompanies hierarchy and position; it relies also on individual competence, understanding, and voluntary cooperation.

5. The better the goals of the program are understood and accepted by those who work for it, the easier it is to secure voluntary cooperation from them.

6. The better the systems of organization and communications, the more likely it is that authority in the sense of domination may be minimized.

---

became a proponent of big government at a relatively early age but never lost his perspective and his sense of humor. Found in *Public Administration Review* 22 (December 1962), pp. 175-181.

7. Where delegation and administration by objectives are a widely held philosophy, voluntary initiative can be relied upon to secure cooperation.

8. Voluntary cooperation is most easily achieved when mutual trust, confidence, and the encouragement of positive incentives offset a natural institutional tendency to isolationism.

9. Even when conditions evoke voluntary cooperation, coordination is difficult because people in a bureaucracy have a natural desire to be left alone. Consequently the application of the techniques of coordination is a time-consuming responsibility of the executive and becomes more so as he rises in the hierarchy.

10. Relatively more time is spent on external coordination than on the internal variety.

## The Relationships and Forces of Coordination

The relationships of coordination constitute a kind of web which on analysis turns out to be more rational than confusing. Thus, in a study of fifty-six assembly-line foremen to determine the relative importance of various aspects of their work and how they spent their time, the evaluation of their peers was that the best supervisors were those who spent most of their time outside their own work group. In other words, the relationships of these men were not only horizontal but also diagonal or lateral in the sense that they had contacts with the subordinates of other foremen. The average foreman tested was in contact with someone else for an average of four hours and thirty-six minutes of so-called interacting time in each eight-hour day. Of this interacting time, two hours and seven minutes were devoted to the foreman's own employees and twenty-eight minutes to his superiors. This left two hours for relationships with other foremen—the lateral or peer relationship—and for dealings with the subordinates of other foremen, the diagonal relationship.[2] And remember that this is first-line supervision, not middle nor top management where the ratio of interacting time is higher.

Why were those who spent relatively more time than others on external relationships voted the better foremen? Possibly because in external relationships it is necessary to rely upon persuasion and human relations rather than on authority. By the softer method a foreman can get more benefits for and from his workers: better quality, better service, better emoluments, better cooperation. The tactful administrator who has what we have called political sense secures cooperation. The executive with enough imagination and sensitiveness to enable him to conceptualize, can think of all the relationships involved in the administrative process and knows how to blend then.

---

2 Frank J. Janinski, "Foreman Relationships Outside the Work Group," *Personnel*, 33 (September 1956), pp. 130-136.

These coordinating skills are much emphasized by Wallace Sayre who relies on what he calls fields of forces in administration to explain his philosophy of leadership.[3] Administration, he says, is a complex of fields of forces and the best administrator is the one who can blend these fields in a way to serve the purposes of the agency and the larger public. For a bureau, which in the federal government is middle management, the arrangement is shown on the accompanying chart.

### FIELDS OF FORCES IN ADMINISTRATION

*(Federal Bureau)*

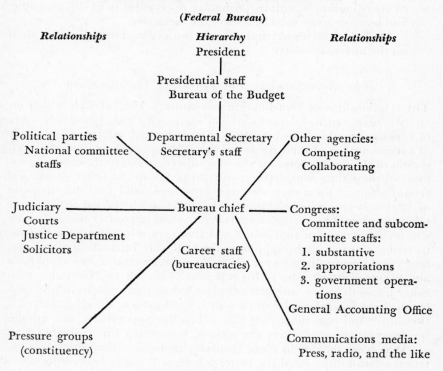

At the center of the constellation is the bureau chief. Above him the hierarchy leads to the President. Below him it leads to career officials who are his subordinates. In starlike relationships are political parties, other agencies, pressure groups, and the media of communication. Serving as his right and left anchor are the judiciary and Congress. He com-

---

[3] The following is based on author's notes taken at a lecture given at Williamsburg, Virginia by Professor Sayre during an executive development conference sponsored by The Brookings Institution.

monly deals with six congressional committees, three from each house. The General Accounting Office is related to the congressional complex, the Bureau of the Budget to the staff agencies in the Office of the President. Some of the agencies with which the bureau chief deals are competitive with his own and he may fear the possibility of being absorbed by them; others are collaborative and make useful allies.

This field theory, suggestive as it is of physics, is a valuable one for understanding the complexity of the forces that circulate in administration and the need to coordinate them. The illustration is not complete in every respect, of course, but it helps to show not only the importance of the subject but also the fact that in the federal government, coordination is not only administrative but also political in the best sense of the word, and hence far from the monotonous function it is sometimes assumed to be.

### Bureaucratic Resistances to Coordination

A common obstacle to coordination is specialization, which produces a splintering effect in administration and often creates a bureaucratic resistence to it.[4] The term "bureaucracy" describes a form of organization that is widespread in the modern world. Large institutions made necessary by the rapid development of science and technology must of necessity make use of the division of labor principle, which is specialization, to a degree never before required. Specialization leads to an intricate, hierarchical organization. But this kind of organization impedes direct communication and replaces face-to-face relationships with rules and regulations reduced to writing. These encourage uniformity and standardization but also tend toward impersonality and a loss of the human relations ingredients in administration.

Being rational, bureaucracy possesses a certain inherent efficiency, but because it is characteristically large, specialized, and impersonal, it also has disadvantages, including loss of energy. Consequently the job of modern management in every aspect of administration is to buttress the weaknesses of bureaucracy, a need that is especially apparent in the area of coordination.

The chief disadvantage of bureaucracy is what has been referred to as isolationism. Excessive specialization encourages exclusiveness, a cloistering of the professional group, an isolationism that, often unconsciously, resists contacts with other groups. But there can be no coordination without such contact. Other factors in the complex are pride, a dislike of having the group's province invaded, an understandable

---

[4] The following analysis is based on Marshall E. Dimock, *Administrative Vitality: The Conflict with Bureaucracy* (New York: Harper & Row, Publishers, 1959), part II.

desire to be left alone and to develop one's own personality and independent existence, and the threat of standardization and excessive conformity: in short, all the elements dealt with by Whyte in *The Organization Man*.

Two other ways in which bureaucracy loses energy are when individuals tend to avoid responsibility, and when they try to compensate for their loss by empire building for the group in an effort to enhance their feeling of security.

The coordinator must understand these bureaucratic excesses if he would turn them to the advantage of his program. The antidote to cloistering is involvement in the determination of higher goals, planning, policy making, decision making—every aspect of administration that might appeal to the specialist group's sense of importance and quicken the pulse. Incentives also may be improved with an appeal to the achievement motive, the challenge of innovation, enterprise, and risk taking. The corrective to bureaucratic indifference and dislike of initiative is again through motivation and getting people accustomed to assuming responsibility as soon as possible. The antidote to empire building is to encourage in people and in groups a sense of their own selfhood and to create normal outlets for prestige and feelings of success.

The fact is that successful coordination is less a matter of technique than it is a philosophy arising out of mature reflection on a number of administrative variables and values that must be combined: bureaucracy and enterprise, the individual and the group, initiative and cooperation, selfhood and the common good, specialization and integration, authority and voluntarism, consistency and variety. Thus approach and method are more important than technique in the sense of gadgetry, which may do more harm than good.

Nevertheless, certain methods, many of which have already been dealt with, are useful. They include goals mutually arrived at, plans jointly made, policies clearly understood and approved, roles clearly assigned, employees with the achievement motive, supervisors who like to see people grow, informal organization and relationships stressing lateral and diagonal associations, training programs, staff conferences, firmness, and knowing who is the boss. In short, there is needed a combination of human relations and decisiveness, challenging goals and voluntary cooperation, individual development and program success.

## Administrative Control

It has been said that administrative control is the means by which management determines whether objectives are being reached efficiently and on time. Thus the administrator measures effort in relation to goals and assures himself that he is attaining his objectives. In a sense, a dependable internal control system is like a report sent to a gunner firing at a target beyond the range of his vision.

Although the current emphasis is on human relations, the importance of the internal control functions is not thereby reduced. It is easy to neglect a former emphasis when a new one appears, but the temptation should be resisted in favor of a new synthesis. As an *attitude*, the concept of control may properly be modified as the human element receives more recognition, but as a *system* of administrative techniques for securing maximum efficiency, control must always play a central role in administrative management, and in public administration it should receive far more attention than in the past.

When those who exercise the control function become officious, a block is placed in the way of sound human relations. The authoritarian personality has no more place in administration—private or public—than in any other part of a democracy. Mary Parker Follett rendered an outstanding service when she underscored the dehumanizing effect of overemphasis on the control concept and so-called ultimate authority. "When writers on business management," said Miss Follett, "speak of 'ultimate authority' and 'supreme control' as two of the functions of administration, I think that expressions are being used which are a survival of former days." [5] More than a generation ago this farsighted woman realized that so many people contribute to the actual making of administrative decisions that the concept of final authority is losing whatever validity it ever had.

To conclude from this, however, that the techniques of internal control may be deemphasized would be an unwarranted misconstruction of what Miss Follett and others of the human relations school have advocated. The desirable combination is a human relations attitude coupled with the most reliable tools for measuring performance that can be devised.

## The Strategy of Control

Control is a practical matter, for it reduces a work program to measurable units and then registers the results instantly and accurately so that everyone in the organization will know precisely where the work stands in relation to predetermined goals at any given time. This is not something that the top executive or the efficiency expert with his stopwatch and layout and motion studies, can do unaided. Rather, like planning, control also is a function in which everyone in the organiza-

---

[5] "The Illusion of Final Authority," *Bulletin of the Taylor Society,* XI (October 1926), pp. 243-246; conveniently reprinted in Lepawsky, ed., *Administration: The Art and Science of Organization and Management,* pp. 326-327.

tion must have a part. The media of control are reports, charts, budgets, standards, and expenditure limitations, all of which are put to use in organization planning, management engineering, research, work planning, budgetary control and cost analysis, and personnel administration.

The kind of control system used depends, first of all, on the type of program being administered, being more or less elaborate as the program requires. Nevertheless, because they consist of a fairly limited range of techniques, most internal control systems have certain characteristics in common. To begin with, a control system is not something worked out in a remote place for the benefit of a theoretical situation; rather, a control system must serve each working unit at each level of coordination. In the installation of a control system, the three main steps are designing the system, creating the norms to be met, and charting the degree to which actual performance varies from these norms. In designing a control system, one must be certain that the information to be gathered is useful, adequate, and measurable.

Furthermore, before the system is put into effect, all who are to be concerned with it must have a chance to discuss it, criticize it, and accept it emotionally as well as intellectually. It is important that those affected be able to answer clearly the question, What does this mean to me in my job? If employees can be shown that a proposed control system is a tool by which they may measure their own progress, improve their performance, take greater pride in their work, and increase their chances for rewards and promotions, then they are likely to show a personal interest in it, which is one of the conditions of success. Consequently, individual employees and their unions must be satisfied that the standards are fair. If the system is regarded merely as a speed-up or as the means of getting more work for the same pay, it may damage employee morale with all that that implies in the way of efficiency, production, public relations, and the like.

Because the operation of a control system rests on accurate reporting, specified information on current operations must be routinely gathered at the working level as a normal part of daily operations and not as an extra burden on employees. Such information must be reported in terms of dollar units, time units, or physical units of some kind; in other words, it must be measurable. This point is often overlooked and much time is wasted in trying to fit unmeasurable factors into a pattern that calls for concrete data. Here is good advice from business experience:

> Executives desire control over their operations. But when they seek to measure the unmeasurable, when they require personal beliefs to be justified in quantitative terms, when they compel the lower ranks to spend time in getting measurable results rather than in meeting actual

operating problems, then control has become self-defeating. *Control of situations by "measurability" may be as inefficient as control over people by arbitrary use of position.*[6]

When the needed information has been reported, it is then consolidated at each successive level of coordination so that officials at every step in the organization may have a complete picture of accomplishment. The test of a proper control system is whether the information provided is sufficiently pertinent, clear, and detailed (including charts where feasible) to show the supervisor where he should make an inquiry or take some kind of action. To learn where the trouble spots are, he must be able to compare accomplishment as reported through the control system with a norm—a standard or a quota—showing where the work should be at a series of given points. Norms are provided partly through a system of budgeting that sets expenditure limitations and forecasts for accomplishment over stated periods in the work year, through an accompanying system of work planning, and through a reliable system of cost accounting.

It has been emphasized that control is based on measurement. In contrast to private enterprise, government performs many duties that defy classification as products or even as services. A municipal police department, for example, protects the lives and property of a city; this is clearly a service in a broad sense, but what is a unit of protection and how much is it worth? The State Department protects nationals of the United States traveling in other countries; this also is a service, but how is it measured and what is it worth? The courts are open to all citizens, but in any year only a small proportion of the people use them; what is their value in terms that can be measured? The difficulty of identifying measurable units in such cases immediately becomes apparent.

Nevertheless, there are large areas in public administration where it is possible to apply standards of measurement comparable to those used in industry, to analyze work units, production units, production centers, and processes so as to ascertain the cost of a finished product or service. The vocabulary may be a little different from the one common in industry but the procedure is the same. At the municipal level, efficiency measurement has been developed for police, fire, education, and library services, and for public works, but in addition a number of control procedures covering the adequacy—as distinguished from the efficiency—of municipal services have also been evolved. At the state level the Institute of Public Administration in New York has pointed the way in areas of highway administration and educational ad-

---

6 Learned, Ulrich, and Booz, *Executive Action,* pp. 136ff. This chapter on "Control and Management" is recommended for its clarity and emphasis on the main issues.

ministration. It must be admitted, however, that most state studies so far have shown that while the *results* of government activity, or its efficiency, are in fact measurable, attempts actually to measure them have fallen short of what is possible.

Should time and motion studies, as conducted in many industries, be used also in government where the work is similar to that of a business enterprise? A reference to scientific management often conjures up a picture of a man with a stopwatch. He may be trying to discover what the standard time should be for the performance of a certain operation like making a connection at a telephone switchboard or turning a strip of steel out of a perforating machine. But in public administration this type of management engineering—which represents the highest degree of specialization among control experts—has thus far made little headway even in activities of a business type in which government engages.

Although time and motion experts may never become very numerous in government, a few measures aimed at accomplishing some of the same results are appearing. Chief among them is work simplification, introduced in the federal government at the end of World War II by the Bureau of the Budget, which has also instituted training courses in the techniques involved. Work simplification is closely related to job methods training and both tie in with supervisory training. Work simplification is also related to work planning and to work control. Hence it is a versatile and useful tool.

The Department of the Army believes that work simplification makes possible a more effective use of manpower, equipment, materials, and space. The five *steps* involved are these: select the job to be improved, record the job details, analyze the job details, develop the improvements, and install the new method.[7] As installed in some other federal agencies, a program of work simplification emphasizes the distribution, sequence, and volume of work.

The five main *techniques* of the procedure—also identified with administrative control—are the work distribution chart, the flow process chart, the work count, motion economy studies, and layout studies. As described by the Army, the work distribution chart is a simple tabulation of the various tasks performed by the individuals in an organization, classified according to the major activities of the program. The time spent by each person on each task is shown and the total chart reveals the total man-hours spent on each activity. The flow process chart traces and highlights the flow of productive effort, recording the steps involved in a particular procedure so as to show up duplicated effort, backtracking, and bottlenecks. The work count indicates the

7 Department of the Army, *Techniques of Work Simplification*, Pamphlet No. 20-300 (Washington, D.C., 1951), p. 1.

effect of the relative volume of an operation on the methods used. Motion economy studies delimit the space area in which an individual doing a particular kind of work can do it with efficiency, and show how that task can be accomplished with a minimum of physical effort. And finally, layout studies examine the relationship of physical layout to the work methods used.

A final point to be emphasized is that an internal control system must rely on a number of elements and not look only to one. Since modern statistical and accounting systems are essential tools, management must be free to use them at any time. But this means that a common tendency to isolate these functions at the overhead levels of goverment must be avoided.

Equally essential are modern cost accounting and internal auditing procedures. In a few areas of public administration, cost accounting has been developed to the point where it is now more progressive than it is in many private business concerns. In government, data are sometimes presented in terms of man-hour and machine-hour costs rather than in terms of dollars. For purposes of cost control at the lowest levels of operation the use of such physical measures is often more revealing and more economical than conventional dollar values. It would be possible to devise a fully coordinated system that would meet all needs, including those of top management and those at the lower levels relative to budgeting and reporting, but this means strengthening the current procedure and giving operating officials more control than they usually enjoy over cost accounting, internal auditing, and statistics if the system is to be fully useful for administrative control purposes. Fortunately, some progress is being made in this direction following a recommendation of the second Hoover Commission that cost accounting methods be extended in the federal government, and the Bureau of the Budget has taken the lead in the matter.

Current progress in administrative control is due in part, at least, to the fact that many public administrators now realize that they are more concerned with deviations from the norms than with the perfection of the norms themselves. Administrators want to be able to sense the situation, to know whether performance is lagging or on schedule, and to know where the soft spots are. To know the trend is sometimes all an administrator needs in order to start looking for what is wrong. And finally, administrators want advance notice—storm warnings—of problems that, if overlooked, might become acute. And throughout, of course, there must be a balance between the mechanical techniques of measurement and control on the one hand, and the human factors of leadership and morale on the other.

## BIBLIOGRAPHY AND CASES

### Annotated Reading Suggestions

A common test of both coordination and control—and, indeed, of most things administrative—is efficiency, a broad and expansible concept. In Dwight Waldo's book of readings, *Issues and Ideas in Public Administration* (McGraw-Hill, 1953), the editor includes excerpts from three writers, Herbert A. Simon, Paul H. Appleby, and Harvey Pinney, all of which relate to the efficiency concept. This is in Part VI, "Efficiency and Responsibility."

Four chapters in Marshall E. Dimock, *The Executive in Action* (Harper & Row, 1945) are relevant: Chapter 12, "The Measurement of Performance," Chapter 16, "Administrative Coordination," Chapter 18, "Unity of Command," and Chapter 19, "Supervision and Control."

One of the best brief discussions of coordination is found in an essay by Harry Hopf, the management engineer: "Administrative Coordination," *Advanced Management*, 5 (April-June 1940). See also George Gant's discussion reprinted in Felix Nigro, *Public Administration: Readings and Documents* (Holt, Rinehart, and Winston, 1951), pp. 125-135.

The philosophical foundation for understanding control is dealt with by Mary Parker Follett in *Dynamic Administration*, her papers collected and edited by Henry C. Metcalf and L. Urwick, (Harper & Row, 1941), in Chapter 9, "The Psychology of Control." See also John M. Gaus's discussion of the subject in John M. Gaus, Leonard D. White, and Marshall E. Dimock, *Frontiers of Public Administration* (University of Chicago Press, 1936) and in *Reflections on Public Administration* (University of Alabama Press, 1947).

Electronic data processing, the latest development in this area, is dealt with in the Symposium, "Electronic Data Processing," *Public Administration Review*, 22 (September 1962).

Pioneering work in measurement has been done by Clarence E. Ridley and Herbert A. Simon, *Measuring Municipal Activities: A Survey of Suggested Criteria for Appraising Administration* (Chicago: International City Managers Association, 1943). See also William R. Divine and Harvey Sherman, "A Technique for Controlling Quality," *Public Administration Review*, 8 (Spring 1948); and Brig. Gen. H. A. Barnes, "Control Activities in the Quartermaster Corps," *Public Administration Review*, 4 (Autumn 1944). Among more recent contributions are John W. Kendrick, "Productivity Measurement in Government," *Public Administration Review*, 23 (June 1963); and Bernard D. Rifkind, *et al.*, "Applying Work Measurement to Personnel Administration," *Public Administration Review*, 17 (Winter 1957).

The use of statistics and accounting for planning and control purposes is dealt with, respectively, by John J. Corson, "The Use of Statistics in Management," *Advanced Management,* 9 (April-June 1944), and by Howard W. Bordner, "The Development of Army Accounting," in *Public Administration Review,* 9 (Spring 1949).

## Case Studies

In the Stein *Case Book, The Air Search and Rescue Program,* written by W. Scott Payne in 1950, twenty-three pages, is a good illustration of coordination methods. A second case, also in the Stein collection, is *Self-Insurance in the Treasury,* also an illustration of coordination as well as of program planning and the choice between private and public enterprise. This case, only thirteen pages long, was written by Kathryn Smul Arnow in 1949 and revised in 1952.

Two other ICP selections offer a variety of subject matter. No. 47, *Reorganization of Philadelphia General Hospital,* thirty-four pages, reported by M. Robinson, illustrates both coordination and control programs. No. 55, *Upstream-Downstream Controversy in Arkansas White-Red Basins Survey,* by I. K. Fox in 1960, illustrates the perennial problem of coordinating certain federal programs.

PART
FOUR

# Working
# Relationships

# 18

## Line and Staff
## Relationships

THIS PART OF the book takes up three special types of relationship in public administration without which no effective performance is possible. The first of these, between line and staff, is the subject of the present chapter. This one also prepares the ground for an understanding of the structure and staffing of overhead administration, which leads in the chapter that follows to a discussion of the relationship between operating administration and overhead administration. In the final chapter in this part, the third relationship, between headquarters and the field, completes the trilogy.

### Issues of Policy and Administration

Generally speaking, line connotes action; staff, advice. Line is hierarchical; staff, collateral. Line is authority, staff, influence. A bureau chief is a line official, his research assistant is a staff officer. What the correct relationships should be between the two types of activity has long been a matter of debate, to the point where students of the subject have come to believe that the right adjustment between line and staff constitutes one of the most difficult areas of management.

There have been notable differences in thinking and practice in this area between business and government, although a somewhat altered viewpoint in government in recent years has brought them more nearly in accord.[1] In both camps theorists are agreed at least on the fact that as organization grows in size and complexity, problems of planning and coordination also grow, not only vertically but horizontally. Operating executives need the help of staff officials to assist in planning objectives, developing programs, affecting coordination, and the like. The main problem is how to organize this relationship.

In government, for example, it has sometimes been proposed to create in the State Department a small top planning and strategy staff, unlike any of its predecessors, to mastermind foreign policy. It is objected that such an arrangement would undermine the work of all the action officials in the Department including, perhaps, even the Secretary. It has also been proposed to solve the nation's economic problems through a small planning staff at the apex of the federal hierarchy. It is objected that such an agency would dilute the responsibility and authority of Cabinet officials.

A former official of General Motors once referred to the invention of the staff activity as "the chief element of progress that we have made in the science of management during the last 3000 years." [2] But Peter Drucker, consultant to General Electric, holds just as decidedly that the popular use of the terms "line" and "staff" to describe different kinds of administrative activity does positive harm. In his view, "It would actually be undesirable to have any staff functions." The concept is destructive because a staff office conveys authority without responsibility. The heads of staff services become empire builders, with the result that they become much too busy running a big unit, much too concerned with perfecting tools and techniques, much too intent on pushing their services. If their real job is to think about the undertaking as a whole and to judge the impact of every decision, then they should become either consultants or operating officials.[3] Stating yet another view, Lepawsky concludes that line and staff are coordinates operating not in a hierarchical relationship of one over the other but on a horizontal plane of authority and responsibility under the chief executive.[4]

But the issue is not merely one of words or of defining functions and roles, for it relates also to public policy. The proper concern of a staff agency, said a pioneer in American public administration, is with "the revision of organization as new needs dictate, and with the re-

---

[1] For an excellent historical survey, see "Staff and Line Organization" in Lepawsky, ed., *Administration: The Art and Science of Organization and Management*, pp. 289-321.

[2] Edgar W. Smith, "Executive Responsibility," *The Society for the Advancement of Management Journal*, 3 (January 1938), p. 32.

[3] *The Practice of Management*, pp. 240-242.

[4] Lepawsky, *op. cit.*, p. 321.

formulation of major policies." [5] Although White would clearly not have gone so far himself, champions of the staff activity sometimes convey the impression that staff agencies should *make* policy, while line officials merely carry it out.

It used to be said that line activity was action and had a monopoly of authority and command and that staff work was merely advice and facilitation and could legitimately express itself only through the line organization. This sharp distinction reflected military dogmas that held "the line" to be of primary importance, with a single commander in every command and every subordinate reporting to a particular superior. Writers then treated the line and staff relationship almost exclusively as an aspect of formal organization. "The staff organization," it has been said, "may be described as a deliberate organization for thought, just as the line organization is the organization for execution." [6] It has also been held that the term "staff" is "strictly one of formal organization, intended to distinguish the mere function of counsel from the scalar [hierarchical] right of command." [7]

With the changed thinking on the line and staff relationship that has occurred in recent years—especially in government where it was most needed—the sharp cleavage between the two functions is no longer stressed, even in military organization. It is now realized that authority is more a matter of influence than of command and that both line and staff work are involved at most levels of operation. Although the key words "authority," "command," and "control" are still used, their connotation is not so authoritarian as formerly because the modern emphasis is on cooperation and teamwork.

Another reason for a different viewpoint is the growing need for an ever more minute division of labor and specialization, which in turn makes staff work increasingly necessary as the indispensable ingredient of a unified and balanced administration. Consequently as the number of staff officials multiplies along with the varieties of staff functions, some of the work shades off into the type of activity traditionally reserved to line officials. Hence staff work becomes in some degree a combination of both direct and indirect activity, including advice as well as direction to line officials. In practice, a function is seldom pure; more often it is an interesting and frequently a troublesome blend.

Some executives try to simplify the problem of the directing and

---

5 Leonard D. White, "Some General Aspects of Organization," in *Introduction to the Study of Public Administration* (2d ed., New York: The Macmillan Company, 1939), pp. 41-43.

6 Oliver Sheldon, *The Philosophy of Management* (London: Sir Isaac Pitman & Sons, 1923), p. 120.

7 James D. Mooney and Alan C. Reiley, *Onward Industry* (New York: Harper & Row, Publishers, 1931), p. 63.

control functions of staff units by saying that any group that gives directions is a line unit, but since both advisory *and* directing functions are almost always involved in the same group, rigid definitions are less useful than an understanding of complicated human relationships. "Some of the confusion and friction that exist between line and staff personnel," say the authors of a Harvard study, "seems to have developed because both groups, in seeking a guide to behavior, have looked to definitions rather than to the situation in which they were working. Quibbling over definitions does not help." [8]

This same group of investigators found that in talking with business executives about their "human problems," the difficulties of the line and staff relationship were mentioned by everyone. Questions often heard were, Do line and staff units ever work together as they should? Should staff services be centralized? When should new staffs be created? Should there be a management committee consisting of top line and staff executives? Difficulties mentioned included the line man who never took advice from a staff assistant to the president of the company or from a staff department, the overeager staff department chief who tried to impose his views on other executives, the department head who invariably agreed in a meeting to do what the line and staff groups had jointly decided and then never did any of it, the staff officer who had been instructed by his chief to convey an order to a subordinate plant manager but who changed the order because he did not agree with it, and the executive who created advisory staff departments but used them as supervisory agencies with consequent friction all around.[9]

In the universities the tendency is to train experts in particular staff subjects—personnel, finance, law, and so on. Such functions are part of every organization of any size and they are easily taught in correlated courses on public administration and business management. Consequently, a disproportionate number of university-trained people, being prepared in staff work, are encouraged to enter those fields and soon acquire a strong vested interest in their own specialty. Hence, in the manner of guild groups generally, staff experts magnify the importance of their work—its power, its influence, and its separate identity—out of all proportion to its just claims in the total administrative situation. This does not mean that training for staff positions should be deemphasized; it does mean that line work should receive at least equal attention, and that promising students should be encouraged either to enter line work directly or to use a staff position as a steppingstone to it.

Nowhere has the danger inherent in an exaggerated staff function been better stated than by Willard N. Hogan when he commented that preoccupation with budgets, limitations, and controls of various

8 Learned, Ulrich, and Booz, *Executive Action,* pp. 158-159.
9 *Ibid.,* pp. vii, 7, 155.

sorts "puts a premium on negativism in public administration." Responsibility for coordination and planning should so far as possible be placed in the operating line in accordance with "the basic management principle of allocating definite functional responsibility with corresponding authority." Management, continues Hogan, must not become submerged in the minutiae of staff functions. "Centralized services and budgetary and personnel controls are giving us a bad case of organizational schizophrenia as the control of mechanics becomes dissociated from, and builds up competing interests with, policy direction." [10]

The original difference in the line-staff function between business and government is that in industry, the staff function has had to fight for its existence, whereas in government it is just the reverse, with staff officials sometimes acquiring a great deal of power of the wrong sort. The greater need for accountability in government, through overhead central control agencies such as budget bureaus and civil service commissions, is the obvious reason that the staff function has become so strong in public administration, but it is not a justification. Public accountability can be secured in other ways without violating administrative principles and cooperative human relationships. Fortunately, the problem is in process of solution by reason of the fact that in both business and government a balance between line and staff activities is an emerging pattern.[11]

## A Proper Boundary between Line and Staff

If drawing the boundary between line and staff functions were simply a matter of arbitrarily determining what work should be assigned to each, the problem would be easier. But no such formal distinction is possible, because the size and complexity of modern organizations have made it necessary to invent categories and subcategories to describe the variety of services performed by staff officials. In the resulting proliferation of labels and units the tendency of one kind of activity to blend with another is intensified and characteristics common to both types of function become more obvious but harder to place on this or that side of a boundary.

In business the simplest kind of staff work is that of a single aide to the top executive. This person may be a private secretary, a personal assistant, or a counselor of some kind, and typically he is outside the chain of command. Assume now that the line executive finds he needs two or even three such assistants. The line-staff relationships now be-

---

[10] Willard N. Hogan, "A Dangerous Tendency in Government," *Public Administration Review*, VI (Summer 1946), pp. 235-239.

[11] Lepawsky, *op. cit.*, p. 307.

gin to be complicated because if the line executive takes enough time to see all three of his assistants as often as he should, he will have less time for the line officials who also report directly to him. At this point, therefore, he stops building up an inner office staff and, if additional assistance is necessary, he develops a special unit at the departmental level. When the organization grows so large that even more staff help is needed, separate divisions or departments are created on a functional basis to deal with matters such as personnel, legal advice, public relations, financial affairs, and the like, each with its own chief.

When this stage of growth is reached, it is rarely possible to describe any staff function as only one of giving advice, fanning the executive's brains, digging up facts for him, or helping with the planning process. In addition to the advisory function, staff departments now begin to get over into the line of action, including issuing orders directly to persons in the line of command. A finance department, for example, performs the staff function of devising better methods of cost accounting but it also performs the line function of keeping books and disallowing expense vouchers. A personnel department discharges the staff function of advising the chief executive on how to improve morale but it also administers the classification system, the efficiency rating system, social security provisions, and the retirement program. The legal division gives staff advice on how to stay within the law and at the same time conducts suits before the courts. The public relations department advises line officials on how to keep workers and stockholders happy but it also administers a war chest of many thousands of dollars worth of advertising via newspapers, radio, television, and so on.

But these large functional staff departments are not the end of the matter. A growing enterprise soon needs staff assistance in many places, at headquarters and in the field, at the departmental level and among the lower ranks. Some of this staff work is departmentalized in the manner described above, and some is carried on by one or two persons horizontally affiliated with a line official and consequently having two bosses: the line executive whom they serve directly and the expert in their own field who is their staff superior at a higher level in the program. Being practical men, administrators usually create staff assistance wherever they need it and are not much bothered by theories of organization as subscribed to by the draftsmen of formal organization charts.

In business, staff work is relatively more dispersed throughout the enterprise than it is in government where the tendency is to concentrate it in the office of the top executive. Moreover, in business the staff function is closely tied in with operations, whereas in government—especially federal—the staff activity is more often a separate function.

In staff work a basic distinction is between that which is *advisory* and that which performs a *service* involving a certain amount of follow-up and action; but both types may be performed relative to the same subject matter and in the same unit. Leonard D. White distinguished the staff function per se and the auxiliary staff function, the latter being a facilitating service more closely related to the chain of command; but again, the difference is more in the *nature* of the work done than in the *structure* of the units that do it. John M. Gaus uses the phrase "auxiliary technical staff services" to describe the facilitating service. After an intensive study of the top management structure of twenty-six American business concerns, Paul Holden, Lounsbury Fish, and Hubert Smith identify four types of staff agencies including control, service, coordinative, and advisory.[12] Even the purist must admit that all four of these functions are often discharged, both in business and in government, by units formally designated as staff agencies.

The larger and more varied the enterprise the more diversified will be its staff services and the more important will it be that interstices between formal line and formal staff organizations be filled in, because the efficiency of a program is often explained by the skill with which the connective tissues of organization are supplied. If the anatomical comparison may be carried a step further, the connective tissue often seems more conducive to smooth operation and ultimate efficiency than the bony structure on which it is built. This is the reason that the staff function increases with the size of the program and why so much confusion results when formal theories and definitions are allowed to check the growth of the staff function when it serves a useful purpose. Sometimes the theory must come after the fact.

Although the foregoing discussion seems to indicate that line work and staff work are not very different from each other, the point must not be pushed to the conclusion that there are no differences worth noting. Not all staff work bears on the directing function, and when it does the staff official must be careful to move through channels and to avoid the temptation to "throw his weight around."

An illustration of this danger concerns a staff official who was supposed to work with several different departments in a corporation in preparing a product for sale.[13] But as a direct action man he did not believe in working through channels if he could help it. "I'm just cocky enough," he said, "to think I'm top management material, and that's the kind of job I'm trying to do. This is a step in that direction." As it turned out, he was so wrong in his approach and attitudes that he alienated the department heads with whom he was supposed to cooperate. It was his practice, for example, to work with subordinate members

12 White, *op. cit.*, pp. 41-43; John M. Gaus, "The General Administrative Staff," *Plan Age*, III (January 1937); Paul Holden, Lounsbury Fish, and Hubert Smith, *Top-Management Organization and Control* (Palo Alto, Calif.: Stanford University Press, 1941).
13 Learned, Ulrich, and Booz, *op. cit.*, pp. 164ff.

of other departments without telling their chiefs what he was doing. He kept his own chief informed and demonstrated a high level of ability and accomplishment, but he got results more by the force of his personality than by doing what his job description called for. Consequently he pleased his chief but not the other department heads, who especially objected to learning from another vice president of the actions of their own subordinates.

The failure of this staff man occurred at the point where he neglected to clear through channels and to establish connections with responsible line officials. His superior also erred because he knew what his subordinate was doing and should have guided him. Although both got immediate results, "it is not entirely reasonable to expect that technical specialists without broad administrative experience will necessarily appreciate the importance of building teamwork. The senior executives concerned, however, might have been expected to understand and to take steps to meet this need without destroying initiative and ability." [14]

This case also underscores the importance of the teaching function in administration:

> In final analysis, senior executives determine the kind of staff work they have. If they consult other departments on interdepartmental matters, they set an example that will be followed. If they ask staff assistants whether they have consulted with other departments, they also encourage them to consult. If they prefer, encourage, and reward this type of consultative behavior, their subordinates will be anxious to follow suit.[15]

## Staff Work at the Bureau Level

In order to understand staff work at the bureau level, the example of one of the smaller bureaus in Washington typifies hundreds of operating agencies in the federal, state, and local governments. Its bureau chief has a budget of $10 million a year and his program employs about 600 people. He has an assistant bureau chief who is responsible for much of the detailed work of administration, leaving the chief himself free to plan, coordinate where special problems arise, and settle matters of policy. The closest staff assistant to the chief is called an administrative assistant in charge of budgets, personnel, and organizational matters. The functions of this man are partly advisory, partly operating. He advises his chief and the division heads within the bureau on questions of organization, procedure, finance, and personnel, but in addition,

14 *Ibid.*, pp. 166-167.
15 *Ibid.*, p. 167.

on instructions from the bureau chief that are made known within the organization, he also carries out organizational changes, position reclassifications, and the like.

Where relationships are properly planned, people in an agency are seldom conscious of the dual functions performed by the administrative assistant nor do they know when the switchover occurs from advisory staff to auxiliary staff activities. So long as the administrative assistant has the backing of the bureau chief, so long as his authority is made clear, and so long as cooperative working relationships are maintained, formal distinctions as to function rarely enter people's minds. To attain so desirable a state of naturalness is an objective of successful top management.

Additional staff functions at the bureau level in this particular case are those of the office manager, who has charge of minor purchases, transportation, and a stenographic pool; a statistical division that constantly feeds the bureau chief and the division chiefs a type of material that this particular agency commonly needs in its daily work; and a public relations man who takes care of the requirements of the Washington office and supervises functionally, but not directly, the work of public relations men in three regional offices. Finally, there are four staff or "utility" men (as the term is used in baseball) to advise division chiefs on major operating programs; these men are experts in their respective lines, one being a physician, for example, and another a social worker.

This is about the limit of staff work in the Washington office of this particular bureau. Other staff functions—legal advice, finance and accounting, the general aspects of personnel work, the purchase of commodities in quantity, and the like—are taken care of by staff units at the higher departmental level through a cooperative relationship with the bureau and are usually handled by the administrative assistant.

In the field offices of this bureau the situation is similar except that the size of individual offices being smaller, staff assistance also is less. In each of the three regional offices, for example, the regional director has an administrative assistant, an office manager, a public relations man, and a statistician. In addition, much coordinating staff work is done by the administrative assistant, thus combining line and staff activities at that level. In the local offices the corresponding staff work is done by the local manager, or an assistant to the manager, or by the manager's secretary, depending on the size of the office and the burden of the work load.

In a typical bureau, therefore, the staff function is distributed throughout the organization, being more concentrated among fewer people at the bottom, however, where more direct action is the rule, than at the top where emphasis is on planning and coordination and the various staff specialities are more highly developed.

### Staff Work at the Departmental Level

Possibly because it is so large, far-flung, and diversified in its operations, the Department of Agriculture in Washington has paid more
attention to the staff function in administration than have most other
government agencies, and offers an interesting illustration of staff organization at the departmental level. The early part of the story is
told by Gaus and Wolcott and also by Paul H. Appleby who was assistant to the Secretary of Agriculture when Gaus and Wolcott made their
study; Wolcott himself became assistant to the Secretary when the study
was completed.[16]

The institutional arrangement where substantial power is vested
in staff officials is explained in this way:

> By necessity, most, if not all, line matters directed to the Secretary must
> clear through the general staff. There were insufficient hours in the day
> to permit the Secretary to give adequate attention to all or even to the
> most important questions. Countless orders, memoranda, letters, and
> other papers required his signature; records of hearings and budget
> recommendations were subject to his review; and questions of policy
> and organization needed his attention. In addition, the demands on
> the Secretary's time by the President, the Congress, his party, interest
> groups, organizations, and individuals were extensive.[17]

At that time the general staff in the Department of Agriculture consisted of the undersecretary and assistant secretary, four assistants to
the Secretary, several officials heading staff agencies dealing with financial, personnel, and other matters, and finally a number of other officials
drawn from the line units to serve from time to time in a staff capacity.
Of all these, however, the most important were probably the four assistants to the Secretary, for they occupied his outer office and were
closer to him in daily contacts than were others more remotely located.
The functions of the general staff were to reduce pressures on the
Secretary; to evaluate each matter in the light of all its relationships,
various departmental functions, and over-all policy; to determine the
merits of each case and pass it on to the Secretary with a recommendation, based on analysis, for action.

In any organization, of course, internal relationships will vary with

---

16 John M. Gaus and Leon O. Wolcott, *Public Administration and the United States
Department of Agriculture* (Chicago: Public Administration Service), pp. 289-377;
Paul H. Appleby, "Organizing Around the Head of a Large Federal Department,"
*Public Administration Review,* VI (Summer 1946), pp. 205-212.

17 Gaus and Wolcott, *op. cit.,* p. 296.

the personality and inclinations of the top executive, and the methods studied by Gaus and Wolcott were those of a particular Secretary of Agriculture. But it is also true that in the long haul the traditions and requirements of an institution will influence methods of organization and procedure. The Department of Agriculture has always emphasized the staff function—more, in fact, than any business concern of corresponding size would think of doing and more than most other government agencies—the reason being that the Department is so large, with a budget during the period under study ranging from $1 billion to $1.5 billion a year and by 1963 exceeding $7 billion.

Under the conditions described by Gaus and Wolcott, staff officials in the Department of Agriculture exercised an enormous influence. The four assistants to the Secretary could themselves virtually determine particular courses of action. Ordinarily they decided who should see the Secretary and what matters did not seem to warrant his attention, including the issuance of press releases quoting him. An assistant to the Secretary could even decide what constituted the Department's function, the acid test applied to every issue. The distinction between staff and line was clear in terms of duties and authority, and the purpose was the common one of furthering the Department's function.

Did the bureau chiefs resent the magnification of the staff function in the Secretary's outer office? Although evidence on this point is incomplete, there seemed to be more objection to coordination interposed by staff divisions located between the bureaus and the Secretary's office than there was to the long-established practice of staff assistants to the Secretary himself. Thus the coordination of bureaus by a division chief in charge of personnel administration, for example, was more of an obstacle in the path to the Secretary than the gantlet of staff officials in his outer office.

In his study of the staff function Appleby agreed that the first requirement of a good staff man is breadth of knowledge and ability— he must be a generalist. Also, he must be self-effacing, he must like people, as a new man in an agency he must be able quickly to assimilate himself in it so as to avoid the jealousy usually accorded an outsider, and he must possess a certain intangible quality that partakes of both integrity and wisdom. A sense of humor helps.

A staff official must be a generalist in order to be able to translate narrow, specialized thinking and action into broader terms that will help the Secretary to discharge his leadership function within the Department and as a member of the President's Cabinet. Furthermore, no director of a particular staff function should be allowed to dominate other staff functions; each should remain within his own field of competence and none become too powerful. Although a chief of staff to coordinate all staff activities is sometimes used—as during the mid-1950s, for example, in the White House Office—Appleby apparently dislikes the device for civilian agencies. If the position is needed at all at the departmental level, it is merely for the sake of staff cross reference and synthesis among different staff people, not as a link between them and the Secretary. A better plan, says Appleby, is to see that the staff acquires a "collegial character in which the principal discipline is the enforcement of cross reference." [18] In addition, the staff should never usurp the role of operating bureau chiefs; it must synthesize its product and that of the bureaus, and it must take the dross and the narrow and refine them into public policy and public administration. Even without explicit authority to do so, a proper staff organization carries out this synthesizing process within the limits fixed by an absence of authority, its strength being logic and not power.

Although job descriptions contained in administrative manuals may seem to define relations between line and staff with great precision, the fact is that people in the jobs described do not automatically develop such relations; rather, they must be led in that direction by a skillful administrator. "One of the most critical tests of the administrative ability of the executive," remark the authors of the Harvard study cited above, "lies in the way in which he uses staff assistance." [19] Here again, a function that does not show up on a formal organization chart is nevertheless one without which a program will lack a chief means to successful operation.

## Staff Assistance at the Top

The staff needs of a chief executive in charge of an entire government —President, governor, or municipal executive—vary with the size and complexity of the jurisdiction, the traditions of the office, its relations with the legislative branch, and the qualifications and personal preferences of the incumbent. And yet it is also true that certain needs inherent in the position itself must somehow be taken care of if the work is to get done.

Compared with those of the bureau chief and the departmental Secretary, the distinguishing need of the head of a government is for greater drafts of manpower to handle staff functions, simply because a greater variety and volume of work is to be planned and coordinated. With wise management, much of this need may be met through existing departments. Thus, legal advice may be secured from the attorney general in federal and state governments and from the legal department in a municipal government, personnel advice from the civil service commission or other central personnel unit, purchasing advice from the central purchasing agency, organizational advice from

18 Appleby, *op. cit.*, p. 211.
19 Learned, Ulrich, and Booz, *op. cit.*, p. 155.

the bureau of the budget or the central finance department, and, in the case of the federal government, advice concerning foreign affairs, military preparedness, and similar matters from the regular executive departments dealing in these fields.

Try as he may to utilize existing departments, however, the chief executive also needs staff advice and counsel in his immediate vicinity. Such advice has to do with broad policy questions that cut across the responsibilities of the respective departments, political considerations, time, public relations, executive coordination, and the work of his own office. Consequently the average head of a government must recruit what we have called generalists, men so well educated and experienced as to be able to offer sound advice on a variety of subjects. If the executive were to surround himself with specialists on every subject with which he is concerned he would soon find himself so occupied with advisers as to have little time for dealing with the outside world. To achieve a balance and draw the line between departmental staff and immediate staff is a test of executive ability that becomes harder, especially at the federal level, as the size of government increases.

## The Principle of Unity of Command

A problem of many administrators is how to secure cooperation and teamwork, which depend so much on informal relationships, and at the same time keep certain formal organizational relationships intact so that people will not be working at cross-purposes. Traditionally the solution of this problem has been to emphasize the principle of unity of command, meaning that in any organization final authority for decisions at each level in the hierarchy must be clearly located and understood.

So far so good, but when as a corollary it is argued that no more than one person should give orders to a particular subordinate, no man should serve more than one master, and a military or similar type of organization is the only defensible one, then it is found that most actual experience diverges from these standards. Under the modern, functional type of organization where both line and staff officials must give instructions from time to time and the accent is on cooperation rather than on obedience, old assumptions have had to be changed.

Staff work is the logical projection of the principle of the division of labor, which in large organizations is an important factor. The more prominent staff work becomes and the more it must be subdivided, the more are inroads made on the principle of unity of command. Thus, "the ideal situation is one in which all the special knowledge and skills of the staff departments are integrated and brought to bear at *all* levels of supervision. For instance, a foreman has problems in many areas: engineering, scheduling, control, and public relations. All the abilities

of the specialized staff groups are channeled through him to employees."
Consequently the foreman must in effect receive orders from staff officers as well as from his immediate line superiors. "The need for getting
knowledge into practice is expressed in the current view that *effective*
personnel administration can be judged by the behavior of the line
better than by the knowledge of the staff." The real problem, therefore, "is not one of the degree to which staffs control line activity, but
it is one of obtaining through the line organization results which em-
body staff skills." [20] Thus, staff activity is interwoven with line activity at
many points in the enterprise, and the principle of unity of command
must be modified to meet the actual conditions that result.

The principle should not, however, be discarded. Rather, the
corollaries to it should be more carefully enunciated. The experienced
administrator knows that someone must be boss, multiple direction is at
best confused direction, and clear lines of relationship, authority, and
organization are essential to proper cooperation. Otherwise the signals
are not clear, wires get crossed, a proper flow of communication
throughout the program is lacking, and all elements necessary for the
performance of a unified task remain scattered. Since the modern
temper, conditioned as it is by the human relations philosophy, is opposed to "command," a solution might be to adopt Mary Parker Follett's suggestion and for "unity of command" substitute "unity of direction," which merely means that for every enterprise there must be a
deciding authority, where all communications are centered and where
full coordination can take place.

## Securing Cooperation between Line and Staff

That conflict rather than cooperation is too often the product of line
and staff relationships in both business and government has already
been noted. Line officials in the federal government, for example, resent what they consider interference in matters of policy and internal
administration by the General Accounting Office or the Bureau of the
Budget or the Civil Service Commission. In private management, the
universality of the problem is illustrated in the statement that "a line
man never takes advice from a staff assistant to the president, or from a
staff department." [21] This attitude of instinctive resistance, compounded
from a mixture of tradition, custom, and ritual, is both psychological
and managerial. What can be done about it?

It is possible to oversimplify both the difficulty and the remedy;
nevertheless, certain points seem clear. The psychological problem arises
when line officials stress the importance of their work and belittle that

20 *Ibid.*, p. 162.
21 *Ibid.*, p. 7.

of staff units, an attitude that creates a feeling of insecurity and resentment on the part of staff officials, and as a result they become overly aggressive. The remedy is to bring each side to understand the essential role of the other and to emphasize their mutual interdependence.

"General-staff personnel," say Gaus and Wolcott, "should . . . be self-effacing. They should be unambitious in a narrow personal sense but thoroughly ambitious to get the job well done, to get problems solved and results achieved. They have no authority of their own except the authority of ideas, which depends upon their competence and their effectiveness in winning consent." [22] This sound doctrine is equally applicable to line officials and accords with the administrative philosophy of men like Ordway Tead and Chester Barnard, who have observed that authority rests on influence rather than on command. At the same time, self-effacement on the part of administrators is not likely to become widespread and, in addition, if a characteristic of line executives in the American habitat is the desire for "success" or to be considered "successful," then it is not reasonable to expect staff officials to behave otherwise. By the same token, it is possible that if the same recognition for work well done that line administrators crave were also offered to staff people, they might be less overzealous and overbearing. This is where management comes in: there is no stimulus to accomplishment like a pat on the back at the right moment, and the boss is the man to do it.

Another technique of management that effectively reduces the attitude barrier between line and staff officials is interchangeable tours of duty, a procedure used by large corporations, notably the American Telephone and Telegraph Company. Line officials are rotated to staff positions at headquarters for, say, three or four years, and then sent back to the field for more line experience. This exchange, which may occur several times during the career of a key individual, tends to foster understanding of the other fellow's point of view and the problems he faces. In some cases the rotation is continued to the point where line officials who have been especially successful in staff jobs are finally retained there in a senior status.

In government, tours of duty are now extensively used in the armed services, in the career service of the State Department, and in the Forest Service, among others. It is an especially valuable experience during the formative years of a man's professional life and is a factor in developing a career service in public administration. The first Hoover Commission strongly recommended an extension of the device.[23] Indeed, tours of duty are becoming increasingly popular, the Civil

22 *Op. cit.,* p. 299.
23 Commission on Organization of the Executive Branch of the Government, *Personnel Management* (Washington, D.C.: Government Printing Office, 1949), p. 21.

Service Commission is taking an active part in the matter, and the device may eventually do more to break down provincialism and entrenched attitudes of exclusiveness than any other single strategy of management.

Are there any significant differences in the personality patterns of line and staff officials? There is no simple answer to this question. It was once believed that such differences did exist and they were assumed to be one reason for the frictions that appeared. The staff employee was supposedly the retiring, studious introvert, and the line executive the dynamic, active extrovert. But if such a distinction was ever valid, it is hardly supported by what facts are known. It is possible that some kinds of staff work—notably research and fact finding—attract the studious type of individual, but even this is a precarious generalization. Neither university professors, insurance salesmen, nor bookies fall readily into a set mold, so why should staff men and line executives? Moreover, in the field of auxiliary or facilitative staff work, where the ideas of staff men are translated into action, the assumption breaks down altogether: the nearer the approach to the action stage of the program, where persuasion and drive are indispensable factors, the more do staff officials resemble their line colleagues. In addition, among staff and line officials alike, the ability to cooperate and to work harmoniously together is a common requirement.

An illustration of a difficult kind of personality in a staff position occurred in a large company where a chemist headed a research laboratory that was a staff unit responsible for many service functions. Cooperation with other divisions of the company was essential but the personality of the chemist made this impossible until a remedy was supplied.[24] The chemist was less interested in people than he was in things, especially higher chemistry, and although he expected line officials to share his interest, he ignored theirs. Typical comments of the department heads he was supposed to serve were these: "He won't discuss anything with us. We have no right to question his judgment, since we don't know anything about the 'higher chemistry'." Or, "He has antagonistic traits and is brusque, but he is a stickler for details and perfection." His attitude was that he was doing a wholly technical job and if management could not use it, that was management's loss.

There are egocentric people of this kind in any large organization. They often have a high degree of personal competence but until they have been retooled, so to speak, their usefulness as a member of a joint enterprise is limited. "Occasionally," remark the reporters of this case, "members of an organization show no awareness of the need for establishing relations on a personal basis. They may be 'in but not of' the company. Instead of feeling a loyalty to any informal group of associ-

---

[24] Learned, Ulrich, and Booz, *op. cit.*, pp. 162-163, 168-171.

ates or to the higher organization, they may be loyal primarily to themselves. They may lack the capacity for cooperative behavior. . . . Often men interested chiefly in *things* are not concerned with *people*." [25]

It cannot be assumed, however, that as a man is, so will he always be. The challenge to management is to smooth off the rough spots on such people so that they may work more easily with others. In the case of the chemist, a wise and sympathetic management was able to change his attitude by involving him in group meetings and discussions where other points of view were expressed, and to teach others to work with him by stressing his contribution to the work of the company. This is part of the large training function in administration that has several times been noted.

Another instance of how cooperation may be secured was encountered by one of the present authors in Washington during World War II. The Recruitment and Manning Organization of the War Shipping Administration was charged with the planning and execution of a certain nationwide program of manpower recruitment in a given period of time. Since the head of the agency had other matters to occupy his attention, in a particular instance where cooperation was needed he designated the chief of a subordinate division to serve as coordinator of activities involving contributions from several staff and line departments. At first glance this action seemed like a violation of accepted managerial practice because it subordinated the heads of equal departments to the direction of one of them, and it also placed staff units, including public relations and personnel, in a position of equal participation with line units.

How could such a course be justified? The answer is that cooperative procedures are the daily menu of administration. Executives are interested in results, and unless they are likely to cause some permanent harm, the methods used are incidental. In this instance, for two reasons the curse was taken off what might have been considered a breach of principle: the top administrator took part in the planning of the joint project and approved what was done; and the delegation of authority to the department head was clear and temporary, and every cooperating unit, both line and staff, was made aware of that fact. Authority remained centered at the top level and was simply delegated to a lower one for a particular purpose and a limited time. Concerning the outcome of this experiment, it was remarked that so long as arrangements of this kind are fully understood, there is no reason why jealousy cannot be avoided or why all department heads should not cooperate as willingly and as fully as they would for the chief executive himself.[26]

---

[25] *Ibid.*, pp. 162-163.
[26] Marshall E. Dimock, *The Executive in Action*, p. 112.

## Top Staff and the Issue of Centralization

The main difference between the typical practice of business corporations and that of government has been noted: In business it is customary to keep staff agencies at the departmental level, whereas in many reorganized state governments and in the federal government the policy has been to institutionalize the office of the chief executive and place staff units under his immediate supervision. This personalizes the office of the chief executive, magnifies his importance, and detracts from the role of the Cabinet where there is one. Where the business practice is to spread authority, government practice is to concentrate and centralize it; where the business practice is to encourage teamwork, government practice where staff activity is concerned is largely one-man rule.

There are deviations, of course, from this typical pattern. Thus, in some large business corporations there has recently appeared a tendency to centralize top coordinating units of line or staff and line officials, but this is not the same thing as the government practice of magnifying the staff activity of the chief executive's own office. Where this magnification does occur in industry, the results are usually unfortunate. The authors of the Harvard study describe such an instance:

> In one case a staff department reported directly to a president because of his personal interest in its activity. The president believed that placing the staff at presidential level would give it more "authority" and would help staff personnel to obtain results. Actually, the arrangement hampered the staff personnel in developing cooperative working relationships with the people in the lower ranks who had the necessary information. As one line subordinate said, "You can't tell what one of those 'quiz kids' may tell the boss." [27]

But exceptions such as these do not alter the basic difference between public and private management in the handling of the staff function.

Does the character of management in business and government differ so much that two separate rules of organization concerning the proper place of the top staff function are warranted? Or will it be found that a concentration of staff activity in the office of the chief executive is undesirable in either case? Both the Brownlow Committee and the first Hoover Commission greatly added to the size and complexity of the staff surrounding the President. Opposing Appleby's contention that a chief of staff is a poor idea and that all staff employees on the same plane should be equal, the Hoover Commission also recommended a coordinator of staff activities in the Office of the President on the ground that "at present there is no one place in the President's

---

[27] Learned, Ulrich, and Booz, *op. cit.*, p. 181.

Office to which the President can look for a current summary of the principal issues with which he may have to deal in the near future; nor is a current summary of the staff work available on problems that have been assigned to his advisers, his staff agencies, or the heads of departments and agencies." [28] To meet this deficiency, the commission proposed the addition of a staff secretary. The commission visualized this official as a career public servant who would not himself advise the President on any issue of policy, nor review in a supervisory way the substance of any recommendation made to the President by another staff officer. The picture is that of a colorless individual mechanically conveying the ideas of others to the President, never adding his own interpretation to the material passing over his desk. If such a person could be found he would be wholly unlike the mere human beings so often encountered in administration.

It seems obvious that when staff agencies are unduly centralized at the top they may in fact need the services of a coordinator at a rank between them and the top executive. But the President must continue to deal directly with the heads of his own staff units in any case, and hence his time is even more taken up than it was before. He comes to be closed around by staff assistants and secretaries constituting what has come to be called a Kitchen Cabinet whose members have a growing influence over him. Decision making in the Office of the President becomes anonymous, the Cabinet is neglected, and cooperation at the departmental level gives way to more or less open combat. The more layers of organization and coordination there are, the more remote do line officials and field offices become from the top office, and the more formal and impersonal are the relationships involved. To avoid such a danger—and it is a danger—the sound rule is not to create more layers of coordination than are absolutely necessary.

After reviewing the recommendations of the first Hoover Commission concerning the proper place of staff agencies in the federal government, Albert Lepawsky doubted the wisdom of what was proposed. "The Hoover Commission," he commented, "thus gave recognition to the long-range American trend toward the integration and strengthening of federal staff agencies. The implications of this trend for efficiency and economy are apparent, but there was some doubt that these measures would leave the line agencies all the freedom they needed to perform adequately vital public functions." [29] A number of other writers agree with this point of view.[30]

28 Commission on Organization of the Executive Branch of the Government, *General Management of the Executive Branch* (Washington, D.C.: Government Printing Office, 1949), pp. 21-23.

29 Lepawsky, *op. cit.*, p. 316.

30 Thus, operating independence was the underlying concern of The Brookings Institution in its report on federal reorganization made at about the same time as the study of the Brownlow Committee and entitled *Investigation of Executive*

Of the two opposing sides to the subject of staff services for the chief executive, therefore, one holds to the constitutional and legal view that vests all executive authority in the man at the top. All administrative structure is then built around him, and the point of departure is from the top down. Emphasis is on undivided authority, the complete integration within a single framework of all units of organization from apex to base, and large staff services available to the President.

The opposing view emphasizes teamwork and focuses attention at lower levels of the organization, on the major operating departments and programs. It is assumed that in any large effort, many men and many programs must work together voluntarily and cooperatively. Instead of underscoring the transcendent importance of the top man, therefore, attention is on departmental leadership, middle management, and the creation of a high morale among all workers and units of the enterprise. This approach from the bottom up does not question the legal and constitutional importance of the chief executive; it merely assumes that his power is a formal distinction with practical implications affecting the constitutional independence of the executive branch in its relationship with the legislature. The newer approach minimizes purely legal questions and concentrates on making a huge, complicated bureaucracy produce administrative results that are businesslike and effective. Obviously, these opposing viewpoints must be reconciled and the best taken from each to form a new synthesis. Many problems have been solved, but those that remain go to the core of constitutional and administrative theory and practice.

---

*Agencies of the Government,* 75th Cong., 1st Sess., Report No. 1275 (Washington, D.C.: U. S. Government Printing Office, 1937). A similar view was expressed by Lewis Meriam and L. F. Schmeckebier in their book, *Reorganization of the National Government* (Washington, D.C.: The Brookings Institution, 1939), and by Schuyler C. Wallace in *Federal Departmentalization: A Critique of Theories and Organization* (New York: Columbia University Press, 1941). It was disagreement with the tendency to centralize top staff agencies that led A. C. Millspaugh to write on "Democracy and Administrative Organization," in J. M. Mathews and James Hart, eds., *Essays in Political Science* (Baltimore: The Johns Hopkins University Press, 1937), pp. 64-73; and the policy was sharply attacked also by Dwight Waldo in *The Administrative State* (New York: The Ronald Press Company, 1948), chap. 8.

## BIBLIOGRAPHY AND CASES

### Annotated Reading Suggestions

A virtual debate on the pros and cons of staff activity took place in the pages of *Public Administration Review* in 1946 and 1947. For a critical view, see Willard N. Hogan, "A Dangerous Tendency in Government," 6 (Summer 1946), and a rejoinder by George W. Berquist, "Coordinating Staffs—Are They Really Dangerous?" 7 (Summer 1947). (The fact that both of these were published in summer may be merely coincidental). For an attempt to discover a middle position, see O. Glenn Stahl, "Straight Talk About Label Thinking," 6 (Autumn 1946).

One of the best treatments of the whole subject is Robert C. Sampson, *The Staff Role in Management: Its Creative Uses* (Harper & Row, 1955).

A number of first-class treatments are sympathetic to an expanded staff activity: Paul H. Appleby, "Organizing Around the Head of a Large Department," *Public Administration Review*, 6 (Summer 1946); Herbert Emmerich, *Essays on Federal Reorganization* (University of Alabama Press, 1950); John M. Gaus, "The General Administrative Staff," *Plan Age*, 3 (January 1937); F. Morstein Marx, *The President and His Staff Services* (Public Administration Service, 1947); these may be taken as representative.

On the other hand, equally respected authorities constantly advise against too much emphasis on staff activity: Peter H. Drucker, *The Practice of Management* (Harper & Row, 1954); Schuyler C. Wallace, *Federal Departmentalization* (Columbia University Press, 1941); and Lewis Meriam and L. F. Schmeckebier, *Reorganization of the National Government* (Brookings Institution, 1939), may be cited as examples.

As stated in the text, however, most current discussions revolve around "what" and "how much," not "whether." Among the best treatments are Paul E. Holden, Lounsbury S. Fish, and Hubert L. Smith, *Top-Management Organization and Control* (Stanford University Press, 1941); and E. P. Learned, D. N. Ulrich, and D. R. Booz, *Executive Action* (Harvard Business School, 1951).

On the federal problem, there is an excellent symposium, "The Executive Office of the President: A Symposium," *Public Administration Review*, 1 (Winter 1941), and a good article by Norman N. Pearson, "A General Administrative Staff to the President," *Public Administration Review*, 4 (Spring 1944). On the influence of personal traits, see Robert A. Walker and William A. Jump, "The Staff Officer as a Personality," *Public Administration Review*, 14 (Autumn 1954).

The reports of the Brownlow Committee (1937) and the two Hoover Commissions (1949 and 1955) may also, of course, be consulted with profit.

## Case Studies

A number of ICP cases bear on the line-staff relationship. No. 11, *The United Nations Publication Board,* thirty pages, written by H. Kaufman, is especially interesting because of its international character; it also shows how vital a reliable staff service may be. No. 60, *Governor Freeman and the Minnesota Budget,* thirty-page pages, reported by T. Flinn, is another interesting case, the more so because Minnesota has a department of general administration to serve the governor. Governor Freeman, of course, later became U. S. Secretary of Agriculture.

No. 54, *Shredded Wheat Property,* twenty-two pages, written in 1960 by H. F. Miller, has an interesting sound reminiscent of children's programs on television. Actually, it concerns Governor Harriman of New York and his budget bureau. Finally, No. 40, *Decentralization of Business Services in the Agricultural Research Service,* forty-six pages, concerns both headquarters-field relationships and staff activities, but may appropriately be considered here.

# 19

# Relationships
# to the Top

A THEME RUNNING throughout this book is that governmental administration is a cooperative affair. No government can be judged by how
well its work is accomplished at a particular point; achievement can
properly be judged only by the total effect, the quality of which depends on cooperation. Barnard's observation will be recalled, that without the cooperation of thousands of people at all levels of organization,
the chief executive is powerless. Because he can do virtually nothing
by himself, his achievement depends not upon authority but on the
degree of cooperation he is able to secure from his colleagues and subordinates.

The real question, therefore, is not who is superior to whom
(hierarchy), but rather, what knowledge and action are necessary at
each level in order to get a particular job done well? Rank is not
personal; it is part of the need to develop consensus.

But it is not always possible to regard hierarchy in so dispassionate
a light. A man's viewpoint is shaped by his vantage point. Thus the
bureau chief—the administrator from whose vantage point this book is
written—naturally considers his job as the center of the administrative
universe. Like most people when developments affect their job, the
question most frequently on his mind is, What does this mean to me?
To the bureau chief, therefore, the Office of the President and the
White House staff surrounding the President seem remote, perhaps

even threatening. Top decisions seem often to be made on the basis of insufficient facts and contrary to what experience at the lower level shows can be achieved. And from the eminence of the Office of the President, the view is distorted the other way; from there it seems as though most bureau chiefs are confined in too narrow a frame of reference in matters that require a broad analysis.

Tempting as it may be, therefore, to champion one viewpoint or the other, contending either that all administration should be oriented from the bottom to the top and the function of top officials limited to serving those at the action level; or alternatively, arguing for the top-to-the-bottom orientation, with top officials making all policies and major decisions and the work of subordinate officials confined to non-discretionary action—clearly neither view is right to the exclusion of the other. The two must somehow be reconciled.

## The Theory of Coordinate Functions

The reason that perspectives differ so markedly, even when officials from different levels view a common problem together, has been suggested by Appleby. Thus, "As business moves up the hierarchy—first of a bureau, then of a department, and finally of the executive branch — . . . it undergoes progressive translation from special-interest and specialized substantive and expert consideration, to more general, more total-governmental, more total-public, more completely political consideration." [1]

In other words, the higher the level of administration, the greater is the number of factors to be considered and the more general is the public interest to be served. Consequently, the wider and more versatile must be the viewpoint of those who make decisions at the top.

The bureau chief, for example, is mainly and properly concerned with the interests that are served by or support his bureau. Staff officers at the departmental Secretary's level or in the Bureau of the Budget, on the other hand, are more involved with how to integrate programs and reconcile divergent policies in order to maintain friendly relations with Congress, political parties, and the public, including the press. Similarly with the approach to problems at these levels: "The more aspects a problem may seem to possess," says Appleby, "the less directly does an expert contribute to its solution." The contributions of experts are most useful when offered at the lower levels where the problem may be seen as relatively simple, relatively specified, and relatively free from the varied, varying, and intense sentiments of those involved. At the top level, by contrast, a problem has many more facets

---

[1] Paul H. Appleby, *Policy and Administration*, p. 53.

to it and the administrator responsible for its solution must be a generalist.[2] At the top, executive skill is partly the ability to arrive at the heart of an issue—even when lacking facts known to the bureau chief—through a kind of sixth sense by which the ramifications, overlappings, and nuances of the difficulty are seen.

Nevertheless, this kind of artistry is not the whole of the matter; there must also be a solid base of accurate information flowing up and down the line concerning the matter under study, the kind of information required, and why decisions are made as they are. In this two-way flow, one line is as significant as the other. The effort is especially important because, as Appleby remarks, ". . . it is not possible at any higher level to have all of the information possessed at the next lower level, and it would be the height of absurdity to imagine that all of the information available everywhere in a large organization could be available to, or used by, the administrator at the apex. The abstraction at each successive level of information needed and useful at that level is of the essence of the administrative performance."[3] In a well-run bureaucracy, therefore, the executive tries to create an atmosphere that will encourage subordinates to offer more information than the minimum expected of them. And, indeed, on this one practice alone does superior coordination largely depend.

The result of shoving more and more complex and difficult problems for decision to a higher level, where coordination becomes the main job of the chief executive, is almost daily mirrored in the press and television. The Secretary of Defense and the admirals are fighting; the Bureau of Reclamation and the Corps of Engineers are at it again; the Secretary of Commerce announces that business is getting better by the hour, the Secretary of Labor warns that the unemployment rate is alarming. Behind these differences that appear to be jurisdictional, and the seeming lack of coordination over policy utterances at the top, is the solid reality of actual differences of policy and divergent views struggling for recognition. "Public controversy," says Appleby, "is simply a moving up of the level of treatment of some particular matter."[4] The issues of ultimate concern to the bureau chief rarely make the headlines; those of the White House generally do. The difference is not merely in the eminence and prestige of the level involved; more basic is the gravity and scope of the issue itself.

Consequently there is a growing realization that in public administration the President as a person is less important than as the holder of the top administrative office in the land and the work it must do. It is not a person that needs to be institutionalized, says Wallace Sayre,

2 *Ibid.*, pp. 49, 62.
3 *Ibid.*, p. 74.
4 *Ibid.*, p. 82.

but the office and its responsibilities.[5] To the same effect is Appleby's observation that the President's position as administrative leader is actually somewhat subordinate to that of Congress, which holds the whiphand over organization, budgets, personnel, and other matters vital to the executive function. The President's only advantage over Congress is that Congress is 531 people, which, by its numbers and organization, is unfitted for administrative duties; whereas the President, being one person, is better able to move and maneuver.[6] But even this statement must be qualified because as things have turned out, the President is now surrounded by a large staff bureaucracy which cannot help but slow him down.

## The Role of the Top Executive

A fateful issue of American public administration is still the problem of how to define the role of the chief executive in the larger state and city governments and especially in the federal government. It is hard to be rational about this because public attitudes are naturally and properly colored by sentiments of patriotism and not a little romanticism.

Evaluations of the office and the definitions of its responsibilities cover a wide range. Clinton Rossiter has concluded that "the Presidency is in a sturdy state of health," that any changes should be confined to small adjustments, that, in short, we should "leave the Presidency alone." Instead of the six presidential roles mentioned in an earlier chapter, Rossiter lists ten: chief of state, chief executive, chief diplomat, chief legislator, commander in chief, chief of party, protector of the public peace, voice of the people, manager of prosperity, and leader of a coalition of free nations. Rossiter admits that this range of responsibilities leaves the President little time as chief executive of a far-flung bureaucracy, but this is not a serious matter so long as he sets the tone for the executive branch and makes the most important decisions. Although skeptical about the wisdom of an elaborate staff apparatus surrounding the President, Rossiter is equally skeptical about the need, mentioned by Appleby, for government-wide integration—the arrangement of departments and agencies in a rational pattern heading up to the President himself. Thus,

> . . . The "perfect pyramid" of administration is more a delusion than
> a panacea; rivalry and friction have virtues of their own . . . the
> President has responsibilities that range far beyond his formless duty
> "to produce a good administration." . . . He has other and more
> important roles to play. . . .

---

[5] In an excellent review of six books relating to the chief executive, *Public Administration Review*, 16 (Autumn 1956), pp. 307-312.

[6] Appleby, *op. cit.*, p. 72.

It may well be time to readjust our thinking about the President's responsibility and authority as Chief Executive. If we cannot level the latter up, perhaps we should level the former down.[7]

By "the latter," Rossiter means our expectations of what the President must do as top administrator.

Howard Lee McBain went even further in depreciating the purely administrative role of the President, when he remarked that "The prime function of the President is not executive at all. It is legislative." The President is not chief executive but chief legislator and we judge him by what he succeeds in getting Congress to do. In the bureaucracy subexecutives look not to the President for the source of their authority but to the law. Hence, says McBain, "To conceive the President as the general manager of a vast administrative organization with his hand of control resting day by day upon all its ramifying parts is to imagine a vain thing." In fact, the day by day activities of the Presidency are carried on quite independently of the President. His main job is to get Congress to cooperate.[8]

Corwin and Koenig note that the presidential power is dangerously personalized in two ways: First, the quality of presidential leadership is altogether dependent on the accident of personality; and secondly, there is no governmental body that can be relied upon to give the President independent advice and which he is nevertheless bound to consult:

> . . . Should one man have available the immense powers that are today the President's for the asking—indeed, for the taking? It seems to the authors that the time has arrived for us to recognize that crisis, and especially international crisis, has become a constant factor of national existence, and that reliance on intermittent recourse to presidential dictatorship is no longer the safe answer. What then is the safe answer? It seems to us that methods must be devised for making the national legislative power more readily available when the need for important action arises.[9]

These authors then recommend a new type of Cabinet, one which, as Corwin suggested in an earlier book, would be capable not only of supporting but also of controlling the President. Rossiter concedes that this plan might be a useful one but warns against the tendency of

---

[7] Clinton Rossiter, *The American Presidency* (New York: Harcourt, Brace & World, 1956), p. 152.

[8] Howard Lee McBain, *The Living Constitution* (New York: The Macmillan Company, 1927), pp. 115-120.

[9] Edward S. Corwin and Louis W. Koenig, *The Presidency Today* (New York: New York University Press, 1956), p. vii.

Congress, through legislation and control of the purse strings, to assume power over vital parts of the executive branch.

In each of these books there seems to be general agreement on the dangers of overinstitutionalizing the Presidency. As Rossiter summarizes the feeling, "the danger [is] that the President might be buried under his own machinery. The institutionalization of the Presidency could be carried so far that the man who occupies it would become a prisoner in his own house, a victim of too much and too rigid organization." [10]

The strongest case for the President as chief administrator and for government-wide integration at the top was made by the Brownlow Committee in 1937. Since the government of the United States is the largest and most difficult task undertaken by the American people, argued the Committee, the key need is for a strong executive at the top. It was further contended that the President is the one and only national officer representative of the entire nation; that if democracy is to succeed, the Presidency must again become as effective as the framers of the Constitution intended. The efficiency of government depends upon two factors: the consent of the governed and good management. Real efficiency must be built into the structure of government just as it is built into a piece of machinery. It was then noted that as of 1937 when the report was published, the chief executive was limited and restricted, the work of the executive branch was badly organized, personnel requirements were neglected, and fiscal and auditing systems were inadequate. Consequently there was much to be done; but above all, "The President needs help."

The first step proposed to this end was to provide President Roosevelt with six key administrative assistants, each "with a passion for anonymity," an attitude becoming to their staff role. Integration was to be secured by reducing some 100 separate departments and federal agencies to twelve main departments and then relating independent commissions and government corporations to this central matrix; by relaying important decisions to the presidential staff and to the President himself through the Secretaries of the twelve major departments; by strengthening the role of the Bureau of the Budget; by having a single administrator for personnel functions and placing him on the presidential staff; and by reforming accounting and auditing systems so as to increase the executive's influence over them. In addition, planning was to be provided for through budget and personnel administration, and for economic affairs through the National Resources Planning Board.

In the years that followed the publication of this report, the rationalization of the many federal agencies was only partially carried through; personnel administration remained with the independent Civil Service Commission; in 1943 the National Resources Planning

---

[10] Quoted by Sayre, *loc. cit.,* p. 311.

Board was allowed by Congress to die for lack of funds; and three years later, as a result of the Employment Act of 1946, the Council of Economic Advisers was established in its place. But for the rest, most of the Brownlow Committee's recommendations were adopted, especially those affecting the Office of the President.

A distinction was and continues to be made between the White House Office, to which the six anonymous assistants were appointed (they are many more than that today), and the Executive Office of the President, of which the White House Office and many other agencies are a part. The creation of this large overhead agency, comparable in size to one of the smaller regular departments of Cabinet rank, has sometimes been called the most important improvement in public administration since the passage of the Budget and Accounting Act of 1921. Since 1937 the number of agencies located in this Executive Office of the President has changed from time to time in line with various reorganization plans, those of the two Hoover Commissions included, and the personal preferences of Presidents. The Bureau of the Budget has been a mainstay from the outset, as have agencies dealing with the national security. Today the total list includes the White House Office, the Bureau of the Budget, the Council of Economic Advisers, the National Security Council, the National Aeronautics and Space Council, the Office of Emergency Planning, and the Office of Science and Technology.

After a slow start, both the White House Office and the Executive Office of the President have grown rapidly in numbers and appropriations. In 1932 President Hoover got along with three secretaries and two-score clerks, but under President Eisenhower the White House Office staff comprised about 250 persons crowded into the two executive wings of the White House and the nearby old State Department building, and expenditures amounted to about $1.5 million a year. Under President Kennedy the trend continued.

## The Range of Solutions

As shown in the foregoing discussion, there is a good deal of disagreement as to whether the institutionalization of the Presidency has taken the right form. Admitted that staff agencies are needed at the top, there are too many of them. Certain complementary solutions might improve the situation.

The White House Office itself is unquestionably a necessary unit and there is general support for the Bureau of the Budget as an essential top agency close to the President. Criticism is chiefly aimed at the *number* of staff agencies immediately surrounding the President and taking too much of his time. During the Eisenhower Administration the number of staff agencies and assistants was so great that Sherman Adams, the equivalent of a chief of staff, was appointed simply to coordinate this type of work, thus setting up yet another level of coordination between the President and his Cabinet.

One remedy is to use the Cabinet itself as a coordinating and policy planning device. The Cabinet has not generally been distinguished in this role but there is no inherent reason why it cannot become so. The Truman Administration made the attempt with some success. The Cabinet performs admirably in other countries, as in Britain and Canada where the form of government is not dissimilar from our own. The objections generally offered here are that every Cabinet member is a potential rival of the President himself and hence cannot be wholly trusted, the President is too busy to coordinate, and Cabinet officials are too concerned with their own departments to have time for government-wide problems of coordination.

Behind these objections, however, are two others that die hard: First, the assumption that staff solutions are better than line solutions and that hence staff functions should be still further added to; and second, that the work of the President is indivisible and therefore he must decide everything himself, although it is admitted that because of his six to ten roles, this is really not possible. As a result, there is still much irrational and confused thinking about the subject.

Another proposed solution is to replace anonymous staff assistants with a few able executives to whom the President could delegate some of his administrative responsibilities. This arrangement would constitute no threat to the President's authority because the tenure of these men, like that of the members of his present staff, would be at the President's will and dependent upon his satisfaction with their work. In support of this proposal is the fact that the device is common in most large business corporations, including great holding companies such as the American Telephone and Telegraph Company, as well as in most national governments where overextended staffs at the top are generally viewed with suspicion. Herman Finer believes that the President should have eleven such executive assistants.[11] One of the present authors has recommended eight, two of whom, as first among equals, would be generally responsible for external and for domestic affairs respectively. Under them the allocation of functions would coincide with policy and program areas in the structure of the economy.[12] This idea of a sort of supersecretary was recommended by Governor Nelson Rockefeller to the Jackson Committee on national policy machinery and is, in fact, a pattern that seems to be developing in the White House

---

[11] Herman Finer, *The Presidency: Crisis and Regeneration* (Chicago: University of Chicago Press, 1960).

[12] Marshall E. Dimock, *The New American Political Economy: A Synthesis of Politics and Economics* (New York: Harper & Row, Publishers, 1962).

Office more or less without conscious design simply because the need is so clear.

Yet another solution would be to encourage comprehensive and long-range planning, similar to that started by the National Resources Planning Board in 1934. Business has long emphasized the planning function because it has been found to reduce the amount of staff work needed in large-scale administration. There is much fumbling and idle work connected with most staff activity simply because no one knows if or when the results of staff research will be put to use. But when planning is adopted, the first step is to determine objectives and the second is to determine the means to attain them. In a real sense, therefore, intelligent democratic planning reduces superfluous staff activity. For this reason an intensified emphasis on planning in government seems inevitable and will probably go far to solve problems of organization and coordination at the top of the federal government.

### How Much Integration?

Underlying all the problems and possible solutions discussed here is what Dwight Waldo has called an inarticulate major assumption of fundamental political theory that is only rarely brought into the open. This assumption is that every formula and solution in administration is derived from or explained by a philosophical proposition, many of which have been a part of human knowledge since the time of the Greek philosophers.[13]

For example, to the question, How much integration shall be brought about at the top of the federal government?, the answer cannot be supplied until a precedent question, Integration for what?, has been dealt with. In a nation that prides itself on pluralism and a loose confederation of interests, does it not seem strange that so much emphasis should be placed on symmetry of organization and ultimate authority for the determination of economic and other public policy decisions? Symmetry is necessary in a Socialist state, but is it necessary or even desirable in a nation where freedom and invidual choice are fundamental concepts?

The next question is, If the American people are not yet prepared to accept responsible political parties (meaning parties able to deliver what they promise), is there really much chance of securing executive responsibility when the legislative branch cannot be relied upon, even in time of crisis, to back the common leadership?

A third question relates to the two previous ones: If the American people want responsibility and integration so badly, why not follow

---

[13] Dwight Waldo, *The Administrative State* (New York: The Ronald Press Company, 1948).

Woodrow Wilson's recommendation and establish a Cabinet form of government, one in which the chief executive, as the actual leader of the party in power and chief legislator as well, is assured of support throughout the whole of the legislative and executive branches so long as the party remains in office? Does anyone really think that institutionalizing the Presidency can accomplish integration at the executive level without prior structural arrangements to make that integration possible?

The fact is that executive coordination is the *last* step in a connected, government-wide process, not the first. Without the means of assuring responsibility in government, it is hard to think that coordination and integration at the top can take place in any real sense. Here is confirmation of Appleby's contention, underscored so effectively in *Politics and Administration,* that so far from being an independent variable, administration is part and parcel of, and limited by, the coordinations and unities found in the government as a whole.

If from the foregoing it may be concluded that the American Presidency as originally constituted is as effectual in the atomic age as it was in the horse and buggy age, then the American people must accept the best of a pluralistic situation and of checks and balances. That such an assumption is valid within the confines of fundamental administrative theory seems clear. Appleby states the proposition in this way:

> . . . any man in the presidential office comes gradually to attempt less in the way of tight control, simply because he finds that tight control cannot be achieved. . . . that President serves most effectively who exercises much less than his theoretical powers, who uses his power as an *ultimate* executive power. It is at that point—and not through the broad exercise of arbitrary, personal powers in a thousand and one directions—that the role of the President is crucial.[14]

In short, in its administrative guise the essence of presidential power is its exercise for decision in only the most difficult issues that come on appeal from the public in outcries of distress and criticism. When this stage is reached, history shows that issues are faced up to, decisions are made, and effective action is taken.

## Relationships Upward from the Bureau Chief

When the bureau chief, who as middle manager is at the center of the administrative process, looks to higher authority, he sees first the Secretary and the Secretary's executive and staff assistants who supply policy guidance and help him to relate his work to that of other programs. In

---

[14] Appleby, *op. cit.,* p. 114.

most cases, the interest and concern of the bureau chief stop there. If his department does its job, there is not much else that higher echelons need to supply. The more questions that can be resolved at the departmental level, the fewer are the issues to be coordinated at the apex of the government.

But when solutions at the departmental level are not possible, then there are a number of ways in which the bureau chief can get additional help. In matters relating to personnel administration, the Civil Service Commission and the presidential assistant in charge of personnel matters for the government as a whole are available. Similarly, the Bureau of the Budget offers a wide range of services through its several divisions that, in addition to budget review, include among others legislative reference, which coordinates legislation on a government-wide basis; and management and organization, which counsels on matters of structure and procedure. These divisions are not supposed to reach into the departments and bureaus to try to do directly what should properly be left to their own officers. Rather, the role of Bureau officials is to assist their opposite numbers within the departments and bureaus when they need help.

Again, the bureau chief may call on the General Services Administration, which helps him in the renting or construction of office and plant facilities, the purchasing of materials in quantity, the provision of transportation and machinery. Here also, officials of the GSA cannot do the whole job even if they were so inclined; their main effort is to help their opposite numbers in the departments and bureaus when outside assistance is needed.

The bureau chief may also turn to the General Accounting Office, but here the situation is a little different because the GAO is the watchdog of Congress and in a technical sense is part of the legislative branch. Nevertheless, as a result of reforms ushered in by the two Hoover Commissions, accounting is now a departmental responsibility and the role of the GAO is comparable to that of the Civil Service Commission in personnel administration: the GAO sets the standards, turns administration over to the departments, and contents itself with policing the results.

Other overhead agencies are useful only in special cases. Thus, the National Security Council coordinates high-level planning and action between the Departments of State and Defense. Useful to the Departments of Commerce and the Treasury, especially, is the Council of Economic Advisers which reports only to the President. Neither of these top agencies is in the main stream of command for most departments, however, and hence their work is not directly pertinent to that of most bureau chiefs.

If direct contacts such as these (and the less formal the better) between bureau chiefs and the overhead levels of government were en-

couraged and hence occurred more often than they now do, the result
would be to facilitate decision and action at the lower levels, thus reducing the number of problems that get pushed up to the presidential
level, adding to the burden, the confusion, and the problem of coordination there. Most large corporations operate successfully on the
basis of direct contact between middle management and particular units
at the higher level. Hence it seems reasonable to suppose that government also might derive substantial benefits from the same practice,
especially if it occurs as informally as possible.

Before such a system can be made to work, however, the top echelon
surrounding the President must accept the arrangement as part of its
philosophy of administration. The President could not do everything
himself even if he were sufficiently inexperienced to attempt it. Too
much decision making at the top, especially of the wrong kind, merely
aggravates officials in charge of operating bureaus and departments,
causing them to become tentative, unsure of themselves, even slothful,
for fear that higher authority might not approve. Instead, they should
be free to make up their own minds, to settle as many issues as possible
themselves so as to keep the workload at the top within a reasonable
range. If, therefore—as Rossiter, Corwin, Koenig, and others have
feared—American government suffers from an overconcentration of
staff responsibility at the top, it is not because constitutional requirements demand it but because our philosophy of administration is wrong.
If the President may delegate to staff officials, he is equally free to
delegate to line officials. It is along some such lines, together with more
planning of objectives and policies, that the ultimate solution to this
vexing problem will probably be found.

## BIBLIOGRAPHY AND CASES

### Annotated Reading Suggestions

Innumerable books have been written about the executive, looking down.
But relatively few look in the opposite direction, from the bureau chief or departmental level upward.

Some books, however, succeed modestly well. Among them may be mentioned Paul H. Appleby, *Policy and Administration* (University of Alabama
Press, 1954), especially Chapters 4 and 5. The same may be said of Mary Cushing Niles, *Middle Management: The Job of the Junior Administrator* (Harper
& Row, 1941), for she looks in all directions, as she should. Prominent place
should also be given to E. P. Learned, D. N. Ulrich, and D. R. Booz, *Executive
Action* (Harvard Business School, 1951), in which the authors deliberately con-

trast the down-from-the-top and the bottom-to-the-top points of view to show that the latter is becoming more common.

On the chief executive and his administrative relationships there is much good material, some of it exciting. Louis Brownlow, for example, on *The President and the Presidency* (Public Administration Service, 1949); Pendleton Herring on *Presidential Leadership* (Farrar and Rinehart, 1940); Clinton Rossiter on *The American Presidency* (Harcourt, Brace & World, 1956); Edward S. Corwin and Louis W. Koenig on *The Presidency Today* (New York University Press, 1956); Harold Laski on *The American Presidency* (Harper & Row, 1940); and Rexford G. Tugwell on *The Enlargement of the Presidency* (Doubleday, 1960).

There are equally good books on the state executive: Leslie Lipson, *The American Governor: From Figurehead to Leader* (University of Chicago Press, 1939); Coleman B. Ransome, Jr., *The Office of Governor in the South* (University of Alabama Press, 1951), and *The Office of Governor in the United States* (University of Alabama Press, 1956). Also relevant to this chapter is New York State Constitutional Convention Committee, *Problems Relating to Executive Administration and Powers* (Albany, 1938).

Interesting books on the municipal executive and his associations are Harold Stone, *et. al., City Manager Government in the United States* (Public Administration Service, 1940); Thomas H. Reed, *Municipal Management* (McGraw-Hill, 1941); and Clarence E. Ridley and Orin F. Nolting, *The City Manager Profession* (University of Chicago Press, 1934).

Books of historical interest showing the evolution of an office are Leonard D. White, *The Federalists* (Macmillan, 1948) and *The Jacksonians* (Macmillan, 1954).

*The Annals* of the American Academy of Political and Social Science for September 1956 has an excellent symposium on the Presidency; especially interesting are the articles by Sidney Hyman and Eli Nobleman, the latter of whom writes on the delegation of presidential functions. See also Cabell Phillips, "Executives for the Chief Executive," *New York Times Magazine,* June 5, 1955. On the role of the Vice President, see Irving G. Williams, *The Rise of the Vice-Presidency* (Public Affairs Press, 1956); and Edgar W. Waugh, *Second Counsel: The Vice-Presidency: Our Greatest Political Problem* (Bobbs-Merrill, 1956). There is also a good article by Don K. Price, "Staffing the Presidency," *American Political Science Review,* 40 (December 1946).

## Case Studies

In the Stein *Case Book,* the *Glavis-Ballinger Dispute* tells the story of the President's difficulties with some of his top lieutenants in the area of conservation policy. Among the actors are President Theodore Roosevelt and Gifford Pinchot, long-time leaders of the conservation forces in the United States. This case is reported in eight pages by Winifred McCulloch, and published in 1952.

A spectacular case in the ICP series is No. 52, **Steel Seizure of 1952,** fifty-three pages, written by G. McConnell. This was the famous seizure of the steel industry by President Truman during the course of a nationwide strike. Still another case, mentioned in an earlier chapter, is No. 60, **Governor Freeman and the Minnesota Budget,** thirty-five pages, by T. Flinn, written in 1961.

# 20

# Relationships
# to the Field

OF THE APPROXIMATELY 2.3 million employees on federal payrolls, nine out of ten employees work in the field, leaving only 230,000 or so at headquarters offices in Washington. Moreover, most of the work performed in the field is directly applicable to a citizen clientele, whereas most of the work done in Washington lacks this direct quality. Accordingly, because nine tenths of all federal administration occurs in the field, a corresponding degree of emphasis should be placed on field administration.

In practice, of course, the principles of public administration are the same at both ends of the line; it is only the problem of securing proper coordination and communication between headquarters and the field that is distinctive and of common concern to both groups of officials. Consequently, the emphasis in this chapter is on that aspect of the problem.

## The Areal Distribution of Power

Relations between headquarters and the field occur in two principal types of arrangement. The first, with which this chapter is primarily concerned, relates to a single governmental program with a headquarters office in Washington and a substructure in the field which may include regional, state, and local offices—at one or more of these levels or all of them in combination. The work of the Bureau of Reclamation is an example of this kind of program. The second arrangement lies at the core of intergovernmental relations and is often referred to as administrative federalism; it concerns a number of different governments at different levels coordinately occupied with a particular type of program, as in the case of public roads, for example.

In the first arrangement, relationships are vertical and occur within the same federal agency. In the second, they are both vertical and lateral because they occur in a line from Washington to related agencies of different governments at different levels (federal, state, and local), and also between federal field units and agencies of other governments at the same level.

The larger issue, of course, is the problem of intergovernmental relations. This matter is of vital concern to the public administrator but the subject is more appropriately dealt with in a course in American government. Nevertheless, some aspects of the question should be noted here, for they are part of the web to be dealt with by administrators in a headquarters-field relationship.

Because of government's need to get a particular job done in a particular place, problems surrounding the area (geographical) distribution of power and authority are as persistent as those relating to the separation of powers among the departments of government. There seems to be no permanent, unchangeable formula for allocating power between one level of government and another, or even among different governments.[1] So-called unitary governments have sometimes tried it, as when Napoleon arbitrarily carved out *départments* in France to replace the older geographical subdivisions that had grown up naturally, his aim being to assure centralization and control throughout the nation. A unitary government is one in which theoretically all power is monopolized at the top, and lesser governments such as counties and municipalities receive only such powers as the central government chooses to bestow. By contrast a federal government is made up of sovereign states that theoretically are at least the equal of the federal government, which enjoys only express powers in certain areas such as foreign affairs, interstate commerce, naturalization, and the like.

But whether a unitary or a federal government is in question, relationships between the many different governments at all levels within a nation are constantly changing. Thus the areal distribution of power is a chronic, persistent problem. In the United States only within the

---

[1] For a good, brief historical survey, see James W. Fesler, "Field Organization," in F. Morstein Marx, ed., *Elements of Public Administration* (Englewood Cliffs, N.J.: Prentice-Hall, Inc., 1959), pp. 246-251; and Albert Lepawsky, *Administration, The Art and Science of Organization and Management*, "The Geography of Organization," pp. 349ff.

last thirty years or so has a concerted attempt been made to develop a body of knowledge and principle that may eventually help to overcome some of these difficulties.[2]

The first main issue has to do with optimum size: Is there a point beyond which the federal government may become so large as to be virtually unmanageable? A few years ago many students of scientific management would have argued that if the principles of management are clearly understood and followed, there is virtually no limit to how large a human institution may become and still be as well managed as a smaller one. Now that some of the results of great size are becoming evident, there is some doubt in the matter. Something equivalent to the law of diminishing returns seems to operate in this area so that beyond a certain point every addition to size and volume tends to be less efficient than earlier units, and if growth continues, the efficiency of the whole operation is endangered.[3]

It seems, therefore, that centralization is bought at a price. Equally apparent is the fact that the end of the trend toward centralization is not yet in sight. Dominant forces in the world, including new technologies and the threat of war, seem to make further centralization inevitable. But along with this development, not only administrative problems become aggravated; even more basic are the effects of centralization on individual freedom and initiative, on the political system, and on the future of economic and cultural interests.

One obvious means of applying a brake to centralization is to encourage decentralization. Of the three principal ways in which this may be done, the first, already noted, is to check the growth of federal power and return as much power as possible to the states. The second is to set up intermediate regional units, such as the Tennessee Valley Authority, for example, where the effect is to devolve work onto the states and out of the reach of competing federal departments. And the third method, which is the main concern of this chapter, is to decentralize departmental administration from Washington so as to give field officials as much freedom and opportunity for initiative as they can handle.

Americans have accepted increasing centralization and great size partly because some degree of administrative decentralization has soothed some of their fears. Moreover, congressmen and senators enjoy the patronage that comes to them from the appointment of federal officials in their home territory. Defense offers the greatest opportunity, with over a million employees, and in addition, defense contracts main-

---

[2] See bibliography at the end of this chapter.

[3] Optimum size is dealt with by one of the present authors; see Marshall E. Dimock, *Administrative Vitality* (New York: Harper & Row, Publishers, 1959), pp. 255ff, and *The New American Political Economy* (New York: Harper & Row, Publishers, 1962), pp. 110ff. For an opposing view, see Frederick R. Kappel, *Vitality in a Business Enterprise* (New York: McGraw-Hill Book Company, Inc., 1960).

tain many a local community. The Post Office has over 35,000 post offices and employs half a million people. The Veterans Administration employs another 167,000. There are more than 500 district offices of Old-Age and Survivors' Insurance under the social security program throughout the nation. All such facilities help the home town. Members of Congress have been heard to argue that economically and politically some of the benefits of decentralization are secured by these means, while at the same time the trend to centralization does not slacken.

Some of the effects of this form of decentralization are: First, since the 1920s the federal aid formula has allowed the federal government to assist the states in one field after another that under the Constitution had seemingly been reserved to the states; as a result, the range of federal activities has greatly widened. Second, most areas of concern are not exclusive but coordinate, with both federal and state agencies involved in a single program or in similar programs in the same field. Third, the effect of this broadening is that many federal programs resemble a holding company type of operation. And finally, a large part of federal administration now consists in setting standards that the states must subscribe to and honor before federal funds are forthcoming.

This last factor, combined with an innate tendency found in all federal programs, has wide administrative repercussions: the 10 percent of federal officials stationed in Washington, generally in a superior hierarchical relationship to field officials, are by the very nature of their work inclined to become specialists. Increasingly do they deal with standards, rules, regulations, policies, and the like, rather than with direct operations, which by contrast involve many aspects in a rounded administrative process. For their part, field officials are chiefly concerned with direct operations and hence, again because of the nature of their work, are inclined to be generalists. In this set-up, it turns out that specialists commonly direct the operations of generalists, although theoretically, of course, just the reverse should be the case. This circumstance is one reason that in the headquarters-field relationship, communication and understanding are often less than adequate and in addition headquarters officials are apt to hold a tighter rein than is desirable on the initiative and independence of officials in the field. In effect, therefore, the ideal headquarters-field relationship has not developed, and both sides must recognize the situation and work to improve it.

Problems of centralization and decentralization are not confined, of course, to the federal government, although because of sheer size they are commonly more serious at that level than elsewhere. The larger cities especially, complain of too tight a control by the state, and problems attending the headquarters-field relationship may be complicated in large departments operating on a state-wide basis.

An interesting aspect of the matter is that today four out of five citizens are employed by others and live in cities, whereas a century ago four out of five were self-employed and lived in rural areas. When cities become so large there is a tendency for a direct relationship to be established between them and the federal government, thus partially or even wholly bypassing the states. The direct relationship was greatly encouraged during the New Deal when the federal government organized vast emergency work and relief programs and in fact, for the sake of speed, became banker to the larger cities where most of the unemployed were located. In 1962 the Kennedy Administration attempted (in vain, as it turned out) to create a separate federal Department of Urban Affairs which doubtless would have strengthened the federal-city relationship still further.

The prospect of checking centralization through a greater federal emphasis on regions does not seem bright. Congressmen and senators are inherently lukewarm or opposed to the plan on the ground that any level of jurisidiction that cuts across state lines would automatically limit their patronage and their total political influence. On the other hand, proposals to create special districts within state boundaries or between particular states, either by means of separate authorities (public corporations) or through the device of the interstate compact, have met with a more friendly response. Indeed, this is one of the most significant recent developments, especially when the objective is to avoid levying new taxes through the operation of a business-type enterprise, as in the case of toll roads, for example. Scores of these special purpose corporate entities have been established in nearly every state since World War II.

The results are noticeable in several directions. Thus, it is harder to hold government accountable for these operations, or even to understand what the arrangement is in the first place. In addition, the number of governmental units in the United States tends to multiply: despite the vanishing of many small, mostly school districts, through consolidation, the total number remains about 100,000. Finally, the problems of governmental organization and coordination are made infinitely more difficult, the power of the chief executive is reduced, and opportunities for legislative patronage are enhanced.

## Difficulties of Communication

Generally speaking, the farther an administrative area is from headquarters, the more freedom its administrators are likely to enjoy, and the nearer it is, the more will they be treated as a combination of child and guinea pig. In the matter of instructions, for example, the common temptation to which Washington officials are exposed is to reduce every procedure, no matter how trivial, to written rule so that every case will be treated alike. But then the field official becomes the victim of what in at least one instance was a five-foot shelf of looseleaf volumes filled with many kinds of instructions that he was supposed to consult before he could be sure that policy and procedure had not changed from the last time he had to make a similar decision. Under the circumstances, and especially if he is located at some distance from headquarters, the local administrator is tempted to ignore the five-foot shelf and do what reason seems to dictate, hoping not to make too many mistakes that will return to plague him. But if he is geographically close to the central office the psychological effect is to assume the presence of a closer tie and tighter supervision.

It is hard enough to exchange ideas and transmit signals that will be understood even when officials can talk face to face and in the same language, but it is infinitely harder when, as constantly happens, the headquarters official and the field man speak what amounts to different languages because each works in a different environment and each in his own mind has a different pattern of information based on geography and local mores. Sometimes these local differences are cultural, as in the case of popular attitudes toward race relations, labor relations, the status of women, or the tempo of work. Such cultural characteristics are deep-set, and although under the eroding action of time they are modified, they do not quickly respond to pressure, especially to outside pressure, which is usually considered "foreign," even—or perhaps especially—when it comes from Washington.

It is hard for a government administrator to understand local points of view unless he is part of the local complex. The inherent danger is that the headquarters official will fail to comprehend the significance of local ways of doing things, while for his part the field official is less sensitive to national objectives than is his superior. Unless remedies are applied, the result may be uncertainty at both ends, delayed correspondence, mutual irritations, frustrated initiative at the local level, and buck passing.

Another factor is a tendency for qualified people to seek the prestige of an administrative position in Washington and to leave positions in the field to people who may be less qualified as administrators and who in addition, are less inclined to find satisfaction in work in a large metropolitan center such as Washington is. Moreover, some people like the work involved in positions of central authority, while others prefer field work as being more active and putting them in closer touch with people. Although the difference in qualifications may be slight, the difference in temperament may be significant and constitute yet another obstacle to mutual understanding, no matter how clearly the written instructions may be worded.

The question of instructions from headquarters is, in fact, a crucial one in a relationship where distance is a factor. There is, to be sure, the danger of exaggerating the extent to which burdensome red tape and overelaborate instructions are found in modern governmental practice because much improvement has been made in a generation and, as noted in Chapter 15, administrative manuals are now mostly of a reasonable size. But since the temptation toward minute prescription remains, here are some examples of what happens at both ends of the line:[4]

**The Disease of Manualitis.**    Manualitis is an occupational disease, generally found in government but often in private enterprise as well, that causes people to assume that every administrative procedure can be reduced to rule and embalmed in a manual for the guidance of all employees. In the present instance, government officials from several districts in the Rocky Mountain region are convened for a conference. In a hotel room after the day's sessions, three district managers are talking shop. The man from Pocatello is saying: "These guys in Washington have no sense of reality. The District of Columbia isn't the United States. Procedures written there just don't fit here. They don't take into account operating realities. I can't follow them and get the job done. They complain if Congress ties their hands on administrative detail and then go ahead and write procedures themselves in such detail that we're supposed to act like robots. It's one thing to sit in a swivel chair in Washington and dictate a new procedure, and another to apply it in Pocatello."

The man from Salt Lake City breaks in: "Another thing—there are a hundred swivel-chair experts in Washington concerned with a hundred different angles of our program and each thinks his own piddling little part is the most important aspect of it and that full time should be devoted to him."

"What you're saying," observes the man from Montana, "is that we're overfunctionalized—that's a Washington five-dollar word—anyway, we're overfunctionalized to the extent that an undivided line of authority over us doesn't exist. We have not one, but a hundred bosses who can't agree among themselves. Most of what they call disorganization in the field exists only in the minds of Washington officials anyhow."

**Instinctive Resistance.**    A staff meeting of regional personnel is in progress in Atlanta. The discussion concerns a new bulletin defining responsibilities of the field staff. Tom Technical is speaking: "I think this bulletin is clear insofar as my duties are concerned. It says that representatives in the field are responsible to the technical divisions in Washington on technical matters, but are subordinate to the regional

---

[4] Illustrations from Graduate School of the United States Department of Agriculture, *Washingtin-Field Relationships in the Federal Service* (Washington, D.C.: Government Printing Office, 1942), pp. 9, 10, 51.

director for administrative matters. All my work is concerned with advising the district offices on their programs and methods. That is all technical work. This means I report to and take my orders from Washington."

To which the regional director replies, "Is *that* so?"

**Crossing Them Up.**    The field official who directly serves both a technical official in Washington and a regional administrator in the field leads a harried existence. A certain field official in the west was on the same day directed by his technical superior in Washington to proceed immediately to San Francisco and by his regional administrator in the field to rush to Butte, Montana. Perplexed, the technical official wired his bureau chief in Washington for instructions as to which superior he should obey, and received the reply, "Cooperate with both fully."

Then, of course, at the other end of the relationship there is the problem of the headquarters official:[5]

**Keeping Him Guessing.**    The director of a federal agency has called a number of his field men to headquarters for a conference. They have accused him point-blank of working in a vacuum in preparing instructions to the field and issuing orders impossible to carry out because of unfamiliarity with field conditions. Says the director, "What have we got field officials for, if not to tell us of conditions in the field? That's one reason you're in here now and another reason why we spent so much time trying to develop a work-reporting program. For two years now I've been hopping on this and the idea hasn't even dented the surface."

**Do It Later.**    The finance officer of a bureau in the Post Office Department is bawling out the chief statistician: "Here it is the tenth of the month and the reports from six regions are still missing. Can't you do something about this?" To which the statistician replies: "Listen, if you have any idea how to make those fellows in the field realize that every month is bound to end sooner or later, let me have it. I have circularized them again and again to prepare the reports promptly, but each time they seem to be taken completely by surprise when the month drops out from under them. Now don't tell me we ought to fire them. The new ones would be just the same."

Hypothetical as these incidents are, they illustrate problems that will continue to exasperate field and headquarters officials alike until more is learned about the possible correctives.

---

5 *Ibid.*, pp. 12-13.

## Creating Harmonious Relationships

What methods have been found effective in dealing with the problem of harmonious relationships between headquarters and the field? A number of rules have been evolved, chiefly by trial and error, and if they are constructively applied, go a long way toward this goal.

The first rule is that *every situation is a distinctive one* and must be separately analyzed to discover how it differs from others. Standard formulas must be avoided. An arrangement that will work in one situation fails in another. In the end the kind of field relationship decided on must depend largely on the degree of decentralization that is permitted, including authority devolved to the regional, state, and local levels; and this, in turn, varies with the job. Administrators are sometimes heard to say that they believe in decentralization or that it is their policy to decentralize, but neither statement represents a mature view of the matter because decentralization is not invariably indicated. In any situation there is a best way to proceed, to organize to do the job, and that best way can usually be determined. If centralization is indicated, then centralization should be instituted; if decentralization seems preferable in a particular instance, then decentralization should be ordered.

The next rule is that decentralization in any real sense is impossible until the *objectives, policies, and plans of the program have been clearly formulated*. These matters have been dealt with in Chapter 10 and it need simply be noted here that anemia in this area is one reason for little effective decentralization in most federal programs. Judging from the usual practice of large corporations, the ideal combination is to centralize policy determination at headquarters and to decentralize operations to the field. In practice, of course, this is a two-way process and not a division of duties, as Donald Stone makes clear in his comment that

> . . . the job of the Washington staff is to formulate programs, establish policy, develop standards and some of the principal procedures, and . . . create a field organization which is competent to administer and permitted to administer the program. These things cannot be done remotely by the Washington staff; field staff must participate all along the line. Policy, programs, and procedures must be developed and constantly re-evaluated in terms of operating and administrative experience. . . . It is futile to set up policy that won't stand up on the firing line. . . . It is a waste of effort to prepare regulations or instructions which field staff aren't in sympathy with or don't understand. . . .[6]

---

6 *Ibid.*, p. 18.

Once the objectives and policies are clear, then if field executives are to be encouraged to exercise initiative and to take pride in their work, they must be allowed to make their own decisions on the job. Consequently, *as much decision making as possible must be devolved to the field.* This point has been well made by two officials of the Forest Service, one of the most competently administered agencies of the federal government: "Decisions should be made at the level of authority which most nearly represents the public affected by the decision. If the decision affects a national activity which concerns either the social or the industrial economy of the entire nation, the decision should be made by a national office. If a decision applies only to a part of the country or to a section of the population, the decision will best be made by officials in that area, who are familiar with the problem from first-hand contact." And then this: "It is as bad to decentralize too far as not far enough, but there is far less danger of doing it." [7]

A delegation of authority to the field that really is a delegation and not just a gesture requires much more than an intellectual appreciation of the need for such a policy. Moreover, the groundwork for delegation must be laid and employees trained. An example of the methods of the Forest Service is found in a letter of instructions from a district forest ranger to a new employee in a local office.[8] Such letters are hard to write, says the district forest ranger, partly because there is always the possibility "that written letters of instruction will be taken so seriously that nothing will be accomplished except what is covered in that letter. This letter," he adds, "is not intended to be a listing of jobs that you will accomplish this year, nor is it an attempt to tell you how to go about doing each job. It is written for the purpose of making it clear to you what your place is in the organization, and an attempt to help you fit into the organization so that it will run smoothly and we can attain maximum results with minimum lost time and effort." He then notes that "Lining up a summer's work on a ranger district necessitates delegation of authority and responsibility. A ranger district is not like a machine shop or factory where the boss can see every machine and every man several times a day."

Going back to the job itself, the district ranger remarks that he cannot go into minute detail about the job because among other objections, he would deprive the new employee of initiative—"you would not have to think." The district ranger then notes certain policies and procedures common to Forest Service districts everywhere, states the new employee's position and title (a very minor one), tells him where in the manual he will find the detailed description of his job, lists a few other incidental responsibilities, and concludes: "In other

[7] *Ibid.*, p. 32.
[8] From District Forest Ranger R. C. Fitzgerald, April 11, 1949.

words, assume responsibility for maintaining our headquarters in a presentable and safe condition. You may enlist whatever help is available to accomplish the job."

The administrator who is emotionally incapable of decentralizing can always find reasons for not devolving authority into the field organization. He is afraid of political influence and financial irregularities. He is afraid mistakes will be made and assumes, somewhat immodestly, that he is less likely to err than his subordinates. Stone remarks that responsible officials in Washington "tend to think it impossible to delegate authority to field offices unless there is a rigid check-control from headquarters. Field Officers, no matter how well they are picked, all make mistakes—so do we all—and they will not always perform as the headquarters official would if he were in the field; and vice versa. That must be taken for granted. But this does not mean that a much better job will not be done in the field if field directors are given authority commensurate with their responsibilities." Indeed, the strategy at headquarters should be to keep matters *out* of Washington as much as possible.[9]

Yet another rule of harmonious relationship is that the more delegation there is, *the more must there be coordination among different agencies in the field* so as to avoid imbalances and cross purposes. This rule is basic and is discussed more fully below.

Next there must be *clear lines of leadership* because only so can responsibility be placed at each level and a high quality of leadership be freed to operate with every necessary tool of management at hand. A basic principle of administration is to get good people and give them all the authority they need to act effectively. Stone remarks that if a field office lacks the right kind of leadership, there is likely to develop a situation bordering on anarchy, with the chiefs of the various field functions or services bypassing the regional director and reporting administratively to their superiors in Washington. Such reporting is likely to cause less trouble in a unifunctional than in a multifunctional program, but even here there will be frustrations and confusion if the field command is a weak one.[10]

Finally, if field offices are to be encouraged to exercise initiative, they must have *the same advantages in the way of management tools as their counterparts at headquarters enjoy.* Important among these are prompt and well-organized channels of communication for instructions and reports, brief but usable manuals of policy and procedure, freedom in budgetary planning and follow-up, personnel management, and program planning, and an adequate staff to assist in direction and coordination.

9 *Washington-Field Relationships in the Federal Service,* pp. 15-16.
10 *Ibid.,* pp. 52-55.

## *Organization at Headquarters for Field Supervision*

Another bothersome problem in the headquarters-field relationship, especially in a multifunctional program, is whether to concentrate or to disperse the authority of officials in the central office to issue instructions to the field. Trial and error has created a wide range of practice depending on the nature of the program, and no practice is satisfactory in every respect.

Where the head of an agency cannot bring himself to delegate and tries to do everything himself, he either prepares instructions to the field personally or has his subordinates prepare them for his signature. But if he has learned to delegate, then he may distinguish between line and staff communications and allow staff instructions to flow out freely so long as they do not impinge on the authority of line officials in the field offices. Or finally, he may appoint a director of field operations either in his own office or as the head of a separate division, and require all instructions to flow through that channel. These are the three main types of organization for field supervision, but there are many variations.

Although there is no one best method for all kinds of programs, there generally is a best one for each; to discover just what it is, however, may be a perplexing matter. Stone states as an abstract proposition that "some operating official in the line of command must be responsible for the *whole* field program," and the italicized word is his.[11] Thus, when the several parts of a diverse program must be coordinated so as to make sense in the field, some one person at headquarters must be responsible for seeing that policy and instructions are consistent.

The Social Security Administration, now a part of the Department of Health, Education, and Welfare but originally an independent agency, is an interesting illustration of a program that insisted from the outset on a high degree of centralization and made successful use of a field operations division.[12] This division had jurisdiction over procurement, budget, travel, space, communications, and all phases of personnel administration for twelve regional and two territorial offices, passing on all outgoing communications from any Washington unit to two or more regions. All of these business management activities were reviewed to ensure their adherence to policy and administrative standards and secure coordination.

This type of organization for field supervision has not generally been regarded with much favor by other agencies that have tried it. To

---

11 *Ibid.*, p. 17.

12 The story is told by W. L. Mitchell in a chapter in *Washington-Field Relationships in the Federal Service*, p. 35.

combine policy review functions with conscientious housekeeping obviously creates an enormous aggregation of power in one place. Headquarters officials resent undue limitations on their freedom of authority; jealousy and frustration set in; delays and bottlenecks develop to the despair of field officials. On the other hand the system has certain advantages: it unifies authority in one place, provides for a thorough review of policy to assure uniformity, acts as a friend in court for field agencies vis-à-vis the functional units in the central office, and by unifying authority at headquarters helps to coordinate the policies of diverse programs in the field.[13]

No better illustration of the complexity of the problem of central office organization for field supervision could be found than in the experience of the War Production Board during World War II, for WPB tried everything in the book to solve that problem.[14] Because it was an emergency program, the administrator did not take time at the outset to study the matter; he might have saved time in the end had he done so. Rather, he agreed to accept office space in each of the twelve federal reserve districts for regional offices of his own, irrespective of whether the areas were suitable to the work of his program. The device was a failure from the start and a crazy quilt of organization developed in the field. Recognizing the chaos, WPB officials then arbitrarily redivided the country into twelve different regions, but resistance developed to this formula also and complaints against overcentralization were constant.

So then a bureau of field operations was set up at headquarters, but almost at once it seemed to create more problems than it solved. When this unit was abolished, field operations were placed under a deputy director in the office of the Director of Industry Operations, but again the device was inadquate. In an attempt to improve it, field liaison men were appointed to represent headquarters in the various regions, but this experiment turned out to be no better than the others. Finally, determined to secure more decentralization, the WPB administrator created an operations council consisting of officials from headquarters and the field.

In the end it was the system of dual supervision that proved most useful. As the plan was applied, the distinction between specialist and generalist was formalized by the fact that policy making and policy interpretation were reserved to the functional divisions in Washington, of which there were approximately forty. It was then an accepted

13 See George F. Rohrlich, "Consolidation of Unemployment Insurance and the Problem of Centralization," *Public Administration Review*, IV (Winter 1944), pp. 43-50.
14 The story is interestingly set forth by William D. Carey in "Central-Field Relationships in the War Production Board," *Public Administration Review*, IV (Winter 1944), pp. 31-42.

principle "that these central functional offices should maintain routine relations with their counterpart in the field offices, although 'administrative' authority and general coordinating power was vested in the regional directors." [15] This is the formula adopted in most large business corporations and is probably about as close to a general rule of guidance as can be devised.

## Interagency Coordination in the Field

With 90 percent of federal programs administered outside of Washington, and with a few large cities—such as New York, Boston, Atlanta, Chicago, Denver, and San Francisco—designated as regional headquarters for many of them, why not try to improve the headquarters-field relationship by concentrating on interagency cooperation in these centers? If organization for field supervision at headquarters is difficult, why not encourage coordination in the field centers where presumably correlations are more apparent and the incentive to work together may be greater?

If the employment service and unemployment insurance may be correlated within a single field framework, why should not the regional directors of a number of other programs—such as public roads and public buildings, agriculture and forestry, business and labor—establish a similar relationship at the operating level? The fact is that on an informal basis much of this already happens because jurisdictional exclusiveness is less than at headquarters and official friendships come about easily. This is explained in part by the principle of oligarchy, according to which the more power vested in particular officials, the more tightly do they try to hold onto it—a principle that operates freely at headquarters and much less so in the field.

Many attempts have been made to secure interagency coordination in the field on a more formal footing, but most of it has been limited to the creation of pooled services such as office and storage space, use of trucks and other equipment, and personnel and purchasing prodecures. Examples are the Federal Coordinating Service, supported by the Bureau of the Budget, which lasted from 1921 to 1933; the National Emergency Council created to coordinate the many field agencies of the New Deal from 1933 to 1939; and more recently the field work of the General Services Administration, the Civil Service Commission, the General Accounting Office, and the Disbursement Division of the Treasury Department. Local post offices also are increasingly used as service agencies for many federal programs.

Nevertheless, none of these goes far enough to cover the whole need. Several possible solutions have been offered but none seems to be with-

---

[15] *Ibid.*, pp. 37-38.

out disadvantages. An early one, advanced in 1935 by the National Resources Planning Board, would have established common regional centers for federal coordination—subcapitals, so to speak.[16] Such an arrangement might do for most purposes but not, for example, for agriculture, which has a different geopraphical base than, say, foreign trade. In addition, of course, politicians will always disagree on site selections: should the regional center be established at Los Angeles, or San Francisco, for example?

Another proposal, but one that was never seriously entertained, was to appoint a kind of supercoordinator at regional centers and authorize him to expedite the coordination of many or even of all departmental programs. It was quickly objected that relations to Washington would become blurred, with results more confusing than ever.

A more practicable plan is to effect coordination through the physical proximity of a number of different agencies in a field center. This is one of the six facilitating factors mentioned by Fesler, the others being familiarity with the work of the other agencies, informal acquaintance with other officials, specific objectives, a limited number of participants, and approximately equal status of participants.[17] When as many federal agencies as possible are placed in the same building, a visit to a lower floor may be all that is needed to effect coordination that otherwise might take days to bring about. Much informal coordination already occurs in this manner among different field units and the attempt is to encourage more of it through the sharing of joint facilities, the organization of luncheon clubs, social clubs, and the like.

Underlying all such thinking, however, is the point amply confirmed by experience that if coordination does not take place in Washington where high policy is determined, there is not much chance that any except cursory and sporadic coordination will occur in the field. There must be a desire to cooperate and it must be backed by official approval if anything like full cooperation is to be effected at the field level.

## A Philosophy of Decentralization

The noted Swedish economist, Gunnar Myrdal, believes that in the long run the question of whether capitalism-representative democracy or socialism-communism prevails will depend upon which system does the better job of effecting decentralization.[18] There is much substance in

---

[16] National Resources Committee, *Regional Factors in National Planning* (Washington, D.C.: Government Printing Office, 1935).

[17] *Washington-Field Relationships in the Federal Service,* pp. 15-16.

[18] Gunnar Myrdal, *Beyond the Welfare State* (New Haven, Conn.: Yale University Press, 1960).

this challenge because in both systems there are strong centripetal forces at work. In addition, creative, spirited administration is everywhere decentralized administration. In the headquarters-field relationship, no one denies that there are great reservoirs of energy and initiative in the field that could be released if central controls were not so burdensome and rigid. In the end, difficulties seem to stem more from basic attitudes than from an ignorance of the administrative principles to be applied.

What, then, is the change in philosophy and outlook that should be encouraged? For one thing, greater modesty on the part of top brass in Washington and a recognition of the fact that there are many men of brains and ability in local centers capable of doing acceptable work. The real job of the Washington staff is to help the field staff do its job, not to do the field job itself. This means elimination of the "directive" approach, line item budgets, transaction reviews, preaudits of cases, and what is worst of all, the writing of voluminous letters and memoranda prior to taking action that is urgently needed. All these things kill initiative. They stifle administration. They give a black eye to government. Delegation of authority must be real, not just on paper. Such delegation of authority must follow the spirit of a top official in one of the federal agencies who recently told his field managers to go ahead and act when action was needed, even violating regulations, if necessary, and to tell their agency about it afterwards. Only with this kind of administration can we expect to attract capable, responsible, broad-gauged officials to the field service.[19]

A new philosophy is appearing in large-scale administration that augurs well for the future. It is what may be called the bottom-up approach in contrast to the top-down approach that prevailed for so long. The trend is confirmed in a comprehensive survey of corporate practice where it was found, for example, that "in many companies executives could have placed a great deal more faith in the capacity of subordinates to assume greater responsibility. Executives who systematically gave responsibility to their juniors, in accordance with the juniors' capacities and interests as well as with the needs of the organization, increased their *own* effectiveness through this process to a degree that sometimes appeared almost spectacular."[20]

It was also found, however, that the problems of working with many people in complex organizations need more study. There must be more effective techniques of teamwork at the top executive level and better methods of securing the participation of subordinate personnel. It is obvious that "the fulfilment of this need requires of the executive not only certain social skills but also *certain fundamental attitudes toward the people around him*."[21]

19 *Washington-Field Relationships in the Federal Service,* p. 18.
20 Learned, Ulrich, and Booz, *Executive Action,* p. 210.
21 *Ibid.,* p. 63. Italics added.

Most of the work in any large organization is done in the field. In recent years much has been heard about the growth of officialdom in Washington, but as already noted, there are roughly only one tenth as many federal employees in Washington as there are throughout the nation and abroad. Except for increases of overseas employees in the last decade or so, this ratio has been maintained for many years. True, as the House Finance Committee and others have pointed out, the Washington ratio has expanded in some notable instances and the tendency should be resisted. There is now needed an attitude of mind that will encourage decentralization not only of staff but also of authority and responsibility to that staff.

Without the positive desire to decentralize, the techniques are slow to develop; but where it exists, there are many things that can be done. Field officials can be allowed to exercise a greater influence on over-all policy determination. Objectives can be more clearly defined. Field officials can be told what the targets are, the accomplishment of them being left to their ingenuity. The number and detailed character of central office instructions can be reduced. Regional centers of coordination can be set up to decrease the supervisory load of the central office. Strong executives with enough self-confidence to delegate on a broad scale can be recruited for headquarters positions. The home office can concentrate on national policy and assistance to the field. The field can concentrate on local decisions and the means of handling local situations.

## BIBLIOGRAPHY AND CASES

### Annotated Reading Suggestions

The principal authority in this area is James W. Fesler. See especially his book, *Area and Administration* (University of Alabama Press, 1949), and his chapter, "Field Organization," in F. Morstein Marx, ed., *Elements of Public Administration* (2d ed., Prentice-Hall, 1959).

On intergovernmental relations in general, the best source is William Anderson, *Federalism and Intergovernmental Relations* (Public Administration Service, 1956), and *The Nation and the States, Rivals or Partners?* (University of Minnesota Press, 1955). See also John M. Gaus, "Federalism and Intergovernmental Relations," *Public Administration Review*, 16 (Spring 1956); and Governor G. Mennen Williams, "Federal-State Relations," *Public Administration Review*, 17 (Autumn 1957).

The working methods in this area are dealt with in *Washington-Field Relationships in the Federal Service* (Graduate School, U. S. Department of Agriculture, 1942), which includes papers by Donald Stone, James W. Fesler, and others. See also Earl Latham, *The Federal Field Service* (Public Administration Service, 1947), and "Executive Management and the Federal Field Service," *Public Administration Review*, 5 (Winter 1945).

There are also a number of studies relating to particular agencies: Emmette S. Redford, *Field Administration of Wartime Rationing* (Government Printing Office, 1947); William D. Carey, "Central-Field Relationships in the War Production Board," *Public Administration Review*, 4 (Winter 1944); these are representative. On practical problems in general, see G. M. Goodrich, "Integration vs. Decentralization in the Federal Field Service," *Public Administration Review*, 9 (Autumn 1949); and William J. Gore, "Administrative Decision-Making in Federal Field Offices," *Public Administration Review*, 16 (Autumn 1956).

New dimensions were given to the problem in two contributions to *New Horizons in Public Administration* (University of Alabama Press, 1945), a symposium edited by Roscoe C. Martin: Arthur W. Macmahon wrote "Function and Area in the Administration of International Affairs," and John D. Millett wrote "Field Organization and Staff Supervision."

## Case Studies

Two outstanding cases in the Stein *Case Book* fall naturally in this area. *The Natural Cement Issue* had to do with federal-state authority, the imposition of standards, and questions of technical judgment. This case was reported by Paul N. Ylvisaker in 1950 and is twenty-nine pages long. *The Battle of Blue Earth County* is the story of a controversy involving a seven-year feud between a county welfare board in Minnesota and officials of the Social Security Administration in Washington. This case also was reported by Paul N. Ylvisaker in 1950 and is told in fourteen pages.

Many other fine cases are available in the ICP series for this chapter. No. 40, *The Decentralization of Business Services in the Agricultural Research Service* was mentioned in the preceding chapter. Another, No. 16, *Three Cases in Field Administration,* offers a variety of illustration. No. 21, *The Department of Commerce Field Service,* thirty-three pages, by K. S. Arnow, also tells an interesting story. No. 19, *The Regional Information Officer,* five pages, by M. Kriesberg, is apposite to both this topic and to public relations. And finally, No. 33, *Coterminous Boundaries Dispute,* fifteen pages, by E. A. Read, illustrates other areal difficulties.

# PART FIVE

# Administration
# and the Public

# 21

## Public Relations

PUBLIC RELATIONS IS concerned with survival because in the long run no enterprise can endure without public support. A characteristic of bureaucracy—even in a small program—is to focus on itself, to turn its attention inward, away from people, away even from its own clients and customers. The purpose of public relations, therefore, is to offset this tendency by encouraging an outward attitude so that the bureaucracy becomes client-oriented and thus can gain and keep the support of the public on which survival depends.

For this reason public relations lies at the heart of administration and is a function for which the chief executive himself must be responsible. But in addition, everyone in the organization must become involved in public relations in some way, and hence the results of a public relations program are not measurable in footage of publicity, the number of mimeographed handouts distributed, nor the bulk of the scrapbook kept by the publicity department. Public relations pay off in only one currency: the survival of the program through sustained public support.

A positive public relations program has these special purposes: First, to keep internal administration outer-directed. Second, to keep employees alive and alert by focusing their attention on objectives, policies, program planning, and the client or consumer. Third, to further democratic education and access to information. And fourth, by these means to assure survival and influence. Hence public relations is at the heart of the political process. In the long run it is an administrative function of prime importance.

There has been a recent upsurge of interest in the public relations of government, due partly to charges by newspapers and other media that access to the news is being withheld, especially by the Pentagon and the State Department. But interest is also due to a recognition by administrators themselves that public relations has been inadequately used in the past. The reporter and the man in government, it is said, "are natural allies." The government man cannot do his job unless the people back him, and it is the reporter's business to make the national situation known to the people. In public administration the issues must be made clear to the people while policies are still being developed; after they are set, it is too late to profit from an expression of public opinion.[1]

Today the decisions that nations must make on short notice are of frightening importance. No longer is it possible to wait for articulate citizens to become informed, for public opinion to jell, and for that opinion to make itself felt in government. Who is to respond to this challenge, the public or the private information channel? Obviously, it is the job of both.

No one has more felicitously stated the opportunities available in public relations than the British political scientist, Brian Chapman:

> . . . the recent awareness [in Europe] of the need for better government public relations has gone no further than communicating to the public what the public service concerned is doing rather than why it is doing it. Only in Sweden are any effective measures taken to ensure the maximum publicity for government business. . . . It may be that no public can be trusted, but since no government in Europe, outside Sweden, has ever tried it, the evidence is incomplete. Public stampedes, to judge from the past, have always been caused by lack of information, or twisted information, not by a surfeit.[2]

And in America? According to a Frenchman, "One is struck by the mass of information published by the American administration in all forms. . . . The American mentality is hostile to secrets." [3]

---

[1] See the excellent summary of William B. Shore, "Developments in Public Administration," *Public Administration Review*, 20 (Autumn 1960), pp. 238-245.

[2] Brian Chapman, *The Profession of Government* (New York: The Macmillan Company, 1959).

[3] Raoul Perol, "La Politique de l'Administration américaine, à l'égard du public," *La Revue Administrative* (March-April 1960), pp. 199-206.

## Public Relations and Administration

Most definitions of public relations have much in common. Rex Harlow, a pioneer in the field, says that public relations is "a science through which an organization can consciously attempt to fulfill its social responsibilities, and to secure the public recognition and approval necessary to success," and elsewhere he calls public relations the process whereby an organization analyzes the needs and desires of all interested parties in order to conduct itself more responsively toward them.[4] In the vocabulary of social biology, public relations is institutional survival and influence—the point that was made at the beginning of this chapter. In less formal terms, it has also been said that public relations is being good and getting credit for it; it is 90 percent doing right and 10 percent talking about it.[5]

In other words, public relations is a planned program of policies and action designed by an administrator to build public confidence in and increase public understanding of his program or agency. Since its purpose is to satisfy all parties of interest—public, employees, and management itself—a public relations plan must be broadly conceived, formulated with the help of everyone in the organization, carried out by every employee, focused on the public, and largely directed from the office of the top executive.

A public relations program may be designed for both defensive and offensive purposes. The defensive aspect of it protects the institution from attack and misunderstanding, and the offensive enhances its prestige and influence. Another purpose is to secure credit for a job well done, which is an aspect of internal morale because people work best when they know they are appreciated. As already remarked, proper public relations programs also make employees consumer- or client-conscious, so to speak, in that the attitudes and desires and rights of the users of the service are taken into account by employees themselves, and in both cases the result is high morale. Service rendered under these conditions is likely to be more appreciated than when both management and employees are self-centered, because a cordial relationship makes the service *seem* better even if it is not.

All institutions must struggle to survive, and it bears repeating that a proper public relations program is a means to that end. All institutions, whether of business or of government, compete for the favor of their master, which is the public, and for the prize, which is favor-

---

4 Rex F. Harlow, *Public Relations in War and Peace* (New York: Harper & Row, Publishers, 1942), pp. x, 130.

5 J. H. Wright and B. H. Christian, *Public Relations Management* (New York: McGraw-Hill Book Company, 1949), p. 3.

able public opinion. If the administrator would secure the permanence and growth of his program, he must make its services known to the various publics that determine its fate. In the field of institutional public relations there is no absolute distinction between industrial, professional, governmental, and other forms of institution, for "all are finally subject to the same force which is in the end superior to any law or tradition"—the force of public opinion when translated into action.[6]

The media of public relations are, first of all, the employees of the organization themselves, and next, its clients and interest groups. Specific techniques are advertising and publicity through press, radio, television; the handling of complaints; the rendering of annual or periodic reports by management; press conferences; and other devices depending on the inventiveness and ingenuity of those who handle the program. Although the use of these media may require specialists like newspapermen, radio and television scenarists, and magazine writers, these are never the top people in a well-planned program. Primary responsibility centers in the top executive assisted by a staff official in charge of public relations. In business this official may be a vice president but in government he is usually the director of a public information section or an assistant to the executive head of the agency. In any case, although he may have had experience in a specialty such as press or television, in his staff work he must be chiefly concerned with the objectives, policies, and morale of the agency and only secondarily with media. As with all tools of management, the media and the techniques of public relations are always subordinate to the objectives of the enterprise and are useful only as they contribute to the broad strategy of management.

More important than publicity in a public relations program is the availability to management of seasoned advice about current and long-range problems that will determine the reputation of the enterprise and assure its future. One intelligent, management-minded staff assistant at a substantial salary is worth more to the top executive than two narrowly trained newspapermen at half that sum each. "Public relations," it has been said, "is not a job for just a few professionals. It is a phase of management. Management sets the policies. The staff and employees carry them out. When the two are working together, public relations is on a sound footing."[7]

Of all of management's staff activities, public relations is the one that the chief administrator can least afford to leave to someone else. The hazards of too loose a rein in this area were painfully learned during the 1920s when public relations was a new field and became a kind of fad. This was the heyday of the publicity expert and the stunt man

6 Harlow, *op. cit.*, p. 3.
7 Wright and Christian, *op. cit.*, p. 3.

whose slogans were "It pays to advertise" and "It doesn't matter what they say about you so long as they talk about you." Businessmen who lived through that era have been heard to comment that public relations is dynamite: let it get out of hand and it will destroy reputations and public confidence almost beyond repair.

## Growth of Public Relations in Government

In democratic governments like those in the United States, there has long been a reluctance to grant administrators very much latitude in the field of public relations. Suspicion has most often been directed at appropriations requested for advertising and publicity, which legislators regard as the means by which bureaucrats extend their power, compete with private interests, and conceal their own failures. In 1919, for example, a so-called gag law prohibited the use of appropriated funds for services, messages, or publications designed to influence any member of Congress in his attitude toward legislation, and also stipulated that no government publication other than spot announcements to the press could be sent except to those who had requested in writing to be placed on a particular mailing list.

When James McCamy made his study of public relations in government in 1939, although the figure was probably incomplete he was able to secure data on only 212 information specialists (as they were called) in the federal government and even this figure represented a considerable increase over what had formerly been allowed.[8] Two years later, Leo Rosten had found only 208 newspaper correspondents in Washington,[9] which meant that even at the end of the New Deal period—a time when public relations in the federal government was considerably stressed—there were almost as many information specialists in federal agencies as there were national reporters representing newspapers and the wire services. Wright and Christian remark that the range of administrative services under the New Deal was so great that without the information provided through public relations activities, most citizens would have been even more confused than they were. The average voter has never had more than a dim idea of the many services his government performs and for which he is taxed. Even during World War II, when the need for information was urgent and the government sought to fill it, there is a question whether the confusion of the public was not sometimes more increased than alleviated.

It is now better understood that publicity is only one aspect of a

8 James L. McCamy, *Government Publicity* (Chicago: University of Chicago Press, 1939).

9 Leo C. Rosten, *The Washington Correspondents* (New York: Harcourt, Brace & World, 1937).

public relations program, and attitudes that were once so unfavorable to such activity in government have begun to change. There are still occasional crackdowns in Congress on appropriations for public relations, but the day of the drastic gag law is apparently over. This fact combined with the urgent need for information that accompanies widespread government activities in time of stress—war and cold war—has caused such a rapid growth of public relations programs in government that already by the end of World War II the federal government was the world's largest employer of professional public relations talent. In 1948 about 2500 men and women were still employed in such work in various federal offices, exclusive of the dwindling war agencies themselves. For a short time thereafter there was a slight contraction due to pressure to economize, but with the onset of the Korean conflict, employment in public relations as in other government activities increased. Today there is hardly an agency of any size in Washington that does not have at least one trained information specialist; it is this group that is responsible for the great volume of newspaper releases, radio and television programs, speeches, information bulletins, and public reports that pour out of Washington every day.

In addition, since the New Deal there have been attempts to establish a government-wide information service with the accompanying threat of high-level censorship.[10] The first effort to create a central clearinghouse for public information was the United States Information Service,[11] set up in 1934 and five years later transferred to the then newly created Office of Government Reports located in the Executive Office of the President. The three main divisions of this new agency were field operations, with thirty-four state and regional offices serving as central contact points for representatives of federal, state, and local governments; press intelligence; and the United States Information Service itself with main offices in Washington and New York and prepared, in theory at least, to answer citizens' questions concerning all branches and programs of the federal government.[12]

The United States Information Service never handled fewer than 44,000 inquiries in any year and the figure was once as high as 100,000. In a single month, some 500 requests for information were serviced for members of Congress alone. During the first eleven months of 1940, no less than 152,799 clippings were sent to congressmen, and in the same year over 1900 requests for research were filled. Programs and

---

10 As a matter of fact, during World War II censorship was actually exercised by the Office of War Information.

11 Not to be confused with the United States Information Agency created in 1953 and whose program is aimed at the peoples of other nations.

12 The story of the Office of Government Reports is told by Lowell Mellett in "The Office of Government Reports," *Public Administration Review*, I (Winter 1941), pp. 126-131.

transcriptions were prepared for radio broadcast. A weekly summary of articles and editorials on governmental affairs from fifty weekly and monthly magazines was distributed to members of Congress and government officials. The Press Intelligence Division provided four different types of services including an index of news and editorial comment on public affairs gathered from 350 daily newspapers of strategically located cities and circulated to hundreds of key government officials.

Like most government agencies, the Office of Government Reports continued to expand. At one time it found itself reporting on measures pending before the state legislatures that were of interest to federal bureaus and departments. Further, where states were trying to qualify for participation in federal programs, such as social security, the Office of Government Reports assumed the function of clearing proposed state legislation, looking into questions of policy, objectives, and possible duplications with other programs in the same state. All this work, important and necessary as it doubtless was, nevertheless contributed still further to federal centralization and to a strengthening of the political party in office. The agency was finally absorbed by the Office of War Information when the latter was created during World War II, and went out of existence in 1948.

Along with the United States Information Service, another early New Deal emphasis on public relations occurred in connection with relief and work relief programs. Being concerned with a humanitarian project and spending billions of dollars for that purpose, the Works Progress Administration in particular was sensitive to criticism, first, that it was doing too little or too much for its relief clients, and second, that it was building a political machine. Consequently there was a press section in the national office, information specialists in the state offices, and every kind of medium then available was used, including press, radio, motion pictures, exhibits, interestingly presented progress reports, and at least three books written by officials of the national office, one of them by the top administrator himself.[13]

While admitting the need for public relations programs in government, "there is no denying," say the authors of a study of WPA, "that the public relations activities of governmental agencies may be dangerous for democratic society. Especially when large resources are involved, an agency should not be more interested in perpetuating itself than in enlightening public opinion. The formula of public relations for modern administration is elusive. The kind of advocacy that prejudices responsible government must be avoided." [14]

A feature of public administration that is little known is govern-

[13] Harry L. Hopkins, *Spending to Save* (New York: W. W. Norton & Company, 1936).
[14] Arthur W. Macmahon, John D. Millett, and Gladys Ogden, *The Administration of Federal Work Relief* (Chicago: Public Administration Service, 1941), p. 292.

ment's widespread promotional activities in behalf of various sections of the economy; a case in point is the mandate recognized by the information section of the Civil Aeronautics Board "to foster and encourage the development of civil aviation" as directed by Congress in the Civil Aeronautics Act of 1938.[15] Similar wording appears in most basic acts including those creating the Departments of Commerce and Labor, the Federal Maritime Board, and others. But the CAB was different in that civil aviation at that time was still a relatively new industry and needed "selling." The government took on some of that responsibility.

The information section of the CAB tried to provide a kind of one-stop service station, handling any reasonable request for aviation information. Originally about as dull as most government publishing, after 1945 the output of the CAB was made more attractive. A triumph was to persuade the Government Printing Office to publish a modern, attractively styled book for forty cents entitled *Path of Flight* instead of a dull tome selling for a dollar and called *Practical Air Navigation.* Using every modern medium of communication, in 1945 the information program of the CAB employed writers, editors, and artists and sold more than 400,000 publications at a price that made the expense of the operation a small one.

Public relations programs at the state and local levels also have increased, in some cases faster than at the federal level. The focus, however, is different, being largely promotional and consisting chiefly of paid advertising and publicity. Even before World War II some forty states had set up promotional budgets in order to attract tourists, permanent residents, and new industries. Advertising appears in magazines of wide circulation and in metropolitan dailies. Some state governments also issue their own publications, those of Vermont and Arizona being outstanding. In addition, a group of neighboring states sometimes collaborate to promote common interests; the New England Council is an association of this kind.

Many city governments also have raised war chests for promotion to attract industries and tourists. A town of 19,000 in New York State, for example, employs a full-time public relations counsel "to keep the citizens informed of everything that is being done, routine or otherwise, in the village." In 1945 the Port of New York Authority opened an office in Chicago "to promote and protect the commerce of the port of New York" by seeking to prevent the diversion of midwestern commerce to Gulf and North Atlantic ports; simultaneously the Authority launched a strong public relations program that included personal contacts, newspaper releases, promotional publications, motion pictures, contacts, and semiweekly radio programs for the New York area. In

15 Philip Lesly, ed., *Public Relations in Action* (New York: A. S. Barnes Company, Inc., 1947), chap. 8.

1949 the Committee of One Hundred in Birmingham, Alabama, began a five-year drive to bring new industries to the city and by 1953 had induced fifty-six concerns to establish national or regional headquarters there. These are all straws to show how the wind is blowing and also how much stronger it is blowing today than even twenty years ago.

Because government public relations programs are now so common, it is more important than ever, of course, that neither Congress nor the public lower its guard so as to ensure their proper use. Granted that as the public receives more information it should be able to increase its own democratic control, nevertheless it is sound democartic policy to scrutinize all government public relations programs with a cold eye. The opposition party can always be relied on to do this for the party in office, of course, because a public lulled into insensitivity to the mistakes of government is harder to win in an election than one that is aroused and dissatisfied. Most laws restricting federal and state public relations programs are the result of this kind of watchfulness. If the result is to curtail inappropriate or improper practices, restrictions are desirable, but if they go too far they can do much harm to the legitimate needs of management.

The chief hazard to public relations in government is the failure of legislators to differentiate between the various aspects of public relations work. Mere publicity and advertising should always be regarded critically, but activities designed to enlighten the public, as well as to keep government employees alert and responsible to the public, are legitmate aspects of the democratic process.

It must be granted that this line of demarcation is often a hard one to draw because many practices that are legitimate in one context are improper in another. Paid advertising by state and local governments to attract industry and tourists is justified and so is the advertising of a government enterprise, such as a municipal light and power plant, where the work is a business-type operation. But advertising to misrepresent or to divert attention from errors is not. Perhaps the line between proper and improper public relations lies in the answer to the question, Is this expenditure designed to conceal mistakes and to make it hard for the opposition party to carry its story to the public? But even this rule of public policy is hard to apply because the concepts of propaganda and information in close cases may be virtually interchangeable, depending on who is using them and for what purpose.

The experienced administrator knows that except in unlikely circumstances, he cannot win the support of all groups at once; hence he must decide whose support to try to win first. His criterion is—or should be—the concept of the public interest. His problem arises when, as sometimes happens, his client-interest group support is oriented toward a policy that he considers too narrow, in which case his integrity may be strained. But loyalty to the program of his political party, to the President, and to the interests of the nation might cause him to challenge and, if possible, convert the interest group to the support of a larger program.

Rex Harlow believes that the question whether public relations is a source of good or of evil in any field depends on the degree to which the ethics of the public relations profession are observed. No institution can conceal its true nature and it is only when a public relations program attempts such concealment that it backfires on management. Irrespective of any idealisms, therefore, the self-interest of management requires that "public relations activities must be honest, truthful, open, authoritative, and responsible; they must be fair and realistic; and they must be conducted in the public interest." [16] Wright and Christian favor this code of ethics but conclude that until public relations is more fully recognized as a profession, it is unrealistic to try to promulgate hard and fast rules. What with the accelerated influence of Madison Avenue in the last decade or so, perhaps that time is now at hand.

The sanction against an improper public relations program is not hard to find because once the word gets around that a certain agency is trying to pull the wool over its employees' eyes, a company's wares are not as advertised, regulated monopolies are attacking government to prevent regulation to protect the consumer, or government is fabricating a story to conceal its mistakes, the management that commits such offenses is through as far as the public is concerned. An indispensable asset of any enterprise is its reputation.

## Public Relations through Employee Morale

The two parts of any public relations program are selling the product and selling the organization. The product can be sold partly through advertising, but the organization itself can be sold only as it is reflected in the high morale of its employees. Moreover, if that aim can be achieved, the product also will be more widely appreciated. This conclusion is the outstanding lesson of the experience of business with public relations programs for the last thirty years. Moreover, the degree of morale that exists in an organization is pervasive: when you walk into a store you feel it, when you receive a letter from a business firm you sense it, when you meet an employee socially you can quickly tell whether his morale on the job is high or low.

John J. Corson tells of two large utility companies in Virginia that, judged by financial results, operated with similar potential efficiency. But what did their employees think? "Sit down in the evening to play bridge with the employees of Company A and they entertain you with stories of their company's efficiency," says Corson. "Have lunch with

---

[16] Harlow, *op. cit.*, p. 73.

them and they speak of its achievements in expanding sales and maintaining low operating costs. Talk with the employees of Company B and you see a sharp contrast. They know little about the company; they talk sarcastically of its officials and resent its profits." [17]

The significance of this finding is that, whether high or low, the state of employee morale spreads through a constantly widening circle of acquaintances. If morale is high, as the circle grows the enterprise acquires a reputation for excellence in the public attitudes formed toward it. This good will must be earned by management in everyday operations because no amount of advertising can buy it. So long as the source of this good will does not dry up, the enterprise can count on a favorable public response. A small firm with a limited number of employees and a desire for a wide market will necessarily have to advertise to make its product known, but many large corporations spend millions of dollars annually on advertising that might more profitably be invested in human relations within their own organization.

The greatest communication defect of a large enterprise may not be that which runs to the public but to its own employees. The three types of internal communication as described in Chapter 12 are orders down the line, reports up the line, and understandings throughout the organization (what we have called lateral or diagonal relationships) concerning common purposes. It is in this third area that management principally fails and it is here that the greatest untapped potential for better public relations exists. Corson does not exaggerate when he contends that poor internal communication decreases production by millions of dollars, that men without incentive or with a knowledge of *why* or *for what* they work, aside from their own salaries, produce less than those who are well informed. Everyone concerned with a particular program should have the basic facts about it and its accomplishments, what the objectives are, and who is on the team.

Some of the more progressive large private corporations have learned the pervasive value of high employee morale better than many government agencies. A case in point is the American Telephone and Telegraph Company which for years has consciously developed a philosophy of management covering every aspect of its operation.[18] The outstanding feature of its public relations program is the clarity with

17 John J. Corson, "Management: Tongue-tied, Deaf and Blind?", *Advanced Management*, XI (September 1946), pp. 101-109.

18 See Norton Long on the subject of AT&T's public relations policy in "Public Relations Policies of the Bell System," *Public Opinion Quarterly*, I (October 1937), pp. 5-22; a convenient summary of this article appears in Wright and Christian, *op. cit.*, pp. 6-8. The subject is also referred to in Marshall E. Dimock and Howard K. Hyde, *Bureaucracy and Trusteeship in Large Corporations*, Temporary National Economic Committee, Monograph No. 11 (Washington, D.C.: Government Printing Office, 1940). See also Frederick R. Kappel, President of AT&T, *Vitality in a Business Enterprise* (New York: McGraw-Hill Book Company, 1960), pp. 35-68.

which objectives and policies are made known to its employees. The corporation was fortunate in having as its first president Theodore N. Vail, a man with a strong sense of right and wrong and an appreciation of his public duty. Consequently, policy was built around certain beliefs: that a nationwide monopoly is a standing invitation to government ownership; that a monopoly must be regulated; that state regulation is preferable to federal regulation; that the greater the monopoly, the greater must be the effort of management to satisfy its own employees and its public; and that a successful public relations program must be a decentralized one.

Based on these clear policies, practical applications were developed. Thus, females were chosen as operators instead of men because it was found that they are less likely to ruffle a subscriber's feelings; linemen were encouraged to make friends with families along the right of way; installers of equipment were taught to be careful of subscribers' floors and walls; and local managers were instructed to follow up consumers' complaints personally. Through all this, decentralization is the key. If a rate case is pending in the courts, local officials handle it so as not to arouse antagonism by bringing in "foreigners"; if labor troubles brew, they are settled on the spot if possible; if money is to be spent on advertising, it is spent locally; and local managers are encouraged to be public-spirited so as to create that kind of reputation for the company. Even the company's major program over a national radio and television network was primarily for entertainment with a minimum of commercial announcement.

In government public relations programs also, the greatest untapped resource is its own employees. To this end, government workers should be motivated and trained in ways which in most jurisdictions, including the federal, have only recently been noticed. The key is improved training and supervision, as discussed in Chapter 15, plus a deliberate policy of treating employees as people and not as more or less mechanical units under the general heading of personnel.

It has been stressed that supervisory training is a means of showing employees that management takes an interest in them and is concerned for their well-being; in this way is morale raised. The example of the Hawthorne experiment, already noticed, is pertinent. Better supervisory training and the attention that accompanies it, therefore, would make it easier for employees to understand their jobs and would stimulate them to do a better one. People with pleasing personalities and an intelligent and courteous demeanor would be placed at reception desks and public counters, employees generally would be more consumer-directed, and citizens would not be shunted around as they often are. People who use the telephone frequently would be instructed in courtesy and friendliness, letter writing would be more simple, informal, and intelligible, and employees would take more pride in their appearance and in their work. A final result would be a heightened morale reflected in greater circumspection in off-duty contacts of public employees with other citizens.[19]

Large corporations and large government agencies have many points in common. Both are often monopolies or near monopolies characterized by bureaucracy. In its worst aspects, a bureaucracy, whether of the public or the private variety, is slow, insensitive to the attitudes and desires of the citizen, rule-ridden, and officious; worships the form instead of appreciating the substance of operations; and has an exaggerated idea of its own power and importance. Of the possible correctives to the evils of bureaucracy, it has already been said that a proper public relations policy based on internal improvements directed by management and designed to heighten employee morale is the most effective. Advertising alone is no answer because the public is not so easily deceived.[20]

## Public Relations by Specific Means

Every government program has some kind of backing from an interest or client group or it would not have been created in the first place.[21] Next to his own employees, these groups and any others related to them constitute the administrator's chief support in the operation of a public relations program.

The relationship between a government agency and its interest or client group is a reciprocal one, each aiding the other and jointly furthering a common purpose. It has already been shown how the Civil Aeronautics Board helps to promote the commercial aviation industry; on their side, the airlines in their own public relations will come to the aid of the CAB if for some reason it is threatened. All government agencies could be analyzed in this way, including the Department of Agriculture's Extension Service and the American Farm Bureau Federation, the Veterans Administration and the American Legion, the Department of Labor and the AFL-CIO, the Office of Education and the National Education Association—and many more. In every case agency and interest group help each other because they have objectives and an-

---

19 Each of these points is interestingly discussed in John M. Pfiffner, *Public Administration*, chap. 36.

20 Spelled out in Dimock and Hyde, *op. cit.*, and in Marshall E. Dimock, "Bureaucracy Self-Examined," *Public Administration Review*, IV (Summer 1944), pp. 197-207.

21 See Pendleton Herring, *Public Administration and the Public Interest* (New York: McGraw-Hill Book Company, Inc., 1936); Avery Leiserson, *Administrative Regulation: A Study in Representation of Interests* (Chicago: University of Chicago Press, 1942); and David B. Truman, *The Governmental Process* (New York: Alfred A. Knopf, Inc. 1951), chap. 14.

tagonists in common. When a government program is faced with a cut in appropriations, or an unwanted reorganization, or if it is severely criticized, it turns first to its interest and client group for help. If a program is so badly administered that mounting complaints threaten its existence, the interest groups are the first to lend a hand to try to straighten it out. If either an administrator or the interest group seeks an extension of functions, they plan a common strategy.

A common mistake of management is to confuse the means with the end, and the field of public relations is no exception. The danger here is that the media of communication will be regarded as the objects of public relations, whereas such media are never more than a means. Success is often uncritically measured by the number of lines of publicity devoted to an enterprise over a period of time, but this is a false yardstick. A more realistic test is the degree to which management is assisted in accomplishing its aims. Moreover, the degree to which each medium is used—or whether it is used at all—depends on its appropriateness as a tool of management at the particular time and under the circumstances that prevail.

A test of professional ability in public relations—one that more than any other divides the men from the boys—is the discrimination with which various media are chosen for certain purposes. The public relations officer who jumps at every chance to get the enterprise mentioned in print or on the air is a dangerous man to have around. The common assumption that the media of public relations are merely the conventional ones of press, radio, television, and the like, is never accepted by the public relations expert who has the management approach, for he knows that the basic media consist of the employees and interest groups of the agency. This is management's point of departure for all of its thinking relative to public relations. The conventional media occupy an important but nevertheless secondary place in the picture.

Where the conventional media are concerned, the priorities must be sorted and chosen with discrimination. The public relations official must have a clear idea of what his priorities and preferences are and then plan his program accordingly. If he is content merely to take what he can get, he will most likely damage the organization. If he seeks publicity first of all and ignores the viewpoints of legislatures and the public, he will not get very far. Generally speaking, a public administrator accomplishes more by playing the game as the legislature and the public want it played than by insisting on his own way.

The bonds between the fourth estate and government administrators should be strengthened. Some of our political columnists and the better public service programs on radio and television are a national asset. Nevertheless, the dean of Columbia's School of Journalism has remarked with much reason that with notable exceptions, journalism is failing to meet the responsibility of keeping the public well informed.

"In all media, the public gets too much froth because too few want substance. In turn, the majority don't want substance partly because they are inadequately informed. The circle is vicious." [22] The cause and effect relationship is something like this: failure to provide more news of the world perpetuates ignorance, and this ignorance leads to lack of interest.

For most administrators the problem is not how to avoid setting up a propaganda machine, but how to arouse the interest of citizens in subjects that it would seem they would or should naturally be interested in.[23]

## Public Reporting and Press Conferences

In all administration, but especially in government, public reporting can be made to play a major role in public relations. Reports are the life of the administrator anyhow, for it is through reports that he checks on the progress of his program and the manner in which delegations of authority are being used. But in addition, it is literally true that public administration rests on a series of public reports on trusteeship and accomplishment. Every government agency prepares an annual report to the legislature and many administrators also issue informal progress reports summarizing accomplishment for the benefit of the President, the legislature, other agencies, and the citizen. Such documents are the raw materials of public relations, offering an opportunity to tell a story in an interesting and newsworthy fashion.

Herman Beyle pioneered in the field of public reporting in 1928 with his study, *Government Reporting in Chicago*. Clarence Ridley of the International City Managers Association campaigned to improve the annual reports of municipalities by creating competition among them, the purpose being to stimulate the citizen's interest in his local government. One of the fruits of this effort was a manual entitled, "Specifications for the Annual Municipal Report," urging fewer pages of solid print and statistical tables and more illustrations, charts, graphs, and photographs. The emphasis has been shifted from clusters of figures to the question, What does this mean to me, the citizen? Not, How have we spent the money? but, What have we accomplished?

Not even the most appealing public reports will be read by very many people, however—that must be granted. But the better the report, the more attractive it can be made to the professional newspaperman and news commentator. Correspondents look to these reports for

[22] Dean Edward W. Barrett, "Journalism Education Today," *Columbia University Bulletin,* February 27, 1960.
[23] Francis R. Rourke, "Administrative Secrecy: A Congressional Dilemma," *American Political Science Review,* 54 (September 1960), pp. 684-694.

some of their copy; in addition, news releases based on them may be prepared in the agency and distributed as handouts to reporters who may be interested. To some reporters such material is enough; to others it is a clue to a story that is worth going after in order to learn about background and possible future developments. The best of all interview sources in the federal government, says James Reston of *The New York Times,* are the specialists just below Cabinet rank,[24] which is yet another reason that public relations programs are best directed from the top.

Thus, the strategy of the public administrator is to establish a friendly relationship with the merchants of information, prepare his own material so well that they will use it, and rely on them to secure a favorable press. This is a more effective and also a more economical formula than building a large staff of ghost writers, newspaper and magazine writers, radio and television scenarists, and motion picture producers who may turn out a lot of publicity but who also put the agency in competition with private enterprise in these areas. In that case private enterprise has only to work through the legislature as an interest group in order to secure reduced appropriations for the public relations program of the competing agency. It is a much more useful policy, therefore, to prepare interesting material for the commercial communications industries and then allow them to take credit for the output. This has the added advantage of keeping the administrator on the good side of the legislature as well as of the commercial communications industries.

Another medium of public relations of special importance in government is the press conference, especially the President's press conference, which is the chief means by which correspondents have access to the President and can learn at firsthand something of what is on his mind. As such, says Richard Strout, the presidential press conference "is a major defense against the built-in danger of the Constitution that the White House will become a water-tight compartment, isolated from Congress and from the man-in-the-street." [25] The rules of the session give the President control at all times. He sets the number of meetings, their time and duration, recognizes correspondents who put the questions, and he can answer or not as he chooses. By custom, the conference lasts only thirty minutes.

Formerly the President could not be directly quoted for anything said at these conferences without permission, which was seldom granted, but since the introduction under the Eisenhower Administration of television and tape recordings, direct quotation has been possible. These films and recordings are not always sent out live on the air, and

---

24 *The New York Times,* April 15, 1953.
25 Richard Strout, "The President and the Press," *New Republic,* January 11, 1954.

are sometimes edited and even censored if national security is in question. Formerly the mood of the presidential press conference (with some exceptions in the case of Presidents Coolidge and Hoover, for example, who required that questions be submitted in writing) has been easygoing and informal; however, the introduction of television has made it much larger and somewhat self-conscious, though much less so under President Kennedy and President Johnson. The advantages of the new procedure are a wider and more direct coverage and, of course, a much larger audience. Since the President often uses his press conference as a kind of sounding board for important announcements, this advantage is a considerable one. And if correspondents and the public learn more about government in this way, the President also learns from reporters things that he should know about what the nation is thinking and what problems are uppermost in people's minds.

The presidential press conference was introduced by Theodore Roosevelt and has been continued as a fairly regular practice, reaching a high point under Franklin D. Roosevelt who was expert in the give and take of such sessions. Some Presidents have had infrequent conferences; Hoover had only twenty-three in his first year and twelve in his last year in office; Truman held an average of forty a year, but Franklin D. Roosevelt held an average of eighty a year. President Eisenhower's preference was for fewer conferences, the rate being about the same as that for Hoover. President Kennedy also preferred fewer conferences than Roosevelt and Truman.

Since no man can have all the answers to the many kinds of questions put to the head of a government, the President is briefed before going to his press conference. As described by President Eisenhower's press secretary, on the preceding day "I get up a list of questions that I think newspaper men are going to ask. We then have a staff meeting on the morning before the President has his press conference where we go over these proposed questions . . . and often we get additional material . . . from the departments. . . . I then go in a half an hour or forty minutes before a press conference and go over these questions with the President just to bring him up to date and refresh in his mind the decisions that have been made on these questions—the actual status of any one problem or any one major field. . . ." [26] Being more of a reader and having a retentive memory, President Kennedy's briefing was less formal than that of his predecessor.

In addition to the President other government officials also hold press conferences from time to time and, as in the case of sessions with the President, their usefulness depends in part on the personality of the man behind the desk and his relationship with the correspondents.

[26] *The New York Times*, February 15, 1954.

This fact was rather sharply pointed up when the Republican party assumed office in 1953 with a preponderance of business executives in official positions. To these men public relations centered on the product of their companies and did not touch relations between top executives and the general public, as is essential in government. There was an assumption, says Marquis Childs, that government could be run in the same manner as a private undertaking in industry and "some of the speech-writing, public relations specialists chosen to serve the President came out of the managerial revolution in journalism, with its stress on the anonymous, pre-fabricated picture of events for a mass audience. But quickly it became apparent that something was missing." Reporters found it hard to gain access to men responsible for policy: "something like a vacuum in the news prevailed," and it was not until some months had passed that the administration began to realize "that in government there is another dimension—the human relations of politics, as contrasted to the specialty of public relations which in business can be laid on by a few experts paid to do the job." [27]

Thereafter members of the Cabinet and other policy officials were more liberal with their time and less unwilling to confer with correspondents. Moreover, in the Eisenhower Administration television was brought to the President's Cabinet meeting on at least one occasion to record a report by the Secretary of State concerning a current mission, and the President himself used television as well as radio to enter the homes of citizens, at their invitation, and to present his programs directly to them. This practice, originated by Franklin D. Roosevelt in his so-called fireside chats, has been carried on since then, but less often in recent years than some people think is necessary in order to keep the people informed of matters of public policy at a time when such matters are more than ever numerous and complex.

## Restricting Access to Information

If it is true, as suggested, that popular control in a democracy is served only so long as government reporting is full and reliable, so that the public may be informed, then it is equally true that the government must not withhold information that the public has a right to know. A growing problem for some time in the United States, it is now a serious one.

The issue that stemmed from the restriction of information coming from the Atomic Energy Commission, which almost everyone agrees is regrettable but necessary, rapidly broadened when in 1951 President Truman signed an executive order withholding from publication in-

27 Marquis Childs, "Public Relations along the Potomac," *The New York Times Magazine,* August 30, 1953.

formation from any government agency that "might be useful to potential enemies." This order set up four grades of so-called classified material: restricted, confidential, secret, and top secret. The President said, hopefully, that the new system "must not be used to withhold nonsecurity information or to cover up mistakes made by any official or employee of the government," and an interdepartmental coordinating committee was created to administer the program. Immediately, however, the American Society of Newspaper Editors protested the order on the ground that the effect would be "to formalize the suppression of much news to which the public is entitled," [28] and in view of what has happened since then it seems that this statement was at least partially correct.

Two years later President Eisenhower directed that the "restricted" classification be eliminated, originating classification authority be withdrawn from twenty-nine agencies, and the authority of sixteen others be limited to the actual heads thereof. The Defense Department, the Atomic Energy Commission, and the Central Intelligence Agency originated a preponderance of classified material and the new order affected these three more than any others.

Nevertheless, two years later a House investigating committee found that many agencies had simply created new labels such as "administratively confidential," "not for publication," "limited official use," "confidential treatment," and the like, in order to avoid giving out information against their wishes. It was also discovered that many agencies were insisting that secrecy was necessary "for reasons of national security" or "in the public interest." The complaint of Washington correspondents was that such labels were used to cover material that by no stretch of the mind could honestly come under security regulations.[29] Meanwhile, as some innocuous classified information leaked out from time to time, Congress became increasingly suspicious that much withheld information was of the same innocent nature.

Something akin to a secrecy problem exists in every administrative agency that operates in any area of controversy even if it is not a "sensitive" one from the standpoint of national security. At congressional hearings in 1955, for example, the Civil Service Commission insisted on its "inherent" right to withhold information from the public, and other agencies appeared to feel the same way about it. But two months later the commission changed its views somewhat and directed its employees to remember that they have a responsibility "to assist in the task of keeping the public informed." [30] The problem here is one of or-

---

[28] *The New York Times,* September 23, 26, and 30, 1951; and January 13, October 1, 3, and 14, 1952.

[29] Reported by Allen Drury in *The New York Times,* November 13, 1955.

[30] *The New York Times,* January 21, 1956.

ganization and the delegation of authority to release information; it is also a problem in control and administrative politics and one that may and often does affect even the lowest level of employees. It is the crucial point in any agency's relation to the channels of communication to the public.

The difficulty becomes especially acute, of course, when a nation is engaged in a war—hot or cold—when there is often an honest difference of opinion as to what might conceivably aid the enemy. A crisis of this nature occurred during President Kennedy's blockade of Cuba in the fall of 1962. The administrator frequently has information regarding situations that the members of the press corps are not fully able to assess because they do not (and many times cannot) know all the background, even though off the record briefing sessions are an increasingly popular feature in Washington. But even in periods of relative peace, the issue is beclouded because of the allegedly "partisan" and "unfair" use of information made by various media of communication. This issue, along with others, was dealt with in 1947 by the Commission on Freedom of the Press.[31]

The problem of secrecy in government will doubtless continue to vex administrators, party leaders, citizens, and the media of communication. Perhaps the most that can be suggested is that all parties develop high standards of fairness and integrity and an attachment to the principle of enlightening the voters as fully, reliably, and impartially as possible. In the cultural milieu of which both administration and communication are a part, the standards for one must be as high as those for the other.

---

[31] Commission on Freedom of the Press, *A Free and Responsible Press* (Chicago: University of Chicago Press, 1947).

## BIBLIOGRAPHY AND CASES

### Annotated Reading Suggestions

Literally scores of books have been written on public relations in general, but relatively little on public relations in government, although at times, and especially in an election year, the subject is a controversial one. A distinction may be made between governmental reporting to the public, and active public relations undertaken to influence public attitudes, although the line between the two is not a clear one.

On public opinion and how it is formed, see V. O. Key, *Public Opinion and American Democracy* (Knopf, 1961).

The International City Managers Association has been active in promoting reporting techniques, even giving prizes to cities for superior annual reports. See Wylie Kilpatrick, *Reporting Municipal Government* (Municipal Administration Service, 1928); Clarence E. Ridley and Herbert A. Simon, *Specifications for the Annual Municipal Report* (International City Managers Association, 1948); and Herman C. Beyle, *Governmental Reporting in Chicago* (University of Chicago Press, 1928).

Two University of Chicago Ph.D. dissertations early opened up the public relations approach: Leo C. Rosten, *The Washington Correspondents* (Harcourt, 1937), and James L. McCamy, *Government Publicity* (University of Chicago Press, 1939).

Zachariah Chafee, whose interest is civil liberties, wrote *Government and Mass Communications* (University of Chicago Press, 1947); John J. Corson has written "Management: Tongue-Tied, Deaf and Blind?" *Advanced Management,* 11 (September 1946); and more recently, David M. Cox has contributed, "How Much Public Relations in Government?" *Public Administration Review,* 21 (Summer 1961).

In the journal of the British Royal Institute of Public Administration, *Public Administration,* two good articles are S. G. Tallents, "Public Relations and Publicity," 37 (Autumn 1949), and "Salesmanship in the Public Service," 11 (July 1933). At about the same time there appeared Marshall E. Dimock, "Selling Public Enterprise to the Public," *National Municipal Review,* 23 (December 1934).

Various fields of governmental activity have also been dealt with: Eric Carlson, "Public Relations in International Technical Assistance," *Public Administration Review,* 16 (Autumn 1956); Elmer Davis, "Security and the News," *Public Administration Review,* 12 (Spring 1952); H. Baker and M. S. Toutzahn, *How to Interpret Social Welfare* (Russell Sage Foundation, 1947); L. V. Howard, "The Agricultural Referendum," *Public Administration Review,* 2 (Winter 1942); Arthur W. Macmahon, John D. Millett, and Gladys Ogden, *The Administration of Federal Work Relief* (Public Administration Service, 1941), Chapter 12, "Politics and Public Relations"; William E. Mosher, *Public Relations of Public Personnel Agencies* (Civil Service Assembly, 1941); National Association of Secondary Principals, *Public Relations in Secondary Schools* (Washington, 1948); National Recreation Association, *The ABC's of Public Relations for Recreation* (National Recreation Association, 1946); G. O. Ward, *Publicity for Public Libraries* (2d ed., H. W. Wilson, 1935); and Elton Woolpert, *Municipal Public Relations* (International City Managers Association, 1940).

Among discussions of the philosophy and techniques of public relations in general, some of the best are Rex F. Harlow and M. M. Black, *Practical Public Relations* (Harper & Row, 1947); Harold P. Levy, *Study in Public Relations* (Russell Sage Foundation, 1943); J. A. R. Pimlot, *Public Relations and American Democracy* (Princeton University Press, 1951); and D. H. Plackard and C. Blackman, *Blueprint for Public Relations* (McGraw-Hill, 1947).

An article of great value is Norton E. Long, "Public Relations of the Bell

System," *Public Opinion Quarterly*, 1 (October 1937). Finally, on the role of interest groups, see Avery Leiserson, *Administrative Regulation: A Study in Representation of Interests* (University of Chicago Press, 1942).

## Case Studies

Two good cases on public relations are found in the Stein *Case Book. The Regional Director and the Press* is a short one, four pages, and relates to an investigation of the National Labor Relations Board. *The Veterans' Gas Station* concerns the Office of Price Administration and gas rationing during World War II. This ten-page case was reported by William H. Riker in 1952.

Another case in the ICP series was mentioned in the preceding chapter: *Defending "The Hill" Against Metal Houses.* One of the most colorful cases, and a short one (seven pages) is No. 45, *Moses on the Green*, by J. B. Keeley, involving Robert Moses of New York City. And finally, No. 19, *Regional Information Officer,* five pages, by M. Kriesberg, involves both public relations and field operations.

# 22

## Cooperation
## and Conflict

MOST ADMINISTRATION, INCLUDING public, operates in an atmosphere of conflict and competition, giving zest to the effort. And yet, paradoxically, the success of any administrative program depends also on a high degree of cooperation within the organization. Cooperation and conflict are complementary phases of group activity. They cannot be opposed to each other because the achievement of one by no means eliminates the other. Consequently, because both are inherent in administration, they must be combined into some kind of working balance.

Conflict, said Mary Parker Follett, cannot be avoided; it occurs everywhere, so why not put it to work? Of the three ways of handling a dispute, the first is for one side to prevail over the other, which is no solution because the weaker side remains unsatisfied. The second is through compromise, but then neither side gets all of what it wants so this also is no solution. The third is to break down the contentions of each side into their components and then bring them together again in a new arrangement, an integration, a new synthesis, in which each side finds satisfaction. Conflict resolved in this fashion is constructive because each side gets what it wants and something new has been created that is beneficial to both.[1]

---

[1] Mary Parker Follett, "Constructive Conflict," in Henry C. Metcalf and L. Urwick, eds., *Dynamic Administration* (New York: Harper & Row, Publishers, 1941), pp.

The public administrator has many opportunities to apply this theory of constructive conflict because his function is the dual one of anticipating and meeting conflict and competition among his public and his subordinates, and at the same time securing their cooperation. Consequently, public administration is far from the comfortable, routine, nondiscretionary, and noncombative occupation sometimes described by civil service reformers who would keep the political element out of the management of government operations. This, of course, is not only impossible but also undesirable. For all of these reasons, public administration demands the highest kind of ability and statesmanship on the part of the practitioner.

## The Administrator as Broker of Influence

Government provides services and promotes new industries; it also imposes controls on industry and acts as policeman. Since these functions are complementary, they cannot be divorced; together they promote the goals of various groups in the community. In each case the common element is a competition for values, services, and satisfactions. Do people want better housing at reasonable cost? Public housing is now an essential service of the community, but when the matter is brought to an issue before the legislature the real estate lobbies are massed against the consumer lobbies to determine how much and under whose control additional housing is to be offered. Do dairy farmers—the largest and most widely distributed of all agricultural interests—desire a better price for milk? They run headlong into monopolists who control retail milk distribution in the large metropolitan centers and into consumer interests that would keep the cost of living down. Do labor unions want to extend organization to additional areas of the economy? They encounter the resistance of management that would limit labor's power and influence. Such examples could be multiplied almost indefinitely, since competition for influence and for available resources runs throughout administration, as it does through all human activity, and is equally accompanied by interdependencies and the exchange of services.

Because of these many wants and needs, and the competition among many groups for who gets what, when, and how through the medium of government, the administrator is at the center of social conflict and social change, and the need is to bring about adjustments as satisfactory to all parties as possible. In his own program and in those it touches, the administrator is a broker of influence for special interests, a reconciler of opposing views in the public interest, and the catalyst of

---

30-32; see also her book, *Creative Experience* (Gloucester, Mass.: Peter Smith, 1951).

group consensus and cooperation. Like the politician, the administrator also dispenses power and influence.

In public administration there are four main types of situation or relationship that are characterized by potential conflict and the clear need for cooperation, and in each case it is the administrator who must bring about an accord and keep it alive. First, there is the social conflict situation in the community, in which different groups, such as business, labor, agriculture, and many others, compete for influence and survival. Second, there is the bureaucratic or jurisdictional situation in which government programs compete with each other, also for influence and survival, as when the Department of the Interior feuds with the Department of Agriculture—as it has for years—over the possession of the Forest Service. Third, there is the guild situation in which various kinds of specialists—lawyers, accountants, personnel directors, general administrators, and the like—compete for influence in the direction and control of particular programs. Fourth, there are labor relations in which management and the unions compete for income, status, and influence within the enterprise.[2] These are the four principal types of conflict involving power relationships—or human relationships, often the same—that the administrator must bring into working accord if his program is to achieve its objective. Like a broker, therefore, he must be a skillful strategist.

In this chapter it is assumed that people divide and struggle because of basic differences of substance and values. It is also assumed that healthy conflicts of opinion in society are normal and useful and that it would be mistaken public policy to try to compress them into a common pattern. It is *not* assumed that technique alone can solve a conflict, but merely that among men of good will, a technique can help.

## Social Conflict and Administration

The social conflict situations encountered by the administrator are those in which his program must compete with others or with the antagonism of particular groups in the community for public support, and in order to maintain a balance among *all* programs in the public interest. To deal successfully with situations characterized by opposing forces, the administrator must understand why people in groups behave as they do, what the various groups in the community are, and why they compete. The clue is an appreciation of what is called the myths or belief systems by which people live.

---

2 In its broadest sense this is an aspect of social conflict (the first category mentioned here), but when considered in the narrow framework of a particular program it is more realistically treated as a separate area of conflict with which the administrator is immediately concerned.

MacIver says that a myth is "the value-impregnated beliefs and notions that men hold, that they live by or live for." [3] He classifies all social behavior as based on myth—what Alexander Leighton calls belief
systems—on the one hand, and on techniques on the other, with the
administrator's falling generally into the second category. The division
is not a sharp one, however, because the two categories merge at many
points.

The social function of the myth is to canalize biological drives and
to give them form and limit. "Every civilization, every period, every
nation, has its characteristic myth-complex," says MacIver. "In it lies
the secret of social unities and social continuities, and its changes com-
pose the inner history of every society. Wherever he goes, whatever he
encounters, man spins about him his web of myth, as the caterpillar
spins its cocoon. Every individual spins his own variant within the
greater web of the whole group. The myth mediates between man
and nature. From the shelter of his myth he perceives and experiences
the world. Inside his myth he is at home in his world." [4]

Does the myth describe reality? Is it real? Is it authentic? Not necessarily. The range of a belief system is from the most penetrating
philosophy of life to the most grotesque superstition of an ignorant
man. Myth is a neutral term and its content varies. So understood, the
myth includes "all human approaches and attitudes, all the modes in
which men face or formulate the business of living." [5] The use of so
broad a concept is justified by its seemingly universal application. Men
have always lived by belief systems that bind them in a cooperative effort in opposition to their enemies. Belief in certain myths may be
morally wrong and may even lead to the destruction of the group holding them, but as long as people characteristically behave in this fashion
it is the beginning of wisdom to recognize it.

A primary characteristic of behavior based on myth is to reinforce
loyalty to the group and its leadership by use of the our-side-other-side
symbolism that is part of all conflict. If there is no handy devil, the
group invents one as the object of a united attack; if no live issue exists,
the group creates one for the sake of inner unity and the feeling of
absorption and security (sometimes more fancied than real, to be sure)
that accompanies it. This statement does not imply a low evaluation of
human nature; it simply describes the way groups characteristically behave under the influence of a belief system.

As examples: To the management of a corporation unsympathetic
to organized labor, the devil is the labor union; to farmers, it is low

3 Robert M. MacIver, *The Web of Government* (New York: The Macmillan Com-
    pany, 1947), p. 4.
4 *Ibid.*, p. 5.
5 *Ibid.*

prices for their produce and high prices for what they must buy; to conservationists, it is the lumberman who skins off the forests; to public utilities, it is competition from cooperatives in the same field and the threat of government ownership; to public health officers, it is poverty and the diseases that thrive on it; to teachers, it is crowded classrooms and low salaries; to the League of Women Voters, it is the political apathy of many women; to labor unions, it is stiff-necked management and racketeers in their own ranks; to the medical profession, it is the threat of a government-sponsored health insurance program.

The point is that every social group tends to magnify conflict as a means of strengthening its own unity. Sometimes these drives are real and necessary; no one would think of criticizing them on moral or other grounds. But at other times group behavior is more like a game of cops and robbers played with toy guns, an act in which each member has a role and from which both actor and group seem to derive a kind of visceral satisfaction.

A technique for resolving social conflict that is coming increasingly into use is called group dynamics: the development of group consensus by concentrating on points of agreement rather than on points of difference. So long as two sets of people think each is on a different side there can be little progress toward agreement, but once they begin to think of each-together-toward-a-common-goal, conflict begins to change into cooperation. Patience, understanding of the opposing viewpoint, objectivity, and the avoidance of false personal and institutional pride—these are the basic elements in the approach to peaceful agreements.

What is the connection between group dynamics and belief systems or myths in promoting cooperation within the ingroup and conflict with the outgroup? Although group dynamics is only a technique and hence carries no *assurance* that substantive issues will invariably be resolved, nevertheless, because it modifies belief systems by creating new groups out of the members of formerly conflicting groups, the technique *might* be the means of solving many kinds of issues. How widely is the formula applicable? Can it be successfully used at the national or even at the international level? At present it is most successfully applied in small groups and where lesser issues are at stake, but its potentialities are not so limited and as experience is gained, it may be equally effective in larger ares of controversy.

Stuart Chase has reviewed some of the more significant experiences with group dynamics and, under the heading of five principles, summarized the techniques that have been found effective. First is the principle of participation, which means bringing everyone concerned into the picture, consulting them, involving them, making them responsible. Second is group energy, which means finding some way to release the reserves of energy created from the interaction of different groups; war releases energy in one way, riot in another, but more constructive methods must be found. Third is clearing communication lines, which means finding improved methods of communication to span the gap between ingroups and outgroups. Fourth is facts first, especially pertinent because emotion so often increases with ignorance. Finally, agreement is easier when people feel secure and well adjusted, because then they are less likely to pick a quarrel; security seems to depend on a sense of belonging, of being wanted.[6] The administrator who understands these principles and can put them to work has a considerable advantage over the man who crashes around in the dark, so to speak.

To help get the feel of a social conflict situation, here is an illustration of how relief is obtained when two sides meet for a discussion of a conflict and open the way to a consensus beneficial to both. During World War II a number of serious work stoppages occurred on allied merchant vessels in American ports. Investigation showed that when Chinese, Indian, Indonesian, or other seamen staged a sit-down strike or deserted their ship, it was not for lack of loyalty but because of group grievances creating tension, deadlock, and finally a strike.

To resolve the conflict, monthly meetings were held in Washington at which all the responsible maritime officials of the allied nations concerned could discuss the common problem. The second step was to discover at first hand at the immigration detention stations just what the men's grievances were. Three principal ones were found: In some cases the seamen felt they were being regarded as racially inferior and that this attitude was reflected in lower pay scales than for white men. The seamen also wanted wages more in line with those paid on American vessels, arguing that since most of the money came out of lend-lease appropriations, there should be equal pay for equal work. And finally, they contended that in some instances treatment and working conditions were substandard and that management was making no effort to improve them.

When all the facts were in, there appeared two strongly opposed views as to policy and remedy. Most of the allied officials felt that the American authorities were too lenient and that if the immigration laws were more severe—jail sentences followed by deportation to the country of origin—the matter could be quickly solved. But the representatives of the seamen themselves felt that such a policy would be a mistake.

For some time negotiations seemed to be stalled and then, as a result of frequent meetings and frank talk, the basis of a solution emerged: Officials of the United States would try to secure congres-

---

6 Stuart Chase, *Roads to Agreement* (New York: Harper & Row, Publishers, 1951), pp. 235-240.

sional approval of more effective immigration sanctions if the allied shipping men would correct the conditions complained of. Agreement was reached on that basis. The background of the problem was explained to the appropriate committees of Congress and the legislation went through quickly. The allied officials carried out their part of the bargain, the seamen were informed of the basis of the agreement, and there were no more desertions and strikes.

## Bureaucratic and Jurisdictional Disputes

A balance of power among programs reflecting group interests in government is no less desirable than a similar balance in the community. Group interests in government may stay within the bounds of the jurisdiction of the public agencies that serve them, but often those limits are exceeded. All institutions expand when given the chance, and this applies equally to business corporations, universities, and philanthropic agencies as well as to government, which, however, usually has the honor of being selected as the scapegoat. When government expands, when many public agencies are confined more or less haphazardly within an over-all framework that can never be made wholly rational, jurisdictions and group interests are bound to overlap and often to compete with one another, generating bureaucratic conflict that the administrator cannot ignore if he would save his own program from predatory colleagues.

In psychological terms, certain factors have been identified as explaining institutional aggrandizement. Thus, every institution is either consciously or unconsciously concerned with survival, and growth seems to connote survival and somehow to safeguard it. Allied to this is the feeling that insecurity may be compensated for by an extension of influence, a show of aggression. Employees are apt to suppose that their jobs are more certain when the program is a growing one. Another factor is that prestige is widely considered desirable, people identify themselves with the prestige of the institution they serve, and in public esteem prestige usually accompanies size. Again, most people seek power in some degree, and power and influence generally increase with size. Also, when an enterprise offers a public service, there is the assumption that it will be a better one if it is a big one. Finally, there is a common fear that if an organization fails to grow, others will move in.

Where competition is the key, the belief system also plays a role. Administration in government is notoriously myth-ridden because the conditions that encourage the growth of myths are present in all institutions. The group is self-conscious, organized around an objective (which may be the group's own rather than that of the agency), becomes professionalized, emphasizes fixed procedures, and feels that it must struggle to retain its just rights and extend its legitimate influence. In short, the group is a bureaucracy, the bureaucracy becomes a guild, and the larger and more professionalized the guild, the greater is the pressure toward conformity and an uncritical acceptance of traditional values and methods.

Following the pattern of social conflict in the community, in government also is the acceptance of a myth by the bureaucracy followed by the invention of a devil, if one is not already at hand. In the case of the military services and the police, the objects of collective hostility are the enemy and the lawbreaker. Although this one is clear, those less obvious are no different. For the National Park Service the devil is the camper who is careless with fire; for the city manager it is the politician seeking patronage appointments; for the Bureau of the Budget it is "unreasonable" demands for more money by government agencies; for the highway department it is heavy trucks that break pavements; and for the stenographic pool it is rush assignments that come in just before quitting time.

In more complicated illustrations there may be more than one devil and the collective adrenalin flows for more than one reason. Thus the members of the public health service are troubled by lax municipal officials who allow garbage to collect in alleys, and by medical associations that seem unfair in the matter of national health insurance. Diplomats sometimes find their troubles multiplied by the attitudes not only of foreigners but also of their own nationals, and these may include congressmen on a junket. Moreover, the devil may change his shape from time to time. When the Children's Bureau was quietly minding its own business in the Department of Labor, for example, its devil was the exploiter of child labor, but when the Bureau of the Budget suddenly announced the transfer of the Children's Bureau to the Federal Security Agency, the enemy—temporarily, at least—became the Bureau of the Budget. And finally, some programs have a greater emotional coloration than others and their devils can be made more striking. Thus for the armed services a splendid devil is always available in the form of a potential foreign enemy with its secret agents, saboteurs, subversives, and propagandists. By contrast, agencies like the Bureau of Labor Standards and the Patent Office must sometimes exercise a good deal of ingenuity to keep a convenient devil on duty. In such cases, although knowledge to overcome ignorance has a certain appeal, the chances are that a sharp jurisdictional dispute will arouse deeper group passions, especially if the enemy is engaged in similar work.

These devils may serve to strengthen group unity but they also intensify jurisdictional disputes because the opposing agency is always a potential devil to replace or to add to those already in existence. Another difficulty is that although group pride and exclusiveness may encourage zeal, loyalty, and even employee pliability, they also easily antagonize other groups, create discord, and eventually weaken the influence and survival power of the agency. Bureaucracies are inherently exclusive in any case, and the administrator who mistakenly feeds this fire may lose more than he gains.

Jurisdictional conflicts reflect underlying group struggles, but aggression is not the only factor. Any program is a composite of many related activities and the neat divisions of organization do not necessarily separate one segment from another. Thus every adminstrator may find functions related to his work that are under the control of someone else; if he is conscientious he will try to extend his control so as to be sure of results. Nevertheless, as one of the present authors has noted in another connection,

> there is a difference between aggrandizement which merely looks to greater financing, more employees, and increased power and prestige, and that which is an integral part of the strategy of performing a unified and rounded function. It is easy to rationalize the one into the other. The executive, therefore, must honestly examine his own thought and motives so as to make sure that his desire for a unified authority is not in reality an avid, if disguised, thirst for power. Nothing will more quickly dissipate the strength of his organization than the assumption of unnecessary and unrelated activity. Similarly, nothing is more indispensable to success than the proper juxtaposition of related parts so that his machine may operate smoothly and with no cylinders missing.[7]

Myths may develop and assist the administrator to accomplish a rounded jurisdiction, but the difficulties of cooperation are not due to phantoms, nor can they be wholly solved by the exercise of good will. Something more is needed, including clear lines of jurisdiction and organization, together with frequent conferences among those concerned to make clear the division of responsibility and the manner in which the parts of a multiplex program add up to something socially worthwhile.

It must be remembered, of course, that overlappings among jurisdictions can never be wholly eliminated, and that some of these interstitial areas are among the more interesting and useful in any field of administration. It is here that energies are generated, innovations occur, and new and exciting syntheses are made. With good will and enough consultation, such areas can be managed without conflict. It is for the sake of coordination, in these cases as in others, that management justifies overhead control agencies such as budget bureaus, civil service commissions, planning boards, and the like.

---

[7] Marshall E. Dimock, *The Executive in Action,* pp. 53-54.

A jurisdictional conflict may be further confused by cloudy policy and faulty administrative coordination within the program itself. If top policies are vague or contradictory, every program that overlaps another, unless it is a formal jurisdiction in itself, is bound to become a battlefield simply because boundaries are fuzzy and the administrator does not know when he is trespassing. Similarly, if controls and coordination are unsatisfactory, overlapping programs are provided with latitude—a kind of no man's land—and they naturally try to move into unoccupied territory before others get a chance at it.

This problem of jurisdiction is likely to be intensified when the institution is large and cooperation at the apex is less than adequate. When congressional enactments are inconsistent or when Congress and the President are at odds, the way is open for bureaucratic infighting at the departmental level. If policies were more clearly understood, if executive-legislative relations were more harmonious, and if coordination were improved at the Cabinet level, then infighting and useless competitions among federal agencies might be measurably less. A wider recognition of the influence of these factors would go a long way to dispel the popular notion of a selfish and power-hungry bureaucracy intent on destroying our liberties.

## Getting Specialists to Work Together

The third problem mentioned at the outset of this chapter is how to get specialists to cooperate instead of fighting with each other. In the eyes of the weary administrator, this feat of integration, as Mary Parker Follett called it, is infinitely more difficult than coping with social conflict situations or ironing out jurisdictional disputes.

The tendency toward exclusiveness that is a characteristic of bureaucracy is also a characteristic of skill groups, and for the same reasons. Each group believes itself to be better than the next and that a means of raising its own prestige is to detract from the competence of another that might rival or compete with it. This common human propensity is so widespread that even nations exhibit it toward other nations. On the individual plane, if a man works in the legal division of a government department, for example, and is not himself a lawyer he must accept a lower social status in the group than his lawyer colleagues. Lawyers are the product of a long, demanding education; in addition, in their trial work they become familiar with many other fields of knowledge, including engineering, administration, medicine, education, patent law, and the like. Consequently, if they did not have it already, they soon acquire a good deal of self-confidence. But when overencouraged, self-confidence becomes a feeling of omniscience, and the result is often an attitude of superiority toward all other specialists.

Soon there is an attempt to arrogate administrative authority and then the battle of the skill groups is on.

In some degree, of course, the same thing is true of every professional group. "While information comes to the expert as fact," comments Mary Parker Follett, "it usually leaves him as opinion." [8] A prime offender is the expert on administration who assumes administration to be a kind of mystery comprehensible only to those who have studied certain subjects in college or graduate school. Similarly, an accountant or financial expert finds himself thinking he knows more about general administration than the chief executive who has no professional handle to his name. This attitude is a frequent cause of conflict in large corporations and is not unknown along the Potomac. Personnel experts also are the victims of this attitude of omniscience, for they often come to feel that what really counts in administration lies exclusively within their province. Engineers also are apt to create a problem in large organizations because their mental set is toward facts and figures and they sometimes have a blind spot when it comes to human relations in its various aspects. Doctors and physical scientists commonly labor under kindred handicaps.

The result is that most experts, in self-defense, belittle the scientific character and importance of the other fellow's specialty and magnify their own, creating social and professional distinctions that interfere with cooperative effort. When a physical scientist holding a high post in the Atomic Energy Commission was asked by a group of social scientists what he thought of the role of social science in government, he replied, "As far as I can tell, social science does more harm than good. Most social scientists seem to be interested in manipulating people with meaningless terms and propaganda instead of adhering to the facts." There is just enough truth to this statement to give it a sting, but if this man had known more at firsthand about the social sciences, he might have had a better opinion of its potentialities if not of the performance of its practitioners in government positions. In fact, he reflected an attitude of superiority that public approbation has tempted many physical scientists to assume.

Specialists are not only social workers, engineers, lawyers, and the like; they may also be specialists within a specialty, as when a doctor specializes in child health or tuberculosis control, or a statistician concentrates on cost of living studies or public opinion polls. Consequently it is not professional specialization alone that is involved, but specialization arising out of organization and the detailed division of labor that must be adjusted in getting cooperation among the personnel of the various skill groups.

---

8 Mary Parker Follett, "Leader and Expert," in Metcalf and Urwick, *op. cit.*, p. 255.

In contrast to the narrow view of the specialist, the general administrator, like other political leaders, must have a composite view —what was referred to earlier as a conceptual view—that takes in the whole organization so as to draw the different specialties into a single driving force. Persons of this caliber at the top are essential if no part of the enterprise is to be neglected. This much is clear. What is sometimes less clear is that every specialist must appreciate what others can contribute to the joint effort.

In the War Shipping Administration during World War II the two main skill groups were the men who had been in shipping and the men who had been in the civil service for most of their lives, and it would be hard to say which group exhibited the greater air of superiority toward the other. Such attitudes are natural, and up to a certain point they may even be beneficial. Each group is justly proud of its lore and its potentiality for accomplishment, and such pride encourages effort. In any group undertaking, self-confidence is more effective than a feeling of inferiority.

From the standpoint of the enterprise, however, self-confidence can be carried to the point where it negates teamwork. Thus the problem of the administrator is to direct the self-confidence of skill groups into useful channels, to convince each group that it needs what the others have to offer, and to try patiently to persuade each one to be more modest and tolerant toward its fellows. He must convince them that so long as specialization is necessary in large organizations, there is an essential and distinctive role for each. And finally, he must get all groups to concentrate on the objective of the enterprise and on teamwork and to think less of their own superiorities in the joint undertaking. These are tests of leadership.

Where a narrow point of view is allowed to dominate an organization the result is frustration and conflict. In a certain company, top management consisted of five functional officials, but the one who dominated the others, including the president, was the controller. Indifferent to the work of the other functional departments, he frequently said, "Just let me have the facts," because to him "a fact was something that could be expressed in figures, and anything that could not be reduced to figures was not a fact at all." A fast thinker, "his mind was a storehouse of figures, he made himself extremely useful to the president, and gave the other executives the feeling that his primary interest was to expose their weak points." His office, for example, prepared cost data on the work of the production and sales departments, and he expected company officials to make use of these figures, but he did not take the trouble to have them arranged in ways that would make them easy to use. The common feeling of the group toward this man was expressed by the director of sales who once remarked that the controller was too much of a tough guy for his own good.

As might be expected, over a period of time the whole organization became figure-minded, so to speak, to the neglect of public relations and all the other ingredients of a balanced operation. The result was harmful to business. In contrast to the controller and the president, the sales vice president had caught hold of the truth that "many of the problems on which he had worked, and most of the decisions which he had to make, involved *relationships with others,* usually a number of others. He had learned, again and again, that his own decisions required the merging and blending of any number of demands from people outside his office." [9]

From the very nature of his training and his work, the specialist is characteristically gaited and wears blinders. He sees the world only through his job. The more specialized the jobs in the agency, therefore, the more attention must be paid to developing executives with a broad viewpoint. This problem of training and supervision has been dealt with in Chapter 15; here it is useful merely to add that a good way to break down professional jealousies and snobberies is to transfer young men from one kind of position to another so as to teach them a number of different gaits. This might make it possible in time to dispense with blinders for the specialist.

## Managers as Specialists

James Burnham, whose book *The Managerial Revolution*[10] caused a stir in the early 1940s, was not so concerned with competition among skill groups as with the dominance of one of them, the managers.

Burnham believes that every society is ruled by an elite or an oligarchy. At one time, he says, it was expected that there would be rule by a class—the laboring class, for example—but this idea is now outmoded. Instead, there will be rule by a skill group—indeed, by a particular skill group composed of professional managers, the men whose profession it is to manage all the companies and programs of industry and government. They are the production men and the chief executives, the men who run agencies like the Tennessee Valley Authority and companies like General Motors. It is this group, says Burnham, that has the power in society; the rest of us, who are owners of corporations and citizens in a democracy, have virtually no power left. This managerial revolution is already well advanced, says Burnham; it is inevitable, it cannot be stopped, and its potentialities are limitless.

Shortly after it was published Burnham's book was reviewed by

[9] Learned, Ulrich, and Booz, *Executive Action,* p. 31.
[10] James Burnham, *The Managerial Revolution* (New York: The John Day Company, Inc., 1941). *Cf.* C. Wright Mills, *The Power Elite* (New York: Oxford University Press, 1956).

David E. Lilienthal who admitted that there was much to support the theory.[11] The findings of others show that today the ownership and control of corporations are widely separated and that power has gravitated from stockholders to paid professional managers.[12] But as Lilienthal points out, there are several things wrong with Burnham's thesis: The assumption that domination and oligarchy are inherent in society; that trends, once started, are unchangeable; and that managers uniformly desire personal power. Nor can such an analysis of the managerial character be squared with H. G. Well's contention that managers are what he calls the learned-priestly type of person, and that like scholars, scientists, doctors, and ministers, they devote themselves unselfishly to knowledge, values, and humanity and desire little power or prestige for themselves. The distinctive element in the learned-priestly type, said Wells, is self-abnegation, devotion.[13] Many will call this characterization overdrawn, and yet it is not without some truth.

Lilienthal disavows Burnham's analysis and thinks it dangerous, but admits its fascination for many people. For one thing it has certainty, which is often a pleasant feeling. The analysis also has a degree of plausibility, and many succumb to the appearance of plausibility even when it is specious. But Lilienthal concludes with the warning that there is "an evil tendency among some individuals within the new mangerial group in America that leads toward exploitation of society by those who should be its servants. This tendency public administrators can scotch if they will but speak out plainly before it has become accepted and habitual."

Later, in his book called *TVA—Democracy on the March*,[14] Lilienthal went even further in an excellent chapter entitled "The Common Purpose," in which he showed how experts, with their limited viewpoints can be encouraged to work together for large social goals. This chapter deserves a wide reading.

11 David E. Lilienthal, "Management—Responsible or Dominant?", *Public Administration Review*, I (Summer 1941), pp. 390-392.
12 See especially Adolf A. Berle and Gardiner C. Means, *The Modern Corporation and Private Property* (New York: Commercial Clearing House, 1932), and Marshall E. Dimock and Howard K. Hyde, *Bureaucracy and Trusteeship in Large Corporations*, Temporary National Economic Committee, Monograph No. 11 (Washington, D.C.: Government Printing Office, 1941).
13 H. G. Wells, *The Work, Wealth, and Happiness of Mankind* (2 vols., New York: Doubleday & Company, Inc., 1931).
14 David E. Lilienthal, *TVA—Democracy on the March* (New York: Harper & Row, Publishers, 1944).

### Employer-Employee Relations

The fourth main area of conflict and cooperation distinguished at the beginning of this chapter is employee relations, also called industrial or labor relations. It is a field that has become one of the most interesting in the whole of the social sciences. In its broadest sense, employee relations are an aspect of social conflict because they involve competitions between groups or classes in the community.

A distinction may be made between employee associations created to bring together those of particular professions or skills such as accountants, engineers, public health officers, and the like, and other associations that are unions. The former exist chiefly to promote the interests of a particular profession, creating standards, disseminating knowledge, holding the profession together. The latter are more interested in working conditions, salaries, the rights of employees, and other matters that labor unions commonly promote. The present discussion centers on unions in government.

Since employees are extensively unionized in industry and relatively less so in government, not nearly so much has been written about labor-management relations in the public field as in the private one. On the other hand, in government the range of practice is as great as it was in private employment before the passage of the Wagner Act of 1935. For several decades or so it was not certain that public employees were legally free to organize, and even where there was no legal barrier, some public employees had been slow to identify themselves with a union. Public attitudes today toward unions in government vary from acceptance to toleration to antipathy.

The first employee union in the federal government appeared in the postal service some seventy years ago; later, others were added, each limited to a particular class of postal employee. The first of the larger unions was created in 1917 on a noncraft basis. Originally affiliated with the American Federation of Labor, it became independent in 1932, at which time the AFL chartered another union as a rival and also set up a corresponding organization to cover state, county, and municipal employees. In 1937 the Congress of Industrial Organizations chartered a union of its own for federal employees and another for state, county, and municipal workers; a few years later the two were joined in a single organization. Then, following the merger of the AFL and the CIO in 1955, a merger at the individual union level also was accomplished.

As the functions of government have enormously expanded in the last generation or so, public payrolls have grown and the question of organization became increasingly pressing. Of some 2.3 million federal employees in 1961, approximately one third belonged to employee organizations, and of these more than half were in the Post Office Department. The largest government union was the National Association of Letter Carriers, with some 150,000 members. Today, therefore, the network of employee organization in government is a wide one, if a little thin in places, and the public administrator has many problems of employee relations similar to but generally less acute than those faced by his counterpart in industry.

Unions of government employees work for the same things that other unions work for: the right to organize and to bargain collectively, improved wages, hours, and conditions of employment, and the like. In recent years, however, some government unions have developed a broader, more statesmanlike viewpoint and have been an important factor in improved government and better administration. In public personnel administration, for example, they have been concerned with a positive approach to classification, service rating systems, pension plans, employee suggestion systems; in some of these areas they can claim most of the credit for the action taken by Congress and the administration.

In the public mind, however,—and understandably enough—main interest centers on the right of public employees to use the traditional weapon of organized labor, the right to strike. In general, there are three main categories of public employees, each operating at a different level of urgency. One is concerned with law enforcement and the protection of the community against emergency. The second works at day-to-day assignments such as filing real estate deeds or keeping tax records. The third is employed at services that may be interchangeably performed by public or private workers, such as those in a shipyard or a liquor store, either of which may be publicly or privately owned and operated. The suitability of the strike weapon among these three groups is in descending order from clearly none at all in the first group to a "maybe" in the last. Public administrators are deeply concerned with this question and most of them realize that something more basic than the right to strike is involved, namely, the responsibility of management for proper and constructive union relations, the extent of the issues that are properly the subject of collective bargaining and agreement, and the degree to which employee organization should be encouraged.

Strikes are a surface manifestation of deeper causes. In the past there have been more of them in government than many people realize. David Ziskind has told of the one thousand strikes that had occurred in American governments prior to 1940, mainly in the areas of protection, education, public health, recreation, public works, publicly owned utilities, and public employment projects.[15] Moreover, during the first

---

15 David Ziskind, *One Thousand Strikes of Government Employees* (New York: Columbia University Press, 1940).

half of 1946-1947 when the Taft-Hartley bill was before Congress, there occurred no less than twelve major strikes among public school teachers in cities as large as Buffalo and New York, involving more than 2000 teachers and affecting 50,000 students. The Taft-Hartley law met threats of this kind with the provision that federal workers who go out on strike face discharge, forfeit their civil service status, and are ineligible for reemployment for three years. A similar trend appeared in the states; only a short time after the passage of the law, ten states had outlawed strikes by some or all public employees.

There have been some interesting discussions of desirable public policy on this issue. Edward L. Bernays, for example, identifies three main prerequisites to cooperation in labor relations: first, the public must understand the value to the nation of sound unions and mature union leadership. Second, the employer must understand the value of unions to him. And third, the worker must understand the industrial system and his relationship to it.[16] Leonard D. White, who for years was a member of the Civil Service Commission, believed that if the consequences were likely to be serious, then strikes by public employees should be prohibited by law; otherwise "the law should remain silent." [17]

In 1950 the Federal Personnel Council formulated a six-point program that is a constructive approach to relations between management and organized public employees:[18]

1. Recognition of the right of employees to organize, but not necessarily recognition of the right to strike
2. Declaration of the open-shop principle
3. Recognition of the duty of administrative officials to confer with representatives of employee organizations and actively to seek the advice and recommendations of such organizations in the formulation of policies on employee relations
4. Recognition by administrative officials, within limits established by law, of a particular employee organization as representing all employees
5. Agreements reached through conference and negotiation to be published and made accessible to all employees affected
6. Administrative regulations relating to the conduct of such meetings to be published and made readily accessible to all employees

In areas where government undertakes a business type of function, as in the operation of a municipal transit system, some of the major

16 Edward L. Bernays, "How to Build Industrial Peace and Prevent Strife," *Advanced Management,* XII (December 1947), pp. 154-158.
17 Leonard D. White, "Strikes in the Public Service," *Public Personnel Review,* X (January 1949), p. 5.
18 Found in W. Brooke Graves, *Public Administration in a Democratic Society* (Boston: D. C. Heath & Company, 1950), p. 182.

programs of TVA, the diversified functions of the Port of New York Authority, and much of the work of the Atomic Energy Commission, employee unrest may become acute and closely parallel to similar disturbances in the private sector of the economy. TVA is generally recognized as a pioneer in the field of employee relations in a government agency. As early as 1935 it enunciated an employee relationship policy that contained provisions for the right to organize and to bargain freely; exclusive bargaining by the majority union in any group, craft, or unit; responsible dealings with TVA directors as a positive aid to improved management; assurances that no one would be forced to join a union against his will; prohibitions against discrimination on account of sex or race; thirty days' notice of proposed changes affecting major working conditions; and voluntary agreement not to use the strike weapon. Appropriate machinery was created to enforce this policy, and each year TVA holds a formal conference with the Tennessee Valley Trades and Labor Council to negotiate a written agreement signed by both parties.

Labor relations are understandably more complicated in the atomic energy field because the work is secret, vital, and relatively new. It is additionally complicated by the use of the contract device, which means that the work is done largely under contract with the government by large private corporations such as Du Pont, General Electric, and Union Carbide. Accordingly, the issues are: Who is the real employer? Where do power and responsibility actually reside? Municipal transit is another difficult area: bus lines may be run by a public corporate body and most employees are members of an industrial union; but they are civil servants and it may be contended that their legal status is no different from that of employees of any other branch of the city government.

In the area of public employee relations, Great Britain for a long time was far ahead of the United States. There, a formal mechanism was created in 1919 to handle employee representation in government administration, when the so-called Whitley Councils were set up following a period of employee unrest both before and after World War I. These councils exist at various levels of administrative organization within the government and culminate in a body of fifty-four members, half appointed by the Chancellor of the Exchequer and half by the unions. Whitleyism has been described as "the endeavor of employers and employees through representative councils to understand each other's problems, establish mutual confidence, and raise the efficiency of the enterprise in which they are commonly engaged." [19]

---

[19] Carl J. Schneider, "The Revival of Whitleyism in British Local Government," *Public Administration Review*, XIII (Spring 1953), p 97; see also Leonard D. White, *Whitley Councils in the British Civil Service* (Chicago: University of Chicago Press, 1933).

Although nothing comparable to the Whitley Councils exists in the United States, with some notable exceptions few governments here prohibit the organization of employee unions. In some areas, especially among public school teachers and other large professional groups, the trend toward organization is spreading. Employee organizations are mainly of three kinds: unions of skilled craftsmen with locals in government as well as in industry; unions confined to a single department of the government; and large, over-all unions covering the whole government and in one instance taking in employees at the state and local levels as well.[20]

On the question of the right to strike, the unions themselves have for the most part recognized the obvious limitations and many have outlawed strikes in their own constitutions. In 1955 a federal law prohibited strikes by public employees—thus strengthening the Taft-Hartley provision—and received the united support of the unions involved. What the unions chiefly wanted was to be recognized for collective bargaining under the National Labor Relations Act and the provision of some kind of grievance machinery. The Truman and Eisenhower Administrations were opposed to such a policy but when the Kennedy Administration came to office the President created a task force to study the matter and in 1962, by executive order, set forth procedures for recognizing and dealing with employee organizations and required the Civil Service Commission to create a system of appeals, including hearings, from actions taken against any government employee.

The field of labor relations is a large one even in government, and no single illustration covers every aspect of it. An interesting experiment, however, concerns the methods used to increase production and to improve labor-management relations in a plant producing war materials during World War II. Among other things, this particular situation illustrates a slogan found on the walls of the Federal Personnel Council in Washington: "No decision becomes really effective until it has received universal acceptance."

In the plant in question, which was a submarginal one, output was increased by 20 percent and morale greatly improved when periodic meetings were arranged between the management and the various functional groups to discuss problems common to all of them. Enough time was taken to talk the matter out, to arrive at a consensus, and to see clearly what each group had to do if raised quotas were to be reached. After a series of experiments of this kind, permanent representatives known as group captains were selected by secret ballot from

[20] The best brief discussion of this subject is in O. Glenn Stahl, *Public Personnel Administration* (New York: Harper & Row, Publishers, 1956), chap. 12. See also Sterling D. Spero, *The Labor Movement in a Government Industry* (New York: Doubleday and Company, Inc., 1924), and *Government as Employer* (New York: Remsen, 1948).

each group of employees; during the war these captains constituted a labor-management committee and their responsibilities came gradually to cover many problems, some of them not immediately related to production. The list included employees' services, wages, hours, employee activities, control of the "music while you work" program, the timing and nature of announcements, and the handling of grievances.[21]

In employee relations as in other areas involving a human relationship, conflict stems from many causes, all of which are failures to do something that is essential to cooperation: a failure to see problems through the eyes of the other group; to understand psychological motivation and to recognize that people can seldom tolerate what they do not comprehend; to create the kind of organization that will enable people to explore areas of agreement and disagreement and to arrive at a consensus or at least at a working compromise; to involve all parties in the work of the organization and to make them feel that they belong and are respected for their contributions; to share power and values so that all stand to gain; and finally, a failure to secure give and take on both sides.

Cooperation is the opposite of these things: it is thinking in terms of real people and vital functions and avoiding emotionally distorted words and phrases; encouraging face to face relationships that dissipate devils, real or imaginary; recognizing the interdependence of all producing groups and checking egocentric drives; building communication lines that allow common sentiments and understandings to flow throughout the circuit; creating an open atmosphere devoid of deviousness; encouraging self-confidence without fear; providing for broad training away from the narrow model; and stimulating constructive action to relax tensions. If these assumptions are correct, or even largely correct, then the qualities of leadership can no longer be regarded as the possession of the gifted few. Rather, they are the common qualities of common humanity vitalized by congenial institutional arrangements.

---

21 R. W. Willmarth and Hollis F. Ware, "An Experiment in Group Dynamics," *Advanced Management*, XII (September 1947), pp. 116-119.

## BIBLIOGRAPHY AND CASES

### Annotated Reading Suggestions

On the role of the administrator as broker of influence there is nothing better than Philip Selznick's **Leadership in Administration** (Harper & Row, 1957), and **TVA and the Grass Roots** (University of California Press, 1949), because Selznick's whole approach to administration is that of relating to tensions and the solution of problems. See also Norton E. Long, "Power and Administration," *Public Administration Review,* 10 (Autumn 1949).

The most comprehensive treatment, relating to all areas of social problem and the use of group dynamics, is Stuart Chase, *Roads to Agreement* (Harper & Row, 1951). There are also some good chapters in Mary Parker Follett, *Dynamic Administration,* her papers collected and edited by Henry C. Metcalf and L. Urwick (Harper & Row, 1941); see especially Chapter 10, "The Psychology of Consent and Participation," and Chapter 11, "The Psychology of Conciliation and Arbitration."

The unresolved tensions in American economic and political life have been brilliantly dealt with by Adolf Berle in *The American Economic Republic* (Harcourt, 1963), especially Part II, "Organization and Structure."

On the resolution of group conflicts in governmental administration, see Symposium, "Collective Bargaining in the Public Service," *Public Administration Review,* 22 (Winter 1962); Sterling Spero, *Government as Employer* (Remsen, 1948); Gordon R. Clapp, *Employee Relations in the Public Service* (Chicago: Civil Service Assembly, 1942); Morton R. Godine, *The Labor Problem in the Public Service* (Harvard University Press, 1951); and Arthur Kornhauser, *Psychology of Labor-Management Relations* (University of Illinois Press, 1949).

The Tennessee Valley Authority has pioneered in the area of cooperation and conflict. See especially *Collective Bargaining in a Federal Regional Agency* (Knoxville, 1941), and *The Employee Relationships Policy* (Knoxville, 1945).

Other useful references are R. J. Roethlisberger and W. J. Dickson, *Management and the Worker* (Harvard University Press, 1940); Robin M. Williams, Jr., *The Reduction of Intergroup Tensions,* Bulletin 57 (Social Science Research Council, 1947); and Donald B. Straus, *The Development of a Policy for Industrial Peace in Atomic Energy* (Washington, D.C., 1950).

One of the few books to deal with the dynamics of trade union leadership is Lois Macdonald and Associates, *Leadership Dynamics and the Trade-Union Leader* (New York University Press, 1959).

## Case Studies

Interjurisdictional conflict is the theme of one of the leading cases in the Stein *Case Book.* Arthur A. Maass tells the story of *The King's River Project,* which involved the traditional rivalry of the Army's Corps of Engineers and the Interior Department's Reclamation Service, in a thirty-six-page account written in 1949 and revised in 1950.

Other cases in the ICP series provide a variety of illustrations. No. 17, *Whittier Narrows Dam,* seventeen pages, is written by D. E. Pearson and revolves around the concept of the public interest. No. 26, *Defending the "Hill" Against Metal Houses,* thirty-five pages, deals with the introduction of prefabricated homes in West Haven, Connecticut, and the social attitudes that were involved. The case is reported by W. K. Muir. No. 39, *"Lonesome Train" in Levittown,* sixteen pages, is not what the title seems to suggest. Rather, it concerns the staging of a controversial cantata in the public schools; written by J. F. Maloney. Finally, No. 63, *Premium Gold Controversy in the International Monetary Fund,* fifty-nine pages, involves relations with another country, the Union of South Africa.

# 23

## Holding Administration
## Accountable

THE MORE POWER concentrated at any point in society, the greater is the need for safeguarding against its abuse. The power vested in public administration in the United States today is great and will surely become greater. Consequently, the question of accountability to the citizen, of democratic control by the citizen as voter and consumer, becomes a central one. To say that without proper democratic controls, the concentration of power in administration might subvert popular government itself seems not to be too strong a statement. The corrective is an old one: every delegation of power to an agent must be accompanied by a corresponding degree of accountability.

This chapter is divided according to the four means by which accountability may be secured: administrative self-regulation, legislative supervision and control of the executive branch, legal remedies offered by the courts, and action by citizens and their groups to secure the compliance of administrators. A final section deals with the question of size in government.

### Administrative Self-regulation

Of all possible methods of holding administrators accountable, probably none is more effective in the long run than self-control on the part of administrators themselves, because they are more likely to act correctly if they *want* to than if they are forced to. Although such restraint

373

cannot always prevent serious breaches of the law, it contributes more than any other factor to a desire among government employees to be courteous and responsive in their relations with the public.

Government administrators are most likely to be public-spirited and honest if they come from a cultural milieu that values these qualities; similarly, if there is no such influence in the background of the administrator, no effective substitute is likely to be found. The home, the school, the church, and all the relationships of early life shape the attitudes that are later carried into public office. The best time to develop a considerate attitude toward people and a regard for ethics on the part of the public administrator, therefore, is before he takes office.

Even if the attitudes of particular individuals are poor, however, much can be done to reinforce ethical standards and to raise the morale and responsiveness of the agency as a whole. The administrator should give his employees a clear idea of the goals and values of the program, make them feel that their personal and vocational interests coincide, consult with them, respect them in their work, reward them for extra effort and attentiveness to consumer desires, provide adequate inservice training, furnish inspired leadership and supervision, and emphasize public relations. These are the morale builders.

Even more important, perhaps, is the influence of the guild, which in any agency has standards of its own that no administrator will defy if he hopes to retain the loyalty and respect of the group. In a bureaucracy, therefore, social and vocational groupings and inclusion as a member of the guild are worth more to the individual than being part of a large, amorphous government agency. To the extent that professionalized government services, such as the Immigration and Naturalization Service or the Internal Revenue Service, develop their own standards of ethics, the beneficial social influences in the background of employees are strengthened and the occasional restraints of legislatures and the courts are rendered that much more effective. Moreover, when as has already happened, professional groups like the city managers develop professional codes of ethics as clear-cut and binding as those of lawyers and doctors, professional self-regulation becomes a powerful force for responsible behavior.

The chief weakness of administrative self-regulation is the parochial, bureaucratic point of view that often accompanies the guild spirit. Professionalism frequently improves ethics but it also fosters self-centeredness. In this event, the corrective must come from outside prodding to keep the bureaucracy alert and consumer-oriented. Internal management also can help in this respect, especially through the supervisory and public relations programs described in Chapters 15 and 21. The citizen advisory committee is a useful device for supplying the outside viewpoint to administration. Granting that such a group often tries to assume too much responsibility, it is worth the risk to get the fresh, citizen approach as a tonic to the self-centered administrator.

Yet another antidote to the parochial point of view is the political and policy leadership of appointed officials at the top levels of government. Nothing would do more to improve executive leadership in public administration than to attract outstanding men and women to careers at the sub-Cabinet level of administration as undersecretaries and assistant secretaries of the departments and agencies in all governments, municipal to federal. Once these people have been recruited and trained, the second need is to find some way to retain them in public employment. To be sure, the longer they stay the less will the fresh viewpoint be present, but infusions of new blood are always possible when vacancies occur. The political parties are capable of supplying experienced executive leadership if the jobs are made sufficiently attractive, especially regarding tenure.

Indeed, it is not too much to say that how to attract and hold appointive officials at the bureau and departmental levels, where executive leadership is most needed, is the single largest unsolved problem of American public administration. A junior executive in Washington who had been working with a group of foreign representatives during World War II was asked at the final meeting, "What will you do now?" The American replied that he planned to return to his private business, which caused the Belgian to comment sadly, "I can't really admire your form of government when it lets good men like you slip through its fingers." It was an attempt to correct this situation that led the second Hoover Commission to propose the establishment of a career service both in appointive policy posts and in the higher civil service in order to attract, train, and reward outstanding people in the federal service.

Administrative self-regulation presupposes a regard for ethical behavior on the part of public administrators, and here there are two points to be noted. First, people seem to expect public servants to have higher ethical values than businessmen, partly because the public service is still regarded as more of a public trust than most businesses. Nevertheless, according to the second point, standards of ethics in government cannot rise much above those of the community because employees are subject to the same favorable or unfavorable influences that control the community and naturally assume that what is good enough for the community is good enough for government. This is not to say that standards in government should not be higher than those in the community generally; it is merely to assert that they are not *likely* to be higher. Furthermore, public administration operates in a political setting and the possibilities of self-regulation are limited by that fact.

Such considerations make it easier to understand the lapses in public morality studied by Senator Paul Douglas's committee in the Eighty-first Congress and the difficulty it had in coming up with practical suggestions for strengthening that morality.[1] All it could offer were certain legal inducements to morality that would have been hard to enforce, and would have constituted unwarranted restraints on the vast majority of public officials who are honest.

Allied to the voluntary restraints that may be encouraged among public administrators is a kind of internal policing conducted by administration itself through central control agencies that exist in most governments of any size. In Washington, for example, the Civil Service Commission, the Bureau of the Budget, and the General Accounting Office are overhead control agencies exercising a general police function over the operating programs of government. These control units have been created to help enforce the law and uphold administrative standards. Consequently, to the extent that they do their job well they supplement the work of external agencies such as legislatures and the courts, and the load on these is relieved. The General Accounting Office, it will be recalled, is known as the watchdog of Congress, and the Bureau of the Budget as the watchdog of the President; both are part of administration but superior to it in some respects, being placed midway between the operating agencies on the one hand and Congress and the courts on the other.

Most public administrators are willing to admit that these overhead control agencies are essential tools of accountability, but draw the line when they interfere in policy and other matters of internal administration in a manner that limits initiative and effectiveness. As remarked on several previous occasions in this book, to find a proper line of demarcation between internal operating independence and overhead control, and to apply it faithfully in every case, is one of the hardest problems of administration. In responsible government, both accountability and internal freedom are necessary conditions, and their successful integration is evidence of the highest kind of administrative skill.

## Officers to Criticize Administrative Action

An interesting device in the area of administrative self-regulation that has been successfully employed in Sweden and Denmark and recommended for experimentation in the United States is the office of the so-called *Ombudsmen*. As described by Kenneth Davis,[2] this official oc-

---

[1] *Ethical Standards in Government,* report of subcommittee, Senate Committee on Labor and Public Welfare, 82d Cong., 1st Sess. (1951).

[2] Kenneth Culp Davis, "Ombudsmen in America: Officers to Criticize Administrative Action," *University of Pennsylvania Law Review,* 109 (June 1961), pp. 1057-1076.

cupies a position of high prestige in the government and his job is to handle complaints from any citizen who is displeased with the action or inaction of any administrator or civil servant. Complaint may be by means of an informal letter and the Ombudsmen may also act on his own initiative if he wishes. He may also exercise discretion in the selection of the complaints he will investigate.

In making his investigations—for which he has the assistance of a small staff—the Ombudsmen may inquire into substance, procedure, delay, convenience, and even courtesy. His criticisms may relate not only to questions of legality but also to matters of good administration, which may be judged on the basis of relevant statutes, regulations, precedents, and custom, as well as on the opinion of the Ombudsmen himself. His only powers are to investigate, criticize, recommend, and publicize. He has no power to change any administrative action and he must, of course, avoid taking positions on questions of political opinion. His effectiveness rests on the fairness with which he does his work, the prestige of his office, and the publicity that accompanies his criticisms and recommendations. However, says Davis, "Being right is not enough. He must be both right and convincing. He can act successfully only when he keeps informed opinion with him. But he can still take strong positions. Because of his great prestige, he can and does lead public opinion on some issues." [3]

There is a considerable difference in the functioning of such an official in a small country as compared with a large one, for obvious reasons, but Davis suggests that with the exercise of the traditional American ingenuity, the device of the Ombudsmen might be adapted to the needs of American government. Already, he says, we have come up with many constructive ideas about official critics of administrative action. To push them further, he suggests the establishment of a permanent Office of Administrative Procedure and Organization, to be located in the Executive Office of the President. A similar plan has already received support from the Senate Judiciary Committee's Subcommittee on Administrative Practice and Procedure and by Dean James M. Landis in his report to President-elect John F. Kennedy on the subject of the regulatory agencies.

Such an office would have two major assignments. First, it would make continuing studies of ways to strengthen the fairness and effectiveness of administrative procedures. In addition, it would receive and investigate complaints about administrative action anywhere in the government, not merely that of the regulatory agencies, and especially in those areas where the citizen is presently unprotected either by procedural safeguards or by judicial review. The office would have discretionary power to select the complaints it would investigate; its stud-

---

3 *Ibid.*, p. 1060.

ies would probably pertain more to regulatory agencies than to other administration and would inquire more into effectiveness (accomplishment of governmental objectives, delay, cumbersomness, expense, and the like) than into fairness.

Davis then describes the proposed office in this way:

> . . . the prestige and status of the Director of the Office are of prime importance; the Director's salary should be no less than that of a cabinet officer. Furthermore, if the job is to be done properly, the Office must have a sufficient budget to allow the Director's principal assistants to operate at a very high professional level. The power of the Office to receive and investigate complaints in specific cases should be widely publicized.
>
> The Director should be appointed by the President with the advice and consent of the Senate, and he should serve at the will of the President. He should have statutory power to compel agencies to make disclosures to him. The powers of his office should be limited to investigating, criticizing, publicizing, and recommending.[4]

## Accountability through the Legislature

The second major instrument of public accountability is the authority of the legislature to empower, limit, investigate, and censure the executive branch. The legislature enacts laws, authorizes administrators to engage in quasi-legislative and quasi-judicial activities, appropriates funds for all administrative programs, and determines the general outlines of administrative organization and procedure. When the executive branch seems to be getting out of hand, therefore, the legislature has many ways to put administrators in their place, if it has the will and the wit to do so.

The legislature also has many ways of checking on the manner in which public administrators discharge their legal mandates. There are hearings on annual budget requests, hearings on proposed new legislation or amendments to existing legislation, and even periodic consultations with administrators in some instances where a public official works closely with his legislative committee. Moreover, if it chooses, Congress can check up on administrative operations through its own agents, chiefly the staff members of its various committees who were greatly increased in number under the Legislative Reorganization Act of 1946.[5] Similar investigations are carried out by the budget, account-

---

4 *Ibid.*, p. 1073.
5 The results of the first five years of the operation of this legislation are summarized by George B. Galloway, "The Operation of the Legislative Reorganization Act of 1946," *American Political Science Review*, XLV (March 1951), pp. 41-68.

ing, and auditing agencies of the executive branch that either supply information to Congress or report directly to it, and these reports also are useful to the legislature.

Although it is true that the routine fact-finding activities of legislatures are improving, they do not cover every need and hence special investigating committees are sometimes required. These are of two kinds. The first consists of experts appointed by the President or some private agency interested in a given subject and seeking remedial legislation. Thus something akin to the British Royal Commission has become a feature of American government as illustrated by the President's Committee on Recent Social Trends in 1932, the Commission of Inquiry on Public Service Personnel (a privately sponsored group) in 1935, the President's Committee on Administrative Management in 1937, and the two Hoover Commissions in 1949 and 1955.[6] Along with the executive branch, Congress also is able to profit from the findings of such groups.

The second type of special investigating committee, and one that has been especially prominent in recent years, is the group created by the legislature out of its own membership to look into a particular situation. In 1929 one of the present authors found that the Treasury and Interior Departments, for example, had been investigated by Congress about fifty times each since 1789, and that of all the purposes served by all congressional investigations since that time, surveillance of the administration was the most prominent.[7] Indeed, no administration in American history had been immune from congressional inquiry, Jackson and Lincoln having suffered equally with Wilson and Roosevelt. In more recent years, both congressional and state investigations have become so numerous and so interesting to the public (especially since the advent of television) that the device is now a prominent feature of the American governmental system. Even in the first two New Deal Congresses, when there was harmony between the legislative and executive branches, 165 congressional investigations were undertaken, of which forty-five were designed to check up on the executive branch and fifty-one sought ways of aiding administration.[8] Since that time the number of investigations has greatly increased and some special com-

---

6 On British Royal Commissions, see Harold F. Gossnell, "British Royal Commissions of Inquiry," *Political Science Quarterly*, XLIX (March 1934), pp. 84-118.

7 Marshall E. Dimock, *Congressional Investigating Committees* (Baltimore, Md.: Johns Hopkins University Press, 1929).

8 M. Nelson McGeary, "Congressional Investigations during Franklin D. Roosevelt's First Term," *American Political Science Review*, XXXI (August 1937), pp. 680-694; and *The Development of Congressional Investigative Power* (New York: Columbia University Press, 1940). The leading case upholding the constitutionality of the investigative power is *McGrain v. Daugherty*, 273 U.S. 135 (1927).

mittees of Congress have become permanent features of the House or Senate organizations.

Legislative investigations are a necessary tool of congressional control and in most cases supply useful and needed information. Nevertheless, a good deal of dissatisfaction with some aspects of investigative procedure has been growing in the public mind. Too often legislative investigations seem more concerned with partisan advantage than with respect for the facts; many of these so-called fishing expeditions keep both the legislative and the executive branch so roiled up as to injure efficiency and morale; and the method is hardly suited to the constructive reform of administration through patient and objective fact finding. Something like the Hoover Commission, the scrutiny of a budget bureau, or a joint legislative-executive council would seem to serve this purpose better. A joint legislative-executive council, which is a kind of policy body composed of members from the two branches, was recommended by a group of political scientists who studied Congress during the early 1940s; the Legislative Reorganization Act of 1946 embodied many of the suggestions of this group, but not the joint council.[9]

Although the techniques of fact finding have improved in the past fifteen years or so, the uses to which the information is put still leave something to be desired. Congress displays much energy and frequently sound and fury as well, but these energies are not always constructively directed so as to get to the root of difficulties and prevent their recurrence. The evidence is that congressional investigations are seldom designed with that purpose in view. The problem is inherent in the political process and the issue is whether party government can be made sufficiently responsible to protect the executive branch from reckless and unjustified attacks that only serve to weaken administration and not to strengthen it. Even the members of the majority party are encouraged to play the game of sectional, pressure group, and selfish interests because of the present weakness of party responsibility.[10] Apart from changing our whole political system from the presidential to the Cabinet form of government, which is presently unlikely, the solution seems to lie in a clear definition of the respective functions of legislatures and administrative agencies.

---

[9] American Political Science Association, *The Reorganization of Congress* (Washington, D.C.: Public Affairs Press, 1945). The legislative council device started in 1933 in Kansas and Colorado and is now found in many other states. The main purpose of the device is to facilitate the fact-finding process on a permanent basis; one of its most prominent interests, as might be expected, is the legislative overseeing of administration. See W. Brooke Graves, *American State Government* (3d ed., oBston: D. C. Heath and Company, 1946).

[10] Committee on Political Parties, American Political Science Association, *Toward a More Responsible Two-Party System* (New York: Holt, Rinehart and Winston, 1950), pp. 23, 66.

If Congress were to emphasize deliberation, fact finding, the education of public opinion, and the careful consideration of policies that are to become laws, and if in addition Congress were to stress orderly and effective methods of holding administration to its stewardship, then the way would be opened to give the executive branch the degree of undivided responsibility it needs as a basis for internal self-improvement. Like a ball team, administration does not play well when too many coaches are calling the signals. Pendleton Herring[11] concludes that legislative interference is probably the greatest obstacle to the improvement of efficiency in both Congress and the executive branch. Largely because of his experience in the field of federal personnel administration, Leonard D. White has advanced the same argument.[12]

Administrators themselves, of course, are not without their share of blame for the situation because the attitude of superiority and critical disapproval that many of them show in their relations with legislators is a goad to legislative intereference.[13] If more administrators could see the advantage of trying to get the legislature on their side instead of regarding it as an antagonist, they would doubtless get further in their legitimate requests for a more rounded authority.

There are certain areas of public administration that the legislature should stay out of. Though it should correct abuses in the conduct of the executive branch, it should not itself try to administer anything except its own organization. Nor should it specify administrative organization in detail, try to control the proper use of funds, determine rules of internal administration except to protect private rights, or make the rules of personnel and financial administration so onerous that no administrator can follow them in the spirit in which they were inacted.

The legislature should be content to get the facts, make the laws, appropriate the funds, and check on the trusteeship of administration without impeding its efforts. The legislature can do all of these things without curtailing the authority of administrators freely to administer. If lawmakers were more often willing to act on the basis of this division of duties, there would be a considerable improvement in the effectiveness of both branches of the government.

11 Pendleton Herring, *Presidential Leadership* (New York: Holt, Rinehart and Winston, 1950), chaps. 1-4.
12 Leonard D. White, "Legislative Responsibility for the Public Service," in the symposium, *New Horizons in Public Administration* (University, Ala.: University of Alabama Press, 1945), and "Congressional Control of the Public Service," *American Political Science Review*, XXXIX (February 1945), pp. 1-11. See also Pendleton Herring, "Executive-Legislative Responsibilities," *American Political Science Review*, XXXVIII (December 1944), pp. 1153-1165.
13 Developed by Marshall E. Dimock, "Administrative Efficiency within a Democratic Policy," in the symposium, *New Horizons in Public Administration*, pp. 21-45.

The invasion of executive power by the legislature is in part at least a psychological problem, with insecurity and jealousy the key factors in the compound. Since the cause is partly psychological, the solution must involve psychological principles. It does little good to reorganize and modernize the various branches of the government if problems of relationship remain unsolved. The area most in need of attention is the point where the legislature and the executive meet, and here the initiative lies with the administrator. The human relations approach to the legislature might produce the same favorable results that it produces in administration generally.[14]

## Accountability through the Courts

When an agency of the executive branch needs help in enforcing the law, when controversies arise that administrative officers are not qualified to settle, or when administrators in the course of their work invade the legal rights of citizens, then the courts stand ready to do their part. Historically, adjudication grew out of administration, and even today, despite the constitutional separation of the executive and judicial branches of the government, adjudication remains functionally connected with the administrative process. The courts provide the remedies when the normal processes of administration are not enough.

Like the surveillance of the legislature over administration, the power of the courts over administration also is a power held in reserve that may be called on to thwart the usurpation of authority by an administrator or the miscarriage of justice when administrative self-regulation breaks down. The federal Constitution specifically limits the powers of government, giving each of the three branches only that amount of authority considered necessary to the performance of its vital functions; and in case that authority is misused or exceeded, the courts have the final word. Constitutional government is limited by law, with administration subject to ultimate control by the courts.

The burden of the judiciary, therefore, is to balance in the right proportions the legitimate needs of social efficiency and individual liberty. In relation to social efficiency Ernst Freund commented that the protection of private rights from the possibility of official error, partiality, or excess of zeal is at least as important as carrying out some

---

[14] That this fact is increasingly recognized is reflected in such books as Thomas K. Finletter, *Can Representative Government do the Job?* (New York: Reynal and Hitchcock, Inc., 1945), Henry Hazlitt, *A New Constitution Now* (New York: McGraw-Hill Book Company, Inc., 1942), Estes Kefauver and Jack Levin, *A Twentieth Century Congress* (New York: Duell, Sloan & Pearce–Meredith Press, 1947), and Wilfred E. Binkley, *President and Congress* (3d ed., New York: Vintage, 1962).

governmental policy. And Frank J. Goodnow, the first of the great writers on administrative law, believed that the importance of and need for administrative efficiency should receive due emphasis as against the inherent natural rights of the individual because effective social control depends on that efficiency.

Chapter 9 covers many of the areas in which the courts protect the rights of citizens, an example being the rules of administrative due process developed by the common law courts long before the passage of the Administrative Procedure Act of 1946. The present analysis, therefore, will summarize what is familiar and deal specifically only with what is new.

In the United States, a principal difficulty of judicial control over administration is that justice is too costly to be accessible to many people who need it. In this country, with a few minor exceptions there is only one set of courts, and it is expensive to take a case before them because it means hiring a lawyer, taking time from one's work, paying court costs, and often enduring a long delay before the case is settled. In countries like France and Germany, on the other hand, where the civil (Roman) law prevails, justice is more widely available through a dual court system, the regular courts being supplemented by a system of administrative courts for a special class of cases.

The administrative courts handle cases that arise when an official tries to stretch the law or to act in excess of his authority, or when he has acted negligently, with bias, or so inefficiently as to deprive some citizen of his property or personal rights. Administrative courts are designed to decide all such cases and to offer this relief quickly and inexpensively. It must be admitted, therefore, that the European system has obvious advantages over our own system of unified courts.

Consequently, interest in and advocacy of an administrative court system for the United States has appreciably accelerated in recent years and several bills to that end have been introduced in Congress.[15] Students of law and public administration began to make such proposals early in the 1930s.[16] Frederick Blachly believes that a system of administrative courts, widely and easily available at a minimum cost, would solve problems that the Walter-Logan bill and the Administrative Pro-

---

[15] One of these, by Senator Logan, proposed a United States Court of Appeals for Administration; Sen. Doc. No. 916, 76th Cong., 1st Sess., introduced Jan. 24, 1939. Senator George Norris had introduced a bill to set up a somewhat different type of administrative court system in the 73rd Cong., 1st Sess.

[16] Marshall E. Dimock, "Some Aspects of American Administrative Law," *Public Administration*, IX (London, October 1931), pp. 417-422; and "American Administrative Law in 1931," *American Political Science Review*, XXVI (October 1932), pp. 543-563; see also Robert M. Cooper, "The Proposed United States Administrative Court," *Michigan Law Review*, XXXV (December 1936; February 1937), pp. 193-252, 565-596.

cedure Act of 1946 tried to solve.[17] Another authority, the late Charles Grove Haines, also supported the establishment of a system of administrative courts.[18] In 1955 the second Hoover Commission recommended the creation of an administrative court in three sections. The first would deal with the limited jurisdiction in the field of taxation now vested in the Tax Court of the United States. The second would have jurisdiction in the field of trade regulation now vested in the Federal Trade Commission, the Interstate Commerce Commission, the Federal Communications Commission, the Civil Aeronautics Board, the Federal Reserve Board, the United States Tariff Commission, the Federal Power Commission, and the Departments of the Interior and Agriculture. The third section would have the jurisdiction now vested in the National Labor Relations Board relative to cases involving unfair labor practices.[19] The Hoover Commission left it to Congress to determine whether the trade and labor sections of the proposed court should have original or appellate jurisdiction. And finally, the American Bar Association has long advocated a system of administrative courts and continues to work toward a transfer of quasi-judicial functions from administrative agencies to such a court system.

How much the device of administrative courts would be worth to the average citizen depends, of course, on the availability of such courts for simple cases involving no great amount of money. If such tribunals were widely accessible and if the skills of both the judge and the administrator could be combined in them, as over a period of time seems to have happened in France and Germany, the plan might substantially add to the safeguards that now protect the individual.[20]

## Government Liability to Suit

Yet another area in which the experience of other nations might be useful to Americans is with regard to the right of the citizen to sue his government if he is wronged as a result of official action. In Anglo-American nations where common law predominates, the traditional view that the king can do no wrong is a constitutional principle in-

[17] Frederick Blachly, "Sabotage of the Administrative Process," *Public Administrative Review*, VI (Summer 1946), pp. 213-227; see also his article in George Warren, ed., *The Federal Administrative Procedure Act and the Administrative Agencies* (New York: New York University School of Law, 1947).

[18] Charles Grove Haines, "The Adaptation of Administrative Law and Procedure to Constitutional Theories and Principles," *American Political Science Review*, XXXIV (February 1940), pp. 1-30.

[19] Commission on Organization of the Executive Branch of the Government, *Legal Services and Procedures* (Washington, D.C.: Government Printing Office, 1955), pp. 87-88.

[20] William Rohkam, Jr., and Orville C. Pratt, *Studies in French Administrative Law* (Urbana: University of Illinois Press, 1947).

terpreted to mean that because the government is sovereign, it cannot be sued unless it gives its consent to such an action. By contrast, in countries where the civil law predominates almost every act of administration, if it injures an individual, may be questioned in the administrative or the civil courts.[21] If we Americans believe what we say about the supremacy of the law and no one's being superior to it, then we almost have to admit that the continental rule of government liability to suit is superior to the Anglo-American rule of nonliability.

But even in the United States there has been a gradual modification of the rule governing nonsuability. Thus, government immunity may be specifically waived in particular statutes through provisions defining the areas in which citizens may sue the government when their rights are invaded as the result of administrative action.[22] And even more could be achieved by this means. In addition, the courts have developed a distinction between actions that are "governmental" in the strict sense, as in police protection, and those that are "proprietary," as when a city owns and operates a water and power business. When a government discharges proprietary functions it is usually held to have descended from its sovereign position into the market place and is therefore suable.[23] Moreover, a section[24] of the Legislative Reorganization Act of 1946 considerably extended the federal government's tort liability (covering an action for damages due to an alleged wrong) and provides a much wider scope of recovery against the government than was previously available. In general it may be said that since the passage of this law the bald assumption that the king can do no wrong is dead so far as the federal government is concerned, although it continues to have influence at the state and local levels.

Before these gradual changes came about, however, the constitutional principle of sovereign immunity caused public administrators to be held personally liable for the invasion of rights—whether deliberate or accidental—through negligence, excess of power, or other illegal action. Thus for a long time the fear of being sued and losing their property was a serious deterrent to men of substance contemplating a career in the public service. Later when it became customary to bond

21 *Ibid.*, pp. 61-106. See also Robert D. Watkins, *The State as a Party Litigant* (Baltimore: Johns Hopkins University Press, 1927), and H. Bethelemy, *Traité Elémentaire de Droit Administratif* (12th ed., Paris: A Rousseau, 1930).

22 The pioneer in this field was the late Edwin M. Borchard; see his articles, "Tort Liability of the State," *Journal of Comparative Legislation and International Law*, XI (January 1930), pp. 1-4; and "Recent Statutory Developments in Municipal Liability in Tort," in *Legal Notes on Local Government* (New York, 1936), II, pp. 89-100.

23 See L. T. David, *The Tort Liability of Public Officers* (Chicago: Public Administration Service, 1940); and James Hart, *Introduction to Administrative Law* (rev. ed., New York: Appleton-Century- Crofts, 1950), part. III.

24 This is the Tort Liability Act which was adopted as part of the main bill.

public officials, the danger was largely obviated. Nevertheless, most authorities on administrative law agree that there remain certain areas where governmental liability should be substituted for officer liability if even-handed justice is to be assured.[25]

In 1955 the second Hoover Commission noted that officers accountable for the control and disbursement of funds were personally liable to the government for the proper performance of their financial duties and that a great number of prohibitory statutes existed, the violation of any one of which could make the accountable officer financially responsible. Consequently, many such officers were overcautious and sought counsel from the General Accounting Office for fear that a claim would later be disallowed by that agency and cause the accountable officer personal financial loss. In the fiscal year 1954, for example, some 29,000 vouchers were submitted in this way to the GAO, causing delay and unwarranted expense. To correct the situation the Hoover Commission recommended that the Comptroller General be authorized to relieve accountable officers from financial liability, "except where losses result from their gross negligence or fraud." [26]

Since in the United States there is as yet no administrative court system, the ordinary courts must supply any redress they can against abuses of administrative power. But no court will take jurisdiction unless there is a case or a controversy, meaning that there must be specific parties and issues. Furthermore, since ours is precedent law developed from case to case and not codified law having general applicability, any decision rendered applies only to the case in question. Nor will American courts issue advisory judgments; they must be final decisions and not subject to review outside the judicial branch. Finally—and this leads into the matter of most concern here—no American court will take a case unless there is an appropriate remedy, some means by which the court may take jurisdiction in the first place and impose a legal sanction to carry out its judgment thereafter.

There are several classes of remedies. Criminal remedies may be but in practice rarely are used in legal actions affecting administrative behavior. Outside the criminal law, ordinary common-law remedies are available in the area that depends on private initiative. Among the most common subdivisions of private law are contracts, torts, trespass, and negligence. Any injured citizen may initiate a legal action under any of

---

[25] John Dickinson, *Administrative Justice and the Supremacy of Law in the United States* (Cambridge, Mass.: Harvard University Press, 1927); J. Roland Pennock, *Administration and the Rule of Law* (New York: Holt, Rinehart and Winston, Inc., 1941); and Walter Gellhorn, *Administrative Law: Cases and Comments* (rev. ed., Chicago: The Foundation Press, Inc., 1947).

[26] Commission on Organization of the Executive Branch of the Government, *Budgeting and Accounting* (Washington, D.C.: Government Printing Office, 1955), p. 45.

these headings against another person, against a public official, or against the government itself if the permission is granted. In other words, where ordinary common-law remedies are available and the government grants permission to sue, the redress of the citizen against an officer of the government is no greater, and no less, than his redress against an ordinary citizen.

In addition to these ordinary remedies, however, there are six so-called extraordinary remedies that the courts have used rather extensively in cases involving administrative action, remedies that are available whether or not the government grants permission to sue.[27] With the exception of habeas corpus, however, they are accorded only in the discretion of the courts and only when no other more conventional remedy is available. Taken together, they are one of the means by which the common law adjusts to social change. Specifically, these remedies are:

*Habeas corpus* (literally, [that] you have the body) is a writ issued to a jailor or to an administrative agency such as the Immigration and Naturalization Service to secure a prompt hearing for an incarcerated person to determine whether he should be kept in custody or released. Consequently, habeas corpus is an important means of testing an administrator's jurisdiction and of checking a tendency to act highhandedly.

*Quo warranto* (by what warrant) also tests jurisdiction, including the right of an official to an office claimed by someone else. In the past this remedy has been used in personnel administration and especially in cases of disputed elections, but today it is seldom invoked.

*Certiorari* (to be certified) is widely used by an appeal court to secure the record of a case from a lower court or from an administrative tribunal in order to determine whether to take appellate jurisdiction. Certiorari is now the principal way in which an individual secures an appeal to a higher court.

*Mandamus* (we command) is a writ issued by a higher court to a lower one or to an administrative agency or official, commanding him to take a certain defined action. Such action is usually ministerial, meaning that the duty has been specifically defined and imposed by law, leaving no discretion to the official. It is the command of a court to "do this" and is therefore an important remedy in the field of administrative action.

*Injunction* (to enjoin or prevent) is the opposite of mandamus in that it prohibits a specific action. It is the command of a court to "stop it," and applies equally to administrative officials and to the public at

---

27 Convenient summaries are found in Hart, *op. cit.*, part I, as well as in Bouvier's *Law Dictionary*, Black's *Law Dictionary*, *Corpus Juris*, and the *Encyclopedia of the Social Sciences*.

large. A common use of this writ has been in labor cases where management seeks injunctive relief against labor unions. Several rules govern
the use of an injunction: there must be a threat of irreparable damage
to vested interests, no other remedy is available, a multiplicity of suits
might otherwise be involved, and so on. This also is a widely used
writ.

*Prohibition* (to forbid) is now little used as a remedy. Its purpose
is to order an inferior court or administrative tribunal not to exceed its
jurisdiction and especially not to exceed it in a particular way. With
the exception of prohibition and possibly also quo warranto, these
remedies are widely available to citizens seeking relief from administrative action.

Briefly to summarize, the citizen may sue for money damages under
the common law and under the criminal law; he may contend that a
particular officer lacks jurisdiction or is acting in excess of his power;
he may get the court to order the official to do a ministerial act; he
may test the exercise of discretion where the official has a clear jurisdiction; he may contend (with a few exceptions) that the official is in
error in interpreting the law; and he may ask the courts to insist on the
rules of administrative due process to which he is entitled.

It would appear, therefore, that the American citizen enjoys a
broad range of legal protections—and so he does. But these judicial
remedies would mean more if justice were more easily accessible and
less costly and if the doctrine of governmental immunity to suit were
not still so largely in effect in some jurisdictions. Many actions that
under present conditions must be brought against a particular officer
might more properly be brought against the government itself. If, as
some people contend, there is no limit to the size to which governments
may attain, then the rights of citizens vis-à-vis government must be
legally increased to compensate for the growing power of government
vis-à-vis the citizen. Only by this means can the relationships be kept
in balance.

## Citizen Control

The potentialities of administrative self-regulation, legislative surveillance, and judicial supervision as media of administrative accountability to the public have now been discussed. But useful as each one
is, they are incomplete even in combination without the fourth medium,
which is control by citizens themselves.

It has already been suggested that the degree to which citizens take
an interest in and participate in the operation of their government
ultimately determines the degree to which the bureaucracy will be
honest and responsive. As Alexander Leighton has noted, the reason is
that administration always reflects the total social complex and cannot
be expected to rise much above or to fall much below the average for

the rest of society.[28] This anthropopsychological position seems to be a sound one.

The importance of citizen advisory committees and of dynamic policy leadership has already been mentioned as two methods by which the citizen point of view may be injected into public administration and help to keep the bureaucracy alert and responsive. Another method is service by the citizen on all kinds of boards and commissions dealing with schools, public health programs, planning, government business enterprises, and many more. An estimated 750,000 public officials hold their mandates directly from the people in this way, most of them as employees of boards and commissions whose members serve without compensation. The willingness of qualified citizens to fill these positions is a measure of the health of a democracy.

Because this kind of citizen participation is so desirable as a method of securing accountability, the tendency of American governments to adopt the short ballot—which substitutes appointive for elective officials—is a mixed blessing. If the public is apathetic toward government, then appointed officials may be more competent than elected ones; but when citizen interest is strong, then beyond a certain point the short ballot weakens that interest and deprives administration of citizen control, however much the administrator may prefer to get along without this control and work under professionalized control instead. Despite its many advantages, not the least of which is a greater attention to ethical behavior, there are disadvantages to professionalism in any field, including a narrow outlook and a tendency to confuse means with ends. And although the seeming naïveté of the layman may sometimes annoy the administrator, the citizen has much to contribute in the way of social outlook and a fresh point of view.

Interest groups are another counterbalance to an excess of professionalism, and here also the citizen may play a major role. Interest groups are themselves professionalized, of course, but in the competitions among them, what emerges is usually broader than the professional viewpoint of any one of them. At many points in this book it has been shown how vital is the role of interest groups in public administration. There is hardly a public program that could exist without their help: they assure the passage of some laws and prevent the passage of others; they fight for proper organization and sufficient funds, and resist harmful reorganizations and budget cuts; they nominate and elect administrative officials to run their pet agencies; they participate in the formulation of administrative legislation; and they are a main bulwark of management in public relations programs.[29]

28 Leighton, *The Governing of Men.*
29 See Avery Leiserson's study, *Administrative Regulation: A Study in Representation of Interests* (Chicago: University of Chicago Press, 1942); and "Interest Groups in Administration," in Fritz Morstein Marx, ed., *Elements of Public*

When interest groups work closely with government officials, the effect is to make administration more democratic. On the other hand, because the outlook of the interest group is usually a narrow or even a selfish one, it could damage the public interest and administrative integrity. In the boisterous 1920s, the depressed 1930s, the power-ridden 1940s, and the complacent 1950s, it is possible that the disadvantages of interest group participation in administration have outbalanced the advantages. If democracy is to survive, it seems as though some of the more blatant domination that has characterized some pressure group activity will have to be modified. Within proper limits, interest groups are an essential aspect of the political process in a constitutional government.

There are many other ways by which the citizen may help to secure accountability from public officials. Thus in addition to serving on policy boards and commissions and working through interest groups, the citizen may vote on election day on issues as well as on candidates, elect the officials who appoint the administrators, run for office himself, support the merit system, make use of the initiative and referendum where they exist, and take part in the recall of public officials when the opportunity arises. In addition, the citizen may serve on grand and petit juries, belong to service and civic clubs, support the League of Women Voters and other nonpartisan groups, belong to a parent-teacher association, subscribe to voluntary programs such as the community chest, and be an active and intelligent worker in his political party. Although each such act of participation may seem insignificant by itself, in combination they help to keep the spirit of democracy alive and to prevent public administration from losing touch with the citizen.

These acts of participation rest on a broad base, which is civic attitude. If the prevailing attitude holds everyone to be selfish and dishonest, participation will be negligible and public administration will conform to dominant expectations, however unpleasant they may be. If the common attitude is to let someone else do it, citizen activities will atrophy and Burnham's theory of control by an elite of professional managers will become a reality. But if the dominant attitude would have government do only what is necessary but do that well, and people are willing to do their share to that end, then voluntary associations and public administration alike will be strengthened and the appropriate role of each will be properly determined. To work constructively in public administration, either as administrator or as citizen devoting a part of his energies to the work of voluntary groups, is a rewarding

---

*Administration* (Englewood Cliffs, N.J.: Prentice-Hall, 1946); David B. Truman, *The Governmental Process* (New York: Alfred A. Knopf, Inc., 1951), chaps. 13, 14; and Pendleton Herring, *Public Administration and the Public Interest* (New York: McGraw-Hill Book Company, Inc., 1936).

attainment because it fulfills a common human need to be a private person with a distinctive and self-developed personality, and at the same time to be a public person contributing to the welfare of the community.

## Growth and Change in Government

Here finally is the last major issue mentioned at the outset of this chapter: the question of size. Is there any limit to the size to which a government may attain and still remain accountable to the people? It will help, perhaps, to explore some of the factors that stimulate growth and change in government and what might be done to guide them or hold them in check.

Conservative citizens often complain that government constantly starts new programs and rarely discontinues old ones, that it has an inherent tendency to expand, to take on new responsibilities, and never to contract. Bureaucrats, one hears, constantly push government into new activities and hence toward collectivism.[30] Thus oversimplified, of course, these contentions are exaggerated and hence untrue. The fact is that aside from the influence of emergencies, such as war and depression, new governmental programs are born because pressure groups want them.

But going behind pressure groups, the basic factor in the expansion of government is social change and the tensions it creates in the community until adjustments can be made, as when the growth of population in large cities creates a need for new hospitals and schools, or there is a demand among farmers for electric power that is not being supplied by private enterprise, or economical methods of food processing eliminate needed nutriments or add harmful chemicals, or a demand for desegregation creates racial tensions. In cases such as these and many more, there is a demand by some pressure group for governmental action, either to meet the problems produced by change or to curtail the factors that create change, and in either case the result is to add yet another program to the burden of government.

If government leaders recognize the symptoms of growing social tensions and act in time to forestall their further development, then government does not have to interfere in the life of the community as much or for so long a time as when the condition is allowed to become aggravated.[31] Unfortunately, such foresight is rare and the result, es-

---

30 The most forceful presentation of this viewpoint is found in Friedrich A. Hayek, *The Road to Serfdom* (Chicago: University of Chicago Press, 1945); and John T. Flynn, *The Road Ahead* (New York: The Devin-Adair Company, 1949). See also Ludwig von Mises, *Bureaucracy* (New Haven: Yale University Press, 1944).

31 The best treatment of tensions in relation to administration is found in Leighton, *op. cit.*, pp. 252-367.

pecially in the federal government, is a kind of "Old Woman Who Lived in a Shoe" on a magnificent scale. In addition, of course, there is an inherent tendency for all institutions—public and private alike—to try to grow because success is so often measured in terms of size and the directors of institutions, being human, naturally want to be known as successful. Government, being an institution, exhibits the same tendency, although its administrators are probably no more acquisitive or power hungry than any other skill group in a position of managerial responsibility.

To control public administrators who see a chance to expand their responsibility is no easy task. Allied as public administrators are with pressure groups and being a pressure group themselves, they are often in a position to determine how new functions shall be added to existing public services and regulations. In the mid-1930s, for example, a group of experts including social workers, architects, economists, engineers, and lawyers united in an effort to formulate a program for public housing. Together they drafted the legislation, secured the agreement of a senator to sponsor it, enlisted the help of his very able secretary, lobbied the bill through both houses of Congress, determined its location in the federal web of agencies, organized the agency thus created, chose its administrator, joined him in running the program, and achieved a high level of program performance.

As public administrators can in some measure control the addition of new functions to government, it seems logical to suppose that they can also exert their influence in the opposite direction. And so they can. But educated in judgment and self-restraint as they may be, it is naïve to assume that they will prune their own powers or refuse to increase them if there is no outside force to compel them to do so. Consequently, if government's functions are to be kept in check through a careful scrutiny of proposed new programs and a determination to discontinue obsolete ones, the processes of democratic control and especially of legislative control must be maintained in full vigor.[32]

The difficulties, of course, are almost as apparent as the need for control. As soon as a particular program is threatened by a conscientious legislator, its pressure groups go into action armed with a full arsenal of persuasions. The administrator of the program in question and his employees join in; they have a vested interest at stake and would hardly be human if they did not defend it. And even if the legislator persists and wins, and the agency is in fact abolished, some modified program often takes its place. During the New Deal, for ex-

---

[32] See especially Herbert Simon *et al., Public Administration* (New York: Alfred A. Knopf, Inc., 1950), two chapters on "The Struggle for Existence." On the role of pressure groups in initiating and continuing governmental programs, see Pendleton Herring, *Public Administration and the Public Interest.*

ample, the Resettlement Administration was created with an elaborate tripartite program of rural resettlement, rural rehabilitation, and so-called greenbelt housing. When the agency was abolished in 1936—to the pleasure, it may be added, of many congressmen—its functions were transferred to the Department of Agriculture and one of its divisions, rural rehabilitation, lives on as the Farmers Home Administration and is larger and also more useful than its parent ever was even in its heyday. Similarly, the Reconstruction Finance Corporation, created under the Hoover Administration to help alleviate the effects of the depression and later used for so many different purposes that it literally covered the national economy, was put into liquidation in 1953; but one of its main functions, loans to small businesses, was transferred to the Small Business Administration and continues to flourish.

If pressure groups and social tensions cause governments to expand, what, then, slows them down? What creates resistance to change, and what makes change less necessary? Sociologists have long maintained, and social psychologists confirmed, that strongly held belief systems or myths and a wide dispersion of private property within the community have a conservatizing effect on society, holding social tensions and consequently government intervention to a minimum.[33]

The danger is that if beliefs are stubbornly rather than intelligently held, and those who hold them shun compromise until it is too late to resolve a conflict, then the result may be a sudden social upheaval with a landslide of government into areas that have previously been free and unregulated. In the 1920s, for example, the so-called era of normalcy was also a blind one; tensions built up under cover of an incomplete prosperity, and when the crash came the result was to thrust government into banking, security and holding company regulation, labor relations, and agricultural production to an extent that it had never occupied before and which proved to be only a beginning.

Alexander Leighton has some good advice, based on principle, for those who would successfully anticipate social tensions, and what he says applies not only to public administrators in their own spheres but also, in some degree, to government as a whole. The administrator who cannot resolve mounting social tensions with a proper remedial action, says Leighton, has only three choices: he can ignore such tensions until all chance to neutralize them is past; he can recognize certain aspects of the trouble and neglect others; or he may discover all the evidences of stress but decide that he cannot do anything about it and "go ahead with his plans as if the people affected would also behave as if the stresses did not exist." The result is easily anticipated: "Administrators are not infrequently caught by surprise when reactions occur that have

---

33 Robert M. MacIver, *The Web of Government* (New York: Macmillan, 1947), chaps. 1, 5-6; Leighton, *op. cit.*, pp. 287-321.

been some time in the process of formation." To the blind, concludes Leighton, all things are sudden.[34]

New government programs are not invariably necessary when tensions appear, but alterations and adjustments of emphasis in existing programs are often desirable. The administrator who is in sympathetic touch with the community he serves and with his own organization will best be able to anticipate the development of trouble and make the necessary changes in his program to forestall a direct appeal by pressure groups for a new government activity.

Where size is concerned, it seems clear that accountability is easier to enforce in a small government than in a large one, and equally clear that governments are going to continue to grow. But there are means of increasing accountability and also of checking rank growth, and it is possible that both may be used to secure a balance at a point where optimum size coincides with maximum accountability. Whether this balance will be achieved seems to depend chiefly on the citizen, on the degree to which he informs himself in matters of policy, takes an active part in government at all levels, and helps to build the kind of community in which honest, responsible, and responsive public administrators may be developed.

[34] *Op. cit.,* pp. 275, 304.

## BIBLIOGRAPHY AND CASES

### Annotated Reading Suggestions

The public service itself has ultimate responsibility for maintaining high standards. In this connection, see Paul H. Appleby, *Morality and Administration in Democratic Government* (University of Louisiana Press, 1952), Chapter 10 on "Political Responsibility." See also Senator Paul H. Douglas, *Ethics in Government* (Harvard University Press, 1952).

Two thoughtful pieces on this subject are Carl J. Friedrich. "Public Policy and the Nature of Administrative Responsibility," in C. J. Friedrich and E. S. Mason, eds., *Public Policy* (Harvard University Press, 1940), vol. I; and John M. Gaus, "The Responsibility of Public Administration" in John M. Gaus, Leonard D. White, and Marshall E. Dimock, *The Frontiers of Public Administration* (University of Chicago Press, 1936). In this connection, see also Marshall E. Dimock, "Forms of Control over Administrative Action," in Charles G. Haines and Marshall E. Dimock, eds., *Essays on the Law and Practice of Governmental Administration* (Johns Hopkins University Press, 1935).

There are a number of good articles: David M. Levitan, "The Responsibility of Administrative Officials in a Democratic Society," *Political Science Quarterly*, 41 (December 1946); Arthur W. Macmahon, "Congressional Oversight of Administration: The Power of the Purse," *ibid.*, 43 (June-September 1943); Herman Finer, "Administrative Responsibility in Democratic Government," *Public Administration Review*, 1 (Summer 1941); Arthur A. Maass and Laurence I. Radway, "Gauging Administrative Responsibility," *Public Administration Review*, 9 (Summer 1949).

Among challenging books dealing with the possibility that Big Government will get out of control, that of Merlo J. Pusey, a Washington correspondent, occupies a high place: *Big Government: Can We Control It?* (Harper & Row, 1945). Books of a similar stature are Thomas K. Finletter, *Can Representative Government Do the Job?* (Reynal & Hitchcock, 1945); Henry Hazlitt, *A New Constitution Now* (McGraw-Hill, 1942); J. Roland Pennock, *Administration and the Rule of Law* (Holt, Rinehart and Winston, 1941); and Dwight Waldo, *The Administrative State* (Ronald, 1948).

## Case Studies

Three cases previously cited from the Stein *Case Book* have relevance to this chapter as well: *The Regional Director and the Press*, involving a congressional investigating committee; *The Cambridge City Manager*, dealing with legislative and voter sanctions; and *The Glavis-Ballinger Dispute*, dealing with accountability to higher administrative officers. Among other cases already cited, the *Van Waters Case*, *The Firing of Pat Jackson*, and the *Closing of Newark Airport* also are pertinent to this chapter.

A case not previously mentioned deals with the watchdog of Congress, the General Accounting Office; this is No. 35, *General Accounting Office: Two Glimpses*, eighty pages, written by C. G. Schulsinger.

# Index

Abegglen, J. C., 36n
Accountability, 373-394
  through citizen control, 388-391
  extraordinary remedies, 387-388
  through the legislature, 378-382
  and line-staff function, 277
  through self-regulation, 373-378
Accounting systems, 156, 267
Adams, Brooks, 20
Adams, Sherman, 301
Administration
  elements of, 48-56
  functional view, 5-6
  and the human factor, 6-7
  interrelationships of, 52
  positivist theory of, 74
  sociological theory of, 70-76
  *See also* Public administration
Administrative adjudication, 122-127
  advantages and disadvantages, 124
  appeals from, 125
  delegation of powers, 119-122
Administrative Analyst Examination, 38
Administrative courts, 383-384
Administrative federalism, 310-313
Administrative law, 117
  development of, 21
Administrative Management, President's Committee on, 379
Administrative manuals, 228-229, 315
Administrative orders, 118

Administrative Procedure, Attorney General's Committee on, 122-123, 125
Administrative Procedure Act of 1946, 123, 125, 383
Administrative Procedure and Organization, Office of, 377
AFL-CIO, 341
Agriculture, Department of, 34, 35, 63, 64, 105, 106, 282-283, 341, 353, 384, 393
Air Force, Department of the, 217-218
Air Force, Secretary of the, 204
Alabama, University of, 23
American Bar Association, 123, 125, 126, 384
American Economic Association, 86
American Farm Bureau Federation, 341
American Federation of Labor, 87, 365
American Legion, 341
American Management Association, 132
American Railway Association, 121
American Society of Newspaper Editors, 347
American Society of Planning Officials, 136
American Telephone and Telegraph Company, 31, 76, 287, 302, 339